Women's Life Writing and Early Modern Ireland

Women and Gender in the Early Modern World

SERIES EDITORS
Allyson Poska
Abby Zanger

Women's Life Writing and Early Modern Ireland

EDITED BY JULIE A. ECKERLE
AND NAOMI MCAREAVEY

UNIVERSITY OF NEBRASKA PRESS   LINCOLN

Library of Congress Cataloging-in-Publication Data
Names: Eckerle, Julie A., 1971–, editor.
| McAreavey, Naomi, editor.
Title: Women's life writing and early modern Ireland
/ edited by Julie A. Eckerle and Naomi McAreavey.
Description: Lincoln: University of Nebraska
Press, [2019] | Series: Women and gender
in the early modern world | Includes
bibliographical references and index.
Identifiers: LCCN 2018040953
ISBN 9780803299979 (cloth: alk. paper)
ISBN 9781496214263 (epub)
ISBN 9781496214270 (mobi)
ISBN 9781496214287 (pdf)
Subjects: LCSH: English prose literature—Irish
authors—History and criticism. | English prose
literature—Women authors—History and
criticism. | English prose literature—Early modern,
1500–1700—History and criticism. | English prose
literature—17th century—History and criticism. |
Women and literature—Ireland—History—16th
century. | Women and literature—Ireland—
History—17th century. | Ireland—In literature.
Classification: LCC PR8723.W6 W68 2019 | DDC
820.9/00409287—dc23 LC record available
at https://lccn.loc.gov/2018040953

Set in Arno by Mikala R. Kolander.
Designed by N. Putens.

For our families,

Michael, Anya, and Katya

and

Martin, Luke, and Nicholas

and

for all the women of Ireland who told their

stories to repeal the Eighth Amendment

CONTENTS

ACKNOWLEDGMENTS

As is often the case, we would not have been able to complete this project without the support and assistance of many people, most significant—of course—the contributors who helped us turn our vision for the volume into reality through their astute observations, skillful archival research, and carefully crafted chapters. We are also grateful to Women and Gender in the Early Modern World series editors, Allyson Poska and Abby Zanger, and University of Nebraska Press editor in chief, Alisa Plant; we are so pleased that our book found a home with this press and series. We have benefited from numerous conversations with other scholars who share our interest in early modern Ireland, especially the audiences at the last few Tudor and Stuart Ireland conferences. Thanks, too, to the many colleagues and friends who have supported us along the way, including Evan Bourke, Danielle Clarke, Marie-Louise Coolahan, Erika Gaffney, Jane Grogan, Jennifer Kolpacoff Deane, Felicity Maxwell, Bronagh McShane, Jennifer Rothchild, and Ramona Wray. Archbishop Marsh's Library, especially keeper Jason McElligott (also one of our contributors) and Maria O'Shea, kindly contributed our cover image. Several funding sources have provided the practical means to research, edit, and produce our volume. We are grateful to the University of Minnesota's Imagine Fund, Faculty

Research Enhancement Fund, and Grant-in-Aid. Finally, we are grateful for our supportive families and—most important—for having found in one another colleagues willing to devote time and energy to a project on the early modern women who found seventeenth-century Ireland as worthy of thought and reflection as we do.

Women's Life Writing and Early Modern Ireland

Introduction

JULIE A. ECKERLE AND NAOMI MCAREAVEY

Several studies of early modern women's life writing have turned much-needed attention to the rhetorical sophistication, narrative creativity, and bold self-expression of women whose writings, often categorized as "personal" or "private," have not heretofore been considered worthy of scholarly consideration.[1] At least, they have not been considered worthy except as sources for data about women's historical lives. As a consequence of the larger scholarly trend toward autobiographical and biographical studies and the more specific interest in early modern women's life writing, however, scholars now have a much better understanding of early modern women's intellectual and introspective habits (including literacy practices, political views, and rhetorical techniques) as well as their varied engagement with the familial, political, and social contexts in which they lived and wrote. Thus, English life writers such as Lady Grace Mildmay; Lady Anne Clifford; Elizabeth Isham; Lucy Hutchinson; Lady Anne Halkett; Lady Mary Rich, Countess of Warwick; Lady Ann Fanshawe; Alice Thornton; Dorothy Osborne; Elizabeth Freke; and Lady Elizabeth Delaval, among many others, have experienced a renaissance of sorts as we turn to their work with a new eye and purpose.

Yet placing early modern women on the map metaphorically has not, in many cases, meant putting them on the map in a more literal sense.

While the Irish connections of Rich, Fanshawe, Freke, and Thornton have been acknowledged—Rich was the daughter of the First Earl of Cork and was born and grew up in Ireland in the early decades of the seventeenth century; Fanshawe resided briefly in Ireland with her diplomat husband during the civil war period; Freke moved to the Irish estate of her in-laws in the 1670s; and Thornton lived in Ireland as a child in the 1630s—they have rarely been the subject of sustained scholarly attention.[2] This is despite the fact that Ireland resonates strongly in the life writings of these women, as contributions in this volume by Raymond A. Anselment, Anne Fogarty, and Amelia Zurcher show.[3] Other well-known women (life) writers spent periods in Ireland, such as Elizabeth Cary, who accompanied her husband to Dublin when he was appointed lord deputy in 1622 and remained there until 1625;[4] Osborne, who married the son of Sir John Temple (author of the influential and controversial polemic *The Irish Rebellion*, first published in 1646) and lived with her in-laws in Dublin in the late 1650s;[5] and Katherine Philips, who spent a highly productive year attached to the viceregal court in Dublin in 1662–63, where her acclaimed play, *Pompey*, was written and performed.[6] The impact of Irish connections and experiences on their life writing is different for each woman: for Philips her stay in Ireland was undoubtedly key to her development as a poet, as her letters testify; while for Osborne, whose surviving letters predate her time in Ireland as well as her marriage, her future husband's Irish connections amount to little more than passing references to elite Irish figures. Still, the place of Ireland in these women's writings needs further scrutiny if we are to reach a more nuanced understanding of the complexity of Anglophone women's life writing.

For some time scholars have been challenging the Anglocentrism of early modern women's writing, with Kate Chedgzoy suggesting in 2006 that "the study of early modern women's writing might benefit from being situated in relation to more expansive, detailed and complex cultural geographies of the period."[7] Her subsequent work has examined women's writing throughout the British Atlantic archipelago, attending to Anglophone writing in early modern England, Wales, Scotland, Ireland, and the Americas.[8] Such "archipelagic" critiques (sometimes called "multi-centered," "Three Kingdoms," or "Four Nations" approaches, or the "New

British History") have gained momentum in early modern literary studies more broadly, with John Kerrigan probably the best-known proponent of what he calls a "devolutionary" approach. "To devolve," he explains, "is to shift power in politics or scholarly analysis from a locus that has been disproportionately endowed with influence and documentation to sites that are dispersed and more skeletally understood."[9] Even though Ireland has been a significant field of early modern literary studies since at least the 1990s, such scholarship has disproportionately focused on the works of Edmund Spenser and William Shakespeare.[10] This means that Ireland and Irishness have continued to be viewed from a largely *English* vantage point that is necessarily self-limiting. Archipelagic approaches, in contrast, "avoid being tied to a core-and-periphery scheme so as to bring out those aspects of the field which were expansive, multilevelled, discontinuous, and polycentric," according to Kerrigan.[11] They therefore facilitate a deeper and more nuanced understanding of the culture of early modern Ireland.

Important work has been done on early modern women's writing in other archipelagic locations. Sarah Prescott, for example, has fruitfully applied Kerrigan's arguments to an analysis of Philips, who—in addition to her productive year in Ireland—lived most of her adult life in Wales; Prescott claims that "by dismantling the framework of center and margin, archipelagic accounts of spatial experience allow not only for a reassessment of Philips as a Welsh poet but also for a revaluation of the ways in which we write women's literary history in Wales and beyond." By attending to Philips's Welshness, yet neither claiming the poet as unproblematically Welsh nor assuming that she experienced Wales as an English exile, Prescott focuses on Philips's "fluid role as archipelagic interface" and in the process emphasizes "inter-connectivity and fluid exchange as constitutive of an experience of place and space."[12] The same argument can be applied to Philips's Irish experiences and for the place of Ireland in the Anglophone Irish writing of many other early modern women.

An interest in the "devolutionary interactivities" (to appropriate Kerrigan's phrase) of early modern women's writing is shared by all the contributors to this volume.[13] But, at the same time, the volume "wears its Hibernocentricity on its sleeve," just like Marie-Louise Coolahan's pioneering study of women's writing in early modern Ireland, which similarly focuses "on texts produced by Irish women and by women who lived in Ireland; its parameters are defined by residence or birth."[14] Our relocation of Ireland from the margins to the center of the scholarship of early modern women's life writing makes an important contribution to the "devolutionary" project. As Kerrigan shows, the Anglocentrism of English literary studies has meant that non-English writers have been either misunderstood because their local contexts have not been considered or ignored because they have been deemed insufficiently "English."[15] In relation to early modern women's life writing, this has limited our understanding of the texts of English women who wrote their lives in Ireland, but it has had an even greater impact on our interaction with writers whom we might call *Irish*. The recovery and examination of those writers who have been neglected is therefore a priority for us in this volume.

Our volume benefits from the huge amount of recovery work that has been undertaken in recent decades by scholars of women in early modern Ireland.[16] The sixteenth- and seventeenth-century material published in *Irish Women's Writing and Traditions*, two groundbreaking volumes added to the three-volume *Field Day Anthology of Irish Writing* in 2002, suggests something of the range of extant material through published excerpts from genres including autobiography-inflected poetry, correspondence, depositions, petitions, diaries, memoirs, nuns' chronicles, spiritual testimonies, and conversion narratives.[17] Yet even this very helpful introduction to women's life writing in Ireland is little more than a glimpse into the variety and amount of surviving material. Scholars have continued to add new Irish voices to the conversation, including the indomitable [Mrs. Francis] Briver, mayoress of Waterford, who wrote of her experiences at the outbreak of the 1641 rebellion.[18] Investigations into women's participation in intellectual communities, such as the Hartlib Circle, have focused attention on the role of Irish women such as Dorothy Moore and Katherine, Lady Ranelagh.[19] And the expansion of the field of early modern letters has provided a context in which the epistolary output of Irish women can be examined.[20] Research is showing that women in early modern Ireland engaged in the full spectrum of autobiographical and biographical genres, including recipe book (Hannah

Alexander);[21] business diary (Elizabeth Petty);[22] commonplace book (Lady Anne Southwell);[23] memorandum book (Elizabeth Boyle, Countess of Cork and Burlington);[24] nun's chronicle (Mary Bonaventure Browne);[25] meditations (Frances Cooke);[26] Quaker travel narrative (Barbara Blaugdone);[27] conversion narrative (John Rogers's Independent congregants);[28] and what Coolahan terms "marginal autobiography" (Mary Trye).[29] One might go as far as to say that the history of women's *writing* in early modern Ireland is a history of women's *life writing*. Yet until now there has been no book-length study of women's life writing and early modern Ireland.[30]

Once one begins to look beyond England and into Ireland, the amount of material to be explored is simply astounding. The 1641 Depositions, recently digitized by Trinity College Dublin, contain the testimonies of many hundreds of Irish women, mainly Protestant settlers of English and Scottish descent.[31] This collection forms the largest single source of women's voices from early modern Ireland. Many more women writers are represented among the voluminous correspondence that survives from sixteenth- and seventeenth-century Ireland and is preserved in public and private collections in Ireland, Britain, and beyond. Within just one collection of letters at Trinity College Dublin (the Lyons Collection of the Correspondence of William King), for instance, reside at least 150 letters by women: these are the subject of Julie A. Eckerle's contribution.[32] Letters by well-connected women like Elizabeth Butler, First Duchess of Ormonde, exist in numerous collections throughout Ireland and other countries: for Ormonde, who is the subject of Naomi McAreavey's chapter, the tally of surviving letters has already exceeded three hundred.[33] Our volume brings these and other new voices to this discussion, including the lesser-known Cork Boyle women (Ann-Maria Walsh), Eliza Blennerhassett (Amanda E. Herbert), Jane Bonnell (Eckerle), and Elizabeth Davys (Jason McElligott). Together we make the case that reading these texts will help us to develop an increased sensitivity to the prevalence of Ireland in seventeenth-century women's autobiographical and biographical accounts; a recognition of the influence of Ireland on life writers' self-understanding, as well as their textual representation of self; a more complicated approach to national identity throughout the British-Irish archipelago; and a more general consideration of the complex and dynamic relationship between place, individual, and text.

This volume—the first critical collection to focus exclusively on seventeenth-century women's life writing in the Irish context—provides an entirely new perspective on both new and familiar texts as we resituate them in a powerful and revealing landscape. We suggest that carefully examining the writings of Irish women helps to focus our attention on the representation of Ireland and its people by better-known (English) writers such as Philips. Not only was her play *Pompey* written and first performed in Dublin under the patronage of the Earl of Orrery (a member of the life-writing Cork Boyle family), but she also dedicated a number of poems to the Irish elite, including several women.[34] Her letters from this period richly illuminate the cultural life of the viceregal court in Dublin Castle at a key moment in its history.[35] They also document her experiences as an Anglophone woman writer in Ireland—one who may have encouraged other women in the country to take the pen, as a poem by the anonymous Philo-Philippa suggests.[36] More important, the letters reveal the ways that Philips used her experiences in Dublin to shape her identity as a writer, particularly by recounting the enthusiastic support her work received from the upper echelons of Irish society. The autobiographical writing (autobiography-inflected poetry as well as letters) produced during her year-long stay in Ireland is therefore critical to understanding Philips's sense of herself as a writer, while also illustrating the significance of Ireland in her flourishing writerly identity. Scrutinizing her life writing alongside that of some of the Irish women attached to the viceregal court (such as the younger women of the Butler and Boyle families who were initiated into her Society of Friendship) is potentially very revealing of the archipelagic interactions of women in early modern Ireland.

At the same time, the reasons for Philips's stay in Dublin point to the limitations of archipelagic readings of the culture of early modern Ireland. Even though David Baker and Willy Maley are exemplary in their suggestion that in the New British History "the obvious fact of England's long-term hegemony is in no way denied," there remains a tendency in the scholarship to downplay the fact that the relationship between England and Ireland was unique in the archipelago because Ireland was a settler-colony of England.[37] Philips herself had come to Ireland in 1662–63 to claim land that had been confiscated from the Irish rebels to reward those "adventurers" (like her father) who had invested in an army to suppress the rebellion. Like Philips, the majority of Anglophone women writing their lives in early modern Ireland were also engaging in some way with the colonial settlement of the country. Some of the women already mentioned had fathers or husbands active in colonial administration; others married, or had friends or relatives who had married, into Irish families; and still others were born in Ireland to English (and Scottish) settlers and administrators. The women's complicity with the colonial project is diversely reflected in their writing.

But, as many of our contributors show, the place of the English colonial project in women's construction of their lives in Ireland was far from simple. This is partly because succeeding waves of colonialism over many centuries had massively complicated the issue of "English" and "Irish" identities in Ireland. "Irish" is for us useful shorthand for any woman who lived a significant portion of her life in Ireland. Yet many of these women would not have identified themselves as "Irish" in any way, and many critical differences, not to mention conflicts (ethnic, religious, political, economic, social, and geographic), are hidden beneath this blanket term. But if identifying these women as "Irish" seems like an act of national appropriation, it is done with the intention of exposing the blind spot in the scholarship of early modern women's writing, which too often relies on "English" as the default subject position for women writing in the English language. This would not be such a problem if it did not also come with some problematic assumptions about the way an "English" woman might write about Ireland, which too often implies that for "English" women Irish experiences are exile experiences and that Ireland and the Irish are Other (a tendency Prescott also notes in relation to Philips's Welsh experiences).[38] Our work shows that for many women this is far from the case. Lady Frances Parker's comment in a 1690 letter to William King that "I have since I was in Ireland lived in hopes of seeing it again" offers just one example of the reality that Ireland was, at least for some women, their home and a place that they cherished.[39] So by deliberately making the choice to identify women *with* Ireland rather than *against* Ireland, we suggest that we might reach a more nuanced understanding about what Ireland meant to the women who lived there.

Clearly, attending to Ireland involves coming to terms with the particular complexity of national identity in that country. As a starting point, it is useful to distinguish between four main groups living in sixteenth- and seventeenth-century Ireland: the native Irish, the Old English, the New English, and (from the mid-seventeenth century) the Cromwellian settlers (or the "New Protestants"). Broadly speaking, the native Irish spoke Gaelic and were Catholic, and their power had gradually been eroded by different waves of settlement; female examples include the "Pirate Queen" Gráinne Ní Mháille (Grace O'Malley) and Rosa O'Doherty, wife of the Confederate commander Owen Roe O'Neill.[40] The Old English were the descendants of the Anglo-Norman invaders of the twelfth century; they retained their Catholicism as well as their allegiance to the English Crown, but they also intermarried with the native Irish, and many adopted Gaelic language and customs: Eleanor, Countess of Desmond; and Mary Bonaventure Browne, Abbess of the Galway Poor Clares, may be counted among this group.[41] The Old English lost much land and power to the New English, who came to Ireland during the Elizabethan and Jacobean settlements and were generally Protestant, English-speaking, and loyal to the Crown: Martha Piggott, whose husband and son were killed at the siege of Dysart Castle during the 1641 rebellion, as well as the daughters of the First Earl of Cork, are considered New English.[42] Finally, the newest arrivals were those who came to Ireland in the aftermath of the civil wars, many of whom reaped the benefits of the Cromwellian land settlement that came with the dispossession of Irish Catholics; these New Protestants, such as Elizabeth Avery, include many of the female members of John Rogers's Independent congregation, which was established in Christ Church, Dublin, in 1652.[43]

But a number of Irish women do not fit comfortably into any of these groups. The First Duchess of Ormonde, for example, was heir to the Old English Ormondes through her mother, but her father (from whom she inherited the title Baroness Dingwall) was a Scot, and she was raised a Protestant. Similarly, Lettice Digby, née Fitzgerald, who engaged in letters with her besiegers at Geashill Castle, was descended from the Old English earls of Kildare, but she was a Protestant and married into an English estate. For those in the mid-seventeenth century, certainly after 1642, when the Old English Catholics joined the native Irish in rebellion, it might be more useful to distinguish individuals in Ireland by religion. Yet this is also unsatisfactory, given the split in the Confederate Catholics along class-inflected ethnic lines. Thus, categories of national identity in early modern Ireland begin to multiply, as well as blur into one another.

Even women who theoretically fit into one of these groups—the New English Boyle women, for example—do not remain there long under scrutiny. How do we categorize someone like Rich, ostensibly a second-generation New English woman who spent her adult life in England? By defining her as a "New English" Irish woman, we privilege her paternity, but by characterizing her as "English," we overidentify her with her husband. Instead we must ask, how did *she* see herself and her relationship with Ireland? How is this explored in her writing? And how is her national identity, and that of other women, shaped and disrupted by their gender? This is ultimately the purpose of our book, which argues for a more nuanced understanding of women's national identity in early modern Ireland, one that must take into consideration geographic issues such as birthplace, upbringing, residence, and mobility; familial issues such as ancestry, parentage, marital status, and offspring; social and cultural issues such as class, language, religion, and political affiliations; and even issues relating to the materiality of the texts themselves, especially the locations of their production, circulation, and reception.

Our contributors make unique cases for how particular women writers represent their Irishness. Ann-Maria Walsh, for example, prefers the term "Anglo-Irish" for the Cork Boyles because the dual importance of their Englishness and Protestantism makes them proto-Ascendency figures. "Anglo-Irish" is less useful for the Ormonde Butlers, with their Old English lineage and extensive Catholic relations, so McAreavey utilizes the term "English-Irish." Conversely, Zurcher adopts the label "Irish-English" in recognition of the Boyle women's ethnic-national hybridity, but where (unlike the Ormonde Butlers) the emphasis is on a dominant English rather than Irish identity. For other contributors, including Jason McElligott and Eckerle, the issue of national identity is moot, with McElligott showing just how difficult it is to identify the marginalia in books found in an Irish library as "Irish" in any way. Ruth Connolly's analysis of the letters of Ranelagh perhaps best sums up the volume's core argument by showing how "Ireland" and "Irishness" are floating signifiers for women, with the potential to mean different things at different times and for different purposes.

The changing circumstances of sixteenth- and seventeenth-century Ireland often provided a stimulus for life writing, with women from all classes finding and asserting their individual and collective voices amid the political crises. In the aftermath of the 1641 rebellion, for example, the Commission for the Despoiled Subject offered an official space in which Protestant women could speak publicly of their experiences in war-torn Ireland. The depositions of women such as Elizabeth Price of County Armagh, whose testimony extends to ten pages, indicate that even as the women answered a series of preestablished questions, they were allowed considerable freedom to shape and develop their own personal accounts.[44] Another deponent, Lady Elizabeth Dowdall of Kilfinny Castle, County Limerick, supplemented her formal deposition with an alternative version of her Irish rebellion experiences, "a true note," suggesting that the deposition process inspired her to engage in more flexible life-writing endeavors.[45] Dowdall defended Kilfinny Castle from Catholic insurgents, and other siege situations generated different autobiographical texts, particularly letters. The epistolary exchange between Lettice Digby, Baroness Offaly, and her besiegers at Geashill Castle is perhaps the best-known example, although there are numerous other letters written from besieged women in seventeenth-century Ireland to a variety of correspondents.[46] There is also a range of life writing extant for Catholic women who offer an alternative version of the events of 1641. The chronicle of the Irish Poor Clares, which was written in Irish but survives in a contemporary English translation, focuses on the nuns' experience of exile in the aftermath of the Cromwellian invasion. The 1650s saw the mass exodus of Catholics and the arrival of radical Protestants who left a range of autobiographical records. For members of Rogers's Independent congregation in Christ Church, Dublin, for example, oral spiritual testimonies were a prerequisite to admission; many of the women's testimonies were recorded and published by Rogers.

The mid- to late seventeenth century also saw the arrival of Quakers like Blaugdone (discussed in Fogarty's contribution), whose travel narrative provides a rich account of the experiences of a Quaker woman in Restoration Ireland.[47] While such women were a minority, their texts offer a valuable female perspective on life in late seventeenth-century Ireland.

To best attend to the complexity and range of women's life writing during this period, we have loosely organized the following chapters by genre rather than by the life writers' national or religious identities. Even here there is a great deal of overlap, since—as is often the case with life writers—many women wrote in more than one genre. Generally speaking, however, the volume moves from the most traditionally understood autobiographical forms such as prose retrospective narratives and letters to less common and thus far less scrutinized forms like inscriptions of book ownership. Throughout, the authors interrogate how Ireland figured in women's life writing: as subject, as character, as influence, and—perhaps most often—as a means through which the life writer's sense of self most clearly developed. Several common themes also become apparent. These include rhetorical techniques like the manipulation of memory and epistolary convention; the self-accounting that is nearly universal in life writing of this period; writers' attempts to come to terms with the economic and political challenges unique to seventeenth-century Ireland; and the invaluable role of networks, whether those of family, epistolary correspondents, or confessional community.

The volume begins, then, with prose narratives. In "Alice Thornton, Elizabeth Freke, and the Remembrances of Ireland," Anselment's analysis of Thornton's and Freke's retrospective narratives, tales in which their memories of Ireland figure large, also incorporates one of our volume's key themes— the role of Ireland in the textual construction of a woman's self. Fogarty's chapter similarly investigates the use of retrospective prose narrative in which Ireland plays a significant role in the writer's construction of self. In "Reading Dislocation and Emotion in the Writings of Alice Thornton, Ann Fanshawe, and Barbara Blaugdone," Fogarty integrates consideration of the unique historical moments experienced by her three writers, as well as the emotional communities in which they were embedded, into her comparative analysis of what she acknowledges are "charged accounts of the colonial experience from a female point of view."

Not surprisingly, epistolary documents receive the most attention in our collection, and several of our contributors demonstrate the extraordinary range of purpose to which seventeenth-century women put their epistolary skills. Among the most prolific female life writers of the period were the Boyle women, or the seven daughters and four daughters-in-law of Richard Boyle, First Earl of Cork. Walsh's introduction to these women in "The Boyle Women and Familial Life Writing" considers them "within the familial context and the larger Boyle archive" to demonstrate how, for individuals like Rich, Ranelagh, Alice Barrymore, Joan Fitzgerald, Elizabeth Burlington, and Margaret Orrery, sense of self involved at least in part each woman's perception of her place *within the family*. Zurcher's "Life Writing in the Boyle Family Network" furthers this analysis with more in-depth attention to sisters Rich and Ranelagh and their place within various familial and Protestant networks. By emphasizing "the complex relation for women between Protestant piety and other intellectual and social concerns in the period," Zurcher's chapter addresses the religious aspect of identity that is so fraught during this time.

The next chapter brings us full circle, as Connolly's further analysis of Ranelagh's letters returns to the subject of Ireland as a space in and against which identity is constructed or negotiated. "The Politics of Honor in Lady Ranelagh's Ireland" focuses specifically on Ranelagh's "rhetorical self-distancing from Ireland's ill-governed spaces," which, Connolly argues, "enabled Ranelagh to create an ethnically inflected defense of her decision to separate from her estranged husband, the New English peer Arthur Jones, Viscount Ranelagh." Although Connolly thus reads Ranelagh's emphatic departure from Ireland (and her husband) more negatively than Zurcher, who sees in this decision a thoughtful retreat from the more public and active life her family led there, both chapters assign extraordinary significance to Ranelagh's physical break with Ireland, as well as how she represents that break in writing. A woman with connections to Ranelagh is Elizabeth Ormonde. In "The Place of Ireland in the Letters of the First Duchess of Ormonde," McAreavey focuses on a transformative period in the lives of both women: the Interregnum. During this period, and with Ranelagh's support, Ormonde successfully petitioned Oliver Cromwell for a portion of her family's confiscated Irish estate after her husband went into exile with the king. McAreavey attends to a range of letters written during and after the long and difficult petitionary process, arguing that during the period Ormonde "mobilized her own lineage and inheritance to establish herself, in her husband's absence, as head of the family." In the process, McAreavey maintains, "Ireland moved to the heart of her epistolary self-representation, where it remained for the rest of her writing life."

The following two chapters turn to letters written by women with far less prestige and power than those in the Boyle and Ormonde families. First, in "English-Irish Social Networks in the Seventeenth Century," Amanda E. Herbert uses the correspondence of Eliza Blennerhassett to explore how "one early modern woman constructed a cross-channel, archipelagic identity by using seventeenth-century Ireland, as both a location and an idea, to influence her sense of self, memory, and place." As earlier chapters make clear, social and epistolary networks are key within large families or coteries like those experienced by more aristocratic women. But Herbert's analysis demonstrates the value of a network for a single individual struggling to make sense of her life in a place she claims to hate. In contrast to Herbert's focus on a single correspondent, Eckerle considers many different women's letters to a single *addressee*. In "Women's Letters in the Lyons Collection of the Correspondence of William King," Eckerle demonstrates how vulnerable women in the position of supplicant manipulated the epistolary genre to at least *ask* for assistance from a man of great power in Ireland and—in the process—provides a useful summary of the range of rhetorical techniques available to women willing (or forced) to avail themselves of epistolary writing, especially in the case of petitionary letters.

Finally, McElligott ventures into the margins of life writing as the genre is traditionally understood, by literally analyzing the marginal notations of female book owners. "Ownership Inscriptions and Life Writing in the Books of Early Modern Women" yields rich conclusions about how the identities of relatively marginal (or at least unknown) figures could be constructed in the margins of a book collection. McElligott makes use of the tools of material studies to analyze the books and signatures of Margaret Ussher for traces of Margaret herself and for clues to female book ownership in early modern Dublin more generally.

McElligott's chapter thus forms a fitting conclusion for a volume that is itself engaged with traditionally marginalized subject matter: life writing, women's life writing, and women's life writing in the context of early modern Ireland. Yet the rewards of such study, we argue, take us to the very center of early modern British and Irish cultures and the questions of both individual and national identity that plagued them. Indeed, although producing a piece of life writing is just one way of understanding or at the least constructing a self, the texts thus created provide remarkable insight into both the process of self-construction and its implications for a fraught and tumultuous historical moment.

In addition to demonstrating the value of life writing to our understanding of early modern Ireland and the women who lived there, however briefly, our volume also reinforces the rich rewards of archival study and, more practically, provides solid overviews of many archives and archival documents that have not heretofore been widely known. For nearly all the contributors, it was only through intimate engagement with and knowledge of a particular set of archival materials that the unique nature of women's (or, in some cases, a single woman's) life writing in the Irish context could be clearly seen. Therefore, in addition to shifting the lens on individual texts and writers in such a way that simultaneously brings gender, nation, and identity into focus, the contributors share insights into archives that will, we hope, contribute substantively to our collective and ongoing conversations about early modern Ireland.

NOTES

1. Book-length studies include Julie D. Campbell and Anne R. Larsen, eds., *Early Modern Women and Transnational Communities of Letters* (Aldershot: Ashgate, 2009); James Daybell's extensive work on early modern women's letters—including *Women Letter-Writers in Tudor England* (Oxford: Oxford University Press, 2006); Daybell, ed., *Early Modern Women's Letter Writing, 1450–1700* (Basingstoke: Palgrave, 2001); and Daybell and Andrew Gordon, eds., *Women and Epistolary Agency in Early Modern Culture, 1450–1690* (London: Routledge, 2016)—Daybell, *The*

Material Letter: Manuscript Letters and the Culture and Practices of Letter-Writing in Early Modern England, 1580–1635 (Basingstoke: Palgrave, 2012); Michelle M. Dowd and Julie A. Eckerle, eds., *Genre and Women's Life Writing in Early Modern England* (Aldershot: Ashgate, 2007); Eckerle, *Romancing the Self in Early Modern Englishwomen's Life Writing* (Farnham: Ashgate, 2013); and Sharon Cadman Seelig, *Autobiography and Gender in Early Modern Literature: Reading Women's Lives, 1600–1680* (Cambridge: Cambridge University Press, 2006). Equally important to the increased interest in and understanding of these life writers are the numerous new or first editions of their texts. These include Elizabeth Freke, *The Remembrances of Elizabeth Freke, 1671–1714*, ed. Raymond A. Anselment (Cambridge: Cambridge University Press, 2001); Mary Rich, *The Occasional Meditations of Mary Rich, Countess of Warwick*, ed. Raymond A. Anselment (Tempe: Arizona Center for Medieval and Renaissance Studies, 2009); David Booy, ed., *Autobiographical Writings by Early Quaker Women* (Aldershot: Ashgate, 2004); Nicky Hallet, ed., *Lives of Spirit: English Carmelite Self-Writing of the Early Modern Period* (Aldershot: Ashgate, 2007); Elizabeth Isham, diary and "Booke of Rememberance," in *Constructing Elizabeth Isham*, ed. Clarke, Elizabeth et al., Centre for the Study of the Renaissance, Warwick University, April 15, 2018, https://warwick.ac.uk/fac/arts/ren/projects/isham/ (web edition of Isham's life writings); Kevin McGrane, ed., *An Account of the Life and Death of Mrs. Elizabeth Bury* (Grand Rapids MI: Reformation Heritage Books, 2006); Joanna Moody, ed., *The Private Correspondence of Jane Lady Cornwallis Bacon, 1613–1644* (London: Associated University Presses, 2003); David George Mullan, ed., *Women's Life Writing in Early Modern Scotland: Writing the Evangelical Self, c. 1670–c. 1730* (Aldershot: Ashgate, 2003); Sarah C. E. Ross, ed., *Katherine Austen's Book M: British Library Additional MS 4454* (Tempe: Arizona Center for Medieval and Renaissance Studies, 2011); Suzanne Trill, ed., *Lady Anne Halkett: Selected Self-Writings* (Aldershot: Ashgate, 2007); Heather Wolfe, ed., *Elizabeth Cary Lady Falkland: Life and Letters* (Tempe: Arizona Center for Medieval and Renaissance Studies, 2001); and Elizabeth Skerpan-Wheeler, ed., *Life Writings: The Early Modern Englishwoman; A Facsimile Library of Essential Works*, ser. 2, pt. 1, vols. 1–2 (Aldershot: Ashgate, 2001). When the lens is widened to include studies of life writing by early modern men as well, a much longer bibliography emerges; see Dowd and Eckerle, "Recent Studies in Early Modern English Life Writing," *English Literary Renaissance* 40, no. 1 (2010): 132–62, for a thorough list. Particularly pertinent to the interests of the present volume is Marie-Louise Coolahan, "Early Modern Irish Autobiography," in *A History of Irish Autobiography*, ed. Liam Harte (Cambridge: Cambridge University Press, 2018), 38–53, which provides a concise overview of male- and female-authored autobiographical writing in early modern Ireland.

2. For the most recent print editions of their work, see Ann Fanshawe, *The Memoirs of Ann, Lady Fanshawe*, in *The Memoirs of Anne, Lady Halkett and Ann, Lady Fanshawe*, ed. John Loftis (Oxford: Clarendon, 1979), 89–192; Alice Thornton, *My First Booke of My Life*, ed. Raymond A. Anselment (Lincoln: University of Nebraska Press, 2014); E. Freke, *Remembrances*; and M. Rich, *Occasional Meditations*. Additional texts by Thornton and Rich are still in manuscript, including the latter's multi-volume diaries and autobiographical narrative: Mary Rich, "Some Specialities in the Life of M. Warwicke," 1625–75, Add. MS 27,357, British Library (BL), London, fols. 1–40; Rich, diary, 1666–77, Add. MSS 27,351–55, BL. On Thornton's complex manuscript corpus, see Anselment, introd. to Thornton, *First Booke*, xvii–lvii.

3. See also Julie A. Eckerle's "Women Representing Ireland in the 17th Century: From English Idyll to Irish Nightmare," *Literature Compass* 15, no. 10.

4. In addition to Wolfe, *Elizabeth Cary Lady Falkland*; see Deana Rankin, "'A More Worthy Patronesse': Elizabeth Cary and Ireland," in *The Literary Career and Legacy of Elizabeth Cary, 1613–1680*, ed. Heather Wolfe (London: Palgrave Macmillan, 2007), 203–21.

5. Dorothy Osborne, *Letters from Dorothy Osborne to Sir William Temple (1652–54)*, ed. Edward Abbott Parry (London: Dent, 1914); John Temple, *The Irish Rebellion* (London, 1646).

6. For a recent edition of *Pompey*, see Katherine Philips, *The Collected Works of Katherine Philips: The Matchless Orinda*, ed. Germaine Greer and Ruth Little, vol. 3, *The Translations* (London: Stump Cross, 1993), 1–91. For her letters, see Philips, *The Collected Works of Katherine Philips: The Matchless Orinda*, ed. Thomas Patrick, vol. 2, *The Letters* (London: Stump Cross, 1992).

7. Kate Chedgzoy, "The Cultural Geographies of Early Modern Women's Writing: Journeys across Spaces and Times," *Literature Compass* 3, no. 4 (2006): 884.

8. Kate Chedgzoy, *Women's Writing in the British Atlantic World: Memory, Place and History, 1550–1700* (Cambridge: Cambridge University Press, 2007).

9. John Kerrigan, *Archipelagic English: Literature, History, and Politics, 1603–1707* (Oxford: Oxford University Press, 2008), 80. The foundational text is J. G. A. Pocock, "British History: A Plea for a New Subject," *Journal of Modern History* 47, no. 4 (1975): 601–28. For a recent critique of the way in which Pocock has been interpreted by historians, see Richard Bourke, "Pocock and the Presuppositions of the New British History," *Historical Journal* 53, no. 3 (2010): 747–70. For Marie-Louise Coolahan's critique of archipelagic approaches, see "Whither the Archipelago? Stops, Starts, Hurdles and Hiccups on the Four Nations Front," *Literature Compass* 15, no. 11 (2018).

10. See, for example, Mark Thornton Burnett and Ramona Wray, eds., *Shakespeare and Ireland: History, Politics, Culture* (Houndmills: Macmillan, 1997); Christopher

Highley, *Shakespeare, Spenser and the Crisis in Ireland* (Cambridge: Cambridge University Press, 1997); Willy Maley and Rory Loughnane, eds., *Celtic Shakespeare: The Bard and the Borderers* (Farnham: Ashgate, 2013); Richard McCabe, *Spenser's Monstrous Regiment: Elizabethan Ireland and the Poetics of Difference* (Oxford: Oxford University Press, 2002); and Andrew Murphy, *But the Irish Sea betwixt Us: Ireland, Colonialism and Renaissance Literature* (Lexington: University Press of Kentucky, 1999).

11. Kerrigan, *Archipelagic English*, 82.

12. Sarah Prescott, "Archipelagic Coterie Space: Katherine Philips and Welsh Women's Writing," *Tulsa Studies in Women's Literature* 33, no. 2 (2014): 52–53, 68, 71. See also Prescott, "Archipelagic Orinda? Katherine Philips and the Writing of Welsh Women's Literary History," *Literature Compass* 6, no. 6 (2009): 1167–76.

13. Kerrigan, *Archipelagic English*, 79.

14. Marie-Louise Coolahan, *Women, Writing, and Language in Early Modern Ireland* (Oxford: Oxford University Press, 2010), 6.

15. Kerrigan, *Archipelagic English*, 10.

16. The historiography of women in early modern Ireland continues to lag far behind England and elsewhere. The defining works remain Margaret MacCurtain and Mary O'Dowd, eds., *Women in Early Modern Ireland* (Dublin: Wolfhound, 1991); and Mary O'Dowd, *A History of Women in Ireland, 1500–1800* (Harlow: Pearson Longman, 2005). The study of the literature of early modern Ireland has fared a little better, with key texts including Deana Rankin, *Between Spenser and Swift: English Writing in Seventeenth-Century Ireland* (Cambridge: Cambridge University Press, 2005); Anne Fogarty, "Literature in English, 1550–1690: From the Elizabethan Settlement to the Battle of the Boyne," in *The Cambridge History of Irish Literature*, ed. Margaret Kelleher and Philip O'Leary (Cambridge: Cambridge University Press, 2006), 1:140–90; and Patricia Palmer, *The Severed Head and the Grafted Tongue: Literature, Translation and Violence in Early Modern Ireland* (Cambridge: Cambridge University Press, 2013). There also have been efforts to make the literature of early modern Ireland available in scholarly editions. Examples include Andrew Carpenter, ed., *Verse in English from Tudor and Stuart Ireland* (Cork: Cork University Press, 2003), as well as volumes in the Literature of Early Modern Ireland series at Dublin's Four Courts Press, including John Flood, ed., *The Works of Walter Quin: An Irishman at the Stuart Courts* (2014); Henry Burnell, *Landgartha: A Tragi-Comedy*, ed. Deana Rankin (2014); William Dunkin, *The Parson's Revels*, ed. Catherine Skeen (2010); Richard Nugent, *Cynthia*, ed. Angelina Lynch (2010); Henry Burkhead, *A Tragedy of Cola's Furie or Lirenda's Miserie*, ed. Angelina Lynch (2009); and Faithful Teate, *Ter Tria*, ed. Angelina Lynch (2007). See also the publications of Dublin's Irish Manuscripts

Commission, including David Edwards, ed., *Campaign Journals of the Elizabethan Irish Wars* (2014); John Lowe, ed., *Letter-book of the Earl of Clanricarde, 1643–1647* (1983); Aidan Clarke and Bríd McGrath, eds., *Letterbook of George, 16th Earl of Kildare* (2013); Elizabethanne Boran, ed., *The Correspondence of James Ussher, 1600–1656* (2015); and Andrew Carpenter, ed., *The Poems of Olivia Elder* (2017).

17. Angela Bourke et al., eds., *The Field Day Anthology of Irish Writing*, vols. 4 and 5, *Irish Women's Writing and Traditions* (Cork: Cork University Press, 2002).

18. [Mrs. Francis] Briver, "An Epistolary Account of the Irish Rising of 1641 by the Wife of the Mayor of Waterford (with text)," ed. Naomi McAreavey, *English Literary Renaissance* 42, no. 1 (2012): 90–118; Naomi McAreavey, "'This is that I may remember what passings that Happind in Waterford': Inscribing the 1641 Rising in the Letters of the Wife of the Mayor of Waterford," *Early Modern Women: An Interdisciplinary Journal* 5 (2010): 77–109.

19. On the women of the Hartlib Circle, see Carol Pal, *Republic of Women: Rethinking the Republic of Letters in the Seventeenth Century* (Cambridge: Cambridge University Press, 2012). On Moore, see Dorothy Moore, *The Letters of Dorothy Moore, 1612–64: The Friendships, Marriage, and Intellectual Life of a Seventeenth-Century Woman*, ed. Lynette Hunter (Aldershot: Ashgate, 2004); Marie-Louise Coolahan, "Irish Women's Letters, 1641–1653," in Daybell and Gordon, *Women and Epistolary Agency*, 174–77; and Felicity Lynn Maxwell, "Calling for Collaboration: Women and Public Service in Dorothy Moore's Transnational Protestant Correspondence," *Literature Compass* 14, no. 4 (2017). On Ranelagh, see Ruth Connolly, "A Proselytising Protestant Commonwealth: The Religious and Political Ideals of Katherine Jones, Viscountess Ranelagh (1614–1691)," *Seventeenth Century* 23, no. 2 (2008): 244–64; Connolly, "Viscountess Ranelagh and the Authorisation of Women's Knowledge in the Hartlib Circle," in *The Intellectual Culture of Puritan Women, 1558–1680*, ed. Johanna Harris and Elizabeth Scott-Baumann (Basingstoke: Palgrave Macmillan, 2011), 150–61; Connolly, "'A Wise and Godly Sybilla': Viscountess Ranelagh and the Politics of International Protestantism," in *Women, Gender, and Radical Religion in Early Modern Europe*, ed. Sylvia Brown (Leiden: Brill, 2007), 285–306; Michelle DiMeo, "Katherine Jones, Lady Ranelagh (1615–91): Science and Medicine in a Seventeenth-Century Englishwoman's Writing" (PhD diss., University of Warwick, 2009); DiMeo, "Lady Ranelagh's Book of Kitchen-Physick? Reattributing Authorship for Wellcome Library MS 1340," *Huntington Library Quarterly* 77, no. 3 (2014): 331–46; DiMeo, "The Rhetoric of Medical Authority in Lady Katherine Ranelagh's Letters," in Daybell and Gordon, *Women and Epistolary Agency*, 96–109; DiMeo, "'Such a sister became such a brother': Lady Ranelagh's Influence on Robert Boyle," *Intellectual History Review* 25, no. 1 (2015): 21–36; Lynette Hunter, "Sisters of the Royal Society: The Circle of Katherine Jones, Lady Ranelagh," in *Women, Science and*

Medicine, 1500–1700: Mothers and Sisters of the Royal Society, ed. Lynette Hunter and Sarah Hutton (Stroud: Sutton, 1997); 178–97; and Betsey Taylor-FitzSimon, "Conversion, the Bible, and the Irish Language: The Correspondence of Lady Ranelagh and Bishop Dopping," in *Converts and Conversion in Ireland, 1650–1850*, ed. Michael Brown, Charles I. McGrath, and Thomas P. Power (Dublin: Four Courts, 2005),157–82.

20. Coolahan, "Irish Women's Letters," in Daybell and Gordon, *Women and Epistolary Agency*, 167–81.

21. Hannah Alexander, *A Book of Cookery for dressing of Several Dishes of Meat and making of Several Sauces and Seasoning for Meat or Fowl*, ed. Deirdre Nuttall (Westport: Evertype, 2014).

22. Elizabeth, Lady Petty, business diary, June and July 1675, Lansdowne Manuscripts, 1228, BL.

23. Anne Southwell, *The Southwell-Sibthorpe Commonplace Book: Folger MS V.b.198*, ed. Jean Klene (Tempe: Arizona Center for Medieval and Renaissance Studies, 1997). See also Marie-Louise Coolahan, "Ideal Communities and Planter Women's Writing in Seventeenth-Century Ireland," *Parergon: Journal of the Australian and New Zealand Association for Medieval and Early Modern Studies* 29, no. 2 (2012): 69–91.

24. Elizabeth Boyle, Countess of Cork and Burlington, memorandum book, Misc. Box 5, Cork Manuscripts, Chatsworth House, Derbyshire.

25. Mother Mary Bonaventure Browne, chronicle, MS, Poor Clare Monastery, Nun's Island, Galway; for a modernized edition, see Celsus O'Brien, ed., *Recollections of an Irish Poor Clare in the Seventeenth Century* (Galway: Connaught Tribune, 1993). For an analysis of the chronicle, see Marie-Louise Coolahan, "Identity Politics and Nuns' Writing," *Women's Writing* 14, no. 2 (2007): 306–320; Coolahan, "Archipelagic Identities in Europe: Irish Nuns in English Convents," in *English Convents in Exile, 1600–1800: Communities, Culture and Identity*, ed. Caroline Bowden and James Kelly (Farnham: Ashgate, 2013), 211–28; and Naomi McAreavey, "Irish Nuns and the Counter-Reformation Movement: The Struggle between Nation and Vocation," in *Representing Women's Authority in the Early Modern World*, ed. Eavan O'Brien (Rome: Aracne, 2013), 221–51.

26. Frances Cooke, *Mris Cookes Meditations* ([London, 1650]).

27. Barbara Blaugdone, *An Account of the Travels, Sufferings & Persecutions of Barbara Blaugdone. Given Forth as a Testimony to the Lord's Power, and for the Encouragement of Friends* (Shoreditch, 1691).

28. John Rogers, *Ohel or Beth-shemesh: A Tabernacle for the Sun*, 2 vols. (London, 1653).

29. Mary Trye, *Medicatrix, or the Woman-Physician* (London, 1675). Coolahan, "Early Modern Irish Autobiography," defines "marginal autobiography" as "the autobiographical fragments that emerge from texts apparently written for entirely different purposes" (50) and cites Trye as an example because she writes herself

into the "paratextual margins" (specifically the dedication) of her text (51). For paratextual materials, especially prefaces, as life writing, see Eckerle, "Prefacing Texts, Authorizing Authors, and Constructing Selves: The Preface as Autobiographical Space," in Dowd and Eckerle, *Women's Life Writing*, 97–113.

30. Life writing is a major strand in Coolahan's *Women, Writing, and Language* but is not her central focus.

31. See the 1641 Depositions database, http://1641.tcd.ie. For an analysis of women's depositions, see Coolahan, *Women, Writing, and Language*, 141–79; Coolahan, "'And this deponent further sayeth': Orality, Print and the 1641 Depositions," in *Oral and Print Cultures in Ireland, 1600–1900*, ed. Marc Caball and Andrew Carpenter (Dublin: Four Courts, 2010), 69–84; and Naomi McAreavey, "Re(-)membering Women: Protestant Women's Victim Testimonies during the Irish Rising of 1641," *Journal of the Northern Renaissance* 2 (2010).

32. William King, correspondence, MSS 1995–2008, Lyons Collection, TCD, Dublin.

33. The majority of the Duchess of Ormonde's letters are preserved mainly among the Ormond Papers in the National Library of Ireland, Dublin; and the Carte Papers in the Bodleian Library (Bodl.), Oxford. Elizabeth Butler, Duchess of Ormonde, *The Letters of the First Duchess of Ormonde*, ed. Naomi McAreavey, is forthcoming with Arizona Center for Medieval and Renaissance Studies.

34. For Philips's Irish contexts, see Coolahan, *Women, Writing, and Language*, 195–212; Catharine Gray, "Katherine Philips in Ireland," *English Literary Renaissance* 39, no. 3 (2009): 557–85; and Rosalinde Schut, "La Femme Forte: Katherine Philips and the Politics of Her Dublin Writings, 1662–1663," in *Early Modern Englishwomen Testing Ideas*, ed. Jo Wallwork and Paul Salzman (Farnham: Ashgate, 2011), 107–20.

35. On her letters, see Paul Trolander and Zeynep Tenger, "Katherine Philips and Coterie Critical Practices," *Eighteenth-Century Studies* 37, no. 3 (2004): 367–87.

36. Philo-Philippa, "To the Excellent *Orinda*," in Carpenter, *Verse in English*, 367–73.

37. David J. Baker and Willy Maley, eds., *British Identities and English Renaissance Literature* (Cambridge: Cambridge University Press, 2002), 1.

38. Prescott, "Archipelagic Coterie Space"; Prescott, "Archipelagic Orinda?"

39. Frances Parker to William King, December 13, 1690, MSS 1995–2008/105, Lyons Collection, TCD. Parker was the second wife of Sir John Parker (d. 1696). Like many Protestants, they had left Ireland in 1688.

40. On Ní Mháille, see Anne Chambers, *Granuaile: The Life and Times of Grace O'Malley, c. 1530–1603*, 3rd ed. (Dublin: Wolfhound, 1998); and Coolahan, *Women, Writing, and Language*, 116–24. O'Doherty's one extant letter is included in Bourke et al., *Field Day Anthology*, 5:30.

41. Anne Chambers, *Eleanor, Countess of Desmond, c. 1545–1638* (Dublin: Wolfhound, 1986).

42. On Piggott, see Dianne Hall, "'Most barbarously and inhumaine maner butchered': Masculinity, Trauma, and Memory in Early Modern Ireland," in *The Body in Pain in Irish Literature and Culture*, ed. Fionnuala Dillane, Naomi McAreavey, and Emilie Pine (London: Palgrave, 2016), 45–50.

43. On Avery, see Crawford Gribben, *God's Irishmen: Theological Debates in Cromwellian Ireland* (Oxford: Oxford University Press, 2007).

44. Elizabeth Price, deposition, June 26, 1643, 1641 Depositions, MS 836, TCD, fols. 101r–105v. For an analysis of Price's deposition, see Coolahan, *Women, Writing, and Language*, 160–65; and McAreavey, "Re(-)membering Women," paras. 23–29.

45. Elizabeth Dowdall, deposition, October 3, 1642, 1641 Depositions, MS 829, TCD, fols. 138r–139v; Dowdall, "A true note," October 6, 1642, MS 1008, Sloane Manuscripts, BL, fols. 66r–69r; also printed in Bourke et al., *Field Day Anthology*, 5:22–24. For secondary criticism on Dowdall, see Coolahan, *Women, Writing, and Language*, 173–78; Chedgzoy, *British Atlantic World*, 92; and Naomi McAreavey, "'Paper bullets': Gendering the 1641 Rebellion in the Writings of Lady Elizabeth Dowdall and Lettice Fitzgerald, Baroness of Offaly," in *Ireland in the Renaissance, c. 1540–1660*, ed. Thomas Herron and Michael Potterton (Dublin: Four Courts, 2007), 311–24.

46. Lettice Fitzgerald, siege letters, in Thomas Pickering, deposition, August 15, 1642, 1641 Depositions, MS 814, TCD, fols. 117r–117v; Fitzgerald to the Earl of Ormonde, January 19, 1642, MS 2, Carte Papers, Bodl., fol. 264. Her letters are printed in Bourke et al., *Field Day Anthology*, 5:25–27. For secondary criticism on Fitzgerald, see Coolahan, *Women, Writing, and Language*, 166–172; and McAreavey, "Paper bullets," in Herron and Potterton, *Ireland in the Renaissance*, 311–24.

47. Blaugdone, *Travels, Sufferings & Persecutions*.

1

Alice Thornton, Elizabeth Freke, and the Remembrances of Ireland

RAYMOND A. ANSELMENT

Among the writing of early modern English women, recollections of life in Ireland are less common than the English presence might suggest. The numerous formulaic depositions recorded in the months following the 1641 Irish uprising offer a vivid testimony of the atrocities and trauma English settlers suffered; personal narratives of several women who defended their property against besieging forces have also survived.[1] Forms of self-writing from less troubled periods of the seventeenth century are not as extensive or as accessible. Letters women wrote from Ireland are now held often among family papers and in archives. Few diaries and memoirs that include accounts of living among the Irish appear to have survived. The remembrances of Ireland of Alice Thornton (1626–1707) and Elizabeth Freke (1642–1714) are noteworthy exceptions. Near the end of 1634, eight-year-old Alice, along with her mother and younger brothers, joined her father, Christopher Wandesford, in Dublin, where he had been appointed master of rolls and where they would live for eight years. Elizabeth Freke was thirty-three when she and her husband, Percy, left England in 1675 for County Cork to "try our fortuns" in Ireland. Over the next twenty years, Elizabeth would live there on five occasions, the shortest eight months and the longest four years. Thornton recalled briefly in "A booke of remembrances" and at greater length in a second manuscript, "My First Booke of My Life," the sense of place she enjoyed with her family during a happy Dublin life. Freke, on the other hand, describes in both versions of "Some few remembrances" the isolation and alienation during her years in Ireland.[2] For both women the Ireland of memory is inseparable from their self-images and subsequent life experiences.

The meaning of Ireland also alters in the revisions of their recollections. The first of Thornton's two manuscripts, each of which begins with her birth in 1626 and ends with the 1668 death of her husband, William, begins as a spiritual memoir. The years in Ireland briefly recalled are occasions of divine deliverance set down in celebration of God's providential mercy. Though the narrative turns more toward her life and family after the return to England, she does not seem at least initially to have a larger audience in mind. Within a year of her husband's death, however, Thornton circulated a personal defense of her honor and that of her family. The revised "My First Booke of My Life" she bequeathed to her daughter significantly expands and refocuses "A booke of remembrances," remembering Ireland anew from an implicitly defensive point of view. The awareness of a larger audience is not apparent in either version of Freke's years in Ireland. Included in manuscripts that contain, among other entries, lists of properties and inventories of possessions, the narratives that begin with her marriage and end within months of her death in 1714 seem another form of accounting. Begun before her husband's death in 1705 and rewritten in the final years of her life, "Some few remembrances of my misfortunes" associate much of her unhappiness with Ireland. Unlike Thornton, whose family contributed significantly to her feeling of belonging, Freke never found in Ireland a sense of place. A stranger and at first frightened, for her Ireland increasingly came to embody the growing separation and estrangement from her husband and son, as well as a place she came to view in widowhood with suspicion and mistrust.

Each account of young Alice's arrival in Ireland begins in essentially the same way. After "safe passage" across the Irish Sea, she arrived in Dublin, "In which place I inioyed great happienesse and Comfort dureing my honoured fathers life."[3] The city where she lived for most of her stay offered a culture not found in north Yorkshire, where she was born. Noted in Raphael Holinshed's *Irish Chronicle* as "Irishe or yong London," Dublin in the 1630s had a population of about fifteen thousand.[4] A traveler through Scotland and Ireland within a year of Alice's arrival praised Dublin as "the fairest, richest, best built city" on his journey, a metropolis "far beyond Edenborough" and most resembling London. Besides "fair, stately and complete buildings," it had in his opinion the "divers commodities" Londoners enjoyed.[5] A resident of Dublin less favorably impressed by the city nevertheless earlier called attention to shops "well replenished withall sortes of wares" rivaling any in London; its citizens were also "wonderfully reformed in manners, in ciuility, in curtesy."[6] Dublin, a cathedral city, possessed the hallmarks of a major urban center. By the beginning of the seventeenth century, Parliament resided permanently in Dublin and Trinity College had been founded. Courts of law, a royal custom house, and the commerce of a significant port increased the city's prominence in the next decades as an administrative, legal, and financial power. Though the majority of the Dubliners were Catholic, English Protestants gained substantial control of trade and during the administration of Thomas Wentworth, later Earl of Strafford, dominated the offices of government and law.[7] When Alice with her mother and brothers joined her father in Dublin, he had an important role in the center of power Wentworth had begun to create, and the family would settle among the prominent residents of Dame Street. They lived in a "very elegant House," according to an eighteenth-century descendant with access to the family papers, "situated conveniently for the Discharge of his high Offices. It was in a very wholsome Air, with a good Orchard and Garden leading down to the Water Side, where might be seen the Ships from the Ring's End."[8]

Almost five years later Alice crossed the Irish Sea again, accompanying her mother to Bath and later sailing back to Ireland through perilous seas. The account in the second manuscript of a life-threatening storm, her safe arrival on the Irish shore, and her response to this deliverance remembers Ireland anew. Though travel across the Irish Sea could take little more than a day if all went well,[9] the tidal streams and winds of the narrow sea, the treacherous shoreline of rocks and sands, and the threat of pirates and privateers were dangerous realities.[10] Sailing from Wexford to Kinsale in January 1650, Frances Cooke and John Cook spent ten days at sea in the turbulent storms described in her *Meditations* and his *True Relation*.[11] While Alice waited in Cheshire with her mother for the stormy sea to change, they witnessed five ships driven onto the shore, only to be caught themselves in a tempest that turned the calm night on which they sailed into winds and waves that threatened to wreck the ship on the Irish sands. Her revised narrative of the harrowing journey in the second of the two manuscripts describes the threat in graphic detail: deliverance from danger includes Alice's rescue from the threat of entanglement in a ship's cable that would have swept her into the sea. Both also end in thanksgiving. Missing from the first version is the family's safe removal from the anchored ship caught on the sands, their reception once ashore, and an extended outpouring of thanksgiving. The additions in the second manuscript modify the emphasis and intent.

Alice's father and her praise of God are notably more prominent. The boat that rescues them from the ship is sent by a Mr. Hubert, who together with his family and friends welcomes them joyfully and entertains them "with abundante affection & kindenesse" (15). Coaches from Dublin with her father and his "many noble freinds" the next day take them back to the city and a reception of further joy. Once again, as Alice had in recounting their first arrival in Ireland, the second manuscript describes a welcoming place: "much peace & happinesse" that would last until her father's death. He, and not Ireland, is the source of this contentment. Mr. Hubert's kindness is an expression of gratitude for the justice received in her father's jurisdiction, having spent twenty ruinous years struggling against a powerful opponent to present his suit. The esteem her father brought to the law is also implicit in the coaches of men who accompany her father and are part of a Dublin she believed that his judicious office helped change. The family's deliverance from the storms of the Irish Sea moves Alice to emulate the thanksgiving of those "that goe downe to the Sea in Ships." Psalm 107 is appropriately central to her stormy journey in the parallels and grateful praise with which she too would "give thanks unto the Lord" (107:1).[12] Her desire to keep the mercy of God in "perpetuall remembrance" is apparent in the long thanksgiving that in the second manuscript complements the greater emphasis on her father (16).

The focus of "My First Booke of My Life" differs from that of the earlier version. Both begin as quite traditional exercises chronicling deliverances covering the span from early childhood to the death of Thornton's husband. The earlier "booke of remembrances" devotes considerably less attention to the stay in Ireland and recalls the decade of the 1640s and the family's return to England for the most part in cursory fashion. Important events that follow in Alice's life are often related in a minimalist fashion. One brief sentence records her 1651 marriage to William Thornton; short paragraphs enter births and deaths of their first children. The narrative and the thanksgiving become more substantial in the last years. Whether this or the revised account was the manuscript Thornton later states that she circulated a year after William died, "My First Booke of My Life" is the manuscript she bequeathed to her daughter.[13] The biographical expansion and prayerful gratitude in this revision reflect more fully the troubled period in Thornton's life in the year preceding her husband's death.

Though the stages of composition in neither manuscript can be dated with certainty, when Thornton recalled her earlier life in a final revision, she had been deeply hurt by the betrayal of a niece who had withheld knowledge of "very great lies & fallshoods against my selfe" and the "Honour of my Family" (181) that might have been countered before the Thornton reputation had been compromised. The scandalous rumors are never clarified, but they appear related to the betrothal of their fourteen-year-old daughter to a local minister and the mother's relationship with him. Rumors about the propriety of the proposed marriage apparently insinuated that the parents were using their daughter to help secure the family's uncertain future. Bruited about was the further suggestion of an improper relationship between Alice and the minister, who had lived with the Thorntons. When the niece's maid revealed the rumors in an emotional confrontation, taunting Alice with the assertion that she, her family, and "all I came on" were "naught," and then both the niece and maid jeered and laughed, the scandal maligning the reputation of the family was all the more hurtful because the Thorntons had supported the niece in her difficult marriage.

Compelled to defend her reputation and that of her family, when Alice expanded the recollections of the Irish years significantly, the revision reflects the defensive tenor.[14] Praise of her honorable father and devotion to a merciful God are an essential part of this vindication.

The initial entry in each manuscript about the years in Ireland begins with the family and not Dublin; the happiness of Alice depends on her parents, especially her father. He "ordered" the traditional education of a young lady in French, dancing, and music; through her father's close relationship with the future Earl of Strafford, Thomas Wentworth, she had the advantage of being taught these and other "qualities" in the company of his two daughters. The "vertuous prouission" of a mother who raised her daughter with a care befitting "her qualitie & my fathers Childe" (10) reinforced their social class and heritage. Above all, through the guidance of her parents and their example, Alice believes she found greatest happiness in the religious life they both embodied and encouraged.

Her "bounden duty" to celebrate God's mercy is apparent in recollections of Alice's Irish life absent from the earlier manuscript. Her fall while swinging with the Wentworth sisters at Robert Meredith's Dublin house is one of the few memories of Alice's early years in Ireland. The account of the accident recalled in the revised manuscript recreates the childhood misadventure from the perspective of the young girl whose new confidence in her abilities turns to fear when she loses her grip. Everyone in the house may have been worried, as Thornton remembers, though probably few if any thought "for a good space of time" that the stunned girl was dead (13). The exaggeration, in any case, enhances her gratitude for her mother's care and her prayerful thankfulness for the mercy of God. Her narrative of another fall, this time when the family coach narrowly avoided sliding into the river on a trip to County Kildare, ends with a similar response. Thornton never describes Kildare, where her father had purchased an estate at Naas and where they would live for at least a while before he sold the property to Thomas Wentworth. The focus on the danger narrowly avoided by the skill of the coachman and the rejoicing of the father, who rode on horseback behind the coach helpless to assist him, occasion prayer as Thornton joins her father in glorifying God for the escape from death (11–12).

Two other additions in the revised manuscript are less immediately related to God's protection of Alice and her family. The vivid narrative of a fire in Dublin Castle, where the Wentworth family resided, traces its cause to a carelessly stored basket of embers and describes the damage to the chapel. The danger to the castle averted by Providence may not have been as immediate as Thornton believes, and she could only have imagined as "terrible to behold" a scene she never witnessed. The cries in the night, the description of the castle setting, and the rescue of the Wentworth family "brought out of bed in blankets" accentuate, however, the providential mercy. Significantly, the rescue of the family includes the deliverance of "all the Kingdom in them," her father, and "his family" (14). This inclusiveness reflects Thornton's belief that on Wentworth's governance rested the well-being of Ireland.

A much longer addition depicting the governance, trial, and death of Wentworth, Earl of Strafford, develops the nature of this relationship and its connection to her Irish memories. Family loyalty explains in part Thornton's departure from thanksgiving and prayer to praise the lord deputy's governance of Ireland and to denounce the malice of his enemies. Alice's father, Christopher Wandesford, would not have been an entrusted part of the administration in Ireland without his ties to Wentworth. They were both friends and kin. An important supporter of Wandesford's career in the English Parliament and Yorkshire government and the godfather of his first child, the newly appointed lord deputy brought his kinsman with him to Ireland, where Wentworth continued to promote his role in the administration.[15] Wandesford also relied on the lord deputy's influence in securing and protecting his possession of the twenty thousand acres of Castlecomer he had negotiated in the county of Kilkenny.[16] After he succeeded the newly ennobled Earl of Strafford as lord deputy, Alice's father tried to circumvent a remonstrance against Strafford in Ireland, proroguing the Irish Parliament and futilely attempting to prevent committee members from going to England to present their case.[17]

The relationship with Ireland—both Strafford's and Wandesford's—is the foundation of Thornton's forceful, uncompromising support of the earl and an implicit defense of her father's loyalty. Strafford's seven years of Irish governance disaffected others through the unbending administration of policies that seemed absolutist and threatening. As lord deputy, he was also believed to have used the office for his own benefit.[18] Before being brought back to England to face charges of treason, Strafford had few supporters.[19] The earl was, in Thornton's judgment, however, "a wise & prudentiall" leader who preserved the dignity and majesty of the monarchy and secured both the church and state on "the right foundations of truth & peace." Thornton scorns his detractors as "factious" and "Seditious," threatening law and peace under the guise of a heretical and popish religion. In her excoriation of the bloodthirsty Irish unworthy of the bountiful peace in the seven years of the "wise & Noble" lord deputy's rule, Thornton adopts the common seventeenth-century English view of the Irish as a "Barbarous People" incapable of benefiting from the civilizing force of English government and law (18). She also accepts without question, albeit with extreme exaggeration, reports of the uprising that began in the years following the death of Strafford and led in her view to the "destruction" and the "martyredom" of "millions of the Poore protestants."[20] But Thornton's denunciation is not limited to the Irish. Unwavering in her commitment to the monarchy and the Church of England, which she unequivocally asserts was upheld by Strafford, Thornton attacks his enemies in the English Parliament as "Mastiues, & blood hounds." The crowds gathering each day in London outside Parliament demanding his death are "Vulger meaner Peopple" easily swayed by lies and "Cruell Malice" (19, 20).

Historians agree that Strafford defended himself well, forcing the parliamentary prosecutors to turn away from impeachment to a bill of attainder, though it is questionable whether "all the world" other than his adversaries shared Thornton's admiration of the "incomparable Wisdome & Abilities" of his gallant defense. She denounces the tactics used in Parliament to inhibit the earl's response to new charges, and she dismisses as "Lies & callumnies" (19) accusations that he encouraged the king in the subversion of law and support of popery. And when in her narrative Thornton accepts the king's decision to sign the bill condemning an innocent Strafford, she recognizes the necessity of this "most Pieous King" (20) to protect his own life. In her interpretation Strafford himself accepts the necessity of his death, absolving the king and hoping his fate will restore a greater peace. Her image of the cheerful, serene, and composed man who went to his death in 1641 forgiving his enemies and praying for the welfare of the nation and its monarch is based on contemporary printings of statements he purportedly made in his last hours.[21] Her belief that years of peace engendered sins that brought down the sword of destruction was a commonplace based as well on hindsight.[22] "Darkenesse & distruction," the eulogy of Strafford concludes, occur when "taken away" are the "Iust & wise men" (21).

The revised manuscript complements and counterpoints the tribute to the Earl of Strafford with that of her father. Both men are ideal public servants whose deaths are a measure of their lives. The earl died on the scaffold with grace and dignity, wrongly sentenced to death for his misuse of office; Wandesford succumbed to a fever in bed with Christian magnanimity, the only lord deputy, his daughter contends, who "died vntouched, or peaceably in theire beds" (25). The earlier manuscript simply notes her father's death in December 1640; the revision relates at length his last days and concludes with a long meditation and prayer. The additions celebrate a public and private life devoted to the good of the Irish people and the happiness of his family that will be blessed in memory for generations. Thornton praises her father as "A true Labourer in Gods Vineyard" (22) and recalls again the reform he brought to courts that had denied justice to the oppressed and unfortunate struggling for years against endless legal delay, corrupt officials, and powerful opponents. His was a "wise, Iust" government, "Legall & right" (21), that won an affection in Ireland unequaled among other English administrators. Extoled for his patronage of the church and support of education, Wandesford embodies in an extended catalog of virtues the "Heroicke Soule"—an "exemplear of Learning, Sobriety, Temporance, chastety, holinesse, patience, humility, Charity, Iustice & clemency" (22). A husband without parallel in the world, a marriage admired by all, and children "infinitly happy, & blessed," the Wandesfords were a rare family exceedingly happy in his love and care.

In the manuscript's recounting, the death of Thornton's father is further affirmation of Wandesford's incomparable life. The narrative that begins with the onset of a sudden fever and ends with the confession of sins, testimony of faith, and prayers commending the soul to God is that of the good death in the *ars moriendi* tradition. The reading of the will and instructions to his oldest son are part of the pattern of the good death, also confirming an abiding concern for the well-being of his family. Less typical is Thornton's further affirmation of her father's concern as well for the welfare of Ireland. Comments about the law he made while apparently asleep similarly recall his concern for an equitable justice to all, whether rich or poor, determined solely by divine and human law. The burdens and responsibilities of the offices he held in Ireland "it was thought" decayed the heart, which was allegedly evident when the body was embalmed. The cause of death seems more than Thornton's fanciful suggestion. Richard Cox wrote later in the century that the lord deputy died suddenly, "heart-broken with his own and the Earl of *Strafford's* Misfortunes."[23] While Cox may have had in mind Wandesford's struggles to control the Irish Parliament and its opposition to Strafford, another event that qualifies, if not questions, Thornton's uncritical view of her father's years in Ireland involved his disputed ownership of Castlecomer. As master of rolls Wandesford used his office to win a favorable claim to the land and his friendship with the lord deputy to protect the holding from the threat of seizure. Strafford's intercession became an issue in the articles of his impeachment, and at Wandesford's death the legal title was again in jeopardy and would remain in dispute until the end of the century.[24] But to his daughter he remained her devoted father honored with great dignity and acclaim: "Such was the loue," the Irish lamented with a hone or outpouring of grief unheard before in Ireland at funerals for the English (26).[25]

The meditation and prayer reaffirm Thornton's tribute to "this Diligent labourour of God" (31) who toiled for the betterment of his family and of Ireland; verses from Isaiah 57: 1–2 offer in the meditation consolation and an understanding of the dying father's premonition, "Ah poore childe, what must thou see & thine Eyes beholde" (24). The righteous and the merciful "taken away" will find restful peace; they are taken from "the euill to come" (26). Thornton often finds solace in the knowledge that death is a liberation from the sorrows of life; in meditating on her father she dwells less on the peace of a "better Place" (29) and more on the "misserable, wrettched world" (27) and the evil he has escaped. Certain that he had "foreseene" and labored in Ireland to prevent a forthcoming evil, Thornton consoles herself with the knowledge that he did not see the destruction of peace and the suffering that she and others believed "was neuer heard of the like" (29).[26] The sins of the nation cried out for God's vengeance, yet "miraculously" divine Providence delivered the family from the Irish turmoil. Without the guiding love of her own father, to whose "Prouidence, caire & wisdome" she unfailingly attributes her former happiness, Thornton welcomes in prayer a greater dependency on God. In her renewed dedication he is "our Father"—in words taken from the Psalm 68:5: "A father to the fatherlesse" (32). God will also be, she prays, her mother's "Husband & guide" (33). And in a sense her mother becomes her father, for strengthened by the spirit of God she led her family out of Ireland and away from the imminent danger.

Thornton's narrative in the second manuscript of the October 1641 plot to seize Dublin Castle and the danger to the family adds considerable detail to her first account. Within days of the conspiracy's discovery, news of the plot to take command of the castle, where ordnances and ammunition were stored, and from this position gain control of the city was widespread. The account is much the same in the numerous reports later printed, the most influential of which were the many editions of John Temple's *The Irish Rebellion* (1646).[27] When one of the conspirators while drinking disclosed the plan to his Protestant kinsman John Connolly, he escaped from their watch, jumped over a pale, and informed the chief justices. In some versions the justices doubted the seemingly drunken Connolly and sent him back for further confirmation of the plot before they then arrested the conspirators. Thornton omits the return and the second escape in a leaner narrative that recreates the drinking scene in the alehouse, the drama of Connolly's leap from a window over a wall, and the urgency of his address to the chief justices.[28] In her lively version, when Connolly voices concern about his Protestant wife, the conspirators reply, "hang her, for she was but an English dogge" and a better Irish wife can be found (36).[29] Where other accounts disagree about whether warnings weeks earlier had been ignored, Thornton places considerable blame on justices Sir John Parsons and Sir John Borlase, "2 old gentlemen" seduced into complacency by years of peace and incapable of fulfilling the vacancy left by the deaths of her father and Strafford.[30] Her vivid recollection lends personal immediacy to the October uprising. The plight of the Dubliners mentioned in some publications is that of her family. During "14 daies & nights in great feares, frights, & hidious distractions & disturbances from the Alarums" and sleepless nights, "fastings & paines," the Thorntons gathered their possessions for the flight to England (37).

With the safe preservation of "my fathers family" from Ireland— curiously described in the manuscript as "a strainge Place" (38)—Alice's mother assumed in England the role her father had held within the family in Ireland. Thornton praises her at great length as the support of the family in a celebration that purposefully counters the later allegations of ruined reputation. Through the dangers of a nation now at civil war, she led her children safely back to her Yorkshire jointure at Hipswell, where she made "a Sanctuary for vs all" (75), and through her determination withstood the military and legal threats to the family estate. Alice remained with her mother until the age of twenty-five, when she reluctantly followed her mother's will and married William Thornton. She and her husband resided for eight years at Hipswell until her mother died; they then moved to Thornton's Yorkshire inheritance at East Newton. Alice Thornton never returned to Ireland, though both manuscripts reveal her efforts to gain the Irish legacy of 1,500 pounds bequeathed by her father. The presence of the family in Ireland would continue, however, in Castlecomer, where Thornton's father had spent a reported 14,000 pounds establishing a plantation of English tenants to farm the land and mine the ore and coal.[31] Along with a manor house east of the Dinin River and a four-thousand-acre deer park, the Castlecomer plantation had a village of some five hundred residents.[32] Alice's brother inherited the property, which stayed in the Wandesford family into the twentieth century, when most of the remaining twenty thousand acres were sold. The house on the bank of the river rebuilt after being destroyed in the Irish uprising of 1798 was lost in a 1966 fire.[33] Alice's remembrance of Ireland memorably endures, however, in manuscript and print.

Elizabeth Freke's experiences in Ireland were very different. Her "remembrances of my misfortuns" begin with her marriage in 1671 to her second cousin Percy Freke and end with the last months before her death in 1714. She began the first recollections before the death of her husband in 1706 and continued writing entries in a vellum-bound manuscript throughout her years of widowhood. In 1712 she revised her remembrances in a wallpaper-bound manuscript, adding further entries during the next year. Unlike the self-writing of Alice Thornton, neither version has a religious focus nor is a personal defense addressed to a larger audience. Though God's providence and mercy are an acknowledged part of the life she recalls, hers is an "unhappy life," and Freke herself remains the focus. The death of her husband and a growing sense of isolation in her later years alter without radically changing the representation of the misfortunes. Freke associates with Ireland separation from her father, her husband, her son, and her money.

Three years after their marriage and an unhappy life in London, where Elizabeth suffered two miscarriages and lost money in a Hampshire property, the Frekes agreed to try their fortunes in Ireland at "his estat."[34] Percy Freke's father had settled in the Munster plantation in County Cork, and the castle at Rathbarry he defended during the 1641 uprising would eventually become his son's; however, the nature of the Rathbarry estate remains in the manuscripts initially undefined.[35] When the Frekes sailed to Ireland in the first of five voyages from England, after being delayed by stormy weather and then the birth of their son, they stayed for eight months at Rostellan. A dangerous Irish Sea threatened their safe landing in 1677 at Cork during a second eight-month stay at an unnamed location. A third return in 1680 of twenty-two months was spent at Rathbarry, as were two further stays, at the estate Percy Freke had secured with the purchase of a reversion on the lease.[36] On the coast of southern County Cork, several miles from the small cathedral town of Rosscarbery, the area around Rathbarry and especially the river valley and town of Bandon to the northeast had been settled by English Protestants.[37] Still decidedly in the minority among the Irish Catholics, the English, according to one study of their presence in seventeenth-century Munster, had "social conditions which would have comforted and reassured."[38] The Ireland of County Cork may not have been "radically different from England," and the city of Cork had become in prominence second only to Dublin, but the Ireland of Rathbarry was not the London Elizabeth Freke had left behind.[39] Her husband, Percy, born in County Cork, was more at home in an Anglo-Irish culture that to his wife would probably have appeared quite foreign.

The Ireland Elizabeth describes in both manuscripts is unwelcoming, with "noe place fitt to putt my unfortunat head" (42). The eight months she and her husband spent at the Second Earl of Inchiquin's Rostellan estate might have eased her transition to Ireland: the O'Briens were related through marriage to the Frekes, with whom they also came to the royalist defense.[40] But Elizabeth, who had another miscarriage during the time at Rostellan, was deeply affected by her mother-in-law's unkindness there. Later a similar treatment, she writes, occurred when she, her husband, and their five-year-old son came to Rathbarry in 1680 after the death of her mother-in-law; her sister-in-law had taken away from "my house" all of any worth—including the seven years of letters between Elizabeth and Percy before they were married—claiming the Frekes' plate and linens were her mother's and leaving them with the bill for her burial.[41] When, after the difficult winter of their next return in 1683, John Hull demanded the fulfillment of a lease on Rathbarry her husband had signed without her knowledge, she claims "we lost neer halfe our goods, the whole country coming to see this cruellty to us" (51/222). The Frekes regained possession of Rathbarry following the war between James II and William III, and Elizabeth reluctantly returned to Ireland in 1692 after eight years "to know more misery" (61). The house at Rathbarry had been burned during the conflict, and in her retelling she found a "deplorable" and "miserable place" with only two rooms, bare walls, and no chair or bed "fitt for a Christion" (61/229). By her reckoning she spent four and a half years "allmost frightned outt of my witts" (229), always seriously ill, and often unable to go down the stairs without assistance. It was "a miserable hard fate" (61/230) and "a miserable life" (232).

But the Ireland of Freke's remembrances does not always appear a miserable place. When on her fourth voyage to Ireland she and her husband arrived at Cork with "none to help us" (50) and were brought before the mayor as suspects in English plots, a Mr. Covett offered himself as security, arranged to have their belongings brought ashore, and welcomed them at his house with the civility "due to our quallity" (221). The estate at Rathbarry her husband then leased to John Hull near the end of this stay in Ireland also seems to befit their quality, and the neighbors in the country appear to have been supportive. A farm in the lease and the number of horses and oxen, a large herd of cows, and a flock of sheep suggest the estate was substantial; neighbors and others in the Rathbarry area came to the Frekes' aid with carts and horses to help them move when forced from their house without adequate notice. However miserable Elizabeth may have been during her last years in Ireland, when their property was restored, they remained a family of some stature, and her life may not have been entirely one of isolation. Percy represented Clonakilty in the Irish Parliament.[42] When he also became a sheriff, "doe all I could to the contrary" (230), Elizabeth accompanied him to the assizes in Cork, which were important social occasions.[43] Twenty-two liveried men attended him; others ran alongside his horses. And when he went the next year as sheriff to Dublin, the Third Earl of Drogheda, Henry Moore, offered a match between his daughter Alice and their son, Ralph. Ireland seemed to have fulfilled the "fortun" the Frekes sought when they first left England, yet Elizabeth was never happy there.

Her initial response to Ireland during the eight months at Rostellan reveals a basic source of Freke's unhappiness when she juxtaposes the unkindness of her mother-in-law in Ireland with the kindness of her father at Hannington. Learning that his daughter was pregnant, Elizabeth's father had sent a coach to Bath for her, where the Frekes were awaiting a ship for their first voyage to Ireland; they stayed with him almost a year, "most kindly treated and used" (40/213), and then left their three-month-old son in his care at Hannington. When Percy Freke later had his wife write to her father for a loan of 1,000 pounds secured on the Norfolk property of West Bilney her father had "settled" on his daughter, he "immediately" sent the money to complete the acquisition of Rathbarry and later waived the loan. And when on a visit from Ireland his daughter seemed to him "a little malloncally," he gave her 200 pounds, telling her not to inform her husband of the gift intended for her own use (49/220).[44] Elizabeth would return from Ireland three times "by the desire of my deer father," the third visit to receive his blessing before he died. At his urging during her final stay she "redily and gladly" promised to remain with him at Hannington, where he assured his daughter that all her needs would be met. The "greatest kindness imaginable" that Elizabeth says she received was "A greatt allterration" from "whatt I found in Ireland from a husband" (49/220), and she adamantly refused to leave when Percy came to Hannington, honoring the promise to her father and protesting the treatment by her husband. Deleted from her first version and omitted in the second is her memory of Percy's parting wish as she left Ireland on her last journey to Hannington that he never see her again. Neither manuscript mentions their reconciliation. The grief and heaviness of heart that Freke says she felt when leaving her father and Hannington doubtless conveys as well a reluctance to return to an Ireland and a husband that had made the last farewell so difficult.

Whatever the differences between them, the revisions reveal in subsequent partings from her husband a changing attitude toward their relationship. Much of her unhappiness in London during their first three years of marriage she attributes to missing her husband, the cousin she married after a long engagement and without her father's consent. Not to have had his company "was no small grife to me" (39/213). Later, alone in the unfamiliar county of Cork and among relatives she thought treated her badly, her loneliness appears to have been great; separation from her husband when she returned to England was a further cause of unhappiness. Percy left his wife in England and journeyed back to Ireland on seven occasions; missing in partings mentioned in the first manuscript is the earlier affection apparent once again in the revisions.

Returning to England after being away three-quarters of a year, Percy in the initial version is angry with his wife, apparently because she chose to remain in England; he leaves in 1686 for two years, angered that she refused to sell the Norfolk property of West Bilney, leaving her "thus thrown off with my son and my deer father dead" (56). When Elizabeth recalls this return and parting in the revision, Percy is no longer an irate husband, and she simply writes, "my deer husband wentt for Ireland" (225). Charged by the Irish proclamation of James II an absentee and prosecuted for refusing to drink to the health of a king's appointee, Percy left Ireland for England and West Bilney in 1688, a decision Elizabeth initially notes was a choice for him between two evils (56). Omitted as well in revision is the belief that her husband later "cruly disgarded" her in London on his return to Ireland (72); deleted, too, is the characterization of another departure, this one for two years, as barbarous (73). Together the changes, all of which were made after Percy faced his final illness, suggest a renewed appreciation of their love brought about by his death.

When Elizabeth did return with her husband to Ireland in 1692, where they were together during the four years of her last stay, Rathbarry embodies a new awareness of isolation. The two rooms and bare walls in the burned house underscore the deprivation and reinforce the memory of her first miserable arrival at least in part because Freke had found a sense of place in England. Left by her husband to shift for herself and, in her telling, with nowhere in England or Ireland to rest her "unhappy head" (223) after her father had died, Freke had taken possession of the Norfolk manor at West Bilney. Unable to occupy the main house until the terms of the lease were fulfilled, she lived in a thatched house for almost seven years before she returned to Ireland. At first without a chair, table, bed, or utensil, the dwelling was reminiscent of the bare-walled house at Rathbarry, but under its thatched roof was an "ease and comfortt" (55) that would have made all the more difficult the return to Ireland. The Rathbarry she says frightened her when she first saw "whatt a place I weere come to" (64) offers none of the contentment of West Bilney. When Freke left Rathbarry for the last time and returned to West Bilney, "againe to bare walls and every thing elce wantting" (66/233), these walls offered a renewed peace and rest. Often the West Bilney hall she later occupied is described in the remembrances as "my own house," "my beloved home," or simply "deerly beloved Bilney." There once again managing for herself, Freke enjoyed the independence and belonging that had eluded her in Ireland. Financial security proved, however, more elusive.

During the three unhappy years in London after the marriage, when her husband lost a considerable part of her money in the Hampshire venture, Freke remembers that she never had control of her funds. "Fearing all my fortune would be spentt" (39/213), she resolved to seek financial security in Ireland, where Percy continued to invest in property with her fortune. Though Freke wrote to her father for 1,000 pounds to complete the ownership of Rathbarry, using the Bilney estate she received from him as security, she later rejected her angry husband's attempt to have her sell the estate so that he could invest in further Irish holdings. She would not "trust to his or any ones kindness" (55). But Freke did give him sums of money. She gave him 500 pounds when he came from Ireland for a three-month visit "to gett whatt mony he could from mee" (56). He left her on another visit to West Bilney "all alone" after he had taken 1,000 pounds she had received from her father. "This I thought very hard usage, butt tis true" (71). When her husband transferred another 1,000 pounds into Irish debentures to acquire additional land in Ireland, Freke was "very unwilling to partt with itt," having saved the money during the many years at West Bilney; "butt I was bound and must obey" (240). She did remove her remaining 360 pounds from the Bank of England without consulting her husband, who refused to see her when he returned for the last time from Ireland, even though by her accounting he had already received the bulk of her 2,000 pounds and interest. And he had taken the money while leaving her with little subsistence. Despite his wife's misgivings, Percy Freke did fulfill the resolve to try their fortune in Ireland. Among the miscellaneous documents in the second manuscript, "A true accountt of what I lent and brought my deer husband" lists only some of the property this money helped buy. Percy Freke benefited especially from the sale of lands forfeited by Catholics and supporters of James II, gaining from the forfeitures extensive holdings that included the village of Baltimore. Among the foremost buyers at the sales and auctions of 1702 and 1703, he became by the beginning of the seventeenth century a major landholder in County Cork.[45]

Money would also contribute to the growing distance in Freke's relationship with her son, Ralph. News from Hannington during Elizabeth's first stay in Ireland that their son had broken his leg, was crippled, and "given over by all" (43/215) brought his parents back to England. Before returning to Ireland a year later, his mother wrote, his leg mended through "my poore, weak endeavours" (42/215), and he walked without crutches. Ralph remained in England until he accompanied his parents on his mother's third voyage to Ireland. During the eight years following the death of his grandfather and her return from Ireland, Ralph would often be with his mother, until she left him in 1692 for her final years at Rathbarry. A year later his father would bring their eighteen-year-old son back to Ireland, where he resided for the rest of his life. Together in Ireland during Elizabeth's last, extended stay, serious conflict with her son arose.

The marriage negotiations between Percy Freke and the Earl of Drogheda occasioned the falling out. Her son was, in Elizabeth's opinion, "quite smitten" (230) and greatly fancied fifteen-year-old Alice; his mother objected initially to her "quality, which I thought too much for a gentleman" (62). The second remembrance clarifies the objection, "~~quality~~ proper for my son, clog'd with seven or 8 brothers and sisters" (230). Both versions stress the mother's reluctance to be separated from her married son a distance of some hundred miles, "which I thought very hard to loose my only child" (63/231). In the second manuscript Freke callously adds, "I cared nott to bee frightnened outt of my mony nor my son too" (231). The terms of the settlement would, she believed, make them servants to the married couple, reducing the parents to the role of "paymasters" and proving "rhuinous" to the family. Prospects for the match ended with Freke's refusal to consider a counteroffer and a son "bitterly angry with me" (63/231). Learning later of her son's marriage in Ireland to Elizabeth Meade, Freke states in both recollections that she forgave him for marrying without her consent and blessing, wishing the couple good fortune; but the self-concern implicit in the accounts of the failed earlier match reemerges in the addition in the revision: "perhaps I mightt have opposed this match, I heering my son wish (to cross me)" (237).

Letters are emblematic of the physical and personal distance. Not hearing from him after Freke left Ireland increased the growing discord between mother and son. Ralph's ingratitude is especially galling. When he wanted 400 pounds for the purchase of land in Ireland, which Freke writes was "imediattly" sent, she further adds, "I never had soe much as a letter of thanks" (241). Several months later she settled on him her rights through marriage to Rathbarry, valued at 300 pounds a year, and again "never had his thanks" (77/241). A similar complaint followed the extended visit of her son and family to West Bilney, compounded by the incivility of not having written once they were back in Ireland. After her son had come to

England to see his dying father, and Freke thought he had left following the funeral only to learn four months later that he was still in England, the aggrieved mother appeals in a letter to his shame and guilt, "troubled thatt your unkindness should add to the afflicttions of my unfortunate condittion" (89). She adds in the second manuscript, "I had only as usuall a rude answer for itt" (254). Another letter written in response to one her son had sent to Elizabeth's attorney and the executor with her of Percy Freke's will, explaining his delays in meeting rents due his mother, complains forthrightly about an "unduttyfull and ungratefull" son who has "broke my hartt" and has "brought mee to the condition I am in." Angered and hurt by her son's "many slights and disrespectts," she threatens to withhold future support and blames the lawyer for misleading her about her son's appreciation when she initially signed the lease (132).

The troubled relationship with her son and with Ireland is further apparent in the relationship with the attorney, her means of being present in Ireland. Within a year of Percy Freke's death, Elizabeth intended to return to Ireland, prove her husband's will, and establish her rights; sickness, however, prevented the journey, and the lawyer sailed to Ireland on her behalf. Though she had never been content during the years she had lived there, Ireland had initially offered Elizabeth and Percy the possibility of finding their fortunes, and she now had a vested interest in the Irish estate, however much she had been happy to leave Ireland. Increasingly suspicious and concerned about her security, Freke's Irish concerns become personal as well as financial. The change is quite obvious in the difference between her first remembrance of the "sad accountt" the lawyer brought back from Ireland and that of the "dismall account" in the considerably later revision.

Initial entries dismiss his three months in Ireland as a stay of "little or noe purposs" other than to inform her that the estate steward had cheated her of 4,000 pounds, tenants had left without settling their obligations, and an ungrateful and imprudent son had encumbered his family with debt (94). Entries in the later version are not merely an account measured in monetary terms. Freke blames the lawyer who "ruiened me in my estate" by failing to deal with the steward, letting her rents fall by 200 pounds, and giving away over 1,200 pounds in arrears (255). The mistrust reveals her vulnerability and even fear; Ireland also seems a place of rejection, if not betrayal. Freke is particularly upset that through the lawyer's bad advice, persistence, and power of attorney, she leased to her son a trust from her husband and only once received the rent due. The 300 pounds paid for this legal service, she adds, cost her a bitter lesson about relying on others (282). The "poor unhappy mother" of an undutiful son, she is now a "wretched self" deceived by those she trusted (257, 255). Illness again prevented her going herself to Ireland in 1709 to undo the "barbarous lease" the lawyer had made with her son (95). In the last years of her life Freke could only rue the folly of heeding the bad advice that misled her into a "fools trap."

The bond with her son remains implicit, however, in responses to letters from her daughter-in-law in Ireland about his illnesses. Learning from his wife that her son is seriously ill of dropsy, she urges them "to hasten over to me for cure" (78/244). Similar fear overcame her after the family's final visit to England. The year-long stay did not go well, she complaining of his "cruell usuage" (198) and he objecting to her condescension; but before her son left, Freke paid over 500 pounds for his baronetcy. When her daughter-in-law wrote three months later that her husband was suffering from gout, one of the last entries of the remembrances welcomes the news that he was alive. Misled by earlier reports that he had drowned in the Dublin harbor, "I have never gone to bed or rise outt of itt with dry eyes" (208).

Besides letters, the news from gazettes and information from published histories further reveal an abiding interest in Ireland inseparable from concern for herself and the well-being of the family. Entries transcribed from the London *Post-Man* in September 1710 report the repairing in Dublin of a defaced monument to the "glorious memory" of William III (155) and in November 1711 a resolution passed at the proroguing of the Irish Parliament, declaring all who speak or write against the principles of the "happy revolution in 1688" enemies of the Crown and church and friends of the pretender (189/277). A long narrative in the first manuscript dated 1710 relates in considerable detail events in Ireland following the revolution that forced James II from the throne and led to the war with William III. Freke drew from contemporary histories for her account of the plight of the Protestants and her extended narrative of the military conflict; she also relied on gazettes for the years following William's triumph. Though she characterizes the series of chronological entries "convenyentt" remembrances about the time in Ireland when her husband was outlawed and they suffered the loss of all their possessions (139), central to the remembrance is William III and the Irish conflict. Where family loyalties determined Alice Thornton's defense of Wentworth, self-interest underlies Elizabeth Freke's support of William. Her history confirms what the entries about Dublin from the gazettes suggest: like Thornton she is committed to the monarchy and Church of England. Freke further sees herself, however, as a "deep sufferer" who claims to have lost through the "mallice of King Jams" and his "black actt" 1,000 pounds a year besides the burning of "our house and castle." She also claims to have "with much adoe saved my deer husbands life" (142). The victory of William, in any case, saved the estate at Rathbarry, for the Frekes regained possession and greatly extended their control of Irish land when Catholics and Jacobites lost their holdings in the Williamite confiscations.

The Frekes and their descendants would continue to control extensive land in Ireland until the first decades of the twentieth century. The farms and acreage of the West Bilney manor were sold by their grandson John Redmond Freke in the eighteenth century. Rathbarry Castle remained a significant part of the Irish estate, which in a 1787 survey encompassed fifteen thousand acres, until the Sixth Lord Carbery, John Evans-Freke, built a new castle in the eighteenth century on a hill in another part of the Rathbarry lands overlooking the sea. With further additions in the next century, Castle Freke would remain the Irish residence of the Carberys, who by 1883 held nineteen thousand acres in Ireland. After a major fire in 1910 destroyed much of the castle, it was rebuilt, sold in 1919, and, following a series of owners in the second half of the century, fell into ruins.[46] Both Castle Freke and Rathbarry Castle are now, however, once again Freke possessions. Stephen Evans-Freke, the son of the Eleventh Lord Carbery, purchased Castle Freke and has begun a major restoration. Renovations he commissioned of Rathbarry Castle are notable especially for the work on the ruins of the castle keep and the integration of new structures on the site of the old.

Reminiscences of life in Castle Freke, the people, and the surrounding Rathbarry area described by Mary Carbery, the wife of the Ninth Lord Carbery, in her memoir, *West Cork Journal, 1898–1901,* portray a pleasure Elizabeth Freke never found.[47] The miserable years she remembers as spent in "noe place fitt to putt my unfortunat head" are also markedly different from the Dublin years of "happienesse and Comfort" that ended for Alice Thornton with the death of her father and the 1641 rising. Neither woman would ever return to the Ireland she left before beginning the first of her remembrances, nor are narrations of daily Irish life their primary intent. Ireland remains, however, very much a part of their self-writing. Though Freke sailed from Cork for the last time a number of years before she appears to have begun writing about this period in her life, she did not leave behind the bitterness of separation from her husband and son that she believes Ireland fostered. The loss of her husband would bring them closer in the remembrances rewritten near the end of her life; the Ireland of her widow-hood, however, reflected anew the estrangement from her son, along with a growing feeling of insecurity and victimization. The Ireland recalled in Thornton's revision of the past, unlike that of Freke's, is a means of coming to terms with the present. Remembrances of Dublin commemorating her father and depicting a family blessed by God are her attempt to fashion and restore a self-image challenged by rumors that questioned her personal and public integrity. To different ends and in different ways the Irelands they remember, and not simply the years lived in Dublin and County Cork, are uniquely valuable expressions of the interrelation between time and place that govern their memoirs. For both women, location and dislocation are especially significant in the dialogue between the past and the present.

NOTES

1. Marie-Louise Coolahan, *Women, Writing, and Language in Early Modern Ireland* (Oxford: Oxford University Press, 2010), 141–79; Naomi McAreavey, "'Paper bul-lets': Gendering the 1641 Rebellion in the Writings of Lady Elizabeth Dowdall and Lettice Fitzgerald, Baroness of Offaly," in *Ireland in the Renaissance, c. 1540–1660,* ed. Thomas Herron and Michael Potterton (Dublin: Four Courts, 2007), 311–24.
2. Alice Thornton, "A booke of remembrances," microfilm, Miscellaneous 326, Ster-ling Memorial Library, Yale University, New Haven; "My First Booke of My Life,"

Add. MS 88,897/1, British Library (BL), London. Elizabeth Freke's remembrances from 1671 to 1714 are included in Add. MS 45,718, BL; her 1671–1713 remembrances are among entries in Add. MS 45719, BL.

3. Alice Thornton, *My First Booke of My Life*, ed. Raymond A. Anselment (Lincoln: University of Nebraska Press, 2014), 10; hereafter cited in the text. The similar entry in the earlier "A booke of remembrances" is on 16–17.

4. Raphael Holinshed, *Holinshed's Irish Chronicle: The Historie of Irelande from the First Inhabitation Thereof, vnto the Yeare 1509*, ed. Liam Miller and Eileen Power (Atlantic Highlands NJ: Humanities, 1979), 39. Estimates of the population range from five thousand in 1600 to thirty thousand in 1660, according to William J. Smyth, "Ireland a Colony: Settlement Implications of the Revolution in Military-Administrative, Urban and Ecclesiastical Structures, c. 1550 to c. 1730," in *A History of Settlement in Ireland*, ed. Terry Barry (London: Routledge, 2000), 168.

5. William Brereton, *Travels in Holland the United Provinces England Scotland and Ireland, MDCXXXIV–MDCXXXV*, ed. Edward Hawkins (London: Chetham Society, 1844), 137, 144.

6. Barnabe Rich, *A New Description of Ireland: Wherein is described the disposition of the Irish whereunto they are inclined* (London, 1610), 70, 59–60.

7. Raymond Gillespie, "Dublin, 1600–1700: A City and Its Hinterlands," in *Capital Cities and Their Hinterlands in Early Modern Europe*, ed. Peter Clark and Bernard Lepetit (Aldershot: Scholar, 1996), 84, 85, 86, 90, 93–94; David Dickson, *Dublin: The Making of a Capital City* (London: Profile Books, 2014), 50, 55, 59; Dickson, "Capital and Country: 1600–1800," in *Dublin through the Ages*, ed. Art Cosgrove (Dublin: College Press, 1988), 63, 67, 70; Smyth, "Ireland a Colony," 168.

8. Thomas Comber, *Memoirs of the Life and Death of the Right Honourable the Lord Deputy Wandesforde*, 2nd ed. (Cambridge, 1778), 75–76. "By the 1630s there was a scatter of aristocratic residences along Dame Gate down to Hoggen Green" (Dickson, *Dublin*, 56).

9. Toby Barnard notes the "quick, cheap and regular" travel, recognizing it could be "frustrating and hazardous." "Crises of Identity among Irish Protestants, 1641–1685," *Past & Present* 127, no. 1 (1990): 43 and n12. See also Barnard, "New Opportunities for British Settlement: Ireland, 1650–1700," in *The Oxford History of the British Empire*, ed. William Roger Louis et al., 5 vols. (Oxford: Oxford University Press, 1998–99), 1:322–23.

10. Ronald H. Buchanan, "The Irish Sea: The Geographical Framework," in *The Irish Sea: Aspects of Maritime History*, ed. Michael McCaughan and John Appleby (Belfast: Institute of Irish Studies, 1989), 3; and John Appleby, "Merchants and Mariners, Pirates and Privateers," in McCaughan and Appleby, *Irish Sea*, 47–58.

11. Frances Cooke, *Mris. Cookes Meditations* (London, 1650); John Cook, *A True Relation of Mr. Iohn Cook's Passage by Sea from Wexford to Kinsale in that great Storm Ianuary 5* (London, 1650).

12. All biblical citations are from the King James Version.

13. See Raymond A. Anselment, introd. to Thornton, *First Booke*, xvii, and the discussion of manuscripts and provenance, xlix–lii.

14. This interpretation is developed in Anselment, introd. to Thornton, *First Booke*, see esp. xxv–xxvi, xxviii–xxix, and xlviii.

15. Anselment, introd. to Thornton, *First Booke*, xx.

16. David Edwards, *The Ormond Lordship in County Kilkenny, 1515–1642: The Rise and Fall of Butler Feudal Power* (Dublin: Four Courts, 2003), 299, 307–8.

17. Richard Cox, *Hibernia Anglicana: or, the History of Ireland From the Conquest thereof by the English, To this Present Time*, 2nd ed. (London, 1692), 60–61, 64; see also Aidan Clarke, "The Breakdown of Authority, 1640–1641," in *A New History of Ireland*, vol. 3, *Early Modern Ireland, 1534–1691*, ed. Theodore W. Moody, Francis X. Martin, and Francis J. Byrne (Oxford: Oxford University Press, 1991), 279–80; and Michael Perceval-Maxwell, *The Outbreak of the Irish Rebellion of 1641* (Montreal: McGill-Queen's University Press, 1994), 83–86.

18. A. Clarke's "The Government of Wentworth, 1632–40," in Moody, Martin, and Byrne, *New History of Ireland*, is especially relevant; Clarke also recognizes the use of office for personal gain (3:252–53, 260–62).

19. According to A. Clarke, "Government of Wentworth," Wentworth had "overreached himself in his treatment of powerful individuals" and had little "local support" (256); see also Dickson, *Dublin*, 60.

20. Thornton is not alone in her assertion about the rebellion's toll. John Temple claims three hundred thousand were victims of rebellion, although not all "cruelly murthered." *The Irish Rebellion* (London, 1646), 6.

21. Thomas Wentworth, *A Briefe and Perfect Relation, Of the Answeres and Replies of Thomas Earle of Strafford: To the Articles Exhibited against him, by the House of Commons on the thirteenth of Aprill, An. Dom. 1641* (London, 1647); and Wentworth, *The Earle of Straffords Speech on the Scaffold before he was beheaded on Tower-hill, the 12 of May, 1641* (London, 1641).

22. Temple recognizes the years of peace (*Irish Rebellion*, 16); as does Cox, who relies on Temple, in *Hibernia Anglicana*, 72.

23. Cox, *Hibernia Anglicana*, 64.

24. Edwards, *Ormond Lordship*, 298–99, 304–5; Jack Burtchaell and Daniel Dowling, "Social and Economic Conflict in County Kilkenny, 1600–1800," in *Kilkenny: History and Society; Interdisciplinary Essays on the History of an Irish County*, ed. William Nolan and Kevin Whelan (Dublin: Geography, 1990), 253–55. For the

dispute, see also Edwards, *Ormond Lordship*, 301–2, 304, 306–7; and Hardy Bertram McCall, *Story of the Family of Wandesforde of Kirklington & Castlecomer* (London: Simpkin, 1904), 99–100, 141–45.

25. Clodagh Tait discusses the nature of the keen, "a usually extempore lament, half-sung, half-spoken." *Death, Burial and Commemoration in Ireland, 1550–1650* (New York: Palgrave Macmillan, 2002), 35–38 and notes.

26. Temple, *Irish Rebellion*, 16; Cox, *Hibernia Anglicana*, 72–73.

27. Raymond Gillespie, "Temple's Fate: Reading *The Irish Rebellion* in Late Seventeenth-Century Ireland," in *British Interventions in Early Modern Ireland*, ed. Ciarán Brady and Jane Ohlmeyer (Cambridge: Cambridge University Press, 2005), 315–33.

28. See also Coolahan, *Women, Writing, and Language*, 248–49.

29. Thornton seems to have read the account in James Cranford, *The Teares of Ireland* (London, 1642): "hang her English Kite, we will get thee a better wife" (7). Cranford's text includes a picture of the escape over the wall (9).

30. Edmund Borlase, *The History of the Execrable Irish Rebellion* (London, 1680), 19. Temple observes, "I could never hear that any English man received any certain notice of this conspiracy" (*Irish Rebellion*, 17).

31. William Nolan, "Castlecomer," in *Irish Country Towns*, ed. Anngret Simms and John H. Andrews (Cork: Mercier, 1994), 122–23.

32. Comber, *Memoirs*, 98–105; McCall, *Story of the Family*, 78, 144–45; Edwards, *Ormond Lordship*, 27–28, 302; Nolan, *Fassadinin: Land, Settlement and Society in Southeast Ireland, 1600–1850* (Dublin: Geography, 1979), 54–56, 66.

33. McCall, *Story of the Family*, 98–99, 144–48; Nolan, "Castlecomer," in Simms and Andrews, *Irish Country Towns*, 129–30. In *Fassadinin* Nolan traces the Wandesfords' residence through the nineteenth century.

34. E. Freke, *Remembrances*, 39; hereafter cited in the text. Citations from the text of the 1671–1714 remembrances are separated by a virgule from similar passages then noted in the 1671–1713 text.

35. Arthur Freke's report of his defense of Rathbarry has been transcribed and edited by Herbert Webb Gillman. Freke, "Siege of Rathbarry Castle, 1642," *Journal of the Cork Historical and Archaeological Society*, 2nd ser., 1 (1895): 1–20. Gillman's description of the nineteenth-century ruins of the castle includes a sketch outlining the area within the walls as well as four 1894 photographs of the keep, curtain wall, and bastion.

36. Richard Barry, Second Earl of Barrymore, held a right that would have reverted to him at the end of the lease.

37. Patrick O'Flanagan, "Three Hundred Years of Urban Life: Villages and Towns in County Cork, c. 1600 to 1901," in *Cork History and Society: Interdisciplinary Essays on the History of an Irish County*, ed. O'Flanagan and Cornelius G. Buttimer (Dublin:

Geography, 1993), 402; Nicholas Canny, "The 1641 Depositions as a Source for the Writing of Social History: County Cork as a Case Study," in O'Flanagan and Buttimer, *Cork History and Society*, 256.

38. Michael MacCarthy Morrogh, "The English Presence in Early Seventeenth Century Munster," in *Natives and Newcomers: Essays on the Making of Irish Colonial Society, 1534–1641*, ed. Ciarán Brady and Raymond Gillespie (Dublin: Irish Academic Press, 1986), 188. He also states that "Easy access from south-west England to Munster might persuade the settler he was hardly venturing abroad" (173).

39. MacCarthy Morrogh, "English Presence," 189; Smyth, "Society and Settlement in Seventeenth Century Ireland: The Evidence of the '1659 Census,'" in *Common Ground: Essays on the Historical Geography of Ireland*, ed. William J. Smyth and Kevin Whelan (Cork: Cork University Press, 1988), 77.

40. William O'Brien, Second Earl of Inchiquin, and Arthur Freke, Percy's father, married members of the prominent Boyle family.

41. Mary, the older sister of Percy, was the wife of Francis Bernard.

42. Percy represented Clonakilty from 1692 to 1699; he represented Baltimore in 1703; see E. Freke, *Remembrances*, 61n77.

43. Toby Barnard, "The Political, Material and Mental Culture of the Cork Settlers, c. 1650–1700," in O'Flanagan and Buttimer, *Cork History and Society*, 312.

44. The miscellaneous documents in the wallpaper-bound manuscript include an account of money received from her father; see E. Freke, *Remembrances*, 316–17.

45. Percy Freke acquired the town of Baltimore as part of the forfeited estate of Edmond Galway he purchased in 1703; see E. Freke, *Remembrances*, 75n118. For the auctions and his emergence as a landowner, see John G. Simms, *The Williamite Confiscation in Ireland, 1690–1703* (London: Faber and Faber, 1956), 148–62; and Dickson, *Old World Colony: Cork and South Munster, 1630–1830* (Cork: Cork University Press, 2005), 62–63.

46. E. Freke, *Remembrances*, 18–19. David Hicks's survey of the history of Castle Freke includes a number of photographs of the castle's late twentieth-century state of disrepair, in *Irish Country Houses: A Chronicle of Change* (Cork: Collins, 2012), 14–25.

47. Mary Carbery, *Mary Carbery's West Cork Journal, 1898–1901*, ed. Jeremy Sandford (Dublin: Lilliput, 1998).

2

Reading Dislocation and Emotion in the Writings of Alice Thornton, Ann Fanshawe, and Barbara Blaugdone

ANNE FOGARTY

Early modern life writings by women about Ireland are inherently variegated and disparate. Yet they may nonetheless be profitably read comparatively because establishing the differences between diverse works allows their specificities to swim into view more clearly and also reveals the determining role played by discrete political and religious positions in their construction. Further, juxtaposing memoirs authored by women permits an interrogation of the effect of gender roles in the formation of identity at particular historical junctures and helps in part to explain commonalities between texts separately conceived. This chapter concentrates on the memoirs of three English women, Alice Thornton (1626–1707), Lady Ann Fanshawe (1625–80) and Barbara Blaugdone (ca. 1609–1704), who spent short phases of their lives in Ireland in the mid-seventeenth century. Their sojourns in the country were prompted by family ties but were also consequent on the midcentury upheavals caused by the 1641 rebellion and the English civil wars.

Thornton's stay in Ireland was occasioned by her father's appointment as master of the rolls in 1633 and was disrupted by his death in 1640 and the outbreak of the 1641 rebellion, after which her family was forced to leave and move back to England. Fanshawe's travels around Ireland with her politician husband, Richard Fanshawe, in 1649–50 were a result of the displacement and enforced exile of royalists during the Interregnum and the second civil war and were cut short by local resistance to the Cromwellian campaigns. Blaugdone distinguishes herself from the other two women in that her journeys to Ireland between 1656 and 1657 were voluntary; as a Quaker she undertook missionary visits to the country in an endeavor to bear witness to her faith and to spread her beliefs by preaching abroad. But the successive instances of persecution that she suffered, as well as the Quaker imperative to remain constantly on the move to spread the divine word, appear to have motivated her return to England. Hence, although these memoirs derive from different historical moments and are insti-gated by varying autobiographical purposes and informed by divergent political and religious apprehensions, they are akin to the degree that the authors experienced political upheaval and exile for familial or religious reasons. Fanshawe's evocative description of the disorientation of her sister and herself, who find themselves like "fishes out of the water" and unable to "act any part" when summoned to join their royalist father in Oxford after his estate had been sequestered by parliamentarians in 1643, may be extended to the experience of colonial exile as well.[1] Even if only assigned a marginal and fleeting part in these narratives, Ireland conceptually and experientially is the scene of dislocation for their authors and a place in which their identity is put under pressure for a variety of reasons.

Additionally, many overarching themes and interconnected rhetorical strategies unite these works, which fasten on moments of transition and crisis. The journey or nautical voyage, particularly the crossing of the Irish Sea, is a dominant and multifaceted motif in these memoirs, as are carefully distilled traumatic memories and sensational mishaps such as the abode on fire or the city under siege that are recounted for their validation of the pains successfully borne by the heroic but beset female subject as well as for their emblematic dimensions. Kate Chedgzoy argues that women's writings in the early modern period tend to eschew the national and concentrate instead on the personal; the omission of any elaborations on Ireland or even glimpses of the authors' everyday life in these texts would appear to sustain this view.[2] The brevity and elusiveness of their accounts of the country are features that unite their work. Ireland is tangential rather than central to these authors' accounts of their lives. Yet even though they do not set out specifically to describe the country or to comment on it in a systematic fashion from the viewpoint of the colonial outsider or functionary, they nonetheless deploy resonant textual maneuvers that obliquely capture its difference. In so doing, they variously elide and foreground the "otherness" of Ireland or the Irish for strategic purposes.[3] Additionally, often it is the very gaps in and silent subtexts of these writings that betray their partisanship or put pressure on troubled notions of national or gendered identity. Further, the accounts by Thornton, Fanshawe, and Blaugdone of their experiences in the country are peculiarly concerned with the portrayal and vindication of fathers and spouses and the upholding and defense of the public dimensions of female honor. It is also evident that they are written with a view to future audiences: they seek to court and answer to the judgments of posterity and to prove the degree to which they have fulfilled the stringent precepts of conduct imposed on women in the seventeenth century and followed the provisos of divine meditation and moral and spiritual stocktaking.

In *A Room of One's Own*, Virginia Woolf notes the ubiquity of the autobiographical "I" in early twentieth-century novels and deplores the fact that it has become an irremovable fixture, masking as much as it reveals.[4] In early modern texts the reverse problem obtains: it is the absence of a recognizable or wholly continuous autobiographical "I" that creates obstacles for the elucidation of works that seem as a consequence often to withhold meaning. Detecting and discerning the lineaments of premodern subjectivity while avoiding the anachronism of imposing post-Freudian apprehensions of the individual or of interiority can prove to be stumbling blocks for the contemporary reader. Two pronounced shifts in the study of early modern life writing, however, have ousted earlier views that the self is merely in abeyance in this era. The inquiry into the multifarious and malleable rhetorical conventions and narrative structures deployed in these texts as well as the recent interest in the history and nature of emotions facilitate the pinpointing of forms of selfhood that otherwise might seem inchoate or wholly imperceptible.

In her overview of early modern life writing, Danielle Clarke rightly urges scholars to look beyond current concepts of autonomous selfhood to discern those that actually held sway in this period.[5] Reticence about selfhood, as she cogently points out, does not preclude the existence of other forms of literary self-construction. Contrary to the twentieth- and twenty-first-century investment in rebelliousness and the deviant as hallmarks of individualism, in this era conformity and an ability to uphold communal and religious values act as prized indicators of worth. Hence, a sense of uniqueness or of particularity may be conveyed in terms that underscore compliance and firmly tamp down any claim to exceptionality. Moreover, the construction of a self in the written discourses of the early modern period is a complex set of negotiations predicated centrally on communal and shared understandings. Indeed, as Thomas O. Sloane avers, the demands of eloquence that required the writer to fabricate a self-image amenable to the audience she envisages facilitates the creation of "rhetorical selfhood," that is, modes of identity discursively mediated.[6] The fashioning of an authorial persona in keeping with the decorum of differing conventions and genres furthers the creation of public masks while ensuring that anxieties about the possible transgression of circumscribed female roles could be allayed.[7] As Michelle M. Dowd and Julie A. Eckerle have persuasively shown, the very instability and hybridity of early modern life writing before the formal emergence of autobiography in later centuries furnish authors with many possibilities for contouring their accounts of their experiences and for subtly insinuating particularist accents into them.[8] Hence, the typicality of the values and lives described is frequently counterpointed or offset by an inventive borrowing from and interweaving of the rhetorical devices and resources of different genres.

The so-called emotional turn in contemporary scholarship affords a further means by which to decipher the apparently clouded or even ungraspable expressive compass of early modern life writings by women about Ireland and the complex constructions of authorship and negotiations with projected readerships that they entail. As most interventions in this ever-expanding field note, commentators appear to be irreconcilably split between the view that emotions are hardwired, innate, and universal on the one hand and that they are socially constructed and mutable on the other. Recently, Jan Plamper and William M. Reddy, however, have persuasively argued that we need both universalist and antideterminist accounts of the origins of emotions to have the ethicopolitical basis on which to assess them and that they should hence not be posited as mutually exclusive stances.[9] The cross-connection of essentialist and antiessentialist viewpoints has proved particularly crucial for the exploration of feelings outside the purlieu of the modern. To boot, akin to the findings that there are modes of selfhood that precede modern notions of subjectivity, the recognition that the study of emotions is by no means to be equated with psychohistory has proved a vital animating principle for the pinpointing and uncovering of emotions in earlier historical periods. Decoupled from notions of a bounded self, the articulation of affective responses is a component of expressivity in every era of human endeavor. Above all, and additionally lending weight to this insight, as has forcibly been argued, emotions, even if they are endowed with certain constants, have a history and alter over time, often disappearing to cede to new categories and conventions.[10]

The slipperiness of emotion as a concept has been a heated but fertile topic of debate, yielding several influential and compelling recognitions. Barbara H. Rosenwein has resolutely contested the view propounded by Norbert Elias in *The Civilizing Process* that emotions are gradually disciplined and reined in during the early modern period.[11] She at once questions Elias's postulate that restraint and the sublimation of the drives are overriding characteristics of Renaissance life and that the medieval period is in contradistinction, as he avers, characterized by wildness, violence, and cruelty. Rosenwein has further validly quibbled with what she terms the "hydraulic" view of emotions that conceives of them as energies that either need to be controlled or explosively seek an outlet.[12] Instead, she posits that feelings are communal and socially constructed and that they are facilitated and given shape by what she dubs "emotional communities."[13] She defines the emotional community as "a group in which people have a common stake, interests, values and goals."[14] Such communities may be both textual and social, and they are qualified for her by the fact that they uphold similar emotional values.

But, as she crucially points out, they cannot simply be equated with or collapsed into rhetorical categories or the laws of genre, even though we are primarily dependent on written sources for knowledge about emotions in earlier historical periods. Words act as vehicles for emotions but do not delimit them or exhaust their significance. Nonetheless, as is evident in the texts under review in this chapter, strategic narrative effects or topoi invariably point to affective nodal points that warrant further inquiry. For Rosenwein, emotional communities play a regulatory role in the enunciation of emotions, but they may also constitute an open ambit within which feelings can be voiced and given a subtly particular or private coloring. It is possible within the context of emotional communities to discern how systems of feeling operate and to discover what affective norms and responses are particularly valued or deplored. Emotions as conceived of in this fashion are inherently relational and social and formulated through shared vocabularies and ways of thinking. Drawing on instructive formulations put forward by Reddy, Rosenwein importantly uncouples emotions from the irrational, preferring instead to see them as forms of cognition and as types of appraisal.[15] By the same token, emotions, as argued in the analyses that follow of the autobiographical texts of Thornton, Fanshawe, and Blaugdone, carry a political charge and are bound up with thorny issues of alliance and fealty thrown into relief and put under pressure by colonial travel.

Recent work on emotion in the early modern period has concentrated on creating taxonomies of emotion; identifying feelings especially predominant, such as melancholy in the seventeenth century; and teasing out the links between violence and affects.[16] My aim in examining emotion in the depictions of Ireland by Thornton, Fanshawe, and Blaugdone is necessarily more restricted and tentative because of the oblique and glancing nature of their writings about Ireland. Their texts are as reticent about emotion as about the self. It is rarely feasible to identify an overt emotional vocabulary in these works or to pick out what Reddy has dubbed "emotives," that is, speech acts that describe emotions and aim to produce an effect on the world. Rather, it will be necessary to conjure with conspicuous rhetorical effects and redolent silences and to tease out the resonances of knotted and dramatically laden events that act as vehicles for emotions indirectly gestured toward but rarely explicitly articulated. My examination of the tantalizingly muffled affective substrata of these accounts of the female experience of seventeenth-century Ireland is centrally informed by Rosenwein's instructive insight, drawing on the tenets of cognitive psychology, that emotions are processes of perception and appraisal. Emotions as she recognizes come particularly to the fore and generate a multitude of differing narratives when individuals set out to discern what is "relevant to their 'weal or woe.'"[17] Moreover, as she also pertinently points out, emotions rarely occur in singletons and may more profitably be seen in sequences.[18] Anxiety about personal honor, worries about physical safety and well-being, and concern with the upholding of family status prompt coded reflections charged with emotion in these distinctive but interrelated autobiographical works. In the face of threats to their existence and to central notions of self-worth, these authors have recourse to conventional morality and religious precepts, but they also momentarily depart from normative views to render complex emotional states that shed light on crucial aspects of the lives of early modern women and of the gendered experience of colonial exile in Ireland.

ALICE THORNTON

Thornton's multiple reworkings of her life story, as Raymond A. Anselment has argued, were motivated by her desire to defend her reputation following the death of her husband, William Thornton, in 1668 and to scotch false rumors about the arrangements that she had made for the marriage of her daughter Naly to the Protestant cleric and family friend, Thomas Comber, who was many years her senior.[19] Because of rumors that had been circulated by her "deadly enemyes" implying that she had a dalliance with her daughter's husband, Thornton recast initial accounts of her life to create *My First Booke of My Life*, the redaction of her life story on which I focus.[20] A central impetus of her work is self-vindication. To that end, she seeks to give an overview of her life that draws out her probity, unwavering virtue, and faith in divine guidance. Her text is conspicuously composite in nature and does not easily settle into any one given genre. It combines aspects of a spiritual meditation, family memoir, commonplace book, and autobiographical story.[21] Some of the lengthier extensions of her original work, such as the descriptions of the deaths of her father and of Thomas Wentworth, Earl of Strafford, use the resources of fiction to mold events. The emotional community that Thornton's text posits are sympathetic family members ready to recognize her plight, to appreciate her pleas, to concur with her values, and to be partisan on her behalf. They are counterpointed by putative hostile others who have cast aspersions on her virtue. As a spiritual memoir, her text, too, is an internal conversation laid bare for public scrutiny that allows the author to inspect aspects of her own belief and to broadcast her conviction that a divine design is discernible in the highs and lows of her existence. Indeed, spiritual and physical trials become the central means by which she proves her faith and attests to the benevolence of an all-shaping providence.

Thornton's narrative, due to the divided nature of the audience that it envisages, at once sympathetic and hostile, is characterized by countervailing aspects, narrative leaps, and occlusions. Yet much of the recent reception of the text has concerned itself less with its literary structure, affective underlay, and rhetorical effects than with its material and sociohistorical dimensions due to the unusual attention it pays to the experience of widowhood, pregnancy, lying-in, illnesses such as smallpox and dysentery, and the deaths of children in infancy.[22] Even feminist surveys, such as *English Women's Voices, 1540–1700* and *Her Own Life: Autobiographical Writings by Seventeenth-Century Englishwomen*, have given prominence in their chosen excerpts to Thornton's portrayal of the female body and drawn attention to her predilection for teasing out the social repercussions of embodied experience.[23] Undoubtedly, the carefully contrived rhetorical nature of the text has become much more apparent as a result of Anselment's uncovering of its complex manuscript history and multiple overlapping phases of composition; his recent edition of Thornton's revised account of her life affords much fuller insights into its structures.[24] My analysis of Thornton's sophisticated deployment of rhetorical effects concentrates on her depiction of physical calamities and dramatic moments of passage, such as the sea voyage or the deathbed scene, to give shape to the narrative of her time in Ireland. Her use of such traditional topoi to heightened ends evinces her skill at subtly insinuating emotions into her expositions and using them to sway our opinion of her.

The prayers and spiritual meditations with which Thornton frames her life story cast her at once as a sinner who wrangles with her failings and a heroic defender of the faith. Dejection because of her "presumptuous sins" (4) is counterpointed with her determination to be "faithfull unto death." She confidently avers that "a woman that feareth the Lord, she shall be praised" (5). In thus asserting her faith, she appeals to the judgment of her audience and the religious sensibilities that bind her to them. Movements from a disconsolate recognition of her sinfulness to the glorification of faith or the euphoric voicing of thanksgiving allow her to set female reticence aside and to assign significance to herself.

Such veering emotions likewise contour her account of her childhood and of her life in Ireland. Thornton opens her story by styling herself in keeping with patriarchal convention as her father's daughter: "Alice Wandesforde, the fifth childe of Christopher Wandesforde Esq, late Lord Deputy of Ireland, Was borne at Kirklington in the County of Yorke the thirteenth day of February." In this manner, she construes her identity in familial and political terms; throughout her account of her experiences in Ireland filial and religious devotion are cross-connected and function as central vectors of her story. The family with its religious and political beliefs constitutes her primary emotional community and forms the resonant ground on which she can spin out aspects of her development. She further announces that her life story will be a recollection of "deliverances" (6), that is, moments at which divine intervention saved her from perdition, at once physically and spiritually conceived.

The "preservations" that Thornton itemizes hinge always on moments of physical endangerment. It is notable, too, that many of her early recollections stem in all likelihood from family lore and not personal memory, as when she recounts how as a toddler, due to the negligence of a maid, she fell and "broke the scull of my fore head in the very top" (7) in the process of entering her mother's room. The unspoken feelings attendant on this happening, implicitly pain, fear, relief, and recrimination, are communal in nature and bear out Rosenwein's observation that the emotions are social and relational in the first instance. Her miraculous survival of the childhood illnesses of measles and smallpox is also depicted in an impersonal fashion and used to indicate how feelings of precariousness or insecurity may give way to ones of certitude.

Thornton strategically uses an oscillation between endangerment and safety, pain and assuagement, to pattern her account of her childhood in Ireland. Notably, she records next to nothing about the events of this happy period, capturing it instead in didactic and affective terms. We learn primarily that she was educated while living in Dublin in the 1630s with the daughters of the Earl of Strafford; that she studied the French language, "Singing, Dancing, Plaieng on the Lute and Theorboe" (10); and that her mother sedulously took care of her moral training. The implicit contentment of this time is drawn out through a prolonged encomium to her parents. An endorsement of familial status and well-being takes the place of any more private shadings of feeling. Likewise, the factionalism of political life in Ireland in the 1630s and the "otherness" of colonial existence are rendered indirectly through the listing of a series of providential escapes from a near-drowning through the fall from a coach in County Kildare; from a fire in the family's home in Dame Street, Dublin; and from the consequences of a more devastating conflagration in Dublin Castle in 1638.

A longer narrative detailing a dramatic rescue of her mother and herself by a vigilant friend from a storm-tossed ship seeking landfall in Skerries, a harbor in North Dublin, draws on a central Irish literary trope, the fateful and danger-laden crossing of the Irish Sea. Allegorically, the deliverance of the king's ship from an Irish tempest by a grateful subject encapsulates a pleasing political lesson. Thornton, however, further embellishes the narrative by appending an account of a "second preservation" (16) due to her own near drowning through almost falling overboard during the rescue operation. This addendum to an already graphically recounted tale of near death and salvation throws her solitary fate into conspicuous relief and underscores the specific anguish of her sense of imperilment. She rounds out this disclosure by voicing gratitude for her deliverance, thus aligning herself with the values and expectations of the emotional community to which she belongs. But this narrative tacked onto the overall symbolic story hints at the difficulty of accommodating female difference within a conveniently symmetrical tale of salvation and royalist faith. Strikingly, here as elsewhere in Thornton's text, the somatic acts as a locus for suppressed or inexpressible emotion. Physical collapse and endangerment mark moments at which she rebels at her lot or balks at the demands made on her and at which doctrines of female submissiveness or religious acceptance break down or elude her. Additionally, her accounts of her illnesses and physical trials allow her to forge a rhetorical selfhood that cannot be otherwise articulated.

In the longest and most entangled sequences in Thornton's records of her sojourn in Ireland, the personal, the political, and the emotional are inextricably connected. They dwell on the summary recall of Strafford from Ireland, his impeachment by the Long Parliament in 1640, his trial in London for treason and subsequent execution in 1641, the sudden demise of her father in 1640 toward the end of his first year in office as lord deputy and his deathbed pronouncements, and the outbreak of the 1641 rebellion in Dublin and elsewhere that necessitated her precipitate return to England with her mother and siblings.[25] In commending Strafford for his heroism and extolling him as a martyr, lauding her father for his virtue and integrity, and condemning the Irish for their barbarism and for rebelling against the king, she is forced to tease out her own affiliations, vexed though they may be. Loyalty and treachery are central concerns of these sections of her narrative, in which its aporias come most to the fore. She cross-associates herself with Strafford and her father as wronged servants to the Crown, implicitly aligning herself with their power and giving ballast to her sense of being unjustly victimized. Her championing of Wentworth as a just ruler, however, covers over the divisiveness of his regime, in which he sought to reshape Irish society and make it conform with English standards, increased the fiscal burdens on landowners to boost state revenues, attempted to reform the Church of Ireland, curtailed the rights of Catholics, and raised an army in the country with a view to fighting the Covenanters in Scotland, all of which alienated the Old and New English alike.[26] Likewise, her defense of the benign nature of the rule of Christopher Wandesford, her father, also papers over his crisis-laden deputyship and the many legal disputes in which he was involved, not least in relation to the estates he had forcibly commandeered at Castlecomer and in the barony of Idough, from which the Gaelic clan, the O'Brennans, had been expelled with the connivance of James Butler, Earl of Ormond, whose holdings bordered on these territories.[27] Thornton describes her father as making numerous edifying pronouncements before expiring, in accordance with the expectations of a good Christian death.

Yet when he specifically summons her for a final audience, these pieties cede to lamentation and a foreboding of the future miseries that await his daughter: "Then would he call on me to his bed side, & stediely looking on me, would sighe and say, Ah poor childe, what thou must see & thine eyes beholde" (24). Her father's terrible dying vision and sudden world-weariness unite him affectively with her. His premonitions are indirect and eschew any uplifting moralism. The bond between father and child overrides all else and endows her helpless witness of his passing with a devastating import that vindicates her into the future. His final, unvoiced recognition, above all, endorses the text that she is currently writing about the misfortunes he foresaw that have subsequently descended on her. Thornton's description of the obsequies for her father in Christ Church Cathedral in Dublin adds further weight to her account of him as an esteemed and benevolent public figure but also involuntarily draws attention to aspects of colonial rule that she resolutely keeps at bay. Her comment that he was such a "worthy Person" that the Irish "did sett up their lamentable hone, as they call it" (26) is a rare instance in which Gaelic culture is alluded to. The "hone" to which she refers is the Irish word *ochón*, "alas," which prefaces or forms part of a lamentation. She projects some of the intensity of her grief onto the anonymous Irish congregation, but she is also careful to maintain the lines of division between herself and them. They serve as an impossible image of political unity and emotional confluence and as a consequence their "otherness" is warily preserved. In this case the imagined emotional community is as much phantom as actual, a momentary consequence of joint mourning.

Thornton's account of the terrors of the 1641 rebellion that drove her mother and siblings from Dublin are concretized in images of sickness, somatic empathy, and religious sacrifice. Her portrayal of the outbreak of the rebellion in Dublin, the outrage of the attacks on Protestant communities, and the dispossession of her family has a novelistic force. She particularly captures the distress of the loss of their possessions and social standing in Dublin and the arduous journey to England through vivid accounts of illness; her brother succumbing to smallpox; and the exemplary death of Frank Kelly, a young Irish boy adopted by her father who had converted to Protestantism. The treachery of the Irish who savagely turn on those around them is counterpointed by the affective interconnections that bind Thornton's displaced and homeless family. The "distemper, brought out of Ireland" (37) that she suffers from and that forces the family to tarry in the port of Neston on their arrival literalizes their plight. The country that had once been a haven has now turned contagious and infects her with its malaise. The second bout of smallpox with which she is infected in Chester one year later in 1642 is of a very different order. In this case she deduces that she has been contaminated by the little dog that she sent to visit her brother who is suffering from the disease. Hence, sibling concern and shared distress appear to precipitate this illness, not malign external forces.

Joy at her brother's survival and her own recovery are contrasted with the pathos of the concomitant death of Kelly, who is tenderly nursed by her mother. The story of the Irish waif who confesses his sins on his deathbed, publicly cements his belief in Protestant precepts, and warns her from approaching him for fear of contagion converts many aspects of her recent experience of atrocity into a morally uplifting occasion and also allows her to salvage a sense of family honor. She gives thanks to God for the opportunity to bring this "poor Soule out of the darknesse and ignorance of his sinfull education" (42) and for her father's perspicacity and largesse in adopting him. Thus Kelly's illness and death indemnify the emotional bonds of Thornton's family, assuage her sense of loss and devastation, and allegorize the rightful links between the Irish and the English, recasting the former as grateful subjects and converts and the latter as benign and just guardians.

ANN FANSHAWE

The memoirs of Ann Fanshawe exhibit many of the quintessential features of female seventeenth-century life writing in their eschewal of personal revelation, the primacy that they accord to family history and genealogy, and their idealization of male experience and virtue. Companionate marriage and conjugal love are affective mainstays of Fanshawe's text rather than any desire for self-portrayal. She confides at the beginning of her composition in a rare moment of emotional disclosure that reminiscing about her marriage "makes my eyes gush out with tears." The emotional community addressed by Fanshawe is familial: she transcribes her work from preexisting records and diaries in 1676 as an act of homage to Richard Fanshawe, her spouse, who had died in 1666. Her narrative posits her son, Richard, as its principal audience and moral sounding ground; he is addressed in the opening pages in which he is exhorted to follow the paths of temperate virtue and to model himself on his father. Fanshawe depicts her marriage as a harmonious one—"we never had but one mind through out our lives, our soules were wrapped up in each other"—but also insists that a hierarchy prevailed whereby she was subservient to her husband's will, noting "he would say I managed his domesticks wholy, yet I ever governed them and myself by his commands" (103). Although the implicit emotional stances of complaisance, disciplined self-control, and self-effacement are the primary cognitive habits determining Fanshawe's worldview, they also regularly come under pressure.

Mary Beth Rose has astutely contended that the civil war, despite the toll that it took on Fanshawe's family and herself, liberated her from ideologies of female conduct insisting on subservience and acquiescence.[28] The sequestration of her royalist husband's estate and the consequent loss of income, his many periods of absence on diplomatic and political missions, and his frequent periods of imprisonment all goad her into action on his behalf but also give her the latitude to assume the male prerogatives of agency and consequential action. One of the most memorable episodes in her narrative is her description of how she resorted to cross-dressing to fight alongside her husband when the ship on which they traveled en route from Ireland to Spain in February 1650 was attacked by Turkish pirates. She weaves this act of derring-do into her overall narrative of marital accord and wifely solicitude, but the emotions that she evinces on this occasion when she was "as free from sickness and fear as ... from discretion" (128) point to countercurrents at odds with the withdrawing demeanor that she invariably adopts.[29]

Fanshawe's text is composite in nature; it straddles the modes of family memoir, hagiographical biography, commonplace book, and ethnographical travelogue. Her style is more muted and pragmatic than Thornton's and, even though she regularly records her pregnancies and the births of her twenty-four children and the deaths of all but three of them, she is much more terse in her commentary on the embodied aspects of female existence. But, like Thornton and Blaugdone, she is drawn to dramatic crises often jaggedly or disjointedly depicted. Her brief recordings on the year, 1649–50, that she spent in Ireland is built around a congeries of such moments. She travels to Cork in the wake of her husband, who had been sent to Ireland to forge diplomatic links with Irish royalists, especially Lord Inchiquin, Murrough O'Brien, with a view to Prince Rupert creating a military base there.[30] Their stay in the country thus has a twofold nature: they are at once on a purposeful mission in Crown territory and, like many other royalists during the Interregnum, they have been driven into enforced exile.

Alternating experiences of solidarity and alienation, of unity and discord, pattern her account of her experiences in Ireland, in which the personal and the political are consistently interwoven. Her joy at being reunited with her husband in Cork is quickly dispersed by news of the death of her second son, of the arrival of Oliver Cromwell in Ireland to begin his merciless campaigns to subdue the country, and of the loss of one of his galleons by Prince Rupert in a skirmish near the Virgin Islands. Cork, a royalist stronghold where she lived for six months, had initially seemed a congenial refuge, but the revolt by the English garrison in mid-1649 in favor of Parliament brings this period of peace to an end.[31] Fanshawe, alarmed by "hearing lamentable scricks of men and women and children . . . stript and wounded and turned out of the town" (123), depicts the crisis as conjointly personal and political. Despite being pregnant and in pain from a broken wrist, she resourcefully packs the family's belongings and manages to get sanction for safe conduct from the city coming "through thousands of naked swords" to travel to her husband, who is absent on business in nearby Kinsale. As in Thornton's work, the somatic acts as a screen for the affective. Fanshawe's throbbing, broken wrist and pregnant body encrypt her feelings of vulnerability and fear that otherwise are censored and unexpressed. Reinforcing this aspect of her preternatural composure and courage, Fanshawe depicts her husband as the emotional center of this war-driven adventure: it is he, the "most disconsolate man in the world for fear of his family" (124), who is terror-stricken rather than she. The joyous reunion of the couple and their family is further posited as a counter to the treachery of Irish alliances, whereby a city that had once seemed friendly turns hostile overnight.

The complex emotional switch points in Fanshawe's narrative are similarly evident in a much-cited passage in her memoirs, in which her husband and herself in the thick of the Cromwellian campaigns stay for three nights in the castle of Lady Honora O'Brien in County Clare.[32] Even though the latter affords shelter to the author and her husband, her slighting comment that she "went for a maid, but few believed it" intimates unease rather than solidarity. The nighttime disturbance on this occasion is not the outbreak of military conflict but Fanshawe's experience of a banshee: "I saw by the light of the moon a woman leaning into the window through the casement, in white, with red hair and pale, gastly complexion. She spake loud and in a tone I never heard, thrice, 'Ahone,' and then with a sith more like wind than breath she vanished, and to me her body looked more like cloud than substance. I was so much affrighted that my hair stood on end and my night clothes fell off" (125). Her vivid tale has many remarkable facets that have been insufficiently examined. It is a rare written record in the seventeenth century of an Irish death messenger and faithfully adheres to the visual and aural components typical of such stories, in depicting a woman at a window, dressed in white, keening or crying in an eerie fashion, who arouses feelings of terror in the onlooker.[33] Banshees were usually seen as followers of certain Gaelic families, prominent among them the O'Briens, and were regarded as tokens of their noble and ancient status. Generally, banshees are sighted by friends of the family, not by those watching over the dying person, and hence have a premonitory function within circles of intimates alerting them to an imminent death. Curiously, Fanshawe internalizes and appropriates this time-honored oral mode that she presumably had picked up during her travels or through reading and renders it as direct experience in her first-person narrative. Views of outsider and native intimate momentarily accord and cross over in her convincing depiction of this harrowing ghostly visitant. Her story seems to deviate from traditional narratives in emphasizing the intensity of her fear, as the detail about the clothes of the spectator falling off does not occur in the multiple later recorded versions of death-messenger visitations.

In the aftermath of the ghostly sighting, she depicts her husband and herself as terror-stricken, but also as pragmatically evaluative. Fanshawe's spouse distances them both from the event in adducing it to be evidence of Irish superstition. In this light Fanshawe has acted as involuntary medium for archaic aspects of Irish culture. A discussion of the story the following morning with Honora O'Brien, however, adds further discomfiting aspects to the occasion, as she confirms that a cousin of hers had died in the night and explains that the banshee who heralded his death was the ghost of a woman who had been raped, made pregnant, and murdered by a previous owner of the castle.[34] Following these divulgences, Fanshawe tersely adds that her husband and herself "disposed ourselves to be gone suddenly" (125). The specter of violence particularly directed against women renders rationalizing distance impossible. In this instance the emotional community implied by the text is put under strain. The Irish royalists with whom Fanshawe and her husband have been making common cause are at once incorporated into their emotional ambit through the experience of the death messenger and then summarily abandoned as they are found, in the case of the Protestant O'Briens of Thomond, to be still dangerously associated with a culture that they find momentarily alluring but ultimately atavistic and suspect. Marital harmony becomes the only refuge from the confused and terrifying emotions of identification and alienation brought to the fore by this visit to a County Clare castle during the uncertainties of the Interregnum and the political and military devastation of the Cromwellian campaigns in Ireland.

BARBARA BLAUGDONE

An Account of the Travels, Sufferings & Persecutions of Barbara Blaugdone: Given forth as a Testimony to the Lord's Power, and for the Encouragement of

Friends was published in 1691 but was probably in circulation in manuscript form prior to that.[35] It is at once a spiritual autobiography hinging on the author's conversion to Quakerism in Bristol in 1654, a travel narrative, and a hortatory record of the salvific effect of belonging to this religious sect. Blaugdone's memoirs cover the years 1654–7 and recount the continuous persecution that she experienced while preaching and proselytizing in England and Ireland and the numerous prison sentences that she underwent because of being viewed as a threat to public order. The Quaker religion, as many historians have observed, granted freedom to women because of its egalitarianism, but the active role they assumed as prophets and preachers also exposed them to public attack, as they openly professed a faith that was feared because of its radical subversiveness.[36] In Blaugdone's compressed description of her travels as itinerant preacher, her experiences in Ireland are given prominence but are also shown to be of a piece with the violent opprobrium that she encounters in England. In her outline of her travails, it is less the "otherness" of Ireland that is of moment than the dividing line that she constantly negotiates between opponents and Friends, hostile adversaries and kindly disposed strangers. The emotional community addressed by her text is once delimited and elastic: her particular interlocutors are the "Friends," other members of her sectary, but she also inclusively invokes those ready to hear the divine messages that she conveys or to show empathy with her plight. Her missionary urge renders her open to others, while also dangerously pitting her against those who do not share her beliefs. To this degree Blaugdone's text bears out Rosenwein's observations that emotional communities are inherently relational but that they are not necessarily static and may on occasion be unbounded.[37]

Blaugdone's construction of a rhetorical self is likewise mutable and exploits countervailing aspects of Quaker life writing, especially the slippages that obtain between the self and the communal, the bodily and the spiritual, the active and the passive. Her brief memoir makes conspicuous use of a first-person narrative to highlight her devotion and tenacity as a purveyor of the divine word. Blaugdone, however, depicts whatever power and resilience she may possess as a concomitant of divine favor. She confides that she endured the sufferings caused by her first experience of imprisonment and the loss of her children and role as teacher because "the Lord so filled me with his Power, that I was preserved through it all" (4–5). Hilary Hinds has argued that female radical sectarian writing in the seventeenth century regularly uses the trope of absence to shield the woman author. In representing herself as a passive instrument of divine ordination, the writer protects herself from accusations of blame.[38] Yet countermanding this rhetorical strategy is Blaugdone's emphasis on the body and her depiction of the frequent distress that she suffers because of the extremes of danger and violent reprisal to which she is exposed. While her way is providentially smoothed for her on numerous occasions, she adverts obliquely to the physical costs involved. Quotidian pain may be dissolved or canceled out by divine aid and subsumed into a narrative of higher purpose, but it is registered nonetheless.

Just such an oscillation between the physical and the spiritual, immanence and transcendence, is evident in her depiction of her two journeys by sea prior to arriving in Ireland in 1656 and 1657. Her subtle recasting of these scenes fuses the hazardous sea crossing that is a staple of narratives about colonial voyages with the biblical story of Jonah and the whale. On her first trip to Ireland, she faces death not due to the stormy weather but to the superstition of the sailors:

> And then the Lord moved me to go for Ireland, and I went in a Vessel bound for Corke, and the Lord so ordered it, that the Ship was carried about to Dublin, and we had much foul Weather, so that the Sea-men said, That I Was the cause of it, because I was a Quaker; and they conspired to fling me over-board; but it being made known to me, I went to the Master and told him what his Men had deigned to do, and told him, that if he did suffer them to do it, my Blood would be required at his Hands. So he charged them not to meddle with me: And Afterwards we were in a Storm upon a First Day, and I was moved to go upon Deck, and speak among them, and Pray for them; and they were all made very quiet, and said, *They were more beholding to me then they were to their Priest, because I did pray for them, and he could not open his Mouth to say any thing amongst them.* (21–22)

It is noticeable that her interventions play those on board against one another: she variously appeals to the master's conscience and position of power and exercises spiritual authority in her own right to win the crew around. Her twofold actions at once forestall the threat of murder and persuade the sailors of the rectitude of her beliefs. Wrested from death, she is reborn as an agent of God, ultimately bringing spiritual enlightenment to the crew while additionally saving their lives as they survive a later and more severe storm before arrival in Dublin. Physical extremity acts as an allegory for spiritual rescue, but simultaneously the narrative captures the riskiness of her position as a Quaker preacher traveling alone. Her intrepid actions are ultimately part of a providential plan, but they nonetheless redound to her as a lone figure in hostile surroundings. The affective dimensions of these events are masked by the moral import of the story. Here, as throughout her narrative, Blaugdone allows her reader to supply the emotions that are intimated but rarely overtly articulated.[39]

Her second voyage to Ireland is likewise cast as a test of faith and a spiritual allegory in which, unlike Jonah, she does not succumb to despair and is rescued as a consequence:

> And in a while after I was moved to go for Ireland again, and then I was in great perils by Sea, where I saw the Wonders of the Lord in the Deep; and there was one man Friend, and one woman Friend then in the Ship besides me, and the Ship was broken near Dungarvan, and it foundred in the Sea, something near the Shore, and we were all alike to be cast away; and I was ordered of the Lord to stay in the Ship, until they were all gone out of her, and the Master and the Passengers got into the Boat, (all save one Man and one Woman, which were cast away) and they got to Shore, and stood there to see what would become of me, who was still in the Cabbin, and the Waves beat in upon me in abundance, almost ready to stifle me: And so when I found freedom I went and stood upon a piece of Deck that was left, and then the Master of the Vessel & the Man Friend called to me, and told me, *If I would venture to leap down, they would venture to come into the Water to save me.* (29–30)

In this dramatic account of the sea voyage as a spiritual passage, Blaugdone's faith and resolution save her from the cowardice of her companions. Their errancy is redisposed and made fit with a tale of providential rescue: "So the Lord's Power and Mercy was wonderfully shown at that time for my preservation" (31).

Catie Gill has contended in her magisterial survey of writing by Quaker women in the seventeenth century that communal narratives and stories of collective selfhood that center on the "we," not the "I," are the predominant modes.[40] Even though it unfailingly sees the self as a counter in a divine plan, Blaugdone's narrative belies Gill's findings, as it consistently stresses the actions of a solitary individual and rarely resorts to the first-person plural. Blaugdone momentarily uses "we" after she persuades the inimical sailors on the ship during her first journey to Ireland of her concern for their spiritual welfare, thus symbolically conjoining their fates. In general, however, her anecdotes emphasize the lone interventions that she undertakes at divine prompting. This muting of the customary communitarian viewpoint may be ascribed to the anomalousness of her trips to Ireland, 1656–7, and the uncertainty that prevailed about the power of religious groupings and the degree of tolerance they should be accorded. In the 1650s the Cromwellian reconstruction of the country was under way and relationships with the Old Protestants, the Catholic royalists, the Presbyterians, and the Quakers were being renegotiated.[41] Even though it was decided that Quaker beliefs were disruptive and should be banned, official attitudes had not totally hardened.

Blaugdone's 1656 trip to Ireland coincided with the expulsion by Henry Cromwell, the lord lieutenant, of two renowned Quaker preachers, Francis Howgill and Edward Burrough, to prevent them from spreading dissent. But when Blaugdone, upon her arrival in Dublin, daringly waylays and accosts Cromwell and the Protestant divine, Thomas Harrison, and berates them for their actions, her words lead to compunction on their part rather than a counterattack. Crawford Gribben notes that their response as recorded by Blaugdone is "a remarkable confession of the Cromwellian ambivalence about early Quaker rhetoric."[42] These divided views are borne out in other predicaments in which she finds herself: in Cork a woman rescues her from a butcher who "would cleave my Head in twain" (27), malice thus ceding to sympathy. But the reverse situation also obtains as she discovers that former friends in the city now accuse her of being a witch. On her second trip to Dublin, she is incarcerated and put on trial and, as she refuses to acknowledge any crime, is returned to the filthy prison where "the Wet and Filth of the House-of-office ran in under my back" (30). This situation is miraculously overturned when friends obtain her release. Her visit to vindicate herself to the benighted judge who had condemned her to jail is followed by his sudden death, thus further reinforcing her self-righteous triumph. This pattern of reversals from endangerment to salvation and from hostility to acceptance signals the providential nature of Blaugdone's missionary work. Her isolated actions prove over time to be part of a divine plan, but the construction of a communitarian "we" is vitiated by the unpredictable and often life-threatening situations in which she finds herself. Instead, she uses her experiences in Ireland to exemplify the fortitude and combativeness required of those cleaving to Quaker belief. Her equanimity though is often counterpointed by her partisan appeal to female friends who can verify her stories. Her narrative ends after a further imprisonment in Limerick; the storm that besets the ship returning her to England and the pirates who rob her of all her belongings but do not harm her seal her account of beset virtue that ultimately triumphs. Her narrative posits Ireland as a space wherein she can discern, after some struggle, the symbolic lineaments of her vocation and calling. Her experiences in the country reinforce her belief and allow her to distil instructive advice for her contemporaries and those who will read her text in the future.

CONCLUSION

The life writings by Thornton, Fanshawe, and Blaugdone about Ireland are lastingly colored by the historical moments in which they are set: Thornton's family through its political alliance with Thomas Wentworth is aligned with an exploitative, divisive, and sectarian colonial regime; Fanshawe, despite taking refuge in the country during the Interregnum and evincing intellectual sympathies for other cultures, struggles to come to terms with royalist

Ireland; and Blaugdone pursues her vocation as a Quaker preacher in a society that views her with deadly suspicion in the main. All three women's depictions of Ireland are terse and oblique yet teasingly laden. Politically and historically, obdurately silent subtexts underpin these texts, which posit more questions than they answer. But pointed rhetorical effects and patterns indicate the preoccupation of all three authors with problems determining their welfare, their weal or woe. By duly identifying and reflecting on the emotional communities that frame their writing and discerning the affective patterns, however conventional, that contour their writing, a contemporary reader may begin to get a measure of these varied and charged accounts of the colonial experience from a female point of view and the differing ideological stances and religious, social, and political cruxes at their core.

NOTES

1. Ann Fanshawe, *The Memoirs of Ann, Lady Fanshawe*, in *The Memoirs of Anne, Lady Halkett and Ann, Lady Fanshawe*, ed. John Loftis (Oxford: Clarendon, 1979), 111. All subsequent references are to this edition and noted in parentheses in the text.

2. Kate Chedgzoy, *Women's Writing in the British Atlantic World: Memory, Place and History, 1550–1700* (Cambridge: Cambridge University Press, 2007), 4–6.

3. For a discussion of the discursive restraints in women's travel writing and the clashing imperatives of passivity and action associated respectively with femininity and colonialism, see Sara Mills, *Discourses of Difference: An Analysis of Women's Travel Writing and Colonialism* (London: Routledge, 1991), 1–23.

4. Virginia Woolf, *A Room of One's Own and Three Guineas* (1928; Oxford: Oxford University Press, 1992), 130.

5. Danielle Clarke, "Life Writing," in *The Oxford Handbook of Early Modern Prose, 1500–1640*, ed. Andrew Hadfield (Oxford: Oxford University Press, 2013), 455. On forms of subjectivity in the early modern period, see Elizabeth Hanson, *Discovering the Subject in Renaissance England* (Cambridge: Cambridge University Press, 1998), 1–23.

6. Thomas O. Sloane, "Rhetorical Selfhood in Erasmus and Milton," in *A Companion to Rhetoric and Rhetorical Criticism*, ed. Walter Jost and Wendy Olmsted (Oxford: Blackwell, 2006), 113–14.

7. On the strictures against female authorship and the ways in which women sought to counterbalance public and private concerns or to play down their presumption in writing, see Wendy Wall, *The Imprint of Gender: Authorship and Publication in the English Renaissance* (Ithaca: Cornell University Press, 1993), 279–340.

8. Michelle M. Dowd and Julie A. Eckerle, introd. to *Genre and Women's Life Writing in Early Modern England*, ed. Michelle M. Dowd and Julie A. Eckerle (Aldershot: Ashgate, 2007), 1–13. For an illuminating exploration of the subsumption of facets of romance into autobiographical texts, see Eckerle, *Romancing the Self in Early Modern Englishwomen's Life Writing* (Farnham, : Ashgate, 2013).

9. Jan Plamper, *The History of Emotions: An Introduction*, trans. Keith Tribe (Oxford: Oxford University Press, 2015); William M. Reddy, *The Navigation of Feeling: A Framework for the History of Emotions* (Cambridge: Cambridge University Press, 2001).

10. For the lively debates about the imperative to read emotions historically, see Barbara H. Rosenwein, "Worrying about Emotions in History," *American Historical Review* 107, no. 3 (2002): 821–45; Rosenwein, "Problems and Methods in the History of Emotions," *Passions in Context: Journal of the History and Philosophy of the Emotions* 1, no. 1 (2001): 1–32; Plamper, "The History of Emotions: An Interview with William Reddy, Barbara Rosenwein and Peter Stearns," *History and Theory* 49, no. 2 (2010): 237–65; and Plamper, *History of Emotions*.

11. Norbert Elias, *The Civilizing Process*, trans. Edmund Jephcott, vol. 1, *The History of Manners* (Oxford: Blackwell, 1978); and vol. 2, *State Formation and Civilization* (Oxford: Blackwell, 1982). For her critique of Elias, see Rosenwein, "Worrying about Emotions," 826–28; and Rosenwein, *Generations of Feeling: A History of Emotions, 600–1700* (Cambridge: Cambridge University Press, 2016), 11–12.

12. For her account of the inadequacy of hydraulic concepts of emotion, see Barbara H. Rosenwein, *Emotional Communities in the Early Middle Ages* (Ithaca: Cornell University Press, 2008), 11–12.

13. For an analysis of the concept of the emotional community, see Rosenwein, *Emotional Communities*, 20–29; and Andrew Lynch, "Emotional Community," in *Early Modern Emotions: An Introduction*, ed. Susan Broomhall (London: Routledge, 2017), 3–6.

14. Rosenwein, *Emotional Communities*, 24.

15. Rosenwein, "Problems and Methods," 8–9.

16. Key studies in addition to Broomhall's *Early Modern Emotions* include Gail Kern Paster, Katherine Rowe, and Mary Floyd-Wilson, eds., *Reading the Early Modern Passions: Essays in the Cultural History of Emotions* (Philadelphia: University of Pennsylvania Press, 2004); Susan Broomhall and Sarah Finn, eds., *Violence and Emotions in Early Modern Europe* (London: Routledge, 2016); and Ronda Arab, Michelle M. Dowd, and Adam Zucker, eds., *Historical Affects and the Early Modern Theater* (London: Routledge, 2016).

17. Rosenwein, "Worrying about Emotions," 836.

18. Rosenwein, *Generations of Feeling*, 8.

19. See Raymond A. Anselment, introd. to Alice Thornton, *My First Booke of My Life*, ed. Raymond A. Anselment (Lincoln: University of Nebraska Press, 2014), xxiii–xxix. All subsequent references are to this edition and noted in parentheses in the text.

20. Thornton, in a third text in which she describes her life since the death of her husband, declares that she has composed it to refute the suggestions of her "deadly Enymys" (qtd. in Anselment, introd. to Thornton, *First Booke*, xvii).

21. Anselment views Thornton's work as following the precepts of the seventeenth-century spiritual self-examination; see "Feminine Self-Reflection and the Seventeenth-Century Occasional Meditation," *Seventeenth Century* 26, no. 1 (2013): 69–93.

22. The following works include commentary on Thornton's accounts of her marriage and pregnancies: Lawrence Stone, *The Family, Sex and Marriage in England, 1500–1800* (London: Weidenfeld and Nicolson, 1977); Sharon Howard, "Imagining the Pain and Peril of Seventeenth-Century Childbirth: Travail and Deliverance in the Making of an Early Modern World," *Social History of Medicine* 16, no. 3 (2003): 367–82; and Will Coster, *Family and Kinship in England, 1450–1800*, 2nd ed. (London: Routledge, 2016).

23. See Charlotte F. Otten, ed., *English Women's Voices, 1540–1700* (Miami: Florida International University Press, 1992), 43–45, 232; and Elspeth Graham et al., eds., *Her Own Life: Autobiographical Writings by Seventeenth-Century Englishwomen* (London: Routledge, 1989), 147–64. For a more recent feminist exploration that also fastens on Thornton's portrayal of illness as a facet of identity, see Anne Lear, "Thank God for Haemorrhoids! Illness and Identity in a Seventeenth-Century Woman's Autobiography," *Women's Writing* 12, no. 3 (2005): 337–44.

24. On the complex evolution of Thornton's life writing and the numerous expansions she undertook, as well as the loss of some of the manuscripts, see Raymond A. Anselment, "Seventeenth-Century Manuscript Sources of Alice Thornton's Life," *Studies in English Literature, 1500–1900* 45, no. 1 (2005): 135–55.

25. For an analysis of the shifting attitudes to Strafford and his transformation into a public martyr, see Terence Kilburn and Anthony Milton, "The Public Context of the Trial and Execution of Strafford," in *The Political World of Thomas Wentworth, Earl of Strafford, 1621–1641*, ed. J. F. Merritt (Cambridge: Cambridge University Press, 1996), 230–51.

26. For accounts of Wentworth's controversial rule in Ireland, see Nicholas Canny, "The Attempted Anglicisation of Ireland in the Seventeenth Century: An Exemplar of 'British History,'" in Merritt, *Political World*, 157–86; Jane Ohlmeyer, "Strafford, the 'Londonderry Business' and the 'New British History,'" in Merritt, *Political*

World, 209–28; and David Lee. Smith, *A History of the Modern British Isles, 1603–1707: The Double Crown* (Oxford: Blackwell, 1998), 98–100.

27. David Edwards vividly outlines the land-grabbing adventurism and political machinations on the part of Ormond that led to Wandesford's seizure of lands in County Kilkenny and the outrage that this caused. See *The Ormond Lordship in County Kilkenny, 1515–1642: The Rise and Fall of Butler Feudal Power* (Dublin: Four Courts, 2003), 299–308.

28. Mary Beth Rose, *Gender and Heroism in Early Modern English Literature* (Chicago: Chicago University Press, 2001), 65–71.

29. Sharon Cadman Seelig argues for a feminist subtext in Fanshawe's memoirs, noting her many deviations from the norms of female conduct; see *Autobiography and Gender in Early Modern Literature: Reading Women's Lives, 1600–1680* (Cambridge: Cambridge University Press, 2006), 90–109.

30. On Irish royalists, see Robert Armstrong, "Ormond, The Confederate Peace Talks and Protestant Royalism," in *Kingdoms in Crisis: Ireland in the 1640s*, ed. Micheál Ó Siochrú (Dublin: Four Courts, 2001), 122–40.

31. On Cromwell's Munster campaigns, 1649–50, see Micheál Ó Siochrú, *God's Executioner: Oliver Cromwell and the Conquest of Ireland* (London: Faber and Faber, 2008), 106–33.

32. Ivar O'Brien notes that the Thomond holding was likely either Clonroad Castle or Clare Castle, County Clare; see *O'Brien of Thomond: The O'Briens in Irish History, 1500–1865* (Chichester: Phillimore, 1986), 179.

33. Patricia Lysaght briefly refers to Fanshawe's text in *The Banshee: The Irish Supernatural Death Messenger* (Dublin: O'Brien, 1996), 48, 373.

34. Lysaght, *Banshee*, notes that only literary versions depict the death messenger as a victim of violence (37).

35. Barbara Blaugdone, *An Account of the Travels, Sufferings & Persecutions of Barbara Blaugdone: Given forth as a Testimony to the Lord's Power, and for the Encouragement of Friends* (Shoreditch, 1691). All subsequent references are to this edition and noted in parentheses in the text.

36. On the assertive social roles played by Quaker women as missionaries and prophets and the harsh treatment meted out to them, see Stevie Davies, *Unbridled Spirits: Women of the English Revolution, 1640–1660* (London: Women's Press, 1998), 249–79; Phyllis Mack, "Women as Prophets during the English Civil War," *Feminist Studies* 8, no. 1 (1982): 19–45; Elaine Hobby, *Virtue of Necessity: English Women's Writing, 1649–1688* (London: Virago, 1988), 26–53; and Hobby, "Handmaids of the Lord and Mothers of Israel: Early Vindications of Quaker Women's Prophecy," in *The Emergence of Quaker Writing and Dissenting Literature in Seventeenth-Century England*, ed. Thomas N. Corns and David Loewenstein (London: Cass, 1995), 88–98.

37. Rosenwein, *Generations of Feeling*, 3.

38. Hilary Hinds, *God's Englishwomen: Seventeenth-Century Radical Sectarian Writing and Feminist Criticism* (Manchester: Manchester University Press, 1996), 108–46.

39. On Blaugdone's positing of a sentimental reader who can supply the deflected emotional subtexts of her work, see Althea Stewart, "Good Quaker Women, Tearful Sentimental Spectators, Readers, and Auditors," *Prose Studies* 29, no. 1 (2007): 73–85.

40. Catie Gill, *Women in the Seventeenth-Century Quaker Community: A Literary Study of Political Identities* (London: Routledge, 2005). See also Gill, "Identities in Quaker Women's Writing, 1652–60," *Women's Writing* 9, no. 2 (2007): 267–84.

41. For an account of the establishment of a new political and religious balance of power in the 1650s, see Raymond Gillespie, *Seventeenth Century Ireland: Making Ireland Modern* (Dublin: Gill and Macmillan, 2006), 182–211.

42. Crawford Gribben, *God's Irishmen: Theological Debates in Cromwellian Ireland* (Oxford: Oxford University Press, 2007), 157.

3

The Boyle Women and Familial Life Writing

ANN-MARIA WALSH

The notion of family preoccupies, inspires, and underlines much of the life writing of the seventeenth-century Boyle women, whose number included Lady Katherine Ranelagh (1615–91) and Lady Mary Rich, Countess of Warwick (1624–78) but also the lesser-known wife, daughters, daughters-in-law, and granddaughters of Richard Boyle, First Earl of Cork (1566–1643). The women's writings, which encompass letters, a diary, an autobiography, a memorandum book, account books, medical receipt books, prose treatises, and pious meditations, form part of the surviving Boyle archive. The practice of keeping records and preserving the family's papers originated with Richard Boyle, who, as a New English Protestant planter, recognized the importance of using textual and other (nontextual) media to legitimize and consolidate his status as a landowner and as a member of the ruling elite in Ireland.[1] Thus, planting, custodianship, and self-publicizing became the bedrock of Boyle's strategy for success, and it was that kind of environment, with an intense focus on fashioning and maintaining an "English" identity, that conditioned the upbringing of the natal Boyle women and shaped the cultural understanding of those other women who subsequently married into the family. The volume, variety, and intergenerational character of the manuscript materials in the Boyle archive attest to the critical importance of the family's writerly skills in enabling them to establish and sustain their authoritative presence in seventeenth-century Ireland and beyond. The purpose of this chapter is to demonstrate through a brief survey and analysis of letters within the Boyle archive how Ireland, the source and mainstay of the family's wealth and privilege, was perceived and represented by the Boyle women in their life writings.

First, it is necessary to situate the Boyle women's writings within the familial context and the larger Boyle archive, as this rich and vibrant writing culture initially prompted the women to pick up their pens and thereafter facilitated and encouraged them to continue developing their literary skills throughout the remainder of their lives. Furthermore, positioning the women's texts within that familial framework also allows us to see more clearly how they responded individually and collectively to their bifurcated existence with homes, landed estates, family connections, and a network of friends located on both sides of the Irish Sea. But it is also pertinent, as Kate Chedgzoy has argued, to study early modern women's writing by "situating it in relation to more expansive, detailed, and complex cultural geographies of the period."[2] Therefore, the second part of this chapter explores specific letters from the archive that illustrate the different ways in which located-ness mattered to the Boyle women. Six letters in particular highlight the competing and often conflicted ways in which Ireland is imagined from a familial perspective: as a home place, as a valuable resource, as somewhere that needed constant minding, as a distraction, as a threat, and as a source of endangerment.[3] This correspondence shows how Ireland challenged each individual female writer to identify and evaluate her core values, not only to cope with the experience of loss but also to recognize and seize those rare moments when she could strive toward achieving her personal objectives. Altogether, this survey and analysis of the archive is aimed at providing a more nuanced understanding of the complex place that early modern Ireland occupied in the imagined lives of the Boyle women as articulated from each of their varying perspectives.

The significant amount of extant material relating to the Boyles can be accessed in the National Libraries of England, Ireland, and Scotland, as well as within the archival collections of various stately homes and a number of other repositories. The sheer size and dispersed character of the archive is a tangible reminder of the Boyle family's impactful presence on what was the Three Kingdoms. The collection known as the Cork Manuscripts is associated with the Boyle family and the earls of Cork and Burlington but also with subsequent dukes of Devonshire and the Cavendish family. Dating from 1586 to 1885, the Cork Manuscripts are composed of the Boyles' private papers and correspondence and is primarily maintained at Chatsworth House in Derbyshire, home to the current Duke of Devonshire. A large proportion of the archive is related to the legal and business side of the estate; it also includes key life writing texts such as the correspondence and papers of the First and Second Earls of Cork, the men's diaries, and— particularly significant for the purposes of this chapter—a memorandum book started in 1659 by the second earl's wife, Elizabeth Boyle, née Clifford (1613–91), containing the countess's handwritten account of the family's history and the key events that shaped her life over a thirty-year period.[4] She begins with her marriage in 1634 to Richard Boyle (Second Earl of Cork) and goes on to describe the circumstances of the births, christenings, marriages, and deaths of her children, grandchildren, and great-grandchildren.[5] Thus, relying on the two earls' diaries and the countess's memorandum book, a picture can be reconstructed of how the Boyle family lived and sustained itself throughout the changes and turbulence that characterized seventeenth-century Ireland.

Most of the Boyle correspondence stored at Chatsworth is addressed, in the main, to the First or Second Earls of Cork, with the exception of the period from 1648 to 1650. At that time the Second Countess of Cork, Elizabeth Boyle, necessarily took charge of the Irish estates to maintain a visible presence and safeguard the Boyles' propertied interests while her husband and other members of the family were absent, living in royalist exile, or fighting on the side of Oliver Cromwell.[6] But the letters that do survive reveal much about different members of the family and their movements as they traveled away from home: to complete their education; to transact business and political matters; or to relocate, often as newly married women, to another estate, county, or country. Moreover, a cursory glance at the Chatsworth holdings can also affirm that every single one of the seventeenth-century Boyle women is represented in some guise and to varying degrees, whether directly as a correspondent or as a diarist or indirectly by way of reference in a memorandum note or in the account books.

The British Library in London also has a number of important holdings linked to the Boyle family, including much of the First Earl of Cork's correspondence and a copy of his autobiography, "True Remembrances," which he began sometime between 1610 and 1611, when he was in his mid-forties.[7] Additional pertinent holdings include the diary, meditations, and memoir of Mary Rich, née Boyle, and several of the family's recipe books, including "Lady Rennelagh's choise receipts, as also some of Capt. Willis'; who valued them above gold."[8] The Ranelagh recipe book is filed among the Sloane Manuscripts, and its survival exemplifies the fate of many other individual items related to the Boyle family that were kept and preserved as part of the British Library manuscript collections of other noble households, such as Althorp, Blenheim, Egerton, Egmont, Hyde, Petty, Portland, Sloane, Southwell, Stowe, and Verney.

The Althorp Papers collection is a special case in point because it includes archival material relating to the Earls of Cumberland, Burlington, and Halifax, each of whom was dynastically connected to Elizabeth Boyle (Second Countess of Cork and later First Countess of Burlington), signaling her importance as the lynchpin within that dynamic.[9] In terms of archival importance, the section of the Althorp Papers that includes the Burlington Papers is particularly significant because it covers an extensive period, from 1627 to 1692, as well as affording a comprehensive view of the Burlington marriage and the next generation of Boyles. In one box of papers alone (Add. MS 75354, covering 1632–78) are ten courtship letters exchanged by Richard and Elizabeth (later Second Earl and Countess of Cork); their marriage settlement; six letters from Elizabeth to Richard, which are undated but estimated to fall between 1664 and 1667; and a number of letters written by Boyle siblings Roger (five letters), Robert (three), Mary (one), and Katherine (thirty to older brother Richard). Another box (Add. MS 75355, covering 1661–82) contains correspondence exchanged between Boyle children Charles (eleven letters), Frances (two), Elizabeth (two), Anne (one), and Henrietta (seven) with their parents, Richard and Elizabeth, along with some correspondence from the respective in-laws. Yet another (Add. MS 75356) relates to incoming correspondence addressed to Elizabeth Boyle, Second Countess of Cork, and includes letters from Mary of Modena, wife of James, Duke of York; Elizabeth Butler, Duchess of Ormonde; and Lady Anne Clifford, the Dowager Countess of Pembroke and Montgomery, a cousin of Elizabeth's and of course a famous diarist in her own right. This material reveals a great deal about Elizabeth Boyle's persona and the kinds of interpersonal relationships she maintained through her epistolary networks and letter-writing activities. On the other hand, another series of letters and papers (these in Add. MS 75357) revolve around Boyle's dealings with the Standing Committee for the East Riding of Yorkshire during 1645 and 1646, when the family's estates were under sequestration and thus testify to her legitimate status as a Clifford heiress and the sole owner of the Londesborough lands. In addition, personal and household accounts, as well as receipts from Ireland for the period 1638 to 1666, reflect the family's high-status lifestyle, as is illustrated with the hefty goldsmith and apothecary bills.

Apart from the British Library, there are several more repositories in London that hold a variety of archival materials relating to the Boyle family: the Royal Society Library, the National Archives, the Wellcome Library, and the National Art Library in the Victoria and Albert Museum.[10] The Boyle Papers at the Royal Society Library are a good example of the generic diversity of siblings Robert's and Katherine's writings; Robert's, for example, include copious amounts of correspondence and papers on matters scientific and philosophical, as well as a copy of his autobiography, "An Account of Philaretus during his Minority," which looks back at his youth in Ireland and the time he spent traveling around Europe in the 1640s.[11] The Royal Society Library also has correspondence between Ranelagh and other members of the Royal Society that reflect both the sophisticated content and geographic scope of her epistolary engagements, starting with her brother Robert and broadening out to include John Beale, John Eliot, and very possibly Samuel Hartlib and Henry Oldenburg.[12] Two further items in the Royal Society Library that represent the multifarious and complex nature of Ranelagh's writing are an extant manuscript treatise, "Discourse concerning the plague of 1665," in which Ranelagh advocates for liberty of conscience, and a medical commonplace book containing several entries filed under Ranelagh's name.[13] Within the Boyle Papers there are also four letters from Boyle sibling Mary Rich to brother Robert.[14]

The Orrery Papers, currently housed at the West Sussex Record Office in Chichester, contain the manuscript holdings of Roger Boyle (1621–79) and his wife, Margaret (1623–89), who after 1660 were known as the First Earl and Countess of Orrery. The massive collection, amounting to more than 750 items covering a thirty-year period from 1660 to 1690, includes copies and drafts of the Orrerys' outgoing correspondence, plus some of the couple's epistolary exchanges.[15] Incoming correspondence comprises thirty-three letters addressed to the Earl of Orrery from his daughter-in-law, Lady Mary Broghill, and twenty-four letters addressed by her to the Countess of Orrery, with as many responses in return to Lady Broghill, concerning outstanding monies due on the marriage settlement, which eventually resulted in a lengthy legal action (Broghill was successful).[16] Apart from the nineteen extant letters written by Ranelagh to her sister-in-law, the Countess of Orrery, there are numerous other letters exchanged between the Orrerys and Richard, Robert, and Mary, the content of which revolves around land, finance, health, and the long-running dispute with Lady Broghill.[17] Various miscellaneous household accounts attest to Margaret Boyle's personal involvement in managing the estate, while a receipt for the purchase of "a bird cage," "two baskets of sugar," "a hundred and a half of oranges," "a box of browne citron," and "two boxes of marmalade" serve as a salient reminder of the Orrery family's privileged existence.[18] Margaret's jointure deeds are listed in the papers, along with a document containing "Rules of Margaret. Dowager Countess of Orrery for the management of the Almshouses at Castlemartyr, Co. Cork, ca. 1680," which sheds some light on how one Boyle woman sought to use her dower money to establish a legacy and substantiate her future reputation as a worthy widow.[19]

One of the archive's gems is the correspondences, before and during the war, of Countess Alice Barrymore, née Boyle (1608–66), who wrote to her friend and member of Parliament Sir Ralph Verney over many years.[20] A reading of the correspondence underlines the importance of letter writing in allowing the women in the family not only a social outlet but also a medium through which they could voice their opinions and concerns about the world in which they lived. Barrymore's younger sister, Ranelagh, similarly conducted epistolary conversations with a wide selection of male and female acquaintances across Europe and the British Isles.[21] The precise locations of some, at least, of Ranelagh's surviving letters are representative of her epistolary network within and across the Three Kingdoms: five letters are spread between the Carte Papers, Clarendon State Papers, and Burnet Manuscripts at the Bodleian Library in Oxford; six more are filed with the Hartlib Papers at the Sheffield University Library; and, farther north, five letters to the Countess of Panmure and another to the Duchess of Hamilton, dated August 6, 1690, are housed at the National Records of Scotland in Edinburgh.[22]

Across the Irish Sea, the Lismore Castle Estate Papers are housed at the National Library of Ireland in Dublin.[23] As already mentioned, the family correspondence of the First and Second Earls of Cork was transferred to Chatsworth House in Derbyshire, but the manuscript calendar summarizing that material is still available on microfilm at the library. After the removal of the family's papers to Chatsworth, some manuscripts, which most likely were misfiled, have since been recovered and remain at the library. Examples include letters written by Ranelagh and the Second Countess of Cork, Elizabeth Boyle, which offer a rare female view of Ireland during and immediately after the 1641 Irish rebellion.[24] Those individual letters are also a tangible reminder that the Boyles had many connections with other noble families resident in Ireland whose libraries and archives might still contain materials related to the Boyle women.[25] Over the course of the seventeenth century, siblings Mary, Katherine, Roger, Francis, and Robert Boyle actively encouraged one another to experiment with new writing techniques and different literary genres.[26] Roger achieved fame and credit as a poet and playwright, but he also demonstrated his literary dexterity by writing and publishing on subjects as diverse as the liturgical festivals and *A treatise of the art of war dedicated to the Kings Most Excellent Majesty and written by the*

Right Honourable Roger, Earl of Orrery.[27] The Boyle men availed of print publication to disseminate their ideas and imaginative outpourings, while the two most intellectually creative female writers in the family, Ranelagh and Rich, were far more limited in the options available to them. Ranelagh's writings never appeared in print under her own name, but her manuscript treatises were often copied, excerpted, translated, and circulated among a European-wide intellectual community.[28] Rich's literary endeavors reached a larger audience by virtue of being published either posthumously or under the name of godly associates with whom she was acquainted. George Berkeley, for instance, persuaded her to write "Rules for holy living" for his collection of spiritual reflections, and her pious meditations featured as an attachment to her funerary sermon, which was printed under the name of her chaplain, Anthony Walker.[29] Two centuries after Rich's death, religious societies published her diary and memoir as an example of a saintly life.[30] Apart from sharing an interest in writing technologies, Robert and Mary also recognized Ireland in their autobiographical texts as the locus where they each were introduced to reading, learning, and pious principles. In a departure from the spiritual, philosophical, political, and scientific themes, Elizabeth Boyle (Second Countess of Cork), like her father-in-law, the First Earl of Cork, constructed her memorandum book around a family-centric model that focused on tracking the Boyles' movements at the apex of Irish and English society. Yet one of the more noticeable attributes that defines the entire Boyle archive is the way in which both the men and women engaged with the familial correspondence network as a way of connecting and maintaining their unity at a time when division and uncertainty were rife. In the next section of this chapter, I consider how Ireland is figured by the Boyle women as an important signifier in delineating their gendered lives.

An initial reading of the Boyle women's archived letters underlines the degree to which mobility was both a central feature of their lives and the justification for much of their writing. As elite early modern heiresses and mistresses of large households, the Boyle women participated in routine progresses around the family's properties, which were located in Cork, Dublin, Waterford, Yorkshire, Dorset, Somerset, and London. Over the course of those sojourns, the women wrote to those at home, giving accounts of their movements and various social encounters.[31] In many more instances, however, the women remained at home while the men traveled abroad.[32] On those occasions letter writing allowed the women to keep in touch with the travelers so that they could allay their anxieties about the men's safety, as well as liaise on more pragmatic issues concerned with the estates, which the women often managed alone for several months at a time.

One example of the latter scenario is evoked in a letter that the First Countess of Cork, Catherine Boyle, née Fenton (1588–1630), wrote to her husband, Richard Boyle, on March 18, 1604/5.[33] The letter was primarily designed as a love letter in its attempt to bridge the emotional and physical gap by reuniting the countess with her husband—in spirit, at least—while he was away traveling around Munster. The materiality of the letter, the impulse to write, and the act of writing are all represented by Lady Cork as reminders of her wifely devotion, figured in "my pen the mes[s]inger of my heart." The letter conveys the experiential reality for the countess and many other noblewomen who lived in Ireland at that time and had to cope with an absentee husband and the accompanying feelings of loneliness. Further enunciating that condition, the writer self-deprecatingly compares herself to a "poure scab," which flatteringly suggests that she was dying of neglect without her husband's life-enhancing presence. Yet the letter is more complex than simply attempting to counteract loss and to underline Boyle's impatience for her husband's return home; the "pen" also empowers the writer to privilege her voice and to highlight her accomplishments, separate from her husband. The catalog of news items reported along with the list of duties performed and the solicitations received and enacted indicate that, in the absence of her husband, Boyle was not pining at home but instead industriously dividing her time fulfilling a number of important roles as well as prompting some initiatives of her own. Accountably, the letter reveals how Boyle availed of the connectivity and disseminating potential of the letter to compensate for her physical confinement and used her husband's absence to draw attention to her own efforts to improve the family's future prosperity and security.

On the other hand, the perspective of a traveling woman (in contrast with the stay-at-home woman) is seen in a letter that Catherine Boyle's grand-daughter, Henrietta Boyle (1647–87), wrote home to her father, the Second Earl of Cork, Richard Boyle, while she was visiting the baths in Kent with her mother and older sisters.[34] On June 16, 1659, Henrietta and her family had departed from Youghal and crossed over to England without the company of Richard Boyle, who was forced to remain in Ireland according to the terms agreed on following his return from royalist exile eight years previously.[35] In a similar approach to that formerly employed by her grandmother, Henrietta uses her geographic distance from the addressee and the occasion of writing to renegotiate her position of favor within the family hierarchy. Determined to set herself apart from her older siblings, Henrietta uses her letter as an outward manifestation of her filial persona. The opening line makes explicit her intentions: "By not drinking the waters I gain the priviledge of writing to your Lordship which I employ the best I can to divert your Lordship with newes."[36] As the letter unfolds, the lively tone and amusing content reflect an acute awareness of the reader, showing Henrietta's understanding of the medium's capacity to connect, while enabling her father to share, even if remotely and retrospectively, in those events and experiences that his family was enjoying. Toward the end of the letter, Henrietta reinforces the favorable impression she has built up by inserting a postscript in which she helpfully presents her sisters' "most humble dutys," reminding her father that the other sisters were "hindered from" writing because they were otherwise preoccu-pied "takeing the water." In a reverse of Lady Cork's response to her situation of isolation, Henrietta exercises her letter-writing skills to command her father's exclusive attention while he remains in Ireland, and, by assuming the role of dependable "eye-witnesse," Henrietta successfully carves out a sepa-rate identity from that of her older Boyle siblings.[37]

When Countess Alice Barrymore wrote to her friend Sir Ralph Verney in 1639 and 1642, she used her presence in her north Cork home at Castle-lyons to positively affirm and pronounce different aspects of her persona as a good and loving mother and as a loyal and courageous Protestant landowner. Barrymore's motives in writing to Verney on February 18, 1639, reflect the relative peace and prosperity that prevailed in Ireland at that time as she sought help in the search for a suitable tutor who might come over and prepare her son to attend school in England.[38] Nicholas Canny and Jane Ohlmeyer have previously noted how settlers who benefited from the plantation of Ireland, like the "New English" Boyles, were encouraged by the Dublin administration to uphold an English way of living through their commitment to English customs, language, law, and the Protestant faith, with the hope that their civilizing influence might also have a positive impact on the native Irish populace. Furthermore, while it was customary for Catholics' heirs to be sent to continental colleges, their Protestant counterparts opted instead for an English equivalent.[39] Therefore, Barrymore's letter served to counteract Ireland's seeming deficiencies by investing in an English education for her son, in addition to signaling her support for the government's policy in Ireland. However, as the request for a tutor is reiterated with some urgency toward the end of the letter, the writer also attempts to protect herself and the boy from any blame in regard to his "Mad" behavior.[40] A distancing effect is achieved when the writer applies a passive verbal construction, calling on the addressee to send over the tutor with "as much speede as may bee[,] for see hee [her son] [is] spoyld for want of one good sarvant."[41] The *Oxford English Dictionary* defines the adjective "spoiled" as "persons, especially children: Injured in character by excessive indulgence, leniency, or deference," but, given the sociopolitical backdrop in which the letter was composed, the term "spoyld" might have connoted the perceived danger and potential spoiling facing "English" children in Ireland at that specific moment in time.[42] Arguably, Barrymore presents her letter as a necessary and timely intervention to correct her son's deviant behavior and to ensure that he is ready to take on the prestigious Barrymore earldom in the not-too-distant future. More fundamentally, the letter underscores Barrymore's civilizing presence at Castlelyons, without whose efforts the Boyle-Barry inheritance might have been permanently destroyed by the effects of the local environment on her young and seemingly innocent boy.

The experience of being surrounded by a dangerous enemy becomes a stark reality for Barrymore when she writes to Verney on March 16, 1642, giving a "full relation of the many miserys this poore Kingdom has been redust to." Writing through the lens of a siege, Barrymore conveys how

Castlelyons has been transformed into a theater of war and how her altered circumstances involve "living everey houer att the mercey of our increasing enemeys."[43] At that point in the Irish rebellion, several of Barrymore's Catholic neighbors and kinsmen of her husband had become the aggressors on the battlefield as well as instigators of violent attacks on the homes and castles of Munster Protestants. Contemporary testimonies confirm that many Protestants were forced to abandon their outlying holdings and seek refuge in garrison towns and fortified properties, and it has been further acknowledged that fifty Protestant families were given shelter at Castlelyons.[44] Barrymore's cryptic comment to Verney that she felt terrified but "dare not, as yet ster, because the safety of so many depends upon my stay heare" hints at the dilemma she faced in having to decide between abandoning Castlelyons to save her family or refusing to surrender her home so that her Protestant neighbors might be afforded temporary protection.[45] The ostensible purpose in writing was to convey the danger and terror that Barrymore and her household faced on a daily basis, but it appears that the letter also had a larger remit in advocating for all Munster Protestants who, like Barrymore, needed English military assistance if both they and Ireland were to survive the "Papists cruelty." Capitalizing on the long-standing friendship between the Boyle and Verney families, while conveniently ignoring the ever-widening gap between her royalism and Verney's support for Parliament, Barrymore makes the most of the remaining lines of the letter to convince the addressee of her dire straits. Part of that process of persuasion involves Barrymore aligning her future with that of Ireland and merging the personal with the political, when she asks the addressee to "send us more aide, which I beg you to doe that you may presarve in Ierland your unconstant enemy, but faithfull friend to sarve you A Barrymore." Thus, by reading Barrymore's 1639 and 1642 letters side by side, it is possible to see how she deliberately and effectively exploits her familiarity with the situation on the ground in Ireland to portray a particular epistolary persona in the pursuit of her evolving list of priorities.

War also provides the background to the letters that Ranelagh wrote from London to her brother Richard Boyle while he was visiting the family's estates in Ireland over the summer of 1667.[46] In early June the Dutch fleet had begun a series of daring attacks, during which they traveled up the River Thames, breaching security lines and setting fire to the English navy ships, with the intention of landing in the capital city and seizing power.[47] Ranelagh's two letters dated June 1 and 15 capture the immediacy and drama of those events, as well as the battles that ensued as part of England's response.[48] Like the other Boyle women, Ranelagh is self-reflexive in her letter, showing how she sought to fill the physical void by capitalizing on her relative proximity to the center of the action and compensating for Richard's absence by supplying him with the most up-to-date news at a time of enormous significance in London, at sea, and throughout the Three Kingdoms. The range of topics that Ranelagh covers in both letters is illustrative of how she exploits the boundlessness of the medium and the multiple perspectives it could afford. Together both letters fill fifteen foolscap pages, and the subjects discoursed include the current state of play in the war against the Dutch, as well as accounts of the French and their latest maneuverings, news of family members and their movements, and reports of recent events inside the royal household. Ranelagh's epistolary accounts also highlight her ease of access to a range of intelligence networks that she uses to gather information, which she then makes available to her eldest brother. On June 1 she notes having seen "a French letter from a very good hand something writ of the easiness of their Kings landing forces & making a disorder in Ireland," to which she adds her own view that she wished "people [there in Ireland] be not to[o] much asleep."[49] That perceived relation of codependency between Ireland and England chimes somewhat with the sentiments expressed by her sister Alice Barrymore when she wrote to Verney at the time of the 1641 Irish rebellion.[50] Perceptibly, Ranelagh adopts a more detached, analytical stance in her letters, which are designed with the readership in mind, and that writerly approach serves to reveal a self that could look beyond her immediate concerns and anticipate those larger issues that might be a priority for Richard as head of a family whose fortunes were deeply intertwined with that of Ireland.

Consolidating many of those points, Ranelagh's letter to Richard on June 15 includes the news that the "French are discovered to be hovering about the Isle of Weight [Wight]" and had joined in "a confederacy" with the Dutch. That news makes the prospect of a French invasion of Ireland even more likely, but additionally it serves to underline the soundness of Ranelagh's previous forecast in that regard. In the closing stages of that same correspondence, Ranelagh makes an explicit request that the addressee "acquaint" their brother Roger (First Earl of Orrery) with the reported events, while urging that they all pray for "poore England" because "in Ireland that wil[l] not be like to subsist when its ruined [England's ruination will also lead to Ireland's demise]."[51] The reference to Roger highlights the way in which Ranelagh expands the remit of her letter and reaches beyond the addressee, knowing that as a more permanent resident in Ireland and as a zealous supporter of the local Protestant cause, Roger needed to be apprised so that the family might be prepared to deal with the implications of an invasion. Altogether the composition of Ranelagh's news reports and the accompanying annotations reflect a desire to use her intellectual prowess for the greater good of the entire family. Not only does this kind of contribution enhance Ranelagh's credibility, but her position at the helm of the family also becomes more firmly cemented because of the constant, voluminous flow of letters sent to her older brother, who is suggestively characterized as closely reliant on her advice, on her judgment, and on her leadership instincts. Because Richard had to divide his time between the family's significant interests in Ireland and Yorkshire and his obligations associated with the Cork and Burlington earldoms and was thus frequently absent, Ranelagh's letters clearly attest to her worth as his trusted representative in London and as someone who had the appropriate political contacts, intellectual capacity, and pragmatic vision to play a prominent part in steering the family safely into the next century.

CONCLUSION

This study of six women's letters within the Boyle archive illuminates an umbilical relationship that bound the family to Ireland throughout the seventeenth century. Yet Ireland is characterized as much more than just an enduring presence in the women's lives. The First Countess of Cork's letter, for example, shows how she responded to her husband's absence in Munster by projecting a marital persona that underscored her sense of self-worth and purposeful intent. Her daughter Alice's letters demonstrate how her rootedness to Castlelyons, in both good times and bad, served to enliven her favorable reputation as a mother, planter, Protestant, neighbor, and Munster landowner. Young Henrietta's letter is representative of how the epistolary medium and tradition within the family afforded the Boyle women fertile ground to demarcate and define themselves apart from both the nucleus of the family and the homeplace. But, additionally, Ranelagh's letters illustrate how her broader understanding of Ireland's politico-religious importance within the dynamic of both the Three Kingdoms and Europe enabled her to earn the respect and confidence of the kin group, therein allowing her a significant say in the running and future development of the family. Thus, altogether the letters reflect and reinforce why Ireland is essentially, instinctively, and appropriately placed at the very heart of the Boyle women's individual and familial conceptions of a life.

NOTES

1. The Boyle motto, "God's Providence is my Inheritance," was inscribed and remains visible on the outer walls of Lismore Castle, County Waterford.

2. Kate Chedgzoy, "The Cultural Geographies of Early Modern Women's Writing: Journeys across Spaces and Times," *Literature Compass* 3, no. 4 (2006): 884–95.

3. Catherine Boyle, Lady Cork to Sir Richard Boyle, March 18, [endorsed 1604/5], vol. 1 (129), Cork Manuscripts, Chatsworth House, Derbyshire; Henrietta Boyle to Richard Boyle, Second Earl of Cork, July 24, [endorsed 1659], vol. 31 (49), Cork Manuscripts, Chatsworth House; Countess Alice Barrymore to Sir Ralph Verney, February 18, [1639], letters, 1639, Verney Papers, Claydon House, Middle Claydon, Buckinghamshire; Barrymore to Verney, March 16, 1641[2], letters, 1642, Verney Papers, Claydon House; Lady Katherine Ranelagh to Richard Boyle, First Earl of Burlington, June 1, [1667]; and Ranelagh to First Earl of Burlington, June 15, [1667], both in Add. MS 75,354, Althorp Papers, British Library (BL), London.

4. In 1864 a manuscript calendar was drawn up to identify and document the correspondence and papers of the First and Second Earls of Cork for the period 1586 to 1774. The material was placed in chronological order and organized into thirty-six volumes, comprising more than five thousand items. The calendar registers incoming and outgoing correspondence while also providing summaries of key documents, including, for instance, excerpts drawn from the two earls' diaries.

5. Elizabeth, Lady Burlington, memorandum book, Misc. Box 5, Cork Manuscripts, Chatsworth House.

6. See, for example, the following documents in vol. 28, Cork Manuscripts, Chatsworth House, confirming that Elizabeth Boyle was present in Youghal and personally involved in the estate: Murrough O'Brien, Lord President of Munster, First Earl of Inchiquin, to the Countess of Cork, July 12, 1648, item 8; Col. William Kingsmill to the Countess of Cork, July 24, 1648, item 9; Elizabeth Boyle, Countess of Cork, petition to the Commissioners for Settlement of Contributions in the Province of Munster, November 27, 1649, item 14; Countess of Cork, petition on behalf of the Earl of Cork to the Lord President of Munster, February 16, 1650, item 16; and "A Note of such writings as my lady took with her into England," May 18, 1650, item 18.

7. Richard Boyle, First Earl of Cork, correspondence, 1632–44, Add. MS 19,832, Boyle Papers, BL, fols. 31–50; "True Remembrances," copy, Boyle Papers, Add. MS 19,832, BL, fols. 23–30.

8. Mary Rich, Countess of Warwick, diary, July 1666–November 1677, Add. MSS 27,351–55, BL; Mary Rich, "Ocasionale Meditationes," 1663–77, Add. MS 27,356, BL; and "Some Specialities in the life of M. Warwicke," 1625–74, Add. MS 27,357, BL, fols. 1–40; and Katherine Ranelagh, "Lady Rennelagh's choise receipts, as also some of Capt. Willis'; who valued them above gold," MS 1,367, Sloane Manuscripts, BL, fols. 1–83.

9. Althorp Papers, [1509]–eighteenth century, Add. MSS 75,351–71, BL.

10. Key documents include Katherine Jones, Lady Ranelagh, copy letter to Elizabeth, Queen of Bohemia, TS23/1/43, National Archives of England (TNA), London, fols. 62–63; Ranelagh to Daniel Finch, Earl of Nottingham, SP3/30, TNA; Ranelagh to Robert Thornhill, E192/14/5 and E192/14/11, TNA; Ranelagh to Joseph Williamson, SP29/197, SP29/230, and SP29/251B, TNA; Boyle Family Receipt Book, Western MS 1,340, Wellcome Library, London; and Ranelagh to Elizabeth, Queen of Bohemia, August 7, 1646, Forster MS 454, 40/1, National Art Library, Victoria and Albert Museum, London, fols. 74–75.

11. Robert Boyle, "An Account of Philaretus during his Minority," R/B/1/37/39, Boyle Papers, Royal Society Library (RSL), London.

12. These RSL documents are as follows: Ranelagh to Boyle, July 29, 1665, RB/3/5/6; Ranelagh to Boyle, September 9, 1665, RB/3/5/7; Ranelagh to Boyle, August 6, 1665, RB/3/5/8; Ranelagh to Boyle, January 7, [1657], RB/3/5/10; Ranelagh to Boyle, September 14, [1652], RB/3/5/11; Ranelagh to Boyle, September 18, [1666], RB/3/5/12; Ranelagh to Boyle, June 3, [1657], RB/3/5/13; Ranelagh to Boyle, [1645], RB/3/5/14; Ranelagh to Boyle, October 12, [1655], RB/3/5/15; Robert Boyle to Ranelagh, November 13, [1648?], RB/3/1/46; Boyle to Ranelagh, August 31, 1649, RB/3/1/54; Boyle to Ranelagh, May 13, 1648, RB/3/1/56; Boyle to Ranelagh, August 2, 1649, RB/3/1/58; Boyle to Ranelagh, [1660?], RB/3/1/73; John Beale

to Ranelagh, September 5, 1660, RB/3/1/23; Beale to Ranelagh, September 6, 1660, RB/3/1/24; Ranelagh to John Eliot, August 13, 1676, RB/3/5/9; Ranelagh to [Samuel Hartlib?], April 3, 1658, RB/3/6/3; Henry Oldenburg, commonplace book that includes extracts from at least one of Ranelagh's letters [1657], *Liber Epistolari*, "Ex.Litt.M.Ra.," MS/1, fols. 190–94; James Gordoun to Ranelagh, June 29, 1680, RB/3/7/32.

13. [Ranelagh], "Discourse concerning the plague of 1665," Boyle Papers, RB/1/14/4, RSL, fols. 27–42. For the medical commonplace book used by Ranelagh and Robert Boyle, see the Boyle Papers, RB/2/8, RSL.

14. Mary Rich, Countess of Warwick, to Robert Boyle, July 30, [1673], RB/3/5/92; Rich to Boyle, December 29, [1677], RB/3/5/93; Rich to Boyle, [late 1663], RB/3/5/94; Rich to Boyle, [late 1656], RB/3/5/95, all in Boyle Papers, RSL.

15. In 1941 Edward MacLysaght compiled and edited the "Calendar of the Orrery Papers" based on the National Library of Ireland (NLI) files MSS 13,177–225: *Calendar of the Orrery Papers* (Dublin: Stationary Office, 1941). The original manuscripts have since been microfilmed and transferred to the West Sussex Record Office (West Sussex RO) in Chichester, where they are attached to the Howard Archive, known as the Petworth House Collection, MSS 13,177–225.

16. Lady Mary Broghill, thirty-three letters to the First Earl of Orrery, MS 13,218, fol. 2; and twenty-four letters to the First Countess of Orrery, MS 13,218, fol. 4, all in Orrery Papers, West Sussex RO.

17. Ranelagh, nineteen letters to the Earl and Countess of Orrery, MS 13,219, Orrery Papers, West Sussex RO.

18. Margaret Boyle, receipt, MS 13,199, Orrery Papers, West Sussex RO.

19. Margaret Boyle, "Rules of Margaret. Dowager Countess of Orrery for the management of the Almshouses at Castlemartyr, Co. Cork, ca. 1680," MS 13,184, Orrery Papers, West Sussex RO.

20. The original manuscripts relating to the Alice Barry, Countess of Barrymore, and Sir Ralph Verney correspondence, 1639–43, have been preserved at the Verney home of Claydon Manor, Claydon, but facsimile copies of the letters are also available in microfilm, under reference MS 636/4, at the BL.

21. Carol Pal, *Republic of Women: Rethinking the Republic of Letters in the Seventeenth Century* (Cambridge: Cambridge University Press, 2012), 142–76.

22. Ranelagh, letters, MS 217, Carte Papers, Bodleian Library (Bodl.), Oxford, fols. 452–59, 66; letters, vols. 78–79, Clarendon State Papers, Bodl., fols. 231, 73–74; letter, Add. MS 191, Burnet Manuscripts, Bodl., Oxford, fols. 113–14; see also the Hartlib Papers database, www.dhi.ac.uk/hartlib/; and letters to the Countess of Panmure, GD 45/14/237/1–5, and letter to the Duchess of Hamilton, August 6, 1690, GD 406/1/3797, both in National Records of Scotland, Edinburgh.

23. MS 12,813, microfilm, POS 8685 (A), Collection List 129, Lismore Castle Estate Papers, compiled by Stephen Ball, 2007, NLI; see Ball's introduction. This archive is one of the largest and most valuable of the NLI's manuscript collections because it provides an uninterrupted view of the estate and the conditions of land ownership in Ireland from the sixteenth to the nineteenth century.

24. Elizabeth Boyle, Second Countess of Cork, to the Right Honourable, Murrough O'Brien, Lord President of Munster, First Earl of Inchiquin, petition letter, May 1648, MS 43,346/3, Lismore Castle Estate Papers, NLI; Katherine Jones to Richard Boyle, First Earl of Cork, December 26, 1642, MS 43,266/20, Lismore Castle Estate Papers, NLI.

25. See, for example, Katherine Ranelagh, four letters to Bishop Anthony Dopping, January to April 1682, P001498149; Anthony Dopping, "Collection of State Papers Connected With Meath, 1633–1733," vol. 1, nos. 10–21, Dopping Collection, Armagh Robinson Library, Armagh, Northern Ireland.

26. Four letters to Bishop Anthony Dopping, January to April 1682, Armagh Robinson Library, P001498149. For example, the dedication is addressed "To The Countess of Warwick. My Deare Sister" in the opening page of Robert Boyle, *Some Motives and Incentives to the Love of God: Pathetically discours'd of, in A Letter to a Friend* (London, 1659).

27. Roger Boyle, *Poems on most of the festivals of the church composed by the Right Honourable Roger, Earl of Orrery* (London, 1681); Roger Boyle, *A treatise of the art of war dedicated to the Kings Most Excellent Majesty and written by the Right Honourable Roger, Earl of Orrery* (London, 1677). See also Toby Barnard, "Boyle, Roger, First Earl of Orrery (1621–1679), Politician and Writer," in *Oxford Dictionary of National Biography*, Oxford University Press, September 23, 2004. www.oxforddnb .com/view/10.1093/ref:odnb/9780198614128.001.0001/odnb-9780198614128 -e-3138; and Kathleen M. Lynch, *Roger Boyle: First Earl of Orrery* (Knoxville: University of Tennessee Press, 1965), 147, 160–61, 165.

28. Pal, *Republic of Women*, 175.

29. Mary Rich, "Rules for holy living," in *Historical Applications and Occasional Meditations upon several subjects written by a person of honour*, by George Berkeley (London, 1670), 131–59; Anthony Walker, *Eureka, Eureka the virtuous woman found* (London, 1678); M. Rich, "Ocasionale Meditationes," BL. Rich's pious meditations were handed down to Rev. Thomas Woodroffe, chaplain to the Earl of Warwick, and thereafter through the generations of the Woodroffe family.

30. Mary Rich, *Memoir of Lady Warwick: also her diary, from A.D. 1666 to 1672* (London: Religious Tract Society, 1847); Mary Rich, *The Autobiography of Mary Countess of Warwick*, ed. T. Crofton Croker (London: Percy Society, 1848).

31. See Elizabeth Boyle, Second Countess of Cork, letters to Richard Boyle, Second Earl of Cork, Cork Manuscripts, Chatsworth House, vol. 31 (33, 35, and 49), spanning the summer of 1659, when the countess was visiting London and the baths at Tunbridge Wells in Kent.

32. Elizabeth, Lady Burlington, memorandum book, Chatsworth House; see fols. 3r, 3v, 4v, 7r, 7v, and 8r, which refer to various journeys the Boyles undertook around their estates. See also letters written by Burlington and her daughters, Anne Boyle and Henrietta Hyde, to Richard Boyle during the summer of 1667, Althorp Papers, Add. MSS 75,354–55, BL.

33. C. Boyle to Richard Boyle, March 18, [endorsed 1604/5], Chatsworth House.

34. H. Boyle to Richard Boyle, July 24, [endorsed 1659], Chatsworth House.

35. Toby Barnard, "Boyle, Richard, First Earl of Burlington and Second Earl of Cork (1612–1698), Royalist Army Officer and Politician," in *Oxford Dictionary of National Biography*, Oxford University Press, January 3, 2008, www.oxforddnb.com/view /10.1093/ref:odnb/9780198614128.001.0001/odnb-9780198614128-e-3135.

36. H. Boyle to Richard Boyle, July 24, [endorsed 1659], Chatsworth House.

37. See Anne Boyle to Richard Boyle, Second Earl of Cork and First Earl of Burlington, July 2, [1667], Add. MS 75,355, Althorp Papers, BL. Anne's letter differs somewhat from Henrietta's letter in approach, as she writes some years later from Scarborough to their father, the Second Earl of Cork, and draws attention to her scribal role, as she alone attended to her sick mother, Countess Elizabeth, who was taking the curative waters as a treatment for her seizures. The image of a dutiful daughter is figured in and through Anne's role as scribe but makes it difficult for the reader to separate out Anne's identity and sentiments from that of her mother, thereby complicating the authorial source of the letter.

38. Barrymore to Verney, February 18, [1639]; David Dickson, *Old World Colony: Cork and South Munster, 1630–1830* (Cork: Cork University Press, 2005). Dickson's first chapter describes the peacetime conditions in Cork leading up to the 1641 rebellion.

39. Nicholas Canny, *Making Ireland British, 1580–1650* (Oxford: Oxford University, 2009), 247, 250, 279, 281; Jane Ohlmeyer, *Making Ireland English: The Irish Aristocracy in the Seventeenth Century* (New Haven: Yale University Press, 2012), 433, 437, 447, 433–34.

40. While it is unclear exactly how young Richard's "Mad" behavior manifested itself, it is known that he did follow in his maternal grandfather's footsteps by marrying and remarrying until eventually he had fifteen children to his name. See "Richard Barry, 2nd Earl of Barrymore," *Peerage*, www.thepeerage.com/p11658.htm#116575.

41. Barrymore to Verney, February 18, [1639], Claydon House.

42. *Oxford English Dictionary*, s.v. "Spoiled, adj.," def. 4, accessed June 21, 2018, www.oed.com.

43. Barrymore to Verney, March 16, 1641[2], Claydon House.

44. Magdalen Faulkner to Sir Ralph Verney, March 8, 1641[2], letters 1642, Claydon House. Faulkner (gentlewoman companion to Alice and kinswoman of Verney) reports that there were fifty families sheltering at Castlelyons and four times as many staying in their Barryscourt Castle.

45. Barrymore to Verney, March 16, 1641[2], Claydon House.

46. Elizabeth, Lady Burlington, memorandum book, Chatsworth House, fol. 13r, confirms Richard Boyle's departure for Ireland on May 20, 1667, and return to Yorkshire on July 8, 1667.

47. James Rees Jones, *The Anglo-Dutch Wars of the Seventeenth Century* (London: Longman, 1996).

48. Ranelagh to Richard Boyle, June 1, [1667], BL; and Ranelagh to First Earl of Burlington, June 15, [1667], BL.

49. Ranelagh to Richard Boyle, June 1, [1667], BL.

50. Barrymore to Verney, March 16, 1641[2], Claydon House.

51. Ranelagh to Richard Boyle, June 15, [1667], BL.

4

Life Writing in the Boyle Family Network

AMELIA ZURCHER

By all accounts the eleven children of Catherine Fenton and Richard Boyle, First Earl of Cork, were an extraordinary seventeenth-century aristocratic family. Their English father's legendary rise, from a penniless adventurer at the turn of the seventeenth century to an Irish landholder collecting more in rents by the 1630s than any other Irish or English aristocrat, put his children in positions of great political and cultural influence. Several of them were also individually very accomplished, most famously the natural philosopher and theological writer Robert Boyle. But after Nicholas Canny's groundbreaking 1982 study of the First Earl of Cork, there has been little attention to the ways the Boyle siblings' experience in Ireland affected the thought of any of the family besides Robert and, beyond some discussion of Robert and Katherine's close relationship as the major context for her interest in natural philosophy, little attention given to the family network as a force in shaping their thought and writing.[1] This chapter takes as its starting point the hypothesis that the life writing of Katherine, Lady Ranelagh, née Boyle (1615–91), and Lady Mary Rich, née Boyle, Countess of Warwick (1624–78), cannot be understood without attention both to their roles in the Boyle sibling network and to their identity and history as members of an Irish-English family. I use the term "Irish-English," rather than subordinate either term to the other as in "Anglo-Irish," to signal the dual residence of much of the family after the 1630s in both kingdoms. "Irish" I place first because all the siblings were born there. In Ireland the Boyles would have been Protestant "New English," as distinct from the Catholic Old English who had settled in Ireland before the sixteenth century, and in the culturally polyglot world that most of them inhabited, it is likely that the Boyles most often referred to themselves simply as "English" for reasons of status. But the historically anachronistic "Irish-English" captures the hybrid nature of their identity and reminds us how deeply the culture of each kingdom was implicated in that of the other.

Cork's incredibly quick accumulation of Irish wealth, made possible by the interval of relative peace in Ireland between the late 1590s and the 1641 rebellion, brought the Boyle family to prominence in the seventeenth century with a speed and definitiveness rarely paralleled. All the Boyle children were born into, and to varying degrees remained connected to all their lives, a distinctively Irish-English planter society that shaped their sense of their place and duties in the world. After a rocky start in Ireland, Richard Boyle was enabled by the intervention of his patron George Carew, president of Munster, to buy all of Walter Raleigh's Irish lands and marry as his second wife Catherine Fenton, daughter of Irish privy counselor Geoffrey Fenton, and these two acquisitions provided the foundation for all his success. For the next three decades he continued to accumulate land and to "improve" his holdings, settling them with English tenants; establishing fortified towns; constructing churches, schools, and almshouses; and installing preachers. Like many English planters in Ireland, Cork professed strong belief in a Puritan providence, a conviction that God would reward those doing his work and that virtue could be measured by the success of one's endeavors. The motto he adopted when he was knighted in 1603, "God's providence is mine inheritance," was described as "humble and Christian" by Gilbert Burnet in Robert Boyle's funeral sermon in 1691, but by the time Cork became wealthy it was not only an appropriately pious nod to his low origins but also a boast of his certainty of God's favor.[2]

Ireland in the first decades of the seventeenth century, for its Protestant English and continental settlers, was a kind of proving ground for piety, a place to establish not only individual virtue but also the progress of God's Protestant kingdom on earth. Such piety rationalized colonialist exploitation of resources and people, and in turn, by the familiar logic of early modern colonialism, Cork and his peers viewed their worldly success as evidence of God's sanction.[3] In political terms their accumulation and development of property in Ireland encouraged the New English aristocrats to develop a sense of themselves as a service nobility, their political virtue defined not by old-style loyalty to the monarch so much as by public service to the Commonwealth.[4] Even as it facilitated their own advancement, this ideology allowed them to imagine themselves aloof from the politics of factionalism in London in the 1630s and afterward. In the uncertain and sometimes hostile environment of Ireland they valued political stability above all else, necessitating steady support from whatever government was in power in England, and their political loyalties throughout the Wars of the Three Kingdoms and the Restoration were dictated by their most firmly held interests, in the security of their lands and the titles by which they were owned. To ensure the viability of their Protestant colonialist project, the landed New English also saw dynastic succession as essential, and Cork's near obsession with advantageous marriages for his children was unusual only because there were so many of them. The marriages he arranged for all the Boyle children (or in Mary's case failed to arrange) largely determined their material and political relation to Ireland in the ensuing decades. Cork married most of his daughters, including Katherine, to Irish nobility, offering large dowries to relatively poor husbands in exchange for social status in Ireland. His sons, in contrast, he mostly married to English heiresses, whose assets helped to build the family's Irish holdings and whose familial connections, he hoped, would give the Boyles political access in England—a hope that was fulfilled, although not in the ways he expected, during the next tumultuous decades. To a greater extent perhaps even than other landed New English in Ireland, the Boyles remained throughout the seventeenth century a family in-between two kingdoms, their familial and political interests determined to a large extent by the complex relationship between England and Ireland.

Ranelagh's and Rich's life writing is not only embedded in this history but also helps illuminate it. Only Rich left writing that can properly be called autobiographical, her brief *Some Specialities in the Life of M Warwicke*, but a rich array of other surviving texts offers a window onto their lives and their complex strategies for making sense of them. For the most part the writing I consider here cannot be said to participate in the historical construction of life writing or autobiography as a genre, because it was private or was written for other rhetorical ends. My goal in this chapter is historical with a different emphasis—to understand how the Boyles represented their selves and their lives' shape and significance, as individuals and also as part of a social network.[5] The Boyle family left a whole host of writing that could legitimately be called life writing in this sense: Cork's *True Remembrances*, widely circulated in manuscript in the 1630s; Robert's very early autobiographical account and autobiographical notes from later life, as well as works such as his *Occasional Reflections* and *Seraphic Love* that frequently foreground his own experience; the books of essays written in old age to make a "strict examination of his own life" by Francis Boyle, Viscount Shannon; the vast romance *Parthenissa* by Roger Boyle, Lord Broghill and eventually Earl of Orrery, as well as some of his poetry; Rich's autobiographical *Some Specialities in the Life of M Warwicke*, her *Occasional Meditations*, and her diary; and a large body of correspondence, sometimes personal and sometimes more public, scattered across many archives, in which Katherine, Robert, and Roger have particular prominence. As a powerful Irish-English Protestant family, the Boyle siblings shared significant interests and assumptions, and Ranelagh's and Rich's life writings are part of a shared familial and cultural project in which the sisters played a still-underappreciated part. Their life writings also offer us a way into the complex relation for women between Protestant piety and other intellectual and social concerns in the period, a relation that in modern histories of women's writing has sometimes been given insufficient attention, and sheds significant light on the gendered nuances of the emergent dichotomy between public and private.[6]

Unlike her father and the siblings to whom she was closest, Katherine Ranelagh left no explicitly autobiographical accounts of herself. In recent years historians of science have become especially interested in her medical thought and her contributions of chemical and medical recipes to receipt books, but in neither of the two in which she's known to have had a major part is it possible to see a persona.[7] Katherine, born in 1615, was one of Cork's middle daughters. Brought up in Ireland and England (in the household of a prospective husband), she was unhappily married at fifteen to Irish aristocrat Arthur Jones, eventually Lord Ranelagh; bore three surviving daughters and a son; and spent all her life after 1641 estranged from her husband, mostly in England. She was especially close to Robert, twelve years her junior, and from 1668 on they shared a house in Pall Mall. In her own time she was unusually prominent among elite women, for her knowledge of natural philosophy and especially for her contributions to religious and political debates.[8] In Gilbert Burnet's reminiscence at Robert's funeral in 1691 (she and Robert died within a week of each other), she was said to have "lived the longest on the publickest Scene" and to have "made the greatest Figure in all the Revolutions of these Kingdoms for above fifty Years, of any Woman of our Age."[9]

The two great contexts for her thought and conversation throughout her life, both of which she shared with various of her siblings, were the Irish-English aristocracy she was born into, many of which joined her in exile in London after the 1641 rebellion, and the intellectual circles she eventually joined in England and Ireland, first through Irish-born Lucius Cary, Viscount Falkland, and the group at Great Tew and then through the Hartlib Circle in the 1640s and 1650s. The latter came together in the famous 1642 pact made by Samuel Hartlib, John Comenius, and John Dury, in which they agreed to dedicate themselves "to the glory of God and the utility of the public," and Hartlib, who called himself the "great intelligencer of Europe" and a "conduit-pipe of knowledge," took as the network's mission the basic principle that "Every one as he hath received any gifft from God (which is a Character of his vertue and glorie) should communicat the same unto others."[10] The linking of God's glory with public utility and the insistence on mobilizing God's gifts sound very much like the Protestant piety espoused by Richard Boyle, First Earl of Cork, and in fact many of the major ideas of the Hartlib Circle had already been held for at least a decade by the Irish exiles who joined it in the 1640s. In the Hartlibean view the pursuit of practical goals was an essential part of piety, and pluralism in methodology—"a certain generosity and liberty in all our Studies," in Hartlib's words—was valued over an attachment to one approach or body of knowledge.[11] Correspondingly, belief in a broadly construed Protestant theology aimed to avoid the excesses of both sectarianism and rigid conformity. All of these were ideas, as Canny shows, central to planter society in the first half of the seventeenth century.[12]

This is not to say that the Irish exiles, much less the Boyles in particular, brought these ideas to Hartlib and his European-English network but rather that the aspirations of Protestants from and in Ireland in this period were quite like those of Protestants from the Palatinate, Bohemia, and the Netherlands and that their confederation around these ideas was all but seamless.[13] Throughout the period that the Hartlib network was active, associates who spent significant time in Ireland and were known to correspond with the Boyles included Cromwell's surveyor general Benjamin Worsley, economist William Petty, physicians Gerard and Arnold Boate, and religious and educational reformers John Dury and Dorothy Moore Dury, the last of whom was Ranelagh's aunt by marriage and in the 1640s her personal friend. As historians have shown, English settlers to Ireland throughout the seventeenth century consistently took Cork's colonialist view of the island as a proving ground for their own piety. Ireland was, in effect, a laboratory for experiments in social improvement.[14] In the deep interest Ranelagh and Robert Boyle took in the religious, social, and scientific projects of the Hartlib network in Ireland as elsewhere, they were effectively sustaining and extending the agenda into which they had been born.

Unlike women such as Elizabeth of Bohemia or Anna van Schurman, Ranelagh did not educate herself as a scholar (she does not appear to have had Latin), and she does not seem to have had the familiarity with or interest in secular continental history and literature characteristic of contemporary *salonnières* such as Madeleine de Scudéry or Marie-Madeleine de La Fayette.[15] The context and intellectual framework for her participation on the "publickest Scene" was instead overwhelmingly the ideology of Protestant piety she was born into in Ireland and thereafter cultivated mainly in London from the 1640s. The Hartlibean program, as has often been noted, in its emphasis on practical "improvement" and empiricism did not require deep traditional humanist learning of its participants, making it more accessible to women and nonelite men than other intellectual networks, and Ranelagh's immersion in Protestant ideology was a sufficient gateway to many of the more ostensibly secular issues with which her Hartlib correspondents were concerned. As she says to her brother Robert in a letter from 1665, lamenting the almost constant recourse to "swords & guns" she has witnessed in recent decades, the proper route to "Mans ruleing the Creatures" is "his Imploying those faculties to that purpose which god himselfe has fitted In their Imployment to make him able to doe, so, & those are his rational ones whereby as he may discover the properties & uses of other things soe he may chuse to aply them thereby to their proper ends."[16] Ranelagh's correspondence suggests that she was interested in a broad range of those proper ends—educational reform, to which she remained committed throughout her life; agricultural development, which she discussed with her close correspondent John Beale; and the medical use of chemical and natural remedies, a project she shared for decades with Robert.

But her particular concern, perhaps her life project, was her dedication to freedom of conscience and therefore to religious toleration across the Protestant spectrum. She stayed within the Anglican Church for the duration of her life, but her house was a meeting place for nonconformists in the 1660s, and she and her sister Mary went to hear preaching by nonconformists as well as Anglicans.[17] In the 1650s, there is evidence to suggest, she and Robert were persuaded by millenarian ideas, almost certainly the context for her decision to learn Hebrew in that decade.[18] She and Edward Hyde, First Earl of Clarendon, intervened on behalf of Quakers and other non-conformists at the Restoration, and her one surviving treatise, "Discourse concerning the plague in 1665", argues against the inhumane imprisonment of nonconformists.[19] Minister Benjamin Denham commented in a 1667 letter to Robert that "I have some times visited, that truly Pi[ous La]dy. Your Sister Rannelo, and have received from her mouth, more Religious discourses in one halfe houre, then I have done from some Bishops table in ten; . . . And shee hath cleerly made mee of her mind, That Relaxing Somewhat of the Penal lawes to Some sober non Conformists, would not drive but bring them to Church, and at last to a sober Condescention."[20] Bulstrode Whitelocke similarly recalled a 1670 dinner at her house at which they "had private discourse about Liberty of Conscience, to wch she was a great friend."[21] One of her last projects with Robert, in the 1680s, was the commissioning and distribution of an Irish translation of the Bible, opposed by the Anglican clergy in Ireland because it seemed to marginalize Anglican, and English, hierarchy and culture in favor of a direct connection between Irish subjects and the contents of scripture.[22]

Ranelagh's commitment to freedom of conscience pointed both outward, toward the goal of uniting the Protestant churches in a worldwide empire that would at last vanquish Roman Catholicism and provide for the reign of reason and justice on earth, and also inward, toward the development of the capacities of every individual subject. As Ruth Connolly astutely notes, the opposite of freedom of conscience in this period, perhaps a little counterintuitively to us, was not oppression or coercion, only one of many forces that might detach one from one's own reason and inner light, but hypocrisy, the disjunction between the soul's convictions and one's words and actions.[23] If religious belief and relation to God was the framework for a relation to the entire world, then the self necessarily made itself through the work of coming to God, and it was crucial for Ranelagh that it be provided the opportunity, the liberty, to do so. Associations of early women's public speech with immodesty, as has been well documented, made them vulnerable to particularly toxic accusations of hypocrisy, challenging their entire ground for speech, and Ranelagh's emphasis on piety as a counter to hypocrisy, whether she intended it this way or not, was probably strategically powerful in authorizing her public voice. (Although it is impossible to know for certain, her commitment to eradicating the conditions for hypocrisy may also echo in her father's struggle in the 1630s against Lord Deputy Thomas Wentworth, who very publicly denounced Cork for his hypocritical profession of dedication to the common good to mask his mere self-interest in pursuing luxury and status.)[24] Ranelagh's resistance to hypocrisy became part of her public persona, not only in the later years of her life but as early as the 1640s, when she functioned as the public guarantor for the virtue of John Dury and Dorothy Moore Dury's marriage by circulating a set of letters among the three of them defending the sanctity and pious efficacy of their union against "scrupulous carnalitie."[25]

Current scholarship bringing new visibility to Ranelagh concurs with Burnet in seeing her as truly exceptional, as a woman, for her participation in conversations and activities that we would now call public. This view seems accurate, perhaps more in the religious than the natural philosophical or medical realms, to the extent those can be distinguished. In Ranelagh's private letters, however, she offered a more complex view of her social role, one that blurs the dichotomy between public and private as we think about them. As life writing, these letters illuminate her negotiation of the gendered constraints she functioned within and the strikingly nuanced speaking positions she constructed for herself. In one pivotal 1658 letter to her brother Roger, Lord Broghill, from Ireland, where she had been living for a couple of years apparently to find some kind of permanent resolution with her estranged husband and negotiate her children's futures, she meditates on her next step now that Oliver Cromwell has died. Broghill has been preferring a petition for her maintenance to Cromwell, who has had "authority and severity against such practices, as my lord's [i.e., her husband's] are," but she has little expectation of a similar response from his son Richard, and first she muses in characteristically wry and balanced fashion on the public implications of his father's death, predicting that "we shall learn to value [Cromwell] more by missing him, than we did when we injoyed him; a perverseness in our nature, that teaches us in every condition, wherein we are, therewith to be in discontent, by undervaluing what we have, and overvaluing what we have lost." Concluding that his death is God's "warneing-piece of great confusions and disorders approaching upon these nations" against which all must make "provisions," she shifts to focus on her own predicament, resolving "as to outward things" to cut unnecessary expenses, which have burdened the friends protecting her from "my lords oppressions." Regarding inward things,

> though I can remove lightly, and need bestow but few thoughts or cares, in getting my wealth together, or considering how to dispose of it, I have some provision to make against this riseing storm, in geting

a greater stabilety of thoughts, and preparedness of mind, than can be descomposed, by the shakeing of the world, and to the making of that provision retyredness is absolutely necessary, and therefore into that I desier to hasten, which not being to be got in this country by me, because of the unkindnes of my friends, and the unreasonablenes of my lord, I shal seeke it, and I hope speedely get into it, in England, . . . [and if there I] find no other provision, I shall have a much experienced providence to depend on, which was all the meanes I had for the greatest part of the time I lived there . . . here I am altogether unserviceable, and yet very chargeable to my friends.[26]

Ranelagh had hoped that her life in Ireland among her friends (i.e., family) would be a kind of retirement, but instead she has put them to great expense, apparently because of the kind of life she has been expected to live there as a landed aristocrat. Clearly she remains concerned about her material support at this moment of personal and political crisis, but equally significant to her in this passage is her preparation of her mind, her quest for internal "stabilety," and for this she requires disengagement from the burdens of her social roles in Ireland.

In a highly interesting conclusion, Ranelagh says that if Broghill confirms that she cannot get from Richard the maintenance she has sued for, she will be

set free to seeke it some other way, wherein my owne honest endeavors may contribute toward it, and show the world I left not my lord upon humour, but upon necessety, and that in soe doing I sought privacy, and submitted to scarcety, rather then pursued a croud, or designed aboundance to my selfe, which, in the way I have hetherto binn, amongst my friends, may have binn suspected, and none has reason to suspect my owne hart than I have, and only upon tryal shal I find, wheather I be mistaken in suspecting it or noe, and since God thus seems to cal me to put it to that, it is my purpose to doe so.[27]

Ranelagh goes from Ireland to London not to move from margin to center, to pursue a more public life, but rather to leave the familial and social network that constitutes the "croud" of aristocratic women's society, to find "privacy" and "scarcety" in a more genuine retirement than she was able to make in Ireland. Toward this end she seems almost to hope that Broghill will not be able to get any concession from Richard Cromwell so that she will have to embark on "my owne honest endeavors." God has called her to retirement as a test of her piety, which is also to say, for Ranelagh, her sincerity—to prove to him and to "my owne hart" by "tryal," in the language of Protestant theology, that she has not left her husband out of mere hypocritical self-interest, to pursue greater "aboundance." Her "honest endeavors," which seem to refer both to means toward material provision and also to some kind of spiritual work in the world, find their meaning not as public, extrafamilial pursuits, as we might tend to read them, but rather as signs of authentic retirement, and in their hoped-for success as indications of her virtue. There are echoes here of her friend and corre-spondent Dorothy Moore, who had written to Ranelagh a decade earlier of her disinclination to marry again so that she could better pursue "that aime . . . of service" that "every Member of Christ ought to propose unto themselves as theire Duty without excluding our Sex," which required the "imployment of our best strength spirituall & corporall."[28] Both effectively single women, both declining conventional aristocratic female roles, Moore and Ranelagh turn to a model of religious trial and service to imagine life projects for themselves that can be justified ethically and culturally.

There is an echo too of Cork's ideology, significantly inverted: Lon-don, not Ireland, is Ranelagh's proving ground for piety, and her virtue will be measured not by her material survival (that "much experienced providence" that in London in the past was "all the meanes I had") but by the thoroughness of her proof, through retirement, that she has not "designed aboundance to my selfe." In the early 1630s, as part of his long-term campaign against Cork, lord deputy of Ireland Wentworth mocked Cork's older daughters, whom Cork had just finished marrying to Old and New English landed wealth, as parodies of real English nobility. Rep-resented on the family tomb, Wentworth scoffed, like "sea-nymphs . . . with coronets upon their heads, their hair disheveled down upon their shoulders," they were the very embodiment of their father's uncultured greed and unwarranted self-importance.[29] Undoubtedly Ranelagh's vigorous disavowal of self-interest in the purer air of London two decades later proceeds in part from her gender; it seems likely that it worked, too, to separate her from the kind of criticism that had shadowed her family during her early adulthood in Ireland.

Ranelagh's private letters also give some insight into the intersections between her personal and more public negotiations of gender. Like Broghill, and doubtless also to some extent through him, alone among her female siblings she seems to have had substantial political access. As early as 1646 she was writing to Elizabeth of Bohemia about the princess's brother Charles I's conflicts with Parliament, and in the 1670s she reported in letters on private visits to the royal family with her sister Mary.[30] After the Restoration she functioned as a representative of Irish landowners, particularly her oldest brother Richard, Second Earl of Cork, at court.[31] Even in the midst of such public activities her more "retired" intellectual and activist role remained fundamental to her identity, and she seems to have acted as a bridge between different parts of her family, linking Richard and Roger's world of Irish landed wealth and political office and influence to her own and Robert's intellectual and spiritual pursuits. In 1681, in the midst of a long power struggle with the Boyles, lord lieutenant of Ireland James Butler, Duke of Ormonde, wrote disparagingly to the Earl of Arlington that Ranelagh still wielded great influence over her brother Richard, and "as for the other branches [of the family] she governs them very absolutely."[32] Ormonde was probably scapegoating Ranelagh, but his complaint also reflects a shared sense, from the outside, of her dominant position among her siblings.[33]

An enormously artful letter to her brother Robert from 1665, three years before he moved for good into her house in Pall Mall, tells a more complex story, illuminating the subtle play of authority and affection between them. From Lees, where she was probably staying with her sister Mary for the duration of an outbreak of plague in London, Ranelagh opens by rebuking Robert, at Oxford, for failing to write to her and then goes on,

> To repair to myself, your absence, as much as I can, next my submitting to the will of the all-wise Disposer, who is pleased so to cast us, I

entertain myself with your books, which yet, by the very few studious persons I meet here, are, as fast as I can suffer them to be, begged or borrowed from me, who lend them willingly, upon the same account I spare you patiently, the hope, that both they and you will do more good abroad, than by being still with me; and I shall ere long have read them all over, as well those I had read before, as the last; and then my fingers will be itching, to look into the sealed roll of papers, written upon, "About religious matters"; and I would fain open them, with your leave, which I hope my being so ingenious a coxcomb as not to do without asking it, will rather bribe you to give, than deny me. But if it should not, I know not what I may be tempted to; and you know I am of a sex, that has long been allowed for an excuse of the frailties of those, who are of it; and, considering how much you believe of those, I must not fear, but you will consider them as tenderly as they require to be considered, and then you will not stick to afford me such a pardon. I am very much pleased with the assurance my experience of God's goodness to you gives me, of your neither being idle, nor ill employed; nor only for your own good; but I should be much more pleased, in having a share in what you are about, that exceeds not my capacity of understanding; and if you would let me receive some such present by the return of this bearer, you would do me a great favour, and give me a profitable employment; for all persons great and fair are not company, nor can give entertainment, that reaches beyond our senses in its pleasingness.[34]

This letter is remarkable, among other reasons, for its extraordinarily sophisticated play with the norms and prejudices informing gender roles and the ways these are negotiated within sibling relationships. Robert had published his *Occasional Reflections* earlier this same year, and Ranelagh had been pushing him to publish another volume, which he had refused to do.[35] Throughout his career she remained particularly enthusiastic about and engaged with his theological work, probably in part because of her sustained dedication, less ambivalent than his, to the English Protestant project in Ireland. Stuck at Lees with company from only "very few studious persons" while he works among his colleagues in Oxford, she cites her itching fingers not just to announce her boredom with the "great and fair" at her sister's house and her appreciation of his more substantive companionship but to remind him, humorously, of her position in their dispute.

In an elaborate joke, Ranelagh suggests coyly that her "ingenious" move to request permission to pry into his sealed papers ("ingenious" might in this period mean clever and discerning, candid, or liberal—all of these would seem possible here) should work as a bribe for his assent. If he won't give it she threatens to look anyway, and she pronounces herself comforted by the prospect of his taking the inherent frailty of her sex as excuse for her excessive curiosity—a claim she then ironizes with her winking assurance that "considering how much you believe" of women's frailties, "you will consider them as tenderly as they require to be considered," which is to say, presumably not at all. Concluding a bit more imperiously that she is pleased to find he is not "idle" or "ill employed," she insists that she would nevertheless be "much more pleased" to "hav[e] a share" in his work—if, and she softens her demand, it will not exceed her "capacity of understanding." Ranelagh's witty presentation of herself here as "so ingenious a coxcomb," an Erasmian wise fool, allows her at once to claim and to disavow authority. She knows, as her joke indicates, that she can count on her brother's shared disregard for misogynist stereotypes, and she assumes herself his match in requiring "entertainment, that reaches beyond our senses in its pleasingness." It is on such authority that she stakes her claim to participate in his religious work even if she cannot persuade him to publish all of it at once. At the same time her imperious manner can guarantee no results. She has not received the letters from him that she expected, and her joking demands construct the rhetorical upper hand she cannot lay practical claim to, marooned as she is at Lees while he works within his circle of male colleagues at Oxford. This wonderful letter offers a close look at Ranelagh's intelligence and wit and the intimacy and equality of her partnership with Robert, but it also reminds us of the limitations her gender placed on her sphere of action and the kinds of concessions she was required to make throughout her intellectual career.[36]

Ranelagh's sister Mary Rich, Countess of Warwick, nine years younger than Ranelagh and two years older than Robert Boyle, was a much less prominent figure than Ranelagh, but the extensive body of life writing she left in manuscript, including both her *Occasional Meditations*, written between 1663 and a year before her death in 1678, and her autobiographical narrative *Some Specialities in the Life of M Warwicke*, begun in 1672 and published in 1848, demonstrates both her sharp intelligence and independence of mind and her embeddedness in the interests of her family. Brought up in Ireland in a foster family from the age of two or three after her mother died, Mary went to London with her family at thirteen; married Charles Rich, younger son of the Second Earl of Warwick; and spent the rest of her life at Lees, the Rich family estate, and at their house in London. Rich's *Occasional Meditations* are a series of pious reflections, most between a half and a full printed page in length. Modeled on the published meditations of Bishop Joseph Hall, circulated broadly throughout the seventeenth century, as well as on the work of Puritan divines Nathanael Ranew and Richard Baxter, whom she knew personally, each meditation opens with an observation from daily life—"Upon blowing of a fire to warme another and finding my selfe heated whilst I was doing it," "Upon my forgettfullnes to wind upe my watch"—which is then made by analogy to signify a spiritual observation or lesson.[37] A total of 182 meditations survive in a single manuscript, edited after her death by a family member of one of the Riches' household chaplains, and thirteen (four of which are also in the manuscript) were published in *Eureka, Eureka the virtuous woman found*, an expanded version of her funeral sermon by Anthony Walker, another Rich family chaplain and one of Mary Rich's closest friends and advisers.[38]

Robert Boyle published his own *Occasional Reflections* in 1665, as noted earlier, at the repeated urging of Ranelagh, to whom his volume is dedicated. According to Boyle's own account, many of those reflections were written earlier, and apparently he kept considerably more in his papers than he published.[39] Rich had a close and affectionate relationship with her brother Robert, who, like Katherine, made extended visits to Lees, and she was the dedicatee of his 1659 treatise *Seraphic Love*, on the practice and virtues of love for the divine.[40] In the introduction to his *Reflections* Robert defined his own practice of written meditation as communal, claiming that he had written them "not to get Reputation, but Company" and urging his readers to "addict" themselves to a similar practice.[41] It seems very likely that Rich saw her own pious practice of written meditation as partly modeled by Robert and anchored by the pious practice of her siblings more generally, as well as by the community of divines associated with her household. Rich's *Meditations* are consistently solemn, but like most pious reflections categorized as occasional in the period, they give the impression of spontaneity, as if they have arisen all at once from a momentary observation. Among others in the genre, including Robert's, they are distinguished by vividness of detail and an unconcern with the scaffolding of erudition.[42] Lacking moralistic tags, alluding directly only to scripture, and focusing consistently on the ordinary and the daily, they seem deceptively artless, as if the coherently signifying world they describe were simply a given. In his funeral sermon Walker called the *Meditations* the "Master-piece" of Rich's life.[43] Although there is no evidence that she circulated them outside her own private devotional circle so that they might have the kind of polemical function that her brother Robert and even her sister Katherine imagined for their own pious writings, nevertheless Rich almost certainly thought of the *Meditations* as her contribution to the project of Protestant piety to which her siblings were also devoted.

As the record of a practice, Rich's *Meditations* offer great insight into her conceptualization of herself and the relation of that self to experience.[44] Like the habit of keeping diaries and what Dorothy Moore called "directories," or schedules for daily life, the practice of occasional meditation was most simply a way to capture and order daily experience, "redeeming" time that would otherwise be lost to lack of awareness and focus and parceling one's day into discrete, intentionally related segments.[45] Occasional meditation was also a continued training in the art of making analogies. Part of the value of pious analogizing in Rich's Protestant context, of course, was recognizing how suffused the created world was with divinity, but her reflections also tend another way, toward not just the consolidation of the world and experience in it into one unified story but also an appreciation of multiplicity. In a meditation on her own reflective practice, "Upon the Consideration of the different manner of the working of a Bee and a Spider," Rich sets the spider, "the Formalist or proud Professor, who works all from himself and his own strength," against the "industrious Bees, that are busily employed in making of their useful Combs" and "do daily fly abroad. . . . And flying from one Flower to another, gather from every of them."[46] As the several surviving volumes of her diary reveal, Rich tended to pray (or to engage in "solemn" or "set" meditation) in her closet, but for her occasional meditative practice she walked most mornings in what she called the "wilderness" at Lees, amid the undomesticated and uncataloged.[47]

Part of the point of occasional meditation was to range in search of new matter, to bring ever more examples into her storehouse. Though, unlike her sister Katherine, Rich did not embark so far as we know on a broad-ranging project of study, it is possible to discern here the influence of the Hartlibean emphasis on the value of reflection and diary writing in making its practitioners "easily Pansophicall," able to set all kinds of knowledge next to one another to derive, as Robert says in the introduction to his *Occasional Reflections*, a whole set of harmonious truths.[48] Interestingly, the natural philosophical terminology of experiment and empiricism also surfaces in the *Meditations*. In "Upon viewing a map" Rich considers how much better a man knows the territory who has "travelled into it and deliberately view'd it, as he makes himselfe more particular observations," and thanks the Lord for the "experimentale divinity" she has learned from "thy old desipulles [disciples]"; in "Upon my keapeing in a rome for som time a bird," which she finally gives its "desired liberty," she remembers how "really advantageous it has proved to me that I have by my own trying things had my esteem taken off from them" and resolves to "lett this which I have experimented make me to allow that" to "those young ones" so that they in turn will be "experimentally able to say with that great and wise experimenter of the world" what is vain and what not.[49] In a moral context, this is the same message Robert Boyle and other new empiricists in the period repeated often, that education through experiment was not an illicit penetration into God's secrets but rather holy participation in a practice modeled everywhere by God himself.

One of the great virtues of occasional meditation was that it mobilized all one saw and experienced for use. So, as Robert Boyle stated in his intro-duction, those who wrote occasional meditations gained "the Satisfaction of making almost the whole World a great *Conclave Mnemonicum,* and a well-furnished *Promptuary,* for the service of Piety and Vertue."[50] The influential Presbyterian divine Richard Baxter, whom Rich knew personally, echoed this idea in a letter to Robert thanking him for a gift of his books, in which he exclaimed, "And your speciall way of *Occasionall Meditation,* I take to be exceeding usefull! Your examples are the translating of the severall Creatures into a language understood; so that it will teach men when they see the *words,* (the *things*) to see withall the *signification* (the *use*)."[51] Rich, too, emphasized this value in her meditation on the spider and the bee, noting that the spider's web is "good for nothing; but is soon brush'd down and flung away," whereas bees make "useful Combs," which "give hony, and become good for something."[52] For these spiritual meditations, of course, use signified particularly in a moral framework: the aim of brother and sister alike in mobilizing the things of the world was explicitly to strive against sin and, by claiming them and the experience of them for the divine, to bring them, as it were, into the shelter of God's logic. The Boyles, like other pious Protestants in the seventeenth century, cultivated piety in themselves and others to engage their minds in the work of becoming conscious of God in the world. The work of redeeming time also redeemed the self, which might otherwise be lost on the one hand to what both Rich and her brother call "dulness," an insensibility to creation, and on the other to Robert's much-noted "raving," by which he meant undisciplined intellectual energy stimulated, for him, by the abstract and fantastically wandering narratives of romance.[53] In both cases the mind was like the spider, disengaged from its environment. Occasional meditation, in contrast, situated the self in the world and in doing so awakened it to presence.

In the introduction to his *Reflections,* Robert Boyle supposed that occa-sional meditation, in particular, required great intellectual skill, "something of Dexterousness and Sagacity that is not very ordinary" in contrast to the "docile" nature of reading a book, but once the occasional meditator got into the habit of "Heavenly mindedness," a Puritan phrase that both Boyle and his sister seized on, she or he "acquire[d] an aptitude and disposition to make pious Reflections upon almost every Occurrence"—even, says Boyle, "oftentimes without particularly designing it."[54] Indeed, the reflections that arise from this disposition might surprise "ev'n him, whose Thoughts they are. . . . For our Instructions are suddenly, and as it were out of an Ambuscade, shot into our Mind, from things whence we never expected them." Written meditations seemed to bypass eloquence and even, imaginatively, language itself: as Boyle declared to Ranelagh in his dedication to her, his goal was to present "Thoughts, rather than Words."[55] In Marie-Louise Coolahan's words in her study of Boyle's *Reflections*, the "relationship between occasion and ejaculation is apparently unmediated."[56] Occasional reflection did not go deep—its goal was not to produce profundity—but for a skilled practitioner it might entirely occupy the mind, sidelining its awareness of itself as observing and writing agent. The middle way between the spiritual, and intellectual, sins of dullness and raving, this suggests, was an oddly unliterary state of mind, if we think of the literary as the inclination of the observing self to be conscious of the *techne*, or skill, by which it *r*epresents our experience of the world. Reflection in the Boyle siblings' sense, as the conceptual mobilization of God's creation, served paradoxically to banish reflexivity.

This imaginary removal of any filter between the observing eye and the world has long been a scientific ideal, what philosopher of science Donna Haraway calls the "God trick," by which we imagine seeing things just as they are, without the inevitable screen of bias.[57] Robert Boyle, as one of the founders of the scientific method, certainly participated in that same historical trajectory of scientific thought by which we dream of erasing the standpoint of the observing self in pursuit of complete objectivity. But Boyle, and even more so Rich, pursued this state not only to achieve mastery but also with a desire to dwell in the world, to become truly God's creatures. Their piety, as expressed in their meditations, adopted not simply an exploitative but also an immersive position in the world. For Rich, especially, the impulse to banish mediation and to participate in the nature or essence of what she observed was in the service of a sincerity one and the same with piety.

Rich's diary records many efforts to arouse herself to "breathe after

God" so that she may present him a "broken and contrite heart" that will allow her access to his love.[58] In her meditation "Upon my forgettfullnes to winde up my watch," she compares her watch to that love, which is "free and unmerited" but when meditated on acts as a "constraineing and most powerfull engine" winding up her "affectiones to the highest pitch" possible.[59] Like many religious women in the seventeenth century, Rich experienced piety as an affective state, of lack in self and desire for other. In her *Meditations* and other pious practices she deliberately conjured constraints that would conduce to that lack and correspondingly to desire. But she was also, inevitably, part of a culture that forced those constraints on her. One particularly apposite example can be found in the 1689 *Discourses and Essays* of Francis Boyle, Viscount Shannon, elder brother of Mary and Robert, produced at another moment of exile for the Boyle family, when Francis lost his lands in the Jacobite risings. His observations are notable not only for the typicality of his misogynist anxieties but also because of the great familiarity of his social world to his siblings. After the loss of his lands, in a nod to the family habit that was perhaps partly ironic, Francis decided to make a "strict examination of my own life, and faults." Chief among them, he decided, was his "ill and foolish distemper of loving and delighting too much in the Company of . . . vain handsome Ladies," which oddly enough led him to produce an entire volume of essays dedicated to the reform not of his own self but of the "Ladies."[60] Like his siblings, interestingly, though in a courtly rather than religious context, he was deeply concerned with hypocrisy, and women for him, as for many early modern observers, were the focal point for his anxiety. In one essay, pondering the difficulty of knowing a woman's "inward intentions" through her words, he inclined initially toward the truism that women's "outward Actions" speak more loudly than their words but ultimately found his way to the far more radical conclusion that a woman must inherently fail to "be a credible Witness . . . as to her own inward intentions."[61] By their very nature women were hypocritical speakers, their female selves getting in the way of authentic utterance. Breaking their own hearts for God was a way for women to neutralize those selves so that their prayers, their most "inward intentions," might be taken as sincere. The kind of play with gender norms that Katherine engaged in with Robert probably would not have found a sympathetic audience in Francis, but occasional meditations were clearly useful in this context, seeming to subordinate or even erase the self in line with Rich's culture's complex set of imperatives for virtue. At the same time, perhaps surprisingly, in Rich's hands the genre may also have offered some compensation for such self-erasure, through its invitation into a relatively unconstrained "wilderness" generative of great thought.

While Rich pointed her analogizing lens in her reflections always toward God, Robert Boyle held in the introduction to his own published reflections that they should not be confined "to Divinity it self, though that be a very comprehensive Subject," but might demonstrate "not onely a Theological and a Moral, but also a Political, an Oeconomical, or even a Physical use."[62] It is all but inarguable that Robert enjoyed a larger discursive theater than his sisters, and although he remained deeply concerned with theology throughout his life, he was less insistent than Ranelagh that it frame all of his inquiry. Probably not merely coincidentally, he spent far less time in Ireland as an adolescent and young adult than she did, and his cultural ties to Ireland seem to have grown more tenuous in middle adulthood than Ranelagh's.[63] But his shift toward natural philosophy in the course of his publishing career was not an abandonment of the habits of thought in his theological work. Headway in science, Claire Preston argues in her study of the rhetoric of early modern science, was accomplished by methods borrowed or repurposed from other kinds of inquiry, and analogy itself was a scientific method. In historical retrospect Boyle's use of analogy was his leading edge, the means he employed to push out of theology into fields that would eventually demonstrate their own integrity. Preston calls the rhetorical figures in Boyle's natural philosophy "literary," but it might be more accurate to see them as connective tissue between different kinds of discourse, signs of methodological continuity.[64] Analogy for Robert was a kind of deep structure, a law that described the created world prior to any particular mode of inquiry into it and that thus constructed as parallel forms of inquiry that we see as distinct.

Similarly, to the extent that Rich's, and Ranelagh's, faithfulness to and indeed extension of their father's pious Irish-English worldview signaled removal or retirement, that removal was not in contradistinction to natural philosophy or other more ostensibly public endeavors. Their life writing is thus not on the margins of cultural discourse but in the mainstream, grappling with the same problems by means of the same methods as their male contemporaries and peers. Since the late Victorian period, which produced a couple of biographies of her, there has been a tendency to see Rich as the small, especially virtuous Boyle sibling, retiring into a gentle, pious private life in England.[65] In her definition of religion as a "form of desire" for women, Mary Ellen Lamb, among others, gives a welcome corrective to outdated contemporary modes of reading early modern Protestant women's piety as simply a renunciation of social agency.[66] As I have suggested, Rich's pious discourse, and the life writing that intersects with it, also share modes of seeing and conceptualizing with other intellectual and cultural discourses, including natural philosophy. Robert Boyle's interest in theology, as historians have increasingly seen, was not distinct from but woven throughout his work in ethics and natural philosophy; similarly, the pious discourse of his sisters and of early modern women more generally was often implicated in large cultural conversations about empiricism, observation, retirement, and the emerging distinction between public and private.

It is not merely coincidental that natural philosophy in the mid-seventeenth century also showed a powerful impulse toward retirement, an "ethos of seclusion," in Preston's phrase.[67] One of the ways natural philosophers defined their new realm of study at midcentury was by declaring themselves members of "colleges," often "invisible," and scholars have tended to anachronize these colleges as more established and institutionalized than they were (in part, since women were participants, to make women's scientific contributions more visible). But such colleges were mainly fictions of sociality, ways to imagine confederations of people—European scholars, English aristocrats, tradesmen, gentlewomen—who had never come together as relative equals before. Natural philosopher John Evelyn calls them, evocatively, "tabernacles in the wilderness," holy places entirely removed from civilization.[68] As that echo of Rich might suggest, they were thus open to those to whom a more established civil structure might deny access, and their nature as hypothesis was one of the reasons they were authorizing for women, whose numbers in natural philosophical circles diminished sharply, as is well known, when the actually institutional Royal Society was founded in the early 1660s. We might also draw a link here between Evelyn's, and Rich's, "wilderness" and the space Ireland afforded to so many members of the Hartlib Circle, both materially and in its nature as cultural crossing ground, for practical experimentation and "improvement." Reading Rich's and Robert Boyle's meditations as two parts of a common endeavor that was in turn indebted to the New English culture of 1630s and 1640s Ireland opens the scope of Rich's ambition and accomplishment to larger questions, situating her life writing in that ambiguous space of generic instability and mixture that fosters so much innovation in seventeenth-century discourse. Her Irish context helps us see, too, the potential stakes of her Protestant piety, which, like her brother's, extended far beyond private virtue.

Rich's *Some Specialities in the Life of M Warwicke*, begun and probably mostly finished in 1672, is a very different kind of text from the occasional meditations she was still composing until close to her death in 1678. One of several autobiographical accounts left by the Boyle family—among them her father's *True Remembrances*, which Rich almost certainly knew, and her brother Robert's "Account of Philaretus during his Minority," written when Robert was twenty-one or twenty-two—Rich's is the most fully articulated, structurally, as an autobiography.[69] Unusually for early modern women's life writing, it construes her life as a whole, beginning "I was born," giving a sequential narrative of major life events, and concluding with the announcement of an "end to my worldly business," as she has discharged her duties both to her nieces and her husband and can now turn entirely toward God for "my remaining days."[70] Most of the interest the account has evoked as a narrative, rather than merely as a source for biographical details, has been for its play between spiritual and apparently more secular aims. On the one hand, it is clearly a conversion story, a relation of her gradual awakening to an inward and personal relation with God, and belongs to the well-documented tradition of early modern self-narratives testifying to God's providence in human life.[71] On the other, Rich devotes considerable attention to her defiance of her father's plans in marrying Charles Rich, younger son of the Earl of Warwick, and some critics have seen in this account of assertive feminine agency an identification with the genre of romance.

In construing romance, justly, as a "mode" available to women writers in the seventeenth century, we tend to emphasize its interest in secular love as psychological motivation and to see this love as a form of rebellion against, or at least relief from, more stringent spiritual models for feminine virtue. Spiritual autobiography, by this logic, in subordinating human agency to divine often constructs the narrativized feminine self as abject, while more secular romance offers agency as an alternative and more modern route to subjectivity.[72] Critics have thus found in Rich's ostensible mix of genres a tension, if not an irreconcilable conflict, in her concept of self, and correspondingly an incoherence in her narrative, a failure, or a disinclination, to build a bridge between her generic models.[73] But we might be better served to remember that our perceptions of conflict and incoherence stem in part from an insufficiently full and precise understanding of seventeenth-century romance as a genre and of the ways her narrative does and does not participate in it. In fact, *Some Specialities* depicts an unambivalently agentive subject, if also one deeply aware of the strictures on women's agency.

In the discursive world the Boyles occupied in the mid-seventeenth century, romance often served as an easy signifier for worldliness and self-interest; hence Rich's repeated use of the phrase "seeing plays and reading romances" almost as a tagline to represent the vanity of her misspent youth.[74] But the term in this period also referred to a specific set of texts, political and international in focus, that were as concerned with history and ethics as with secular love. This genre had strong ties to France, which is one of the reasons scholars have misidentified it as mainly royalist in its politics, but also, tantalizingly and as yet insufficiently explored, to Ireland and Scotland. Roger Boyle, of course, wrote and published most of *Parthenissa*, probably the most celebrated midcentury romance in English, while fighting for Cromwell in Ireland; the obscure Judith Man translated and epitomized Barclay's *Argenis* probably while living in the Irish household of Thomas Wentworth; and Francis Quarles wrote *Argalus and Parthenia*, the only romance in his extensive body of writing, while in Dublin. George MacKenzie's *Aretina* is explicitly Scottish, and Percy Herbert's *The Princess Cloria* deals at length with the wars at midcentury in Ireland and Scotland. And Robert Boyle, although he identified romance early in his life with the intellectual "raving" that he had to subdue in his quest to achieve true reason, remained interested in the genre throughout his life, incorporating romance elements into his treatise *Seraphic Love* and revising and publishing his religious romance *The Martyrdom of Theodora, and of Didymus*, as late as 1687.

For Roger and Robert romance was not distinctive so much for its subject matter as for its approach. Like occasional reflections as Robert imagined them, romance was a capacious genre with a wide variety of uses: in the words of the anonymous author of the 1661 *Eliana*, it included not only "Amatory" matters but "things Oeconomical, Ethethical [*sic*], Physical, Metaphysical, Philosophycal, Political and Theological"—that is, the entire gamut of subjects covered by prose discourse in the seventeenth century.[75] Its particular virtue as a genre was its courtly, aristocratic style, as Robert acknowledged to Roger in the 1661 dedication to *Some Considerations Touching the Style of the Scriptures*, trying to convince his brother to extend his authorship from romance to theology. At its best, he conceded, romance possessed "some pleasing *Je ne scay / quoy*, something of Easie Genuine and Handsom that's peculiar to It." Romance's authors, courtly, or at least presenting themselves as such, and thus ostensibly freed by their social status from the motives of professionalism and publication, occupied the realm of true amateurs, and their work consequently made "Deeper Impressions" in their readers, not only by ranging over a wide field of knowledge but by detaching from ordinary self-interest: "by being suppos'd," as he argues, "more Disinteress'd, and look'd upon not as Suggested by their Profession or Self-ends, but as the Sincere dictates of their Unbribed souls."[76] The value of sincerity was also championed at a thematic level, where lovers' extravagancies proved the authenticity of their attachments and where, for instance, one of *Parthenissa*'s signature moves is for even its antagonists to establish their fitness, were the plot another way, for "disinterested friendship."[77]

It would not be going too far to say that in its effort to provide a "shining example" against the dissimulation and hypocrisy of courtly rhetoric, romance served in this era as the worldly analogue for pious discourse, as an argument for and an occasion to practice sincerity.[78] In this sense, as I've argued elsewhere, it was a fundamentally ethical genre, taking as its subject and mission the establishment of possibility for authentic relations between people.[79] It is probably for related reasons that, like pious discourse, romance in this period was also distinctive for its friendliness to the agency of women, who could find in the rules and strategies of the genre's social world means to protect themselves from accusations of self-interest and hypocrisy. For the Boyles, then, romance was useful especially for its rhetorical ethos, its appeal to a broadly interested, relatively inclusive audience that wished to imagine itself as unbound to any particular interest and also sincerely devoted in its ethical attachments. Such a version of aristocratic liberality was different from the ideological commitment that united the Hartlib network, but in their similar relation to the values of pious discourse there were also obvious parallels between the two.

Rich's *Some Specialities* does tell the story of her marriage to Charles Rich for love rather than money, which has persuaded some readers to call it romance, but in neither form nor content does it show many similarities to romance as employed by her brothers or other contemporary writers: uninterested in the rhetoric of courtesy and compliment, it is also resolutely demystificatory about marriage, and it seems almost deliberately to frustrate romance plot trajectories.[80] Figuring herself as a romance protagonist or narrator would have created a perfect setting for an apologia, if Rich had been interested in one—an admission of guilt for defying her father or a justification of her own choices, either one ethically validated for the reader, in the mode of romance, by the narrator's expression of affective ties to the appropriate subject, whether husband, friend, or father. About Charles's unexpected inheritance of the Warwick estate after the deaths of his elder brother and nephew, Rich's narrator does assure her readers, and perhaps herself, that "I never had so much as a wish for it. . . . It was [Charles's] person I married and cared for, not an estate."[81] This is the closest she comes to ethical justification through affect—though if she means to argue that providence has rewarded her for it, that remains implicit. Although she does not enact rhetorically the mortification of her heart in this text as she does in the diary and her *Occasional Meditations*, in describing her conversion she also declares directly to God her love and gratitude, and it would be inaccurate to say that in this account she turns away from affective piety. She also presents herself as having a kind of genius for building substitute familial relationships—Ann Clayton, with whom her father fosters her in Ireland until she is about eleven, is like a "kind mother"; her father-in-law, the Earl of Warwick, was "to me the most civil, kind, and obliging father that ever any person had"; and with both her mothers-in-law she lived "as lovingly as it was possible for an own mother and daughter to live."[82] Nonetheless, the signal move of *Some Specialities*, against romance practice, is the establishment not of Rich's embeddedness in social relations but, to a truly striking degree for a female-authored narrative of the period, of her independence. Repeatedly she turns away from the social structures into which she was born to construct her own—a repudiation of her father, perhaps, but also a recapitulation of his life's trajectory.

Richard Boyle married his first two daughters to Irish-English nobility on the same day in 1621; after that, the next period of family marriages began with a nearly all-family sojourn in London in 1628, during which the children were presented to the king and queen, and Cork made arrangements for Lettice Boyle's marriage to (English) George Goring in a deliberate attempt to facilitate his access to court. Two more daughters (one of them Katherine) were married within another year, and one two years later, all to Irish nobility. Cork aimed to expand his family's holdings, in all senses, by his daughters' Irish marriages, and he managed in several cases to build substantial control over the assets of his sons-in-law. In 1634 he bought the English estate of Stalbridge, eventually inherited by Robert Boyle (his only untitled son), and in 1639 the entire family, including married daughters and sons-in-law, was again in London for an extended period. During this stay or because of it he married three sons at court, one to a maid of honor to the queen in the royal chapel, with a wedding dinner hosted by the royal family; one to a Villiers connection; and the last, Roger, to Margaret Howard, daughter of the Earl of Suffolk, with a strong financial settlement. During this time Cork also attempted to complete negotiations he had begun "some years before," according to Mary, for an Irish match for his youngest daughter, in London for the first time, but alone among her sisters she refused that match and several others and then arranged for herself a marriage to Charles Rich, a younger son at that point without much wealth or the prospect of it.[83]

Extraordinarily for a girl of fourteen, Mary refused the Earl of Clandeboye's son and defied her entire family, she says, because of an "aversion" that, characteristically, she cannot explain either to her father or to the reader.[84] The refusal of this first match was also a refusal of the family pattern for Boyle daughters—perhaps in part because she was aware of the marked marital unhappiness, well documented in family correspondence, of her sisters Katherine and Lettice. It was a refusal as well of the Irish destiny her father had charted for her; for the rest of her life, as far as we know, alone among her siblings she never visited Ireland again. As a gesture of independence from her family and from an entire generation of their history, her refusal cleared the ground for autonomous action: after noting that Cork had acquiesced to a marriage for Roger that he hadn't desired (though the union was later aborted), she committed to marry Charles Rich on her own, subsequently engaging in a complex negotiation with her father that she won at every step. Faced with her father's strong displeasure after he was approached by Charles's father, she told him through her brothers that she would refrain from marrying without his consent but also would not marry "any other person in the world" but Rich—interestingly a vow that, like other frustrated parents in the period, he apparently believed he would have to honor.[85] After she had spent ten weeks in isolation from her own family (but visited near constantly by the Riches) at Hampton as a gesture of penance, Warwick and Lord Goring, Lettice's father-in-law, brought her to apologize formally to her father, at which point he reinstated her dowry of 7,000 pounds and gave consent for an immediate marriage. In her portrayal of these events Rich no doubt plays up the heroic nature of her stand, a point made all the more emphatically when, as she tells it, she defied her father's wishes yet again, "being a great enemy always to a public marriage," and wed "without my fathers knowledge" in a private ceremony outside London, a "fault" that once again his "great indulgence to me made him forgive me."[86] At several moments in the rest of the narrative, as also in her diary, Rich expresses her contrition for defying her father's wishes, but she never regrets her actions.[87] Describing her own negotiations for the marriage of her niece at the very end of her account, as an extension perhaps of her own willfulness she makes a point of noting that she gives the niece "her free choice to choose or not, to do as she liked or disliked."[88]

Similarly, at the beginning of her account of her extended religious conversion, Rich includes an episode that emphasizes her independence in this process even from her much-loved husband. During her young son's illness, she had promised God that she would "become a new creature" if he restored her child to health, and after her son recovered she found in herself a new desire to leave London for the Warwick estate at Lees. On the road she met Charles, on his way back to London with a parliamentary force, and though he asked her not to go on to Essex alone for fear of her safety, and "though I found in myself a loathness to deny going with my husband (having never before left him hardly, when I could conveniently be with him)," she so much desired solitude that she asked him "to leave me to myself, which he did." It was when she went alone to Lees that she first grew acquainted with Anthony Walker, the priest who much later delivered her funeral sermon and who ministered to her through the first stages of her turn toward God. (Again characteristically, she also notes the secular angle, explaining that her decision to go on to Essex was "well for the house" because she was in residence when a parliamentary force led by Lord Goring, now "one of my best friends," stopped at Lees for munitions, and "I was upon that account used so well that, bating some arms they took, there was not anything touched.") Although Charles soon joined her again at Lees, her inclusion of this episode clearly is meant to distinguish between her roles as wife and as convert, highlighting her spiritual independence.[89] Rich's diary details later conflict between her and Charles, and some readers have seen in her accounts of his shouting and her tears evidence that he was abusive, but their fights as she recounts them consist entirely of her insistent counsel that he piously accept and even welcome his own suffering during his long and painful struggle with gout, countered by his just as insistent refusal to do so.[90] Clearly she believed that her piety gave her the responsibility to evaluate and improve her husband's spiritual state even or perhaps especially during his illness, and, though he resisted locally, in a more general sense he acquiesced. *Some Specialities* consistently records her affection for him, and when he died, which "afflicted" her more "than ever before for anything in my fore-past life," including the wrenching death of her twenty-one-year-old son, he showed his respect for her by "giving me his whole estate for my life and a year after, and making me his sole executrix," a role that she discharged, Walker says in his funeral sermon, with "indefatigable pains," "scrupulous exactness, and admirable prudence."[91]

One of the most pronounced effects, or perhaps stimulants, of Rich's conversion in *Some Specialities* is social withdrawal, a refusal of the "vain and idle pleasures" characterizing her aristocratic society in preference for the quieter world of clergy gathered at and around Lees.[92] Such withdrawal might seem on the surface to involve a rejection of agency, but the collective effect of both sisters' writings is to question that too simplified notion of the public as the only significant field for action. Viewed through the lens of the Boyle sisters' experiments in life writing, Rich's *Some Specialities* can be read as a culmination of a narrative trajectory toward solitary independence, as she sheds first much of her identity as an Irish-English Boyle daughter, then her dependence as a young wife and secular mistress of a great house. At the end of her account she asks God to make her a "widow indeed," entirely detached at last from worldly ties, but also the sole and final inheritor of a substantial patrimony.[93] Her turn to God and her preference for solitude, as I have suggested, are not a repudiation of her rebellious bid for independence in her youth but an extension of it; like Ranelagh, she retires in search of her "own honest endeavors." With most of his daughters, Cork's plans were successful; marrying and bearing children to Irish nobility, they furthered his dynastic ambitions and solidified the family's worldly success. Ranelagh and Rich seized on a different part of the New English inheritance, its colonizing piety, which leveraged Ireland as a theater for ambition even as it ostensibly renounced self-interest. In ways Cork could not have intended, but that must have had some connection to the world he helped construct, both women found in that piety potential and authorization for broad and independent thought.

1. Nicholas Canny, *The Upstart Earl* (Cambridge: Cambridge University Press, 1982). On Cork's economic and political influence, see also David Edwards and Colin Rynne, eds., *The Colonial World of Richard Boyle, First Earl of Cork* (Dublin: Four Courts, 2018).

2. For Cork's motto, see the 1632 version of his *True Remembrances*, printed in the introduction to Robert Boyle, *The Works of Robert Boyle*, ed. Thomas Birch, 5 vols. (London, 1774), 1:vi–xi, xi; see also Canny, *Upstart Earl*, 19. Gilbert Burnet's "A Sermon at the Funeral of the Honourable Robert Boyle," originally published in 1692, is reprinted in Michael Hunter, ed., *Robert Boyle by Himself and His Friends* (Brookfield VT: Pickering, 1994), 36–58; for "humble and Christian" see page 47.

3. Canny, *Upstart Earl*, 22–29; Marie-Louise Coolahan, *Women, Writing, and Language in Early Modern Ireland* (Oxford: Oxford University Press, 2010), 256–57; Carol Pal, *Republic of Women: Rethinking the Republic of Letters in the Seventeenth Century* (Cambridge: Cambridge University Press, 2012), 159–60; Patricia Coughlan, "Natural History and Historical Nature: The Project for a Natural History of Ireland," in *Samuel Hartlib and Universal Reformation*, ed. Mark Greengrass, Michael Leslie, and Timothy Raylor (Cambridge: Cambridge University Press, 1994), 298–317; Toby Barnard, "The Hartlib Circle and the Cult and Culture of Improvement in Ireland," in Greengrass, Leslie, and Raylor, *Universal Reformation*, 281–97.

4. For the social and political identity of the landed peerage in Ireland in the seventeenth century, see Jane Ohlmeyer, *Making Ireland English: The Irish Aristocracy in the Seventeenth Century* (New Haven: Yale University Press, 2012).

5. For life writing's concern with the negotiation of shared and conflicting interests with others, see Douglas Catterall, "Drawing Lives and Memories from the Everyday Words of the Early Modern Era," *Sixteenth Century Journal* 36, no. 3 (2005): 651–72.

6. See Ronald Bedford, Lloyd Davis, and Philippa Kelly, eds., *Early Modern Autobiography: Theories, Genres, Practices* (Ann Arbor: University of Michigan Press, 2006), esp. Lloyd Davis, "Critical Debates and Early Modern Autobiography," 19–34; Conal Condren, "Specifying the Subject in Early Modern Autobiography," 35–48; and Helen Fulton, "Autobiography and the Discourse of Urban Subjectivity: The Paston Letters," 191–216.

7. For Katherine Ranelagh's receipt books, see Michelle DiMeo, "'Such a sister became such a brother': Lady Ranelagh's Influence on Robert Boyle," *Intellectual History Review* 25, no. 1 (2015): 21–36; DiMeo, "Lady Ranelagh's Book of Kitchen-Physick? Reattributing Authorship for Wellcome Library MS 1340," *Huntington Library Quarterly* 77, no. 3 (2014): 331–46; and DiMeo, "Katherine Jones, Lady Ranelagh (1615–91): Science and Medicine in a Seventeenth-Century Englishwoman's Writing" (PhD diss., University of Warwick, 2009). For receipt books

as self-writing, see Catherine Field, "'Many hands hands': Writing the Self in Early Modern Women's Recipe Books," in *Genre and Women's Life Writing in Early Modern England*, ed. Michelle M. Dowd and Julie A. Eckerle (Aldershot: Ashgate 2007), 49–63, esp. 49–50.

8. For Ranelagh's work and social persona in medicine, see Michelle DiMeo, "The Rhetoric of Medical Authority in Lady Katherine Ranelagh's Letters," in *Women and Epistolary Agency in Early Modern Culture, 1450–1690*, ed. James Daybell and Andrew Gordon (New York: Routledge, 2016), 96–109.

9. Burnet, "Sermon at the Funeral," in M. Hunter, *Robert Boyle by Himself*, 52.

10. Samuel Hartlib, qtd. in Mark Greengrass, "Archive Refractions: Hartlib's Papers and the Workings of an Intelligencer," in *Archives of the Scientific Revolution*, ed. Michael Hunter (Woodbridge: Boydell, 1998), 36.

11. Samuel Hartlib, qtd. in Greengrass, "Archive Refractions," in M. Hunter, *Scientific Revolution*, 46.

12. Canny, *Upstart Earl*, 145–50.

13. Canny, *Upstart Earl*, 149; see also Pal, *Republic of Women*, 159–60; and Ruth Connolly, "'A Wise and Godly Sybilla': Viscountess Ranelagh and the Politics of International Protestantism," in *Women, Gender, and Radical Religion in Early Modern Europe*, ed. Sylvia Brown (Leiden: Brill, 2007), 287–88.

14. Coolahan, *Women, Writing, and Language*, 256–57; Coughlan, "Natural History," in Greengrass, Leslie, and Raylor, *Universal Reformation*, 302; Frances Harris, "Ireland as a Laboratory: The Archive of Sir William Petty," in M. Hunter, *Scientific Revolution*, 73–90.

15. See William Robertson, *The First Gate or, the Outward Door to the Holy Tongue, Opened in English* (London, 1654), dedication "To Vice-Countess Ranalaugh," in which Robertson says that her speed in learning Hebrew by his method has shown him both that women are capable of learning the language and that students of Hebrew need not have Latin, A2v.

16. Katherine Ranelagh to Robert Boyle, July 29, 1665, in *The Correspondence of Robert Boyle*, ed. Michael Hunter, Antonio Clericuzio, and Lawrence M. Principe, electronic ed., 6 vols. (Charlottesville VA: InteLex, 2004), 2:499.

17. Ruth Connolly, "A MS Treatise by Viscountess Ranelagh, 1614–91," *Notes and Queries* 53, no. 2 (2006): 171n4.

18. See Ranelagh to Robert Boyle, September 14, [1652], in Hunter, Clericuzio, and Principe, *Correspondence of Robert Boyle*, 1:138; see also Malcolm Oster, "Millenarianism and the New Science: The Case of Robert Boyle," in Greengrass, Leslie, and Raylor, *Universal Reformation*, 140, 142–43; and Connolly, "Wise and Godly Sybilla," in Brown, *Radical Religion*, 297–99.

19. Connolly, "MS Treatise"; see also Connolly, "Wise and Godly Sybilla," in Brown, *Radical Religion*, 289–91.
20. Benjamin Denham to Robert Boyle, [August 1667?], in Hunter, Clericuzio, and Principe, *Correspondence of Robert Boyle*, 3:327.
21. Bulstrode Whitelocke, *The Diary of Bulstrode Whitelocke, 1605–1675*, ed. Ruth Spalding (Oxford: Oxford University Press, 1990), 751.
22. See Betsey Taylor-FitzSimon, "Conversion, the Bible and the Irish Language: The Correspondence of Lady Ranelagh and Bishop Dopping," in *Converts and Conversion in Ireland, 1650–1850*, ed. Michael Brown, Charles I. McGrath, and Thomas P. Power (Dublin: Four Courts, 2005), 157–82.
23. Connolly, "Wise and Godly Sybilla," in Brown, *Radical Religion*, 291.
24. For Wentworth's political and propaganda campaign against Cork, see Canny, *Upstart Earl*, 9–18.
25. For an explanation of the exchange, see Dorothy Moore Dury to Samuel Hartlib, March 28, 1645, in Dorothy Moore, *The Letters of Dorothy Moore, 1612–64: The Friendships, Marriage, and Intellectual Life of a Seventeenth-Century Woman*, ed. Lynette Hunter (Aldershot: Ashgate, 2004), 64; see also John Dury to Katherine Ranelagh, December 14, 1644; and Dorothy Moore, copy letter to Katherine Ranelagh, July 8, 1643, both in D. Moore, *Letters of Dorothy Moore*, 114–17, 17–20.
26. Katherine Ranelagh to Roger Boyle, Lord Broghill, September 17, 1658, in *A Collection of the State Papers of John Thurloe*, ed. Thomas Birch, 7 vols. (London, 1742), 7:395–97.
27. Ranelagh to Roger Boyle, September 17, 1658, in Birch, *State Papers*, 397.
28. D. Moore to Ranelagh, July 8, 1643, in D. Moore, *Letters of Dorothy Moore*, 18–19.
29. Thomas Wentworth to Archbishop Laud, qtd. in Canny, *Upstart Earl*, 12.
30. For Ranelagh's letters to Hyde and Elizabeth and her political activity and opinion more generally, see Ruth Connolly, "A Proselytising Protestant Commonwealth: The Religious and Political Ideals of Katherine Jones, Viscountess Ranelagh (1614–1691)," *Seventeenth Century* 23, no. 2 (2008): 244–64; Connolly, "Wise and Godly Sybilla," in Brown, *Radical Religion*, 285–306; and Pal, *Republic of Women*, 173–75.
31. Harris, "Ireland as a Laboratory," in M. Hunter, *Scientific Revolution*, 85.
32. Ormonde to Earl of Arlington, qtd. in Pal, *Republic of Women*, 220.
33. See also Pal, *Republic of Women*, 219, on her friend Clarendon's possible irritation at what Pal calls her "politicking."
34. Ranelagh to Robert Boyle, November 14, [1665], in Hunter, Clericuzio, and Principe, *Correspondence of Robert Boyle*, 2:583–84.
35. See Ranelagh to Robert Boyle, September 9, 1665, in Hunter, Clericuzio, and Principe, *Correspondence of Robert Boyle*, 2:583–84, 2:499, 2:525.
36. See DiMeo, "Such a sister," for a reading of the working relationship between the two primarily having to do with his work in natural philosophy.

37. Mary Rich, *The Occasional Meditations of Mary Rich, Countess of Warwick*, ed. Raymond A. Anselment (Tempe: Arizona Center for Medieval and Renaissance Studies, 2009), 107, 102. All subsequent references to Rich's *Occasional Meditations* are to this edition.

38. Anthony Walker, *Eureka, Eureka the virtuous woman found* (London, 1678).

39. See Raymond A. Anselment, "Robert Boyle and the Art of Occasional Meditation," *Renaissance and Reformation* 32, no. 4 (2009): 74.

40. See Mary Rich to Robert Boyle, [late 1656]; December 29, [1677], both in Hunter, Clericuzio, and Principe, *Correspondence of Robert Boyle*, 1:205, 4:482; Robert Boyle, *Some Motives and Incentives to the Love of God (Seraphic Love)* (1659), in *The Works of Robert Boyle*, ed. Michael Hunter and Edward B. Davis, electronic ed., 14 vols. (Charlottesville VA: InteLex, 2003), 1:52. All subsequent references to Robert Boyle's works are to this edition.

41. Robert Boyle, introd. to *Occasional Reflections* (1665), in Hunter and Davis, *Works of Robert Boyle*, 5:20.

42. See Anselment's excellent introduction to his modern edition, Rich, *Occasional Meditations*, 1–39, esp. 3–4.

43. A. Walker, *Eureka*, 61.

44. For a discussion of Rich's meditations as autobiographical writing, see Julie A. Eckerle, *Romancing the Self in Early Modern Englishwomen's Life Writing* (Farnham: Ashgate, 2013), 149–50.

45. Dorothy Moore Dury to Katherine Ranelagh, June 12, 1645, in D. Moore, *Letters of Dorothy Moore*, 76; Marie-Louise Coolahan, "Redeeming Parcels of Time: Aesthetics and Practice of Occasional Meditation," *Seventeenth Century* 22, no. 1 (2007): 124–43; Anselment, "Art of Occasional Meditation," 76–77.

46. Rich, "Upon the Consideration of the different manner of the working of a Bee and a Spider," in *Occasional Meditations*, 176.

47. For the distinction between solemn or set and occasional or extempore meditation, see Anselment, introd. to Rich, *Occasional Meditations*, 22. For examples of Rich's recourse to the "wilderness," see *Memoir of Lady Warwick, also her diary, from A.D. 1666–1672* (London: Religious Tract Society, 1847), 74, 75, 78, 80, 81, 83, 156, 163, 241.

48. Samuel Hartlib, qtd. in Greengrass, "Archive Refractions," in M. Hunter, *Scientific Revolution*, 44; Robert Boyle, *Occasional Reflections*, in Hunter and Davis, *Works of Robert Boyle*, 5:28.

49. Rich, "Upon viewing a map," "Upon my keapeing in a rome for som time a bird," both in *Occasional Meditations*, 102-3, 142–43.

50. Robert Boyle, introd. to *Occasional Reflections*, in Hunter and Davis, *Works of Robert Boyle*, 5:19.

51. Richard Baxter to Robert Boyle, June 14, 1665, in Hunter, Clericuzio, and Principe, *Correspondence of Robert Boyle*, 2:476.

52. Rich, "Upon the Consideration," *Occasional Meditations*, 176–77.

53. For "dulness," see Robert Boyle, *Occasional Reflections*, in Hunter and Davis, *Works of Robert Boyle*, 5:52; and Rich, *Memoir of Lady Warwick*, 103, 217. For "raving," see Boyle, "An Account of Philaretus during his Minority," in M. Hunter, *Robert Boyle by Himself*, 8, 12.

54. Robert Boyle, introd. to *Occasional Reflections*, in Hunter and Davis, *Works of Robert Boyle*, 5:27, 5:52. On heavenly mindedness, see Anselment, "Art of Occasional Meditation," 80–81.

55. Robert Boyle, *Occasional Reflections*, in Hunter and Davis, *Works of Robert Boyle*, 5:27, 5:7.

56. Coolahan, "Redeeming Parcels of Time," 127.

57. Donna Haraway, "Situated Knowledges: The Science Question in Feminism and the Privilege of Partial Perspective," *Feminist Studies* 14, no. 3 (1988): 58–62.

58. Rich, *Memoir of Lady Warwick*; for "breathe after God," see, for example, 84, 85, 93, 103, 110, 133, 136, and 199; for "broken and contrite," see, for example, 140, 145, 171, 203, and 213.

59. Rich, "Upon my forgettfullnes to wind upe my watch," *Occasional Meditations*, 102.

60. Francis Boyle, *Discourses and Essays* (London, 1689), Epistle (n.p.).

61. F. Boyle, *Discourses and Essays*, 18.

62. Robert Boyle, introd. to *Occasional Reflections*, in Hunter and Davis, *Works of Robert Boyle*, 5:30.

63. For an example of his apparent disavowal of Ireland as a useful context for him, see the exasperated letter from Samuel Hartlib to Robert Boyle, February 28, 1654, in Hunter, Clericuzio, and Principe, *Correspondence of Robert Boyle*, 1:159, in which Hartlib urges Boyle, then in Ireland to resolve problems with his inheritance and complaining of the country's "barbarousness," to contact other members of the network also in Ireland.

64. Claire Preston, *The Poetics of Scientific Investigation in Seventeenth-Century England* (Oxford: Oxford University Press, 2015), 4–5.

65. Mary E. Palgrave, *Mary Rich, Countess of Warwick* (New York: Dutton, 1901); Charlotte Fell-Smith, *Mary Rich, Countess of Warwick, Her Family and Friends* (London: Longmans, Green, 1901).

66. Mary Ellen Lamb, "Merging the Secular and the Spiritual in Lady Anne Halkett's Memoirs," in Dowd and Eckerle, *Women's Life Writing*, 94.

67. C. Preston, *Poetics of Scientific Investigation*, 147.

68. Evelyn, qtd. in C. Preston, *Poetics of Scientific Investigation*, 149.

69. See Eckerle, *Romancing the Self*, 148–49, for a full account of Rich's autobiographical antecedents.

70. Rich, *Some Specialities in the Life of M Warwicke*, in Mary Rich, *The Autobiography of Mary Countess of Warwick*, ed. T. Crofton Croker (London: Percy Society, 1848), 37–38. For the unusualness of serializing, totalizing life writing by early modern women authors, see Megan Matchinske, "Serial Identity: History, Gender, and Form in the Diary Writing of Lady Anne Clifford," in Dowd and Eckerle, *Women's Life Writing*, 65–80; and Sharon Cadman Seelig, *Autobiography and Gender in Early Modern Literature: Reading Women's Lives, 1600–1680* (Cambridge: Cambridge University Press, 2006), 6–7.

71. Coolahan, *Women, Writing, and Language*, esp. 219–21. See also Bruce Hindmarsh, *The Evangelical Conversion Narrative: Spiritual Autobiography in Early Modern England* (Oxford: Oxford University Press, 2005).

72. See Eckerle, *Romancing the Self*, 12; and Ramona Wray, "[Re]constructing the Past: The Diametric Lives of Mary Rich," in *Betraying Our Selves: Forms of Self-Representation in Early Modern English Texts*, ed. Henk Dragstra, Sheila Ottway, and Helen Wilcox (London: Macmillan/St. Martin's Press, 2000), 148–65.

73. See esp. Wray, "[Re]constructing the Past"; see also Sara Heller Mendelson, *The Mental World of Stuart Women: Three Stories* (Amherst: University of Massachusetts Press, 1987), 62–115.

74. See, for example, Rich, *Some Specialities*, in Rich, *Autobiography*, 4, 21; and Rich, *Memoir of Lady Warwick*, 129, 221, 259.

75. *Eliana* (London, 1661), A3v.

76. Robert Boyle, *Some Considerations Touching the Style of the Scriptures*, in Hunter and Davis, *Works of Robert Boyle*, 2:384.

77. See Amelia Zurcher, *Seventeenth-Century English Romance: Allegory, Ethics, and Politics* (New York: Palgrave, 2007), 131–35.

78. The phrase "shining example" to describe romance is Robert Boyle's, in the preface to the second part of his martyrology-romance *Theodora*, which he published without the first part in 1687; see Hunter and Davis, *Works of Robert Boyle*, 11:8.

79. Zurcher, *Seventeenth-Century English Romance*, 4–17.

80. Rich avoids the kind of "extravagant" language of courtesy and compliment characteristic of *Parthenissa* and other seventeenth-century romance, and she is explicit about and accepting of the financial goals of aristocratic marriage; see *Some Specialities*, in Rich, *Autobiography*, 3, 7–8. The narrative about sister-in-law Elizabeth Killigrew's role in her marriage, which I do not have space to discuss in this chapter, begins as a standard romance plot but then dwindles away without resolution.

81. Rich, *Some Specialities*, in Rich, *Autobiography*, 28.

82. Rich, *Some Specialities*, in Rich, *Autobiography*, 27, 16.

83. Rich, *Some Specialities*, in Rich, *Autobiography*, 2.

84. Rich, *Some Specialities*, in Rich, *Autobiography*, 3.

85. Rich, *Some Specialities*, in Rich, *Autobiography*, 13. Lamb, "Secular and the Spiritual," discusses a similar vow by Anne Halkett and her mother's obligation to respect it, 85–88.

86. Rich, *Some Specialities*, in Rich, *Autobiography*, 14.

87. See, for example, Rich, *Some Specialities*, in Rich, *Autobiography*, 15; and Rich, *Memoir of Lady Warwick*, 213, 220, 247.

88. Rich, *Some Specialities*, in Rich, *Autobiography*, 36.

89. Rich, *Some Specialities*, in Rich, *Autobiography*, 18–20.

90. See, for example, Rich, *Memoir of Lady Warwick*, 103, 217. For abuse, see Wray, "[Re]constructing the Past," 149–50.

91. Rich, *Some Specialities*, in Rich, *Autobiography*, 33–34; A. Walker, *Eureka*, 47.

92. Rich, *Some Specialities*, in Rich, *Autobiography*, 22.

93. Rich, *Some Specialities*, in Rich, *Autobiography*, 38.

5

The Politics of Honor in Lady Ranelagh's Ireland

RUTH CONNOLLY

Ireland does not come out well in the letters of Lady Katherine Ranelagh (1615–91). She strove to shape its economic and spiritual conditions for over half a century, but in her letters she refers to Ireland as "that country" or, in sympathetic mood, "that poore country."[1] Unlike her brothers, the natural philosopher Robert Boyle or the politician Roger, First Earl of Orrery, she never writes of "our poore country" or "my Countrey."[2] Yet her Irish origins were well known enough that, in the only mention of Ranelagh's nationality in any surviving correspondence, she is described by Samuel Hartlib, a German Prussian emigré, to his correspondent John Winthrop as an "incomparable lady of Irish extraction," meaning here of Irish "origin, lineage, descent."[3] So why is Ireland "that country"? My argument here is that Ireland is crucial to her identity but as a place against which she constructs herself as measured and reasoned, a persona Ranelagh called that of a "wise man." These acts of rhetorical self-distancing from Ireland's ill-governed spaces (which were not continuous with the whole of Ireland itself) enabled Ranelagh to create an ethnically inflected defense of her decision to separate from her estranged husband, the New English peer Arthur Jones, Viscount Ranelagh. As she strove to safeguard her personal and familial honor, endangered by her decision openly to separate from him, she cast her husband as unequivocally Irish and mapped his dishonor-able conduct onto preexisting assumptions about treachery, disorder, and inadequacy among the "native" Irish. Her struggle to separate from Arthur was concurrent with her efforts to affirm Ireland's political status as a colony in permanent need of rule by "the English." Her history vividly illustrates how gendered experience can inform a colonial enterprise and vice versa.

In Ranelagh's correspondence, her ideal vision of a potential Ireland—Anglicized and secured for the Protestant faith—emerges against and relies on a reading of Ireland as a porous space of "plots," "fixtion," and fantasies of power. The latter space becomes irremediably associated with Arthur, who has taken on his "native" country's coloring. Indeed, "native" here means a set of behaviors as much as a place of birth. Ranelagh presents these behaviors as requiring condemnation and reform, not toleration or acceptance. Ranelagh thus exploits the slipperiness of identity with which Ireland was associated to designate Arthur as one of those settlers who have corrupted or have been corrupted by Ireland, who have failed in moral and material improvement, and who need to be brought to "reason." She represents his failure as one of honor, touching on a particularly vulnerable point for the New English in Ireland.[4] Ranelagh's rhetorical insistence that she did not belong to "that country" is, then, based on the argument that Ireland and its inadequate governors violated the standards of behavior to which she held herself but to which it needed to be brought to conform. Arthur served as the paradigmatic example of a governor gone native. Ireland-as-Arthur and Arthur-as-Ireland becomes crucial to Ranelagh's own justification for keeping her moral and geographic distance from both country and husband. The gendered experience of marriage in which a wife is governed rather than governor is thus challenged by invoking an ethnic hierarchy that legitimized her disruption of that relationship.

SETTLER IDENTITY IN EARLY MODERN IRELAND

John Kerrigan's thoughtful comment about Ranelagh's brother Orrery, that "history and place foster[s in him] an archipelagic sensibility that is more than Irish or English and not yet Anglo-Irish" is a useful place to begin to think about the political and confessional dynamics behind Ranelagh's relationship with Ireland.[5] Ranelagh's generation were the offspring of settlers who had arrived in Ireland as part of plantations of the late sixteenth century. She was the daughter of Richard, later First Earl of Cork, one of the most effective of that wave of English settlers, and his Irish-born wife Catherine, the daughter of Sir Geoffrey Fenton. With Edmund Spenser, Fenton had arrived in the train of the lord deputy Arthur, Lord Grey, in 1580 and rapidly rose to become one of the country's most influential policy makers, as his son-in-law became one of its wealthiest magnates. Ciarán Brady and Jane Ohlmeyer summarize the settlers' goal as making "a little England in Ireland," and maintaining their distinctive confessional and national identity was imperative to the task.[6] The settlers were expected to introduce the material civility that, combined with the spiritual advantages of Protestantism, would eventually transform the whole island in landscape, manners, and confession.[7] The simplicity of this vision of reform did not survive contact with the realities of attempting to achieve it, and Ranelagh's generation had, in addition, to begin to grapple with questions of whether their identity was, in the words of Toby Barnard, "colonial, provincial or a special Hibernian hybrid."[8] Some members of the "English in Ireland" or of the "English and Protestant interest in Ireland" (the self-descriptions that occasionally occur in some of this generation's writings) could readily reconcile an identity as native of Ireland with being English and Protestant. Ranelagh's exact contemporary, Dublin-born Arthur Annesley, First Earl of Anglesey, wrote feelingly in his manuscript history of Ireland of his obligations to his "native country," which led him to be "cordially desirous that the place of my birth should be as much English and Protestant as the stock and country from whence I came."[9] Annesley's separation of national identity from geographic space suggests the former is both portable and secure, resistant to the assimilation of any influence from Ireland's notoriously enfeebling material and moral environment.

Ranelagh's letters, which date from between 1642 and 1690, repeatedly return to the same goal as Annesley's: how to reform and govern Ireland in the English Protestant interest. This is a persistent topic in this half century of correspondence, sometimes glanced at in half lines, sometimes the focus of entire exchanges, and she grapples in those exchanges with the questions of who, and what, comprises the English Protestant interest. Over this half century the nature of the English Protestant interest was molded and riven by the political and religious dynamics of the Three Kingdoms. Waves of "New Protestants" entered Ireland in the 1640s and 1650s either at the instigation of Parliament or with Oliver Cromwell's forces, and their claims to land and political power posed a threat not only to the estates of settled "Old Protestants" (the new name for the 1580s planters and their descendants) but also to the royalist government restored in 1660. Attempts to maintain a de facto unity led occasionally to the use of the term "British Protestant subjects," as Orrery did in 1662, when he used the term strategically as a blanket term for the loyal settler class in Ireland.[10] This, as he later acknowledged, concealed the significant doctrinal divides between Scottish and English Protestantisms, whose political consequences, bitterly experienced across the Three Kingdoms in the 1640s, continued to trouble Irish Restoration politics.[11] The Duke of Ormonde, the restored king's governing representative, was the Protestant head of a largely Catholic Old English family, who had loyally gone in exile with Charles II. For Ormonde, the divide was royalist versus nonroyalist rather than Catholic versus Protestant, a political divide that no appeal to confessional unity might bridge. These fissures, and the problems of how to negotiate them, come clearly into view across the history of Ranelagh's writing about Ireland. She was a committed Cromwellian of "Old Protestant" stock whose vision of Ireland as an improved, Anglicized space was materially exemplified by the Boyle family's vast holdings in Munster and whose tolerationist vision of Protestantism was informed by the need for settlers to maintain a common denominational front against Catholicism in Ireland. Ranelagh's personal and political negotiations of the settler imperatives of civility, Anglicization, and reform were closely informed by her gendered experience of government in Ireland.

POLITICAL AND DOMESTIC COLLAPSES IN IRELAND

From her childhood Ranelagh's experience of transition between England and Ireland was closely linked with reputation-damaging and emotionally taxing movements between changing marital statuses. She was born in Ireland and lived there until the age of nine, when she was sent by her father to live in England at the home of a proposed husband; the match eventually collapsed over demands for a larger dowry, and she was summoned home, aged fifteen, her father complaining she "had lost the foundation of religion and civility wherein she was first educated."[12] Having been swiftly married to Arthur, she then lived between England and Ireland for a decade but departed with fellow refugees in 1642, after the outbreak of the Irish rebellion threatened the settlers' control of the island. She was in Ireland again in 1656, but after her final break with her husband she moved permanently to England in 1659; the surviving record indicates she returned only once more for her husband's funeral in 1670. The first failed match that entailed a return to Ireland is thus mirrored by a failed marriage that sees her move to England, returning again, once widowed. Her decisions to leave Ireland in 1642 and 1658 prompted her to write defenses of her conduct that segue into larger political reflections on the characteristics of governors in, and of, Ireland. The letters, addressed to her father and her brother, respectively, reveal how these moments of leave-taking become sites for Ranelagh's negotiations of the gendered experience of patriarchal and political power within an Irish context.

The first letter, addressed to her father, is dated December 26, 1642, and written just before she sailed from Dublin, following her negotiated release from the besieged garrison town of Athlone.[13] Ranelagh portrays herself as leaving Ireland impoverished and angry, with the Irish ship of state about to run aground. Athlone had been under the command of her father-in-law, Roger Jones, Viscount Ranelagh, but the town itself had been partially occupied by the Catholic Irish commander Sir James Dillon and the townspeople and soldiers forced back into the castle. Ranelagh described her experience in Athlone briefly as a "most myserable captivety." More detail is provided by the lengthy deposition of the curate Thomas Fleetwood, which reported brutal killings within Athlone itself; random attacks on women, children, and soldiers who went outside the garrison walls to gather food; the murder of a Protestant minister, Mr. Burton, and the expulsion of his wife and children from the town, "which Children (as this deponent was credibly informed) perished and dyed"; and the fate of one English woman, sent by Viscount Ranelagh to carry a letter from

Athlone to Dublin, who was subsequently captured and then "stoned" to death by women in the town.[14]

Nonetheless, Ranelagh's departure with at least one of her children from Athlone on Dillon's promise of safe conduct, "which indeed he kept with mee most punctually & civilly," did not, she assured Cork, mean she had a "confidence in, or a kindness for the rebelles."[15] Rather, the "sperit & the interest both my bloud and religion [gives] me in this cause" would have led her to refuse had she not been compelled to accept because "those by whom I am governed thought that the best way I could come by." For herself, she told Cork, the siege conditions, the difficult and disobliging company she found at Athlone, the sufferings of "the English" in the town, and the opportunity of advocating for them at Dublin all prompted her to accept the safe conduct. Ranelagh's nervousness that she might be deemed a collaborator by her father, who had just lost his son, Viscount Kinalmeaky, at the battle of Liscarroll, is revealing of how unstable loyalties had become.[16] Her letter continues with a fierce reassertion of the importance of the Boyle family's role within Ireland.[17] Her praise of the First Earl's commitment to "this bleeding & well neere ruined commonwealth, which is already soe destetute of any that seriously take its distractions to hart" is accompanied by a condemnation of the disputing factions at Dublin who are unable or unwilling to take heed of her pleas to relieve Athlone: "I find those who sitt at the helme here, soe ill advised as to let the generall good fall to the ground between their perticular dissentions, that I am not able to endure it any longer then I can prepare myself to goe for [the English port] Chester, where I intend to setle my selfe in a way of living suteable to that fortune that it has pleased god to reduce me to, & in which I humblely thanke him I find as much satisfaction, as ever I did in a more plentyfull one."

Her reversal of settler narratives of "improvement" point to failings that stretch from the private household to Dublin Castle and from which she, in principled frustration, will remove herself. The narrative and tropes that underlie Ranelagh's subsequent representations of Ireland emerge clearly in this letter. Her natal family are cast as self-sacrificial, principled, and honorable, while other settlers in Ireland, especially the administration at Dublin and perhaps those who "governed" Ranelagh—her husband

and father-in-law—have proved unable to unite to defend it or succor the vulnerable "English" inhabitants of Athlone. Some have degenerated to the point where a Catholic rebel has a greater care for Protestant women and children. The vulnerabilities of women and children to physical, material, and reputational damage through errors of judgment by male governors is a powerful subtext. Her departure from Ireland means the loss of material wealth, but the accompanying gain in spiritual riches is expressed through another of Ranelagh's favored rhetorical strategies: a triumphant resignation to God's will that introduces the aspects of choice and agency that are otherwise missing from her experience. Sixteen years later, back in Ireland, as the Three Kingdoms rapidly approached another set of political convulsions following Oliver Cromwell's death, Ranelagh returns to the same themes of failed local and household governance as a metonym for failed public governance, with women and children again the principal victims, this time using her estranged husband as the illustrative example.

Sometime in the late 1650s Ranelagh permanently left her husband's household and returned with her daughters to the main seat of the Earls of Cork at Lismore to live with her brother Richard, the Second Earl. The ensuing tensions are evident in a letter sent by Richard to Arthur and surviving in a copy in Ranelagh's hand. It presents a dispute between two male heads of household that pivots on the question of female obedience to their fathers and husbands. The letter is not about Ranelagh's marriage, however, but about Arthur's failure to conclude ongoing marriage negotiations probably for the Ranelaghs' second daughter, Elizabeth, because Arthur, as Richard put it to him, "should be very loath to preffer daughters that would not be obedient as you feared." The direct and irate tone, a relative rarity in Ranelagh's autograph letters but often characteristic of Richard's, suggests the letter is principally his composition, though the explicit expression of ill feeling toward Arthur probably reflects both siblings' attitudes. Richard argued forcefully on behalf of his niece, bringing the weight of his own standing as peer and family head to bear on his recalcitrant brother-in-law: "and what you intend by your loathnes to prefer daughters that wil not be obedient is another kindle to me since [she] has your Lordship's consent under your hand to my Lord Lieutenant for her stay with her mother."[18]

Richard's attempt to compel Arthur to act as he wished positioned Arthur as a subservient member within the extended Boyle dynasty under the command of its head. This relied on a practice begun by Ranelagh's father. Nicholas Canny, the biographer of the First Earl, noted that Cork sought to have his daughters Alice and Joan "focus their loyalty on himself as head of a kinship group rather than on their husbands as heads of their respective households."[19] Arthur is positioned as a rebel within his wife's family rather than an independent head of household who might expect to find his demands for wifely or daughterly obedience reinforced. Ranelagh's separation was unquestionably eased by her brothers' emphatic support of her; their actions reinforced her position within her natal family and resisted the expectations of her role as Arthur's wife. Yet this proved insufficient to defend her reputation and actions, and as Arthur is edged toward the boundaries of the Boyle family, Ranelagh expressly codes his behavior as dishonorable, the action of an "Irish breed."[20] This attack on her husband's honor is the crucial step that enables Ranelagh to map the newly drawn divisions between her and Arthur onto an ethnic distinction that reverses the hierarchy between them.

LAND WITHOUT HONOR?

Ranelagh's strategy sought to position Arthur as resistant to reason and in need of correction by English courts and English governors. Exploiting doubts about how honor was practiced in Ireland provided Ranelagh with the means to contest her marriage and secure her reputation. She pursued this strategy through appeals to the most senior government officials in England: first, the lord protectors, Oliver and Richard Cromwell, and later the vice-chancellor, Edward Hyde, Earl of Clarendon. That this was interpreted as something more than a local dispute, and as having implications for the wider government of Ireland, is suggested by the exchanges of letters about the separation and settlement between the Duke of Ormonde, the lord lieutenant of Ireland, and Clarendon. The latter's unequivocal view of Arthur as deeply dishonorable was countered by Ormonde's refusal to countenance any proposition to order Arthur to travel to England, including refusing a royal letter of summons. It is unsurprising that he proved so resistant to Ranelagh's claims of domestic dishonor; for him, as for Ranelagh, these claims mapped directly onto a partisan and highly politicized vision of how, and by whom, Ireland should be governed.

In Richard Cust's brilliant definition, honor "reflected the ways in which individuals were evaluated in the eyes of the societies to which they felt they belonged."[21] Competitions over honor were competitions to maintain or assert power and status. Nor were they solely individual: the "collective honor" of a household, family, or larger community hung on their adherence to mutually maintained standards. In an illuminating study of early modern honor politics in Ireland, Brendan Kane has characterized the culture of honor in Ireland as subject to a unique set of tensions stemming from the rapidly acquired wealth and perceived religious and ethnic superiority of comparatively lowborn groups of English settlers, and the native and Old English nobility, better-born but typically handicapped by Catholicism.[22] In his analysis of the variety of languages of honor practiced and experienced in Ireland, Kane argues that incoming Crown officials, anxious to assert their rule, used concerns about honor to target New English governors, who often, like Richard Boyle and Roger Jones, originated (at best) from the lower levels of the English gentry classes. Since honor was the principle that underpinned appropriate behavior in both domestic and public spaces, internal family relationships proved a useful if controversial theater of action when reinforcing "English" standards of civility among the New English.

In 1636 a threat by the Irish lord chancellor, Adam Loftus, to disinherit his eldest son in the context of a dowry dispute provided an opportunity for the then newly arrived lord deputy, Viscount Wentworth, to assert his authority by publicly lecturing Loftus in the honorable treatment of his offspring. Wentworth's actions encoded presumptions about honor as it was practiced in an Irish context that justified a political governor's challenge to an Irish peer's paternal authority over his dependents, something Kane suggests could "only seem possible in an Irish context; only there where the nobility were already suspect in honor, civility and loyalty."[23] Ormonde's refusal to intervene when Clarendon made a similar demand some thirty years later asserts his capacity, as the king's representative and the head of an Old English family of impeccable lineage and only-too-recently demonstrated loyalty, to determine honorable behavior. Ormonde's main aim may have been to deliver a firm rebuff to Ranelagh's principal advocate, Orrery, Ormonde's most significant political rival in Ireland, but his action also asserted an identity between standards of honor in England and Ireland and the capacity of Ireland's governors, in his person, to reinforce that standard. This domestic clash reveals two different visions of Ireland and how it should be governed, as kingdom (Ormonde) or as colony (Ranelagh), and sheds light on the ongoing tensions within the Protestant communities in Ireland.

That Ranelagh was relying heavily on the principle that English government officials might continue to intervene to correct recalcitrant Irish peers in their household affairs is revealed in the letter she wrote to Orrery, then Lord Broghill, almost a fortnight after Cromwell's death in 1658. It is not clear when Ranelagh's initial link with Cromwell was established, but it was firmly consolidated by the time Broghill was serving in Cromwell's government. Broghill's biographer, Patrick Little, notes that Ranelagh acted as Broghill's personal intermediary with Cromwell while she lived in England and Roger in Ireland. Writing from Lismore, she tells Broghill, himself newly arrived in Ireland, of her intention to leave and "seeke a maintenance for me and my children" from Arthur through private petition to Richard Cromwell in England.[24] Such private settlements were in England "a tried and tested mechanism familiar since at least the time of Queen Elizabeth" and functioned as an often preferred alternative to formal separation *a mensa et thoro*, which could be granted only by the now defunct ecclesiastical courts.[25] Roger had brought a letter with him from London from Oliver Cromwell, seemingly intended for Arthur. Ranelagh noted that the "persuasions and advice" Cromwell supplied were aimed at "bringing him [Arthur] to reason either here or there." But Cromwell was dead, and with him any hope of a resolution: "his now highness [Richard Cromwell] seemes not to me soe proper a person to summon my lord [Arthur], or deal with him in such an affayre, as his father did, from whose authorety and severety against such practices as my lord's are, I thought the uttmost would be done."[26] Some sixteen years after her letter to her father, Ranelagh once again teeters on the brink of an undeserved reputational disaster, one that could be avoided only by accepting personal poverty and the loss of her daughter's marriage as its price.

The letter articulates very precisely what Ranelagh understood as the action necessary to safeguard her own reputation. Within the letter she reveals she had petitioned Oliver Cromwell about acquiring some leases of land that would have established a propertied relationship to Ireland in her own right. This in fact forms the major motivation for leaving. She had, she wrote, no reason to remain, as Cromwell's death and the consequent uselessness of his letter "takes away what engagement lay upon me to stay in this country [Ireland], in expectation of what effects its delivery would produce." Losing the leases ensures her dependence on her brothers and thus leaves her in a morally dubious and reputation-damaging environment while she remains in Ireland. Living off the large Boyle rent rolls could not make clear to the world that she left Arthur "upon necessity." Trusting to a "much experienced providence" in England restores the moral authority of which she is deprived in Ireland.[27] Ranelagh's resolution of this dilemma articulates the relationship between women's honor and real and symbolic property. Legal disability means Ranelagh cannot hold real property in her own right, yet her actions reinforce Garthine Walker's assessment that "non-sexual morality was a crucial component of women's honour."[28] That morality centered on the household, and the good head of household maintained honor by protecting her family's material worth and its moral credit. In her letter Ranelagh stresses that she must provide for her household without sacrificing that moral credit. By leaving Ireland Ranelagh is able to perform a strategic recuperation of this aspect of her honor and safeguard her household. These are the actions, she tells Orrery, of a "wise man" ruled by what "al good laws make my duty, use honest endeavors in order to provideing for myselfe and famelly." Yet despite this appropriation of a masculine identity, and her renewal of her own agency, Ireland's capacity to disturb and cast doubt on her actions remains intact.[29] On the defensive about her reputation and involved in a complicated negotiation between men represented as models of political and personal integrity (herself, her siblings, Oliver Cromwell) and men positioned as their mirror images (her manifestly inadequate husband and the politically and morally feeble new lord protector), Ranelagh sees Ireland as a space that mercilessly exposes any weaknesses of its and England's governors and visits the consequences on those unlucky enough to be governed by them. Yet by conflating questions of domestic and political governance she was also able to use the opposition between Irish and English, governed and governor, to reverse roles with her husband and make herself the head of household.

ENGLISH HONOR AND IRISH LAND

By making her dispute with Arthur principally a question of honor as it was practiced in Ireland, Ranelagh had hit on a seam with rich yields in England but that met considerable resistance in Restoration Ireland. Once in England Ranelagh turned to her brother-in-law, the English peer Charles Rich, Earl of Warwick, to harass her husband through law courts.[30] She grimly told Richard of Arthur: "he is of an Irish breed which commonly proues fatal to such English as come amongst them."[31] Resonating behind this phrase is the New English contempt for the Old English, who were deemed to have degenerated from their original English stock and become "mere" or pure Irish.[32] Ormonde became a crucial figure in resolving the dispute, and Ranelagh sought to utilize some of the moral credit she had accumulated with the Duchess of Ormonde. Ranelagh had considerable influence with Henry Cromwell's governing council in the 1650s, and she used it to assist the duchess in holding onto the Butler estates when the duke was in exile with Charles II. Clarendon, a fellow royalist exile, told Ormonde that Lord Broghill's "obligations and civilities to your family haue been very extraordinary, as likewise hath my Lady Ranelagh's, to whose interests with the present gouernors *the* preseruation of *the* fortune is much to be imputed and *the* protection that is now enioyed."[33] However, as a Boyle with Cromwellian sympathies, Ranelagh was automatically suspect in the eyes of the Ormonde administration and Ranelagh sought to intensify the pressure on Ormonde by bringing the influence of Clarendon, her friend of long standing, to bear on him.[34] Writing to Ormonde, Clarendon denounced Arthur's behavior and declared that he "must be the worst man in the world and shee the most unworthily oppressed by him." In an echo of Wentworth's intervention, he explicitly accused Arthur of significant breaches of honor, including public lies, failing to provide for his daughters, and "makeing bold with his wifes cabinet," that is, that Arthur had searched his wife's papers and correspondence without her permission, which Clarendon found indefensible.[35] Arthur should, Clarendon advised, "be exposed in his true colours what kind of man he is" and "be sent hither, where no doubt he will be brought to reason" by the English courts.[36] In making these demands, Clarendon mapped honor and the proper provision for, protection of, and behavior toward wives and children onto a hierarchical division between the Irish and English peerage and their systems of honor and justice.

But Clarendon's echo of Ranelagh's own terminology of reason fell on deaf ears. Ormonde declined to dispatch Arthur to England, even after a royal letter of summons was received, claiming Irish parliamentary privilege protected Arthur and citing the latter's ill health and the bad weather as further excuses. These prevarications appalled Clarendon, already angered at Arthur's cavalier rejection of Crown authority, which seemed only to confirm the claims about him.[37] Ormonde's subsequent appointment of Arthur as a member of the Irish Privy Council in 1667 suggests his own opinion.[38] Ormonde or his wife appears to have eventually brokered a settlement, and Ormonde wrote dryly to Clarendon that "his Lady may be sure of all just and reasonable satisfaction, and in truth I think shee had receaued it sooner but for the animosity between my Lord of Orrery and her husband."[39] Ormonde's comment implies Ranelagh's loyalty to her brother rather than her husband is the source of the disorder, the same reasoning Ranelagh feared in 1658, but, crucially, it also firmly grounds the dispute as a local one fostered by internal family politics. Ormonde's refusal to allow issues of Irish honor to be determined elsewhere was making a political point about the efficacy of Ireland's political administration and delivering a rebuff to Orrery. Ranelagh's household dispute was evidently understood by him as inextricably bound up with larger political tensions across the archipelago and within Ireland. Ranelagh's subsequent interventions in Irish politics from London demonstrate her success in securely reestablishing her moral authority and credit on the foundation of Ireland's instability.

Power struggles in Irish politics were increasingly played out in London, where Ranelagh was now the Boyles' preeminent political agent, and her political activity in the 1660s deliberately sought to undermine the decisions of Ormonde's administration at Dublin. Ranelagh observed to Richard in July 1659, having left Ireland five months earlier: "One of *the* misfortunes of *that* place is *that* it seldome lights upon proper Instrum*e*nts for *the* worke they have to get donn."[40] The letter was addressed to Lismore, so her use of the phrase "that place" measures not only her geographic but their mutual moral distance from Ireland's ill-governed spaces. It is moral rather than geographic boundaries that distinguish communities. The implicit point was that Ireland needed to be governed and reformed as Richard governed, reformed, and cultivated his impeccably Anglicized Irish estates.[41] What this meant was Irish land in reliable and reforming Protestant hands. So while Ranelagh was calling on Ormonde to assist her to a personal settlement with Arthur, she was working in London against his government to support the threatened land titles of two waves of Protestant settlers that had entered Ireland after 1641.

Many post-1641 settlers had come in response to Parliament's attempt to privatize the suppression of the rebellion through an act granting lands expropriated from the rebel Irish to English Protestant "Adventurers" willing to fund the military forces needed to do so. The next wave came in 1649 with Cromwell's army, whose soldiers likewise received pay arrears in expropriated Irish lands. With the Restoration of Charles II, all these actions were technically illegal, and all Irish land confiscated since 1641 was vested once more in the monarch. It "could only be divested by decree of the court of claims" staffed by English commissioners and set up by an Act of Settlement.[42] These confiscations included lands possessed by the Second Earl of Cork and many others in the larger Boyle affinity. Irish landowners, particularly those who had remained loyal to the Stuarts, immediately seized the opportunity to demand restitution of their lands from the forces of the Cromwellian "usurpers" and parliamentarian "rebels" against the English Crown. This led to fierce protests from the existing proprietors. Ormonde wrote gloomily to Clarendon in early 1663 that "reports of the King's favouring Papists and the worst of the Irish rebels spreads when any Irishman is restored to his estates."[43] In his detailed discussion of the act's effects on landholding in County Dublin, L. J. Arnold argues that there was "a deeply held conviction which existed among Protestants that the commissioners of the court . . . were intent on dismantling the entire settlement and that this process must be reversed and the Act of Settlement amended."[44]

Ranelagh emerged as a central figure in coordinating these protests.[45] She worked to support aggrieved adventurers in petitioning the English government and used her personal influence with Clarendon and his son Henry, Lord Cornbury, to communicate the anger of Ormonde's opponents. The Irish member of Parliament Dr. Robert Gorges, formerly the clerk of Henry Cromwell's council and Cromwell's secretary, wrote from Dublin partly in cipher to Cornbury to tell him that Gorges had through an "enclosure" sent to Ranelagh sought "to present [the] Lord Chancellor [Clarendon] with his thoughts of Ireland" on behalf of a resentful portion of the Irish House of Commons.[46] Gorges added that the actions of the commissioners in openly inviting claims to lands had set the House "in a flame." Gorges was deeply influenced by Ranelagh and continued her work of transmitting the Irish House's complaints to London through her; Ranelagh's son Richard wrote to Ormonde's heir, Lord Ossory, in 1670 to tell him he was "often conversant with Dr Gorges with whom I have frequent meetings as my mother [is his] Chief agent and Councellor, and on whom I know he depends for all his calculations."[47] A former commissioner of the court of claims, Sir Allen Brodrick, witheringly assessed Cornbury's grasp of the situation to Ormonde: "My Lords deference to my Lady Ranilaugh who hath long assumed to Her self the Direction of these affayres, his singular opinion of the Doctors honesty, & his small understanding of Irish pretentions, made his whole discourse unintelligible." Brodrick's subsequent comment that he expected no more from Gorges in this "then I should haue found when he was secretary to Harry Cromwell" confirms the impression that Brodrick considered the petitioning adventurers and Ranelagh as former Cromwellians intent on undermining Ormonde and the king's authority.[48]

A later 1667 petition against alleged abuses of the act, which took place shortly after Clarendon lost office as chancellor of England, was also the opening salvo in an attempt, allegedly led by Orrery, to impeach Ormonde.[49] While Anglesey assured Ormonde that "my Lady Ranelagh purges her selfe of hauinge any hand in *the* Adventurers petition," Brodrick reported to Ormonde the events surrounding the reading of the petition in the English House of Commons, the intention being "to unravel as much of the settlement [created by the act] as possible. My Lady Ranelagh is still said to have many designs and indeed all the sectaries grow to a high degree in confidence and promise themselves an interest in government very speedily."[50] The political implications of these actions from England are made explicit in comments by another Ormonde agent, Col. Edward Vernon. Writing on December 28, 1667, he reported an argument with Lord Edward Conway, an Irish peer and an Ormonde ally on the Irish Privy Council. Conway had his views altered because Ranelagh, who was

> a woman (as he *said* of an Excelent judgment,[)] said the petition was altered, and was then a very wise and well penned petition; I replyed [to Conway] I was not of thes opinion for I considered [no] petition could be soe that drew any thing of the Settlement or conserne of Ireland into debate before the House of Commons of England being, it would bring all lawes, & soe greate an incertainty, that noe wise person would either purchase or plant in Ireland if an Irish Act of Parliament should not be thought final.[51]

From an Ormonde point of view, Ranelagh was not functioning as an agent of a Protestant or a collective "English interest in Ireland," as Orrery framed it in his (anonymous) protest against the act, *The Irish Colours Displayed* (1662), but as the figurehead of a faction associated with the Cromwellian usurper and radical models of Protestantism.[52] Her activities were politically extremely problematic because they rendered the acts of the Irish House of Commons subject to overrule by their English counterparts. Ranelagh's position in relation to Ireland is thus transformed from a woman shuttled between two nations at the behest of fathers and governors to an agent making skilled and influential interventions in Irish politics who sought to ensure the country occupied a subordinate position as a colonial possession. That systems of honor formed the basis for her judgement of what was appropriate rule in Ireland is apparent from her most detailed surviving account of how Ireland's settler and native communities should interact.

This was written at another moment of acute crisis for Irish Protestants, the accession of the Catholic monarch James II in 1685. Possibly because of this context, her assessment, contained in her notes on the manuscript treatise of Sir William Petty's "Speculum Hiberniae," is remarkably consistent with the more radical visions of Elizabethan settlers.[53] Petty, who had arrived in Ireland as a physician with Cromwell's army, was both a "principal architect" and a "prime beneficiary" of the land redistribution from Catholic to Protestant that took place in Ireland in the 1650s.[54] Ranelagh had known Petty since at least 1652 from their shared membership in the Hartlib Circle. She and he were the only Hartlibian experimenters to last into the changed political climate of the 1680s, and she and he were practiced participants in that group's moral and experimental incursions into Ireland.[55] Petty found her a willing supporter of his attempts to defend the post-Restoration land settlement against further potential encroachment through the treatise's reassessment of the Cromwellian conquest. Petty's argument sought to recast the Cromwellian army, in which he had served, as a coalition of displaced English Protestant settlers, cavalier soldiers of fortune, and "moderate Irish papists" horrified by the "cawseles Crueltyes of theire CountryMen" who produced an "absolute conquest." Their loyalty to the English Crown had been visibly demonstrated by their voluntary surrender of all Irish lands possessed by them to the returning Charles II, giving him "cleere and absolute title" to Ireland.[56]

Petty's coalition was of the willing incorporated soldiers of differing religious, national, and political affiliations joined by unshakable loyalty to the Crown. Ranelagh's notes were quick to build on this. She writes on a firm presumption that native insurrection and foreign invasion were always imminent. Her recommended additions to Petty's treatise included a request that "*the* armes" and "corporate towns" were kept in "*the* hands of *the* English," a right looked on as "an ancient & uninterrupted trust reposed in *them* by *the* crowne of England euer sin[c]e *the* acquisition of

that country." This will reinvigorate English application to "*the* aduance-
ment of their trade & *the* improuement of their riches" and defend against
foreign invasion "since without mentioning into whose protection *the*
natiues may endeavour to throw *themselues*, it is doubtles not capable of
an Argument *that the* English can ever seeke any other *than that of the*
Crowne of England."[57] The "native" population is reliably treacherous, and
an identity with England is the guarantee of the settlers' honor. But for the
fact that the hinted-at invasion is French rather than Spanish, Ranelagh's
lines might readily have been written in the 1590s or the 1640s, even though
she carefully and necessarily avoids invoking any confessional divides. By
casting the loyalty of the English settlers into the lap of James, Ranelagh
followed her well-worn route of appeal to the English ruler to reassert "a
contract which bound the king to respect the rights of those who took risks
to defend the security of his realm by settling in Ireland," a contract that
relies on the king's own role as the fount and exemplar of honor.[58] Her note
on the treatise envisages a secure and united English community in Ireland.
Its continuity is rooted in the possession of property legitimately theirs
on the basis of both conquest and their sustained trust in the monarchy.
Through invoking these old certainties, she circumvents any need to reflect
on the complex politics of the 1640s, which exposed divisions between
and within the "English of Ireland," or the ironies of former Cromwellians
extolling loyalty to a Catholic monarch.

CONCLUSION

In this context Ranelagh's characterization of Arthur as an "Irish breed" forms
part of a larger understanding of Ireland as a colony whose reformers need
to exercise constant vigilance over their communities and themselves. The
situation where Ranelagh could successfully stigmatize her husband as of an
"Irish breed" in an attempt to reverse the power relationships between them
may be unique to this context, reliant as it is on a model of Irish degeneracy
that assumed its capacity to infect even English settlers.[59] The dangers of
slippage, inevitable when an identity is defined as a set of behaviors, take
on a greater danger in the context of mid- and late seventeenth-century
Ireland. The threat was not only to women and children, though it was

felt immediately by them, but it also was a threat to the entire goal of the settlement. Honor provided Ranelagh with a means of connecting the domestic and public weakness she perceived. Her actions exposed, exacerbated, but also relied on divisions within the Protestant community about Ireland's precise status in relation to England. Those actions were shaped by her gendered experience of Ireland. It was the location where she experienced the greatest powerlessness, losing control over her marriage, movements, and reputation, which she was able to win back only through leaving. Ireland both established and periodically endangered Ranelagh's laborious self-construction as an honorable woman. To say therefore that she did not identify with Ireland cannot negate its central role in how she saw herself and how others saw her.

NOTES

1. Lady Katherine Jones, Viscountess Ranelagh, autograph letter signed (ALS) to Edward Hyde, Earl of Clarendon, June 4, 1663, MS 79, Clarendon State Papers, Bodleian Library (Bodl.), Oxford, fols. 270–71; Ranelagh, ALS, to Richard Boyle, Second Earl of Cork, July 24, 1659, vol. 31 (50), Boyle Papers, Chatsworth House, Derbyshire.

2. Robert Boyle, copy letter to Andrew Sall, January 21, 1682, no. 11, Dopping Collection, Armagh Robinson Library, Armagh, Northern Ireland; [Roger Boyle], *The Irish Colours Displayed* (London, 1662), 3.

3. *Oxford English Dictionary*, 2nd ed. (1989), s.v. "Extraction"; Samuel Hartlib, copy letter to John Winthrop the Younger, March 16, 1660, MS 7/7/1A–8B, Hartlib Papers, Sheffield University Library, Sheffield.

4. See Brendan Kane, *The Politics and Culture of Honour in Britain and Ireland, 1541–1641* (Cambridge: Cambridge University Press, 2010). For a superb discussion of Ranelagh's uses of honor in her correspondence, see Elizabeth Anne Taylor [Betsey Taylor-FitzSimon], "Writing Women, Honour and Ireland, 1640–1715" (PhD diss., University College Dublin, 1999).

5. John Kerrigan, *Archipelagic English: Literature, History, and Politics, 1603–1707* (Oxford: Oxford University Press, 2008), 267.

6. Ciarán Brady and Jane Ohlmeyer, "Making Good: New Perspectives on the English in Early Modern Ireland," in *British Interventions in Early Modern Ireland*, ed. Ciarán Brady and Jane Ohlmeyer (Cambridge: Cambridge University Press, 2005), 4.

7. On the complications and disruptions that ensued, see Brady and Ohlmeyer, "Making Good," in Brady and Ohlmeyer, *British Interventions*; and Toby Barnard,

Improving Ireland: Projectors, Prophets and Profiteers 1641–1786 (Dublin: Four Courts, 2008).

8. Toby Barnard, "The Political, Material and Mental Culture of the Cork Settlers, c. 1650–1700," in *Cork History and Society: Interdisciplinary Essays on the History of an Irish County*, ed. Patrick O'Flanagan and Cornelius G. Buttimer (Dublin: Geography, 1993), 311.

9. See Sean J. Connolly, *Contested Island: Ireland, 1460–1630* (Oxford: Oxford University Press, 2007), 398; and Arthur Annesley, First Earl of Anglesey, "Heads and Memorandums for an Intended General History of Ireland by Arthur, Earl of Anglesea," April 6, 1682, Add. MS 4,816, British Library (BL), London, fols. 30r, 48r–v.

10. [Boyle], *Irish Colours Displayed*, 2.

11. Kerrigan, *Archipelagic English*, 259.

12. Richard Boyle, qtd. in Nicholas Canny, *The Upstart Earl* (Cambridge: Cambridge University Press, 1982), 60.

13. Ranelagh, ALS, to First Earl of Cork, December 26, 1642, MS 43,266/20, Lismore Castle Estate Papers, National Library of Ireland (NLI), Dublin.

14. Thomas Fleetwood, deposition, March 22, 1643, MS 817, 1641 Depositions, Trinity College Dublin, Dublin, fols. 37r–40v, 37r, 38v.

15. Ranelagh to First Earl of Cork, December 26, 1642, NLI.

16. See Kerrigan, *Archipelagic English*, 246–47.

17. Ranelagh to First Earl of Cork, December 26, 1642, NLI.

18. Richard Boyle, Second Earl of Cork, copy letter to Arthur Jones, Viscount Ranelagh, December 28, 1658, vol. 30 (56), Boyle Papers, Chatsworth House.

19. Canny, *Upstart Earl*, 120. The Second Earl reproached another brother-in-law, the Earl of Kildare, for similar reasons. See Patrick Little, *Lord Broghill and the Cromwellian Union with Ireland and Scotland* (Woodbridge: Boydell, 2004), 199.

20. Lady Ranelagh, ALS, to Second Earl of Cork, September 2, n.y., Add. MS 75354, Althorp Papers, BL, fol. 50.

21. Richard Cust, "Honour and Politics in Early Stuart England: The Case of Beaumont vs. Hastings," *Past & Present* 149, no. 1 (1995): 59.

22. Kane, *Politics and Culture*, 1–15.

23. Kane, *Politics and Culture*, 266.

24. Katherine Ranelagh to Lord Broghill, September 17, 1658, in *A Collection of the State Papers of John Thurloe*, ed. Thomas Birch, 7 vols. (London, 1742), 7:395–97.

25. See Tim Stretton, "Marriage, Separation and the Common Law in England, 1540–1660," in *The Family in Early Modern England*, ed. Helen Berry and Elizabeth Foyster (Cambridge: Cambridge University Press, 2007), 18–39.

26. Ranelagh to Broghill, September 17, 1658, in Birch, *State Papers*, 396.

27. Ranelagh to Broghill, September 17, 1658, in Birch, *State Papers*, 396.

28. Garthine Walker, "Expanding the Boundaries of Female Honour in Early Modern England," *Transactions of the Royal Historical Society* 6 (1996): 243.

29. Ranelagh to Broghill, September 17, 1658, in Birch, *State Papers*, 396.

30. Felicity Heal notes in her case study of Elizabeth Russell that "as a woman the only effective defences of her honour were her family or the law courts." See "Reputation and Honour in Court and Country: Lady Elizabeth Russell and Sir Thomas Hoby," *Transactions of the Royal Historical Society* 6 (1996): 169.

31. Lady Ranelagh to Second Earl of Cork, September 2, n.y., BL.

32. See Edmund Spenser, *A View of the Present State of Ireland*, ed. Andrew Hadfield and Willy Maley (Oxford: Blackwell, 1997). There is no evidence that Ranelagh read the *View*, but Orrery cites it in [Boyle], *Irish Colours Displayed*.

33. Sir Edward Hyde, ALS, to James Butler, Marquis of Ormonde, October 15 and 25, 1659, vol. 65, Clarendon State Papers, Bodl., fols. 237–39, 238v.

34. Lady Ranelagh, ALS, to Elizabeth Butler, Duchess of Ormonde, March 2, [1666], MS 217, Carte Papers, Bodl., fols. 452–453r. For her relationship to Hyde, see Ranelagh, ALS, to Sir Edward Hyde, March 3, 1644, vol. 23, Clarendon State Papers, Bodl., fols. 113–15.

35. Clarendon, ALS, to Ormonde, January 30, n.y., MS 47, Carte Papers, Bodl., fols. 104r–106r.

36. Clarendon, ALS, to Ormonde, August 31, [1665], MS 47, Carte Papers, Bodl., fol. 98.

37. Charles II, copy letter to Ormonde, August 18, 1665, MS 43, Carte Papers, Bodl., fols. 450r–451v; Clarendon to Ormonde, August 31, [1665], Bodl.; James Butler, Duke/ Marquis of Ormonde, ALS, to Clarendon, September 18, 1665, MS 217, Carte Papers, Bodl., fol. 448r; Richard Jones, Viscount Ranelagh, copy petition to Clarendon, December 21, 1665, MS 48, Carte Papers, Bodl., fols. 372–73.

38. Charles II, copy letter to Ormonde, January 11, 1668, MS 43, Carte Papers, Bodl., fol. 639r.

39. Ormonde, copy letter to Clarendon, January 10, 1666, MS 49, Carte Papers, fol. 319r, Bodl.

40. Lady Ranelagh to Second Earl of Cork, July 24, 1659, Chatsworth House.

41. For these estate practices, see Toby Barnard, "Land and the Limits of Loyalty: The Second Earl of Cork and the First Earl of Burlington (1612–98)," in *Lord Burlington: Architecture, Art and Life*, ed. Toby Barnard and Jane Clark (London: Hambledon, 1995), 167–200.

42. L. J. Arnold, *The Restoration Land Settlement in County Dublin, 1660–1688* (Dublin: Irish Academic Press, 1993), 54. See Geraldine Tallon, ed., *Court of Claims, Submissions and Evidence, 1663* (Dublin: Irish Manuscripts Commission, 2006).

43. Ormonde, ALS, to Clarendon, February 21, 1663, vol. 79, Clarendon State Papers, Bodl., fols. 80–81.

44. Arnold, *Restoration Land Settlement*, 87.

45. One vulnerable settler was the member of Parliament Sir John Clotworthy, her sister-in-law's husband, who had almost eleven thousand acres in Antrim. Ranelagh lived with him in London after arriving in England in 1642. See Aidan Clarke, *Prelude to Restoration in Ireland* (Cambridge: Cambridge University Press, 1999), 170.

46. Dr. Robert Gorges to Henry Hyde, Lord Cornbury, February 18, 1663, vol. 79, Clarendon State Papers, Bodl., fol. 75r.

47. Viscount Ranelagh, ALS, to Thomas Butler, Earl of Ossory, October 14, 1670, MS 37, Carte Papers, Bodl., fol. 546v.

48. Sir Allen Brodrick, ALS, to Ormonde, December 31, 1667, MS 36, Carte Papers, Bodl., fols. 63r–63v.

49. See Earl of Ossory, ALS, to Ormonde, December 7, 1667, MS 220, Carte Papers, Bodl., fol. 310.

50. First Earl of Anglesey, ALS, to Ormonde, January 4, 1667, MS 217, Carte Papers, Bodl., fol. 433r; Brodrick, ALS, to Ormonde, December 14, 1667, MS 36, Carte Papers, Bodl., fol. 31r, qtd. in Arnold, *Restoration Land Settlement*, 121.

51. Col. Edward Vernon, ALS, to Ormonde, December 28, 1667, MS 36, Carte Papers, Bodl., fol. 53r. Lord Conway was Edward Conway, the Third Viscount Conway and Killultagh.

52. [Boyle], *Irish Colours Displayed*, 14. For an overview of the Orrery-Ormonde rivalry, see Raymond Gillespie, *Seventeenth Century Ireland: Making Ireland Modern* (Dublin: Gill and Macmillan, 2006), 222–25.

53. Sir William Petty, "Speculum Hiberniae," [1686], Add. MS 72,884, vol. 35, Petty Papers, BL, fols. 1–54.

54. Barnard, *Improving Ireland*, 51.

55. Patricia Coughlan, "Natural History and Historical Nature: The Project for a Natural History of Ireland," in *Samuel Hartlib and Universal Reformation*, ed. Mark Greengrass, Michael Leslie, and Timothy Raylor (Cambridge: Cambridge University Press, 1994), 298–317.

56. Petty, "Speculum Hiberniae," BL, fol. 12v, fol. 13r.

57. Lady Ranelagh, autograph notes, Add. MS 72,884, vol. 35, Petty Papers, BL, fol. 7r.

58. Gillespie, *Seventeenth Century Ireland*, 261. See also Canny, *Upstart Earl*, 132.

59. Lady Ranelagh to Second Earl of Cork, September 2, n.y., BL.

6

The Place of Ireland in the Letters of the First Duchess of Ormonde

NAOMI MCAREAVEY

The First Duchess of Ormonde, Elizabeth Butler, née Preston (1615–84), is little known to scholars of early modern women's writing, yet she is the author of the largest body of extant correspondence of any woman from seventeenth-century Ireland and was arguably the most powerful and well-connected Irish woman of her time.[1] As Countess, Marchioness, then Duchess of Ormonde, as well as high-ranking Stuart courtier and three-times Irish vicereine, she sat at the pinnacle of Irish society through more than six decades of extraordinary social and political upheaval, unmatched by any other Irish woman of the period in terms of her wealth, social standing, and political sway. Her substantial correspondence reflects her importance within the Ormonde Butler family and in the social, cultural, and political life of seventeenth-century Ireland. Her three-hundred-plus surviving letters are addressed to her husband and family, agents and servants, and friends and clients and span the years between 1630 and 1684, traversing the 1641 rebellion, the wars of the Three Kingdoms, royalist defeat and exile, the Interregnum, the Restoration, and beyond. Together they offer an important Irish female perspective on these key decades of Three Kingdoms history; they illuminate the duchess's crucial involvement in the protection and advancement of Ormonde family interests;

and—most important for this chapter—they demonstrate the centrality of Ireland in her life and writing.

My chapter focuses specifically on letters written during the Interregnum (1649–60), a period that is crucial in establishing the importance of Ireland in the Duchess of Ormonde's epistolary construction of self. These were the years when the Three Kingdoms were radically transformed in the wake of royalist defeat, and Elizabeth Ormonde reconstituted her status in the family, as her husband's exile led to her compounding for a portion of their confiscated Irish estates. My chapter examines her epistolary life writing in the context of the changing dynamics of the Three Kingdoms, exploring her shaping of life-changing experiences, first during her own royalist exile in Caen; then as she petitioned the protectorate government for her family's confiscated estate; then during her retirement at her house in Dunmore, County Kilkenny; and, finally, as she received news of the Restoration and prepared to be reunited with her husband in the London court. My chapter thus tracks her independent rise to power in her family and in Ireland through the process of successfully reclaiming part of the family's Irish estates. Obtaining her lands with the right conditions to make it possible to retire to Ireland forced her to become a political agent in her own right, operating between England and Ireland as she negotiated between Oliver Cromwell in London and his commissioners in Dublin and utilizing political networks spanning the Three Kingdoms. When she finally settled in Dunmore, she functioned effectively as matriarchal head of the Ormonde Butler family, managing the estate, controlling the purse strings, overseeing improvements to the estate, and developing an Ireland-centered client base that she activated on her husband's behalf at the Restoration. As Elizabeth Ormonde mobilized her own lineage and inheritance to establish herself, in her husband's absence, as head of the family, Ireland moved to the heart of her epistolary self-representation, where it remained for the rest of her writing life.

Elizabeth Butler, née Preston, was born in 1615, the only child of Elizabeth Butler (d. 1628), sole surviving legitimate child of Thomas Butler, Tenth Earl of Ormonde (d. 1614); and Richard Preston, Baron Dingwall, later Earl of Desmond (d. 1628), a Scottish court noble and favorite of James VI and I.[2] After the death of her maternal grandfather, the tenth earl, her father laid claim to the Ormonde title and estate in his wife's name. Although he failed to obtain the earldom (which was entailed in the male line), thanks to the personal interventions of the king, Preston and his wife were controversially awarded more than half of the Ormonde estate at the expense of the eleventh earl, a prominent Catholic dissident.[3] Ten years later, in October 1628, the estate was inherited by the couple's thirteen-year-old daughter when she was bereaved of both parents. The orphaned girl was taken as a ward of the court and placed into the care of Henry Rich, First Earl of Holland. Plans were quickly made for her to marry her second cousin, James Butler, grandson and heir to the Eleventh Earl of Ormonde, who had also been brought up as a Protestant after being claimed as a ward of the Crown upon the death of his father and put into the care of the archbishop of Canterbury. The couple married in December 1629, and the reunification of the Ormonde title and estate in Protestant hands was secured when the groom inherited the earldom in 1633. In the years that followed, the new Earl of Ormonde rose from relative obscurity to become lord lieutenant of Ireland for the first of three times in November 1643. He commanded the king's forces in Ireland during the wars of the Three Kingdoms, went into exile with Charles II after his defeat, and during the Restoration was lavishly rewarded for his loyalty with a dukedom.

Typical of the Irish elite of the period, the Duke and Duchess of Ormonde spent their lives between Ireland and England. Like her husband, the duchess was born in London, was raised in England, spent long stretches of her married life in England, and died and was buried in the English capital. Yet the couple had significant interests in Ireland, and their lives involved frequent journeys across the Irish Sea as well as long periods of residence in the country. They owned extensive land and several homes in Ireland, including the family seat at Kilkenny Castle, Ormond Castle in Carrick-on-Suir, and the duchess's favorite house at Dunmore; they also occupied Dublin Castle during the duke's three terms as lord lieutenant. During their lifetimes they owned or rented several homes in England, including a country residence at Moor Park and a London townhouse in

St. James's Square, and they had apartments in Whitehall, where the duke served Charles II in various roles, including the lord stewardship. The duke rose through the ranks of the Irish peerage (earl in 1633, marquis in 1642, duke in 1661), ultimately becoming a duke in the English peerage in 1682. The duchess shared her husband's titles as his consort but also held the Scottish title of Baroness Dingwall in her own right. In Ireland the couple presided over a large and overwhelmingly Catholic kinship network, with the duchess's correspondence revealing the substantial role she played in sustaining relationships with her Catholic in-laws. Her letters also provide evidence that she maintained contact with her father's Scottish family, acting as advocate for her paternal cousin Sir George Preston and remaining close friends with Anne Hume, the widow of a friend of her father, who later married her husband's half brother, Capt. George Mathew. The duke and duchess enjoyed significant Welsh connections through the duke's half siblings, including Mathew, who, as the couple's estate manager, was the recipient of the majority of the duchess's surviving letters. Mathew, Hume, and Preston each enjoyed Welsh or Scottish ancestry, but their interests, as clients of the Duke and Duchess of Ormonde, lay squarely in Ireland.

Throughout her correspondence the Duchess of Ormonde consistently represents Ireland as part of the composite monarchy of the Stuart kings, but she only once describes England, Ireland, and Scotland collectively as the "Three Kingdoms": upon hearing news of Charles II's Restoration, she wrote to her husband to share her joy that "that Bondage under which the three kingdoms as well as my selfe has Sufferede, shouldbee now by his Mercye removede, and our Longe wisht for Blessinge of the kings restoratione at the Length Establishede to uss."[4] Elsewhere in her correspondence she occasionally refers to England and Ireland as "this kingdome" or "that kingdome," depending on where she is writing. There are nineteen uses of the word "kingdome" throughout her letters; in contrast, the word "nation" appears only three times, and this includes two references from the Interregnum. Her conception of the relationship between the Three Kingdoms is fundamentally royalist, and she sees Ireland as one of the dominions of the Stuart kings. For her the relationship between Ireland and its neighbors is mutual; she does not assume the centrality of England (except as the location of king and court). In fact, throughout her correspondence the Duchess of Ormonde refers explicitly to Ireland nearly three times as often as to England (ninety-six to Ireland against thirty-six to England). If we add to this her allusions to specific Irish locations like Kilkenny (fifty-nine), Dunmore (thirty-seven), Carrick [Carrick-on-Suir] (ten), and Dublin (seventy-six), it is clear that Ireland is at the heart of her epistolary concerns. There are only two references to "Scotland" and one to the "Scots," all of which are impersonal, which suggests that her interests in Scotland are focused on the Preston kin who had settled in Ireland; Wales is mentioned only when she describes her routes to England from Ireland via Holyhead. Ultimately, the Duchess of Ormonde's "Three Kingdoms" model for the relationships within the archipelago is one in which only England and Ireland matter, and where (for her) Irish concerns are central and English concerns peripheral.

Although she lived her life between the two countries, the Duchess of Ormonde never describes herself or her family as "English" or "Irish." "Irish" is used a mere three times in her correspondence, entirely reserved for Catholic natives; and "English" is used only ten times (five from the same Commonwealth testimony in which she remembers experiences in the 1641 rebellion), applying exclusively to settlers and newcomers. The duchess's understanding of both the "English" and the "Irish" is strongly inflected by her perception of their relative social and economic status; in both cases she refers specifically to members of the middling and lower ranks of Irish society, with the possible implication that such categories do not apply to the highly mobile Irish elite. She tends to associate the lower-ranked "English" with positive qualities, while the "Irish" are repre-sented negatively: for example, she once seeks a "good English responsable Tenant" for Dunmore, while elsewhere she accuses "tow Irishe Men" of thieving on her lands.[5] Yet even these examples may better illuminate her sensitivity to distinctions in social rank rather than nationality and betray the fact that in early modern Ireland non-elite settlers generally occupied higher positions than non-elite natives and were therefore more likely to enter an aristocratic estate as tenants than as poachers.

The Duchess of Ormonde avoids religious categories in her letters even more than national ones. She never uses the term "Protestant," although she does write to her husband in 1660 sharing her fears about the malevolent "Sectories and Phanatickes" that might threaten his life.[6] Only once does she refer to the "Roman Catholiks," again in a letter to her husband, this time about local resistance to the couple's establishment of a Protestant school in Kilkenny.[7] The duchess uses confessional labels only when they are absolutely necessary and certainly never as shorthand for national affiliations. Since the Duchess of Ormonde and her husband were Protestants vastly outnumbered by their Catholic kin, it is not surprising that she avoids the heavily fraught issue of religious identity in her letters, especially those written to Catholics (such as her brother-in-law Mathew). Instead, she overwhelmingly focuses on the beliefs that she and her correspondents share, and a nondenominational "God" is cited forty-four times in her letters. Even still, she rarely discusses religious matters, and there is little evidence in her letters that she was especially pious.

If the Duchess of Ormonde herself eschewed the labels of "Irish" or "English," "Catholic" or "Protestant," it remains difficult to place her within such binary categories. The Ormonde Butler family from whom she descended and into which she married are commonly described as Old English—that is, the descendants of the Anglo-Norman invaders of the twelfth century who had remained loyal to the English Crown but over the centuries had become increasingly assimilated with the Irish natives, sharing much of their language and culture and especially their religion. The Catholicism of the Old English is what marked them apart from the New English settlers who came to Ireland in the sixteenth and seventeenth centuries and who were promoted to positions of power at the expense of Catholics. When the Old English joined their co-religionists in rebellion in 1641, they indicated a stronger affinity with Irish Catholics than English Protestants. The Duchess of Ormonde and her husband opposed the rebellion, but they more fundamentally diverged from other Old English in their Protestantism. Acknowledging this distinction, historians have sometimes labeled the Duke of Ormonde "Anglo-Irish."[8] However, as a term that is most associated with the later Protestant Ascendancy, it is not only slightly anachronistic but perhaps also overemphasizes his Protestantism, which if not ambivalent was certainly not something he was particularly keen to highlight.[9] "English-Irish" might be a preferable label since it acknowl-edges the couple's dual national allegiances without specifically evoking their Protestantism. By also suggesting that "English-Irish" is a variant of a broadly "Irish" identity, the term also usefully privileges the Irishness of the Ormonde Butlers.

Even though she never uses the term to describe herself, I consider the Duchess of Ormonde "Irish" because Ireland, if not Irishness, is at the heart of her self-representation. Whether she writes *in* Ireland or *to* Ireland, all her surviving letters are *about* Ireland, its land, its people, its politics, and above all her family's interests in the country. There is no doubt that for the Duchess of Ormonde Ireland is home; it offers safety and security, financial stability, and deep connections. England, in contrast, more often represents marginalization, alienation, disempowerment, and insecurity; her seemingly interminable stays there (1655–57, 1668–73) are marked by frustration, disenchantment, and an overwhelming desire to return home. This is distinctly *her* experience, however: her husband seemed at ease in both places and certainly appeared to feel more at home in England than his wife ever did. That this difference was shaped by the gendered division of roles and responsibilities in the marriage—the duke managing the family's political position vis-à-vis the king, and the duchess looking after their landed interests—is the concern of the rest of the chapter, where I suggest that the couple's different relationships with Ireland have their roots in the Interregnum and the journeys husband and wife take, literally in opposite directions from each other, as the duchess returned *to* Ireland from continental exile and the duke left Ireland *for* continental exile. As the couple swap places at the beginning of their decade-long separation, their distinct but mutually beneficial priorities are reflected in the duke throwing in his lot with the king and the duchess with country.

The Duchess of Ormonde's relationship with Ireland was transformed by the circumstances of royalist defeat and exile. Since September 1648, the then Marchioness of Ormonde had lived in Caen, France, among other Irish royalists, where she had maintained a regular correspondence with Sir Edward Nicholas, secretary of state to Charles I (and later Charles II), and other key figures in the exiled court, sharing information pertaining to the ongoing wars in Ireland.[10] Her letters reveal her role in mediating between the court in exile and her husband in Ireland as he fought for the last remaining Stuart kingdom. The eventual defeat of the king's army forced the marquis to flee the country, but rather than the couple abandoning the family's Irish interests altogether, Lady Ormonde stepped into the space left by her husband's departure to ensure that the destruction of royalist interests in Ireland did not lead to the neglect of her family's. She thus sought to safeguard the significant Ormonde estates from the moment her husband could no longer do so.

As she prepared to start the petitionary process, the marchioness wrote to Secretary Nicholas explaining the reasons for her decision. First, she described the circumstances that led to her husband's flight from Ireland; insisting that the marquis refused to be a "furthar wittness of *that Pepells* disobedianse and Contempt of the kings othoritye," she attributes his defeat to the disloyality of the Confederate Catholics.[11] This is disingenuous, however, given her knowledge of the king's culpability for his Irish Catholic subjects' loss of faith. In January 1649 the marquis had concluded the Second Ormonde Peace with the Confederate Catholics, which promised religious toleration in exchange for troops to fight for the king. But on May 1, 1650, Charles II signed the Treaty of Breda with the Scottish Covenanters and under the terms of the treaty pledged to abolish Catholicism in his realms. The king's betrayal of the deal that her husband had brokered precipitated the collapse of the precarious royalist alliance in Ireland and the final destruction of royalist interests in the country, but the marchioness skirts over these issues, instead scapegoating the Confederate Catholics for the failings of the king and his lord lieutenant.

Elizabeth Ormonde carefully distinguishes her husband from his erstwhile Confederate allies, whom she dismisses as disloyal and self-interested, and establishes the marquis as an exceptional figure and the only true representative of Irish royalism. The marquis is characterized by his selfless devotion to the king, with his wife claiming that his unwavering royalism, even in defeat, meant that he "did absolutlye refuse to Treate or acsept anye Conditions from Cromwells Partye; though very good ons have bine offerede hime Consarninge his Estate." She draws attention to his considerable financial losses and emphasizes their family's ensuing destitution when she points out that her husband acted "with soe Litell Consideratione to what might Consarne his Future ^Subsistanse^ as hee hass made noe kind of provitione for it."[12] Although grounds for complaint, her husband's lack of concern for his family's welfare is more positively construed as an instance of his commendable—and self-sacrificing—devotion to the king.

While claiming that her husband's actions have effectively subordinated her family's needs to those of the king, the marchioness suggests that responsibility for their family's welfare now falls on her shoulders. "I begine to See that my Nesesities will Ere Longe Forse mee to what of all the things in the world is the most Contrarye to My inclinatione," she confesses to Nicholas, her insistent use of the first-person singular implying that a decision that was in fact made in consultation with her husband was entirely hers.[13] She therefore ensures that as she moves to negotiate with Cromwell and his Commonwealth government, her husband's impeccable royalist credentials are upheld. She, on the other hand, is forced to abandon her own royalism as she sets her sights on the family's estates in Cromwellian Ireland. In her formal petition, dated May 2, 1652, circumstance and epistolary convention force her to humble herself before the lord protector. She writes with ostentatious deference, addressing Cromwell as "My Lord" twice and "your Lordshipp" nine times, using double negatives in expressing her wish that she will be thought "not uncapabill" of receiving his favor, and signing herself "your Lordshipps humbel Sarvant."[14] Yet she perhaps adds a subversive flourish if the black wax with which her letter was sealed was meant to signify her continued mourning for the martyred King Charles I.

Certainly, it seems that Lady Ormonde felt under less pressure to renounce her own royalist sympathies than to disavow her Cavalier husband in communications to Lord Protector Cromwell. In the wording of her petitionary letter, she effectively writes her husband out of Ormonde Butler family history, instead justifying her claim to Irish lands through her own matrilineal descent from the family. She makes no claim to her husband's estate; instead, she explains to Cromwell that "thar desendede to mee ane Estate of inheritanse in Irland" and requests that *this* is used to provide a portion for her maintenance. She contends that, like the rest of the Ormonde estate, the land of her inheritance "is now by warr and pestelanse very much depopulatede and not Like to bee without much troubill profitabill for a Longe Time."[15] Yet she implies that she alone has the will and know-how to generate an income from these lands—an income that she suggests will benefit the Cromwellian state as much as herself. She reminds Cromwell of how "great ane obligatione you have in your power to plase upon mee" and tentatively suggests that their relationship might become an alliance through which her Irish connections and experience are the reward for his benevolence. Thus committing herself and her children to long-term settlement in Cromwellian Ireland, Lady Ormonde (rhetorically at least) abandons her husband to his own resources on the continent.

Although between the lines of her letter Lady Ormonde implies her high status in Ireland and potential value as an ally, her primary rhetorical strategy nevertheless emphasizes her vulnerability. This frames her approach to the petitionary process overall: as an heiress, her settlement should not have been sequestered along with her husband's, but she chose (or was advised) to overlook this right and instead sue only for relief.[16] Throwing herself on the "generositye" of the lord protector, she stresses the precariousness of her situation as one now "in Niede of protectione and assistanse." She foregrounds her responsibilities as a mother and insists that if her request was granted, the estate would be used only "to raise a Subsistanse for my Selfe and Chilldren."[17] Her affiliation with her royalist husband is comprehensively erased as her needs as a woman and a mother are stressed.

The extent to which this rhetorical strategy was of her own making can be seen in the contrast with two earlier letters written on her behalf by her husband when she was in Caen and he still in Ireland. With a note inscribed on the first letter by a secretary stipulating that "My lord would have my lady to write this letter to Sir Thomas fairfax to which purpose you are directed to Send it to her decyphered by a Safe express speedyly," the letters are addressed to the parliamentarian general Lord Fairfax and his cousin, the Earl of Mulgrave, respectively, and dated March 1649. They were handwritten by the marquis, and, given the evidence of judicious revisions, he composed the letters with great care with the intention that his wife should copy them to send in her own name. In the letter to Sir Thomas Fairfax, the marquis ventriloquizes his wife's voice, requesting the general's intervention so that "my lords servant may receive the mony ^remaineing^ due to him to his according to the termes set downe by the Commitee at Derby house without which without which I shall bee wholy disapoynted of the meanes of subsistence designed for mee and the family left with mee."[18] By deleting "to him" and "to his," the marquis cautiously eliminates any suggestion that the money is due to him, instead emphasizing that it is solely for the use of his wife and children. But the first draft suggests that his impulse was to stress his role in providing for his wife and children. In the revised draft his wife remains scripted into a passive voice and position, as she is required to speak as the subject of her husband's care or "design." In stark contrast the marchioness claims in her own letter to Nicholas that her husband left Ireland without having made adequate provision for his family, which points to her deliberate reworking of the model her husband provided.[19] While he is keen to emphasize his fulfilment of duties as husband and father, she highlights his neglect, and in doing so she balances her husband's loyal devotion to the king with her uncompromising dedication to her family.

In making her claim the Marchioness of Ormonde was fortunate to have the support and assistance of many high-ranking figures in the Commonwealth government in England and especially in Ireland. The Dublin-based commissioner of revenue, Sir Robert King, for example, wrote, "It is hard that she that was born to a great inheritance shall want bread for her children because of her Lord's delinquency, and I believe was not practiced by her."[20] These comments suggest that he and others were willing to consider Elizabeth Ormonde's estate and politics separately from her husband, and although the marquis should be punished by confiscation of his estate, his wife should not suffer the loss of her own inheritance. Her claim was successful, and on February 1, 1653, the commissioners of Parliament in Ireland were instructed to set aside Dunmore House, near Kilkenny, with 2,000 pounds per annum out of the lands of her own inheritance for the use of her and her children on the condition that no part of the revenue should be diverted to her husband.[21]

But when the schedule of lands and rents assigned for her maintenance were examined in December 1653, it became clear that the income produced fell far short of the promised 2,000 pound annuity; in some cases taxes absorbed between 50 and 80 percent of the rents.[22] The Marchioness of Ormonde therefore spent the middle years of the 1650s between London and Dublin, trying to negotiate the conditions that would make her much anticipated retirement to Dunmore possible. These negotiations involved the navigation of complex political situations in London and Dublin, particularly between Cromwell and his Irish commissioners. Letters sent during what turned out to be, unhappily, a protracted stay in England from 1655 to 1657 showcase the challenges the Marchioness of Ormonde faced in her dealings with Cromwell and his government in England and Ireland. The circumstances were particularly fraught given that the Down Survey of Ireland was being taken at the time, which sought to measure all the land to be forfeited by Irish royalists, mainly but not exclusively Catholic, to facilitate its redistribution to merchant adventurers and English soldiers.[23] Elizabeth Ormonde was keen to ensure that her settlement was not included with forfeited land, and her letters shed light on the challenges of reclaiming confiscated land, as well as the struggles between landowners and the adventurers, which would persist for decades.[24] Her experience shows how little difference was made between Catholic and Protestant royalists in Cromwellian Ireland. That she did protect her settlement was attributable to her political connections as much as the hard work of her agent, John Burdon. The marchioness's letters reveal her particular indebtedness to two members of the Boyle family: Katherine, Lady Ranelagh (referred to as "the Lady"), and her brother Roger, Lord Broghill, later Earl of Orrery, one of the trustees of Lady Ormonde's estates, both of whom wielded influence with Cromwell.[25] Their patronage ensured that by autumn 1657 the Marchioness of Ormonde was finally able to take her three younger children to Dunmore, having safely dispatched her elder sons to the continent.

A letter written to Burdon, in Dublin, as she was about to depart from Bristol gives rare access to her emotional turmoil during what had been probably the most difficult period of her life. She looks back on the preceding years as having "Cast greater diffeculties upon mee, then canbee well imaginede, but by thous [those], whoe has bine a wittnes what a Laborious and Sad time I have had, to suport my selfe, and Familie." Her hopes for a new life with her youngest children in Dunmore were modest: "that God has designede mee, though I Covete Not great wealth, yet such a Competensie with a private Life, as may inabell mee to pay my depts and reward my such of My Sarvants as has Sarvede mee industerouslie and fathfullye"; Burdon is identified as "one of the prinsepall" of these. In this, her last letter written on English soil before the Restoration, the marchioness expresses her hope and belief that at last "the worst of my ^ill^ Fortune is Past."[26] Her optimism seems to have been justified, as her retirement in Dunmore brought a measure of comfort and security, and she immediately set about improving the house and estate.[27] Settling into the home she inherited from her mother, it seems that Lady Ormonde expected to remain in Ireland, in her own right, for the foreseeable future.

Despite being barred from contact with her husband, the Marchioness of Ormonde maintained a clandestine correspondence with him throughout her time in Dunmore. Letters bear witness to a power struggle between the couple, showing that in her husband's absence the marchioness assumed a new position of authority in the family based on her location in Ireland and, more important, her sole ownership, occupation, and management of what remained of the Ormonde estate. The marchioness's assertion of power was facilitated by the material conditions of maintaining a secret correspondence with her husband, which necessitated the concealment of her identity and that of her family circle. In the letters she disguises her handwriting, addresses her husband as "Sir" (once specifically naming him as "Mr Benss" and once as "Mr James Johnson"), and signs herself as his "frind and Sarvant," "JH." Through this persona she refers to herself in the third person, either as the anonymous "frind" of the addressee or variously named as "Mrs Beckett," "Mrs Rashlye," or "Mr Dallison," and she constructs "JH" as a disinterested agent or intermediary between her husband and herself. The reconstituted relationship with her absent husband is signified materially on the letters as she eshews the deferential space between text and signature that would be expected in a letter from wife to husband, instead pointedly placing her "JH" signature immediately underneath the text to emphasize their equality.[28] This performed equality is facilitated by their physical distance and specifically the political circumstances of their separation and her residence in Ireland. In conversations between the couple that take place in the letters—mainly about their sons' education and the prospective marriages of their eldest son and eldest daughter—the epistolary persona of male friend seems to liberate Elizabeth Ormonde from obligations of wifely deference, while the facade of the emotional distance and objectivity of a third party enables her to be less self-censoring than she might have been had she written the letters in her own name. And, as important, it seems, particularly as relations become more strained, is the fictional agent's proximity to the Irish estates and their owner.

The license that the pseudonym of "JH" gives for free and open communication with her husband is borne out when she addresses the contentious issue of their eldest son's marriage. Thomas, Earl of Ossory, had fallen in love with Emilia van Beverwart, daughter of Lodewyk van Nassau, governor of Sluys in the Netherlands. Ossory's father had given his cautious approval to the match, but the agreement of his mother was needed to approve the financial settlement, and the marchioness vigorously opposed the marriage. In the first letter to her husband on the topic, she mobilizes the persona of "JH," saying "I showede your frind the proposals of a mach for hir elldest sone," before listing her several objections to the marriage. She writes that she "consevede just cause of exseptione as to the desent of the ladys father, which however not perhapes the less estimede in another contrye, would make it of reproach heare." From her location in Ireland, she disparages the lineage of the van Beverwarts, perhaps because the family was an illegitimate branch of the ruling house of Orange. She also rejects a Dutch connection more broadly, comparing it unfavorably with other matches closer to home, which she claims are "more sutabell in respect of the advantages of thar allianse, then what this stranger cane bringe."[29] While her exiled husband seems to have supported Ossory's marriage partly because of the Dutch alliances that it would bring to the king, she, writing from Ireland, explicitly favors a match closer to home. Whereas her husband places his family's long-terms hopes with the exiled king, she locates them more practically within Commonwealth Ireland.

But more important for her is the issue of money. The marchioness was struggling to maintain her family on a much reduced estate, so in her letter she reminds her husband of the mortgage on the estate, the expense of recovering it, and the dowries needed for her two daughters. She speaks rationally and practically, letting the evidence speak for itself, and so concludes, "for which considered, as shee hopes it will bee seriouslie by hir sone, and shuch of his frinds as are ther, will shee hopes give a stope unto his rueninge of his familie, to please his fancye."[30] Adopting the voice of a disinterested intermediary, she is forthright in her rejection of the proposed marriage, allowing no room for debate, and simply listing her objections without qualification or apology. Although occasionally she betrays some anxiety about her forthrightness, particularly when it involves "displeasinge" her husband, she rarely wavers in her sense of her own authority, which emerges as strongly in her direct response to her son. In this letter she reminds Ossory of his and his father's absence from the estate and the day-to-day business of generating an income and insists that in these circumstances only she can make an informed decision on such an important family matter.[31] Her role safeguarding the Irish estates confers on her an authority above that of her absentee husband and son.

Even when she finally conceded to the match, she continued to drag her feet. With her formal approval and signature necessary for the negotiations to proceed, she simply refused to provide either, exploiting the difficulties of getting letters between Ireland and the court in exile, as well as other practical constraints in letter writing, as a way of avoiding charges of obstinacy or neglect. Her husband was evidently attuned to these manipulations, as several months into the discussions and during the formal negotiations in The Hague in May 1659, she wrote to "vindecate" herself. The letter she received from her husband admonishing her is not extant, but her response from May 19, 1659—four months to the day since her last extant letter—protests against any "misconstroctione" of her motives, explaining that she was "not at this time soe well in hir health as to write hir selfe by reson of a Cough that has troubled hir of Late." Elizabeth Ormonde's resentment of her husband and son's persistence is thinly veiled, the defense unconvincing, and an apology unforthcoming. Moreover, when she insists that she "never as yet did declyne the owninge and payinge of a respect ~~where~~ and obligation where it was soe much dew," the revision of her text reveals the reluctance with which she complies with her husband's wishes. This is not simply a "respect"; it is also an "obligation," and the speed with which she adds the word "obligation" (it is an immediate addition rather than a later insertion) lays bare the resentment that she barely attempts to conceal.[32] Overall, the letters betray her frustration that her expertise in estate matters is not fully recognized by her husband and son and also show how she exploits her Irish-based authority to champion her new status over the displaced men in her family.

Letters written in the wake of the Restoration of Charles II in May 1660 reflect how family dynamics shifted once again, as Elizabeth Ormonde prepared to leave Ireland to be reunited with her husband in London. The new balance of power is registered materially on the first letter she writes to her newly "avowede" husband, as she offers due deference in the significant space created by his "most affectionat wife." The marchioness professes her joy that the "Bondage under which the three kingdoms as well as my selfe has sufferede, shouldbee now by [God's] mercye removede" and describes the Restoration as "such a motive of admiratione and joy to all, and perticularlie to mee, as is unexpresabell." Yet while bringing an end to the "Bondage" she has endured is undoubtedly a cause for celebration, since it guarantees a massive improvement in her family's fortunes, the Restoration leads to her displacement from the position of authority she enjoyed, as the locus of Ormonde Butler power and authority moves away from Ireland. As her family's prospects relocate to her husband and the restored court, Elizabeth Ormonde begins to rewrite recent history. First, she reimagines her years in Dunmore as no longer a period of relative contentment but as an experience of enslavement. She depicts herself as having been a co-participant in an exile experience that she had in fact prudently avoided. She also revises the period of the couple's estrangement as an "8 yeares absense," but representing herself, not her husband, as having been away. Making significant deletions in her letter (she cancels "from you" after mentioning her "absense"), the marchioness suggests that her separation was not just from her husband but from the king and his court also, her suffering compounded by her displacement from the royalist community. Celebrating "our longe wisht for blessinge of the kings restoratione at length establishede to uss," she attempts to reintegrate with the royalist community. She professes her "dewtye for your Master" and admits to her husband that her "reveranse" "forbides the presomtione of anye congratulorye addrese," beseeching the marquis to be "soe just to mee as to let hime know untell I may have the honner to kiss his hands."[33] The marchioness thus recognizes that she is dependent on her husband to facilitate her reentry to the court.

The flurry of letters sent to her husband as Elizabeth Ormonde made preparations to join the court on its triumphant return to London expresses a combination of exhilaration, disorientation, and anxiety as she contemplates the seismic changes that the Restoration will bring to her, her family, and the Three Kingdoms. The last letter sent to her husband just before she leaves Dublin brings these different emotions together, and what particularly emerges is her trepidation about facing the hubbub of London after the relative peace and quiet of Dunmore, and she shares her preference for lodgings in Chelsea or Richmond, where she would be away from "the Hurye of pepell, and the Noysomnes of that great Towne."[34] She insists that her eldest son and his new wife find their own home because "the troubell of haveinge a Nothar Familie in My House is; from Comminge from a retyrede life a troubill I cannot undertake."[35] Morbid fears sit alongside social unease as the marchioness shares her concerns over the possibility of attempts against the life of the king or the marquis himself.[36] For Elizabeth Ormonde, it seems, relocating to London is neither easy nor desired; Ireland is where she is most at home.

Letters to her husband are mainly concerned with the distribution of patronage, and Elizabeth Ormonde takes upon herself the responsibility for recommending clients in Ireland to her husband in the restored court. One of these letters of recommendation stands out for the way it manifests materially the excited chaos of this period. The main body of the letter recommends one Captain Power; then a postscript acknowledges correspondence received but overlooked in the main body of the letter, "The good Neuse haueinge made mee allmost as wilde, as it has done many wisser persons"; then she writes, "I pray turne the leafe," and inserts a new leaf on which a recommendation is made for a second man, Walter Plunkett; yet another postscript is then added after the letter has been folded and sealed.[37] The letter showcases the marchioness's status at the helm of a wide-ranging Ireland-based patronage network, indicating that she can barely keep up with the demands of her new role mediating between clients in Ireland and her husband at court.

The Marchioness of Ormonde invariably cites her clients' loyalty to her husband and the king, highlighting their role in maintaining the king's interests in Ireland. She implies that she is best equipped to identify those Irish men who should be rewarded for loyal service. Often she brings favored clients to her husband's notice as bearers of her letters, writing of one hopeful gentleman that she "couldnot oblidge hime more then by giveinge hime the oppertunitie of it, have chossene hime to bee the mesenger of this." She also advocates for this client not only because he has proven himself loyal to the king and to Ormonde but also because he "has in your absense, and my nesesities, bine frindlie to mee." Among those recommended to her husband's service is her "ould Sarvant," John Burdon, "whoe is Now as Sober and abbell a Secretarye as anye that I doe beleve you Cane light upon and willbee very ussfull to you upon Sondrie ocations."[38] In a list of remembrances that she intended to be delivered to her husband by her close friend, Anne Hume, the marchioness asks that her husband "show a respect unto my Lady of R[anelagh] upon the account of her kindness to me."[39] Indeed, as she anticipated the formal announcement of the king's Restoration, her first priority was to acknowledge the network of female friends who had supported and sustained her during the previous decade, directing her husband (via an agent, Stephen Smith) to visit the Dowager Lady Devonshire, the Lady Marchioness of Dorchester, Lady Strafford, the Dowager Lady of Peterborough, the Dowager Lady Derby, Lady Ranelagh, Lady Anne Savile, and the Countess of Dysart, all women whom she identifies as being "soe perticularlie kind and Frindlie to Mee."[40] All these women are based in England, and all her important clients she sends to London: this indicates her sense that, for the moment at least, Ormonde Butler family interests lie in England.

While the Marchioness of Ormonde exploits her husband's newfound power in the revived court, she apologizes for making use of it and also proposes a novel way of dealing with the number of requests for patronage that she receives. In the memorandum to Hume, she asks for her husband to be acquainted that "such as recommendations as comes from mee, in the behalfe of Persons done rathar out of Complianse then respect, shallbee subscribed with the the leaving out of the ^leter^ E, at the Ende of the word ormond."[41] The spelling of the Ormonde title was flexible—her husband used both spellings, while she routinely adopted the (feminine) terminal "e"—and the marchioness exploits this flexibility to develop a secret code for communications with her husband: through this mechanism she later cues the marquis that a (halfhearted) recommendation for one Mr. Burneston was written under duress.[42] With the rudimentary code allowing the marchioness to maintain strict control over the family's distribution of patronage while at the same time placating hopeful clients, she is shown to be highly attuned to the precarious and sensitive political situation in Ireland. Although Elizabeth Ormonde ultimately defers to her husband's judgment when the people arrive at court, she does the initial filtering of their Irish client base. Her Irish-based patronage is key to putting Ireland firmly on her husband's political agenda in the restored court, but it is entirely dependent on her husband's proximity to the king. The couple's political position at the Restoration is thus dual-centered, with the marquis overseeing critical developments in the English capital and the marchioness doing the same in Ireland.

The Duchess of Ormonde's experiences during the Interregnum resonated for the rest of her life. Whether due to habit, interest, or expertise, from thenceforth she assumed primary responsibility for overseeing the management of the couple's sprawling Irish estates.[43] Her letters also demonstrate her lasting emotional and material investment in Dunmore House, which she continued to improve; at her insistence Dunmore provided the location for the marriage, in October 1662, of her younger daughter, Mary, to the grandson of the Dowager Lady Devonshire, one of the women who supported her during the Interregnum.[44] Elizabeth Ormonde continued to remember and reward those who had helped her during her husband's exile. As late as April 1672 she extended the lease of the son of an old servant who had been "Frindlie to mee, in Times when Few appiered Soe." And in spring 1666 she repaid the many favors of Lady Ranelagh by becoming her advocate following the contentious separation from her husband.[45] The duchess also preserved a warm friendship with Sir Edward Nicholas, who had supported her financially during her time in Caen.[46] Other relationships that trace their origins to the Interregnum did not fare so well. Her friendship with Ranelagh's brother, the Earl of Orrery (formerly Lord Broghill), soured to such an extent that in March 1669 she describes him as "the most false and ingratfull Person ^Man^ livinge" after he conspired with her husband's enemies at court to have him removed from the lord lieutenancy.[47] She also never warmed to her daughter-in-law, Lady Ossory, whom she often criticized for failing to meet her high standards of conduct, going so far as dismissing her as a "healples wife" when Ossory was serving as lord deputy after his father was summoned to the court to answer charges of misconduct.[48] Letters written during the couple's extended stay in England following the duke's dismissal from office once again show the duchess's abiding wish to return to Ireland, a place that for her continued to represent security, stability, and safety for her and her family.

The enduring legacy of the Interregnum for the Duchess of Ormonde might be found in the history of the vault in which she was buried in Westminster Abbey.[49] Now known as the Ormond vault, it was formerly called Cromwell's or Oliver's vault because this was where the lord protector had been buried before his body was exhumed for a posthumous execution at Tyburn in January 1661. That the duchess and her family came to occupy Cromwell's grave shows just how much life had changed for her family since the Interregnum. But as much of an honor as it was for the Duchess of Ormonde to be buried alongside English royalty in Westminster Abbey, it is unlikely to have been the resting place she had planned for herself. She had prepared Dunmore for her dowager house, and in her last letter written within weeks of her sudden death in July 1684 she shared plans for the couple's imminent return to Ireland.[50] This is a fitting end to a correspondence that, despite being overwhelmingly written in England, was always directed, literally and figuratively, across the Irish Sea to her home in Ireland.

NOTES

1. My edition of *The Letters of the First Duchess of Ormonde* will be published with the Arizona Center for Medieval and Renaissance Studies. For an assessment of the Duchess of Ormonde's significance in her family, see Eleanor O'Keeffe, "The Family and Marriage Strategies of James Butler, First Duke of Ormonde, 1658–1688" (PhD diss., University of Cambridge, 2000).

2. Timothy Wilks, *Of Neighing Coursers and Trumpets Shrill: A Life of Richard, 1st Lord Dingwall and Earl of Desmond (c. 1570–1628)* (London: Lucas, 2012).

3. This account is indebted to David Edwards, "The Poisoned Chalice: The Ormond Inheritance, Sectarian Division and the Emergence of James Butler, 1614–1642," in *The Dukes of Ormonde, 1610–1745*, ed. Toby Barnard and Jane Fenlon (Woodbridge: Boydell and Brewer, 2000), 58–64.

4. Elizabeth Ormonde to James, Marquis of Ormonde, May 11, 1660, Dunmore, MS 30, Carte Papers, Bodleian Library (Bodl.), Oxford, fol. 645.

5. Elizabeth Ormonde to Capt. George Mathew, September 13, 1673, MS 2,503, Ormond Papers, National Library of Ireland (NLI), Dublin, no. 122; Elizabeth Ormonde to John Burdon, June 24, 1658, Dunmore, MS 2,323, Ormond Papers, NLI, p. 305, no. 1288.

6. Elizabeth Ormonde to James, Marquis of Ormonde, June 4, 1660, Dunmore, MS 214, Carte Papers, Bodl., fols. 227–29.

7. E. Ormonde to James, Duke of Ormonde, June 18, 1669, Kilkenny, MS 243, Carte Papers, Bodl., fols. 24–25.

8. See, for example, Brian FitzGerald, *The Anglo-Irish: Three Representative Types: Cork, Ormonde, Swift, 1602–1745* (London: Staples, 1952).

9. Raymond Gillespie, "The Religion of the First Duke of Ormond," in Barnard and Fenlon, *Dukes of Ormonde*, 101–14.

10. On the Irish exile community, see Mark R. F. Williams, *The King's Irishmen: The Irish in the Exiled Court of Charles II, 1649–1660* (Woodbridge: Boydell, 2014).

11. E. Ormonde to Sir Edward Nicholas, January 19, 1650/51, MS 2,534, Egerton Manuscripts, British Library (BL), London, fol. 44 (emphasis added).

12. E. Ormonde to Nicholas, January 19, 1650/51, BL.

13. E. Ormonde to Nicholas, January 19, 1650/51, BL.

14. E. Ormonde to Lord Protector Cromwell, May 2, 1652, Caen, MS 138, Society of Antiquaries, London.

15. E. Ormonde to Cromwell, May 2, 1652, Society of Antiquaries.

16. Antonia Fraser, *The Weaker Vessel: Woman's Lot in Seventeenth-Century England* (London: Weidenfeld and Nicolson, 1984), 251.

17. E. Ormonde to Cromwell, May 2, 1652, Society of Antiquaries.

18. E. Ormonde to Sir Thomas Fairfax, March 24, 1648/49, MS 24, Carte Papers, Bodl., fol. 202.

19. E. Ormonde to Nicholas, January 19, 1650/51, BL.

20. Sir Robert King to William Basil, October 6, 1652, in Historical Manuscripts Commission, *Calendar of the Manuscripts of the Marquess of Ormonde*, n.s., 8 vols. (London, 1902–20), 1:266.

21. See Historical Manuscripts Commission, *Calendar of the Manuscripts*, 2:373–75. See also Conleth Manning, "The 1653 Survey of the Lands Granted to the Countess of Ormond in Co. Kilkenny," *Journal of the Royal Society of Antiquaries of Ireland* 129 (1999): 40–66.

22. This account is drawn from Winifred Gardner (Lady Burghclere), *The Life of James, First Duke of Ormonde, 1610–1688*, 2 vols. (London: Murray, 1912), 1:438, where more details can be found. Official documents relating to E. Ormonde's settlement can be found in MSS 2499–2501, Ormond Papers, NLI.

23. See the Down Survey of Ireland database, http://downsurvey.tcd.ie.

24. E. Ormonde to John Burdon, September 21, 1655, [London], MS 2,321, Ormond Papers, NLI, p. 225, no. 1,147.

25. E. Ormonde to John Burdon, August 8, 1657, MS 2,322, Ormond Papers, NLI, p. 385, no. 1,236.

26. E. Ormonde to Burdon, September 16, 1657, [Bristol], MS 2,322, Ormond Papers, NLI, p. 413, no. 1,240.

27. Jane Fenlon, "The Duchess of Ormonde's House at Dunmore, County Kilkenny," in *Kilkenny: Studies in Honour of Margaret M. Phelan*, ed. John Kirwan (Kilkenny: Kilkenny Archaeological Society, 1997), 79–87.

28. Jonathan Gibson, "Significant Space in Manuscript Letters," *Seventeenth Century* 12, no. 1 (1997): 1–10.

29. E. Ormonde to James, Marquis of Ormonde, November 26, 1658, [Dunmore], MS 213, Carte Papers, Bodl., fols. 168–69.

30. E. Ormonde to J. Ormonde, November 26, 1658, Bodl.

31. E. Ormonde to Thomas, Earl of Ossory, [October 1658], [Dunmore], MS 213, Carte Papers, Bodl., fol. 449.

32. E. Ormonde to J. Ormonde, May 19, 1659, [Dunmore], MS 213, Carte Papers, Bodl., fols. 244–45.

33. E. Ormonde to J. Ormonde, May 11, 1660, Bodl.

34. E. Ormonde to J. Ormonde, June 4, 1660, Bodl.

35. E. Ormonde to [Anne] Hume, [May 1660], MS 214, Carte Papers, Bodl., fols. 221–22.

36. E. Ormonde to J. Ormonde, June 4, 1660, Bodl.

37. E. Ormonde to J. Ormonde, May 21, 1660, Dublin, MS 214, Carte Papers, Bodl., fols. 87–88.

38. E. Ormonde to J. Ormonde, May 21, 1660, Bodl.

39. E. Ormonde to Hume, [May 1660], Bodl.

40. E. Ormonde to Stephen Smith, May 7, 1660, MS 2,324, Ormond Papers, NLI, p. 199, no. 1,334.

41. E. Ormonde to Hume, [May 1660], Bodl.

42. E. Ormonde to J. Ormonde, May 20, 1660, Dublin, MS 2,324, Ormond Papers, NLI, p. 235, no. 1,339.

43. See her correspondence to the couple's estate manager, Capt. George Mathew, MS 2,503, Ormond Papers, NLI, nos. 1–130.

44. James, Duke of Ormonde, to the Earl of Devonshire, October 20, 1662, Dublin, MS 199, Carte Papers, Bodl., fol. 117.

45. E. Ormonde to Mathew, April 20, 1672, NLI; Katherine, Lady Ranelagh, to E. Ormonde, [April 1666], MS 217, Carte Papers, Bodl., fols. 452–53; Ranelagh to E. Ormonde, March 2, [1666], MS 217, Carte Papers, Bodl., fols. 454–456.

46. See, for example, E. Ormonde to Sir Edward Nicholas, January 5, 1663/64, MS 2,538, Egerton Manuscripts, BL, fol. 239.

47. E. Ormonde to Mathew, March 9, 1668/69, MS 2,503, Ormond Papers, NLI, no. 15.

48. E. Ormonde to J. Ormonde, June 20, 1669, Kilkenny, MS 243, Carte Papers, Bodl., fol. 26.

49. I am very grateful to Ann-Maria Walsh for this information.

50. E. Ormonde to Richard, Earl of Arran, July 5, 1684, Hampton Court, London, MS 2,439, Ormond Papers, NLI, p. 119, no. 8,491.

7

English-Irish Social Networks in the Seventeenth Century

AMANDA E. HERBERT

In the 1650s a woman named Eliza Blennerhassett (pre-1639–76) wrote a series of lonely letters from Ireland to England. Penned over the course of about five years, the letters were addressed to a family that Blennerhassett called "the only suports of my spirits."[1] In her correspondence Blennerhassett worked to maintain social ties with these people living in England and attempted to preserve her friendship with them. The letters were seeded with pieces of gossip, gift objects, political intelligence, medical and culinary recipes, and expressions of the love and affection that she claimed she felt for this distant family. She showered them with compliments and assured them of her continuing commitment to their bond. And in her letters Blennerhassett cultivated and crafted a very specific kind of English-Irish identity by inserting strategic complaints about Ireland and the people she encountered while living in that country. Through close examination of Blennerhassett's correspondence, we are able to see how one early modern woman constructed a cross-channel, archipelagic identity by using seventeenth-century Ireland, as both a location and an idea, to influence her sense of self, memory, and place.

Despite her close association with England and her clear disdain for Ireland, Eliza Blennerhassett could have chosen to define herself as an "Irish" person. Members of her family had lived in Ireland for decades, having settled in both the north of Ireland in County Tyrone and along the western coast in County Kerry from the fifteenth century onward. Blennerhassett participated in the mid-seventeenth-century Cromwellian settlement, traveling to Ireland in 1656 in the company of her brother. In 1660 she got married in Ireland, to one of her English-Irish cousins. She bore children in Ireland, and she lived in that country until her death. It is likely that she was buried there. Her connections to Ireland were durable and enduring.

People like Eliza Blennerhassett traditionally have been overlooked by scholars, because concepts of primogeniture privileged, and have often continued to privilege, the study of early modern families. Blennerhassett was born into two well-known, and frequently studied, aristocratic English-Irish families—the Mervyns and the Blennerhassetts—but was tied to only minor branches of each of those groups. She was the daughter of Deborah Mervyn and Leonard Blennerhassett. Her mother was related to the Barons Audley, but through two maternal lines, which limited her access to the wealth, property, and privilege possessed by that family. And although her father, Leonard Blennerhassett, was descended from Richard de Blennerhassett of Carlisle (ca. 1450) and was knighted in 1635/36 at Dublin by Lord Thomas Wentworth, then lord deputy of Ireland, he was also a very minor scion of that family: the third son of a second son of a third son. The Mervyns and Blennerhassetts owned property in many different Irish counties, with their most significant holdings in Counties Dublin, Fermanagh, Kerry, and Tyrone. But while Eliza Blennerhassett might have visited some of those locations, she consistently wrote only from two rather small homes: from Trillick Castle, a "defended" or fortified house in County Tyrone, and from a residence in the city of Dublin.[2]

Eliza Blennerhassett also left a very faint archival footprint. She is difficult to trace because, like many members of her family, she signed her letters in different ways: Eliza and Elizabeth and then Blennerhassett, Haysett, and (after she married) Mervyn. Although it is likely that she wrote hundreds of letters over the course of her lifetime, I have been able to find only seven that have survived.[3] These seven letters, the first dating from October 29, 1656, and the last from February 11, 1660/61, are held at the Huntington

Library in San Marino, California, as part of the remarkable Hastings Family Papers, a collection of approximately fifty thousand manuscripts, including accounts, correspondence, court records, catalogs of books, deeds, estate and manorial papers, and household books, dating from circa 1100–1892. The letters were written to five members of the Hastings family: to Lucy Hastings, Countess of Huntingdon (1613–79), and to four of Lucy's children, Eleanor, Elizabeth, Mary, and Theophilus.

The Hastings family represented one of Blennerhassett's most important social and familial connections: Eliza Blennerhassett was first cousin once removed to Lucy Hastings and second cousin to Eleanor, Elizabeth, Mary, and Theophilus Hastings, as Blennerhassett's grandmother (Christian Touchet Mervyn) and Lucy Hastings's mother (Eleanor Touchet Davies) were sisters. Like the Blennerhassetts, the Hastings family had a long history in Ireland. Lucy Davies Hastings was born in Dublin, the daughter of Eleanor and her husband, Sir John Davies.[4] And, like the Blennerhassetts, the Hastings family owned land and buildings in Counties Fermanagh and Tyrone. Echoes of their mutual ties in Ireland can be found throughout the Hastings Family Papers. An anonymous Hastings letter, dating from circa 1650 and written to a man named John Blennerhassett (relationship to Eliza Blennerhassett unknown), explains that the author was "ready to goe to a Tryall about some off my interest in the Countie of Kiery" and asked for John Blennerhassett's help in "getting me a good Jury in that Countie that will bee sensible . . . in order to recover that which is myne owne."[5] Another revealing letter, from William Davys (a cousin of Lucy Davies Hastings and one of the Hastings family's agents in Ireland) to Lucy Hastings in 1657, explains that Davys had been working to put "Mr. Henry Bleverhayssett [probably Eliza Blennerhassett's brother] and Mr. Ferdinando Davys into the Commission of Assesment for the Countyes of Fermanaugh and Tyrone (which will be some advantage to your honors interest in both Countyes)."[6] Although we cannot confirm the identities of all the people writing or mentioned in these letters, the two missives—joined together with the Hastings Family Papers' many pieces of correspondence to solicitors, stewards, and tenants in Ireland—speak to the Hastings' and Blennerhassetts' mutual engagement with Irish law, property, and politics.[7]

Despite the hundreds of letters that the Hastings family sent back and forth across the Irish Sea, important divisions separated Lucy Hastings and her children from Ireland itself. Lucy Hastings left Ireland for England at the age of five and completed her education and training in England. She married in England and spent most of her time in that country. During the 1650s, when Eliza Blennerhassett's surviving letters were written, Lucy Hastings and her children were living full-time at their Donington Park estate in Leicestershire, and this is where Blennerhassett sent her correspondence. The 1650s were a tumultuous time for Lucy Hastings and her children, as that decade saw the deaths of Lucy's oldest son, Henry Hastings (d. 1649), as well as her husband, Ferdinando Hastings, Sixth Earl of Huntingdon (1609–56), and the Hastings' involvement in many lawsuits, as their properties had been sequestered during the English civil wars. Through all this turmoil, and despite the difficulties the royalist Hastings family faced with the Interregnum and Commonwealth governments, Lucy Hastings remained resolutely in England. By the 1670s she had even sold off all of the Hastings family's Irish properties.[8]

We thus know a lot about Lucy Hastings and her children, but we know almost nothing about Eliza Blennerhassett and her family, who lacked the power and privilege of their Hastings cousins. We don't know exactly when, or even where, Eliza Blennerhassett was born, nor do we know where she was raised, although it is clear that she spent at least part of her early years in England, as she references her "coming over into [Ireland]" several times in her letters to the Hastings family. We don't know when or where or under what circumstances she became acquainted with Lucy, Eleanor, Elizabeth, Mary, and Theophilus Hastings. There is one sparse reference to Eliza Blennerhassett in *Burke's Irish Family Records*, which explains that she was born sometime before 1639, the date that her mother, Deborah Mervyn, died. *Burke's* states that she married one of her English-Irish cousins, Henry Mervyn, who was elected, first, to a position as member of Parliament for Trillick Castle and then, later, to act as high sheriff of County Tyrone. *Burke's* also mentions that Eliza Blennerhassett died in 1676, "leaving issue," but we don't know the names or genders of her children, when or where they were born, or even how many she had.[9] Eliza Blennerhassett has very nearly disappeared.

For all the gaps in our knowledge of Eliza Blennerhassett's life and experiences, her seven letters are remarkably revealing. Blennerhassett's letters begin shortly after her emigration from England to Ireland and chronicle the next five years of her life. They record her earliest impressions of Ireland, of the plantation movement, and of her role as an English-Irish woman. They provide a rare firsthand account of a person who was, while certainly not poor, also not "noble": Blennerhassett inherited no estates, held no title, and possessed little to no official influence over early modern politics, religion, law, or the state. The letters are rich in detail about Blennerhassett's feelings, inviting scholarly analysis of the ways that she described and deployed her emotions.[10] And they offer a telling glimpse into the ways that the women and men who participated in the Cromwellian settlement wrote and thought about themselves: how they related to family and friends living in England; how they described their national identity; how they worked (or did not) to fit into Irish society; and how they felt about their homes, old and new. Before exploring the content of Blennerhassett's few, but richly detailed, letters to the Hastings family, it is worth pausing to discuss the idioms and languages that she used in her communications.

When Blennerhassett wrote to the members of the Hastings family, she wrote to five very different people: Lucy Hastings was in her late thirties when she received Blennerhassett's letters, a recent widow responsible for running the Hastings estates as well as overseeing the education and care of her children. Her daughters, Eleanor, Elizabeth, and Mary, would have been in their twenties when they received their letters from Eliza Blennerhassett; at the time of this correspondence they were all unmarried and living with their mother at Donington Park. Blennerhassett's youngest Hastings correspondent was Theophilus, Lucy Hastings's son and the Seventh Earl of Huntingdon. Theophilus was very young—from six to ten years of age—during the period covered by Eliza Blennerhassett's surviving letters.[11] Despite the significant differences in the ages, life stages, and genders of her Hastings correspondents, however, Eliza Blennerhassett approached the members of the family in very similar ways, as she employed consistent sets of phrases, tropes, and positions in all the letters.

We cannot know precisely how Blennerhassett felt about any of the members of the Hastings family, but she chose to present herself as a loving ally.[12] Passion, affection, humility, fidelity, sincerity, and constancy were traits expected of early modern women, and by using them Blennerhassett positioned herself as an ideal feminized subject while simultaneously attempting to convey to the Hastings family how important their alliance was to her.[13] In 1658 Blennerhassett offered her "unfained and most faithfull affection" to Elizabeth Hastings and expressed her delight that Elizabeth Hastings was willing "to concerne your selfe with so much afection in me" in return.[14] Her mother, Lucy Hastings, received similar treatment, being told by Blennerhassett that "there is not a persone in the world that hath a more affectionat passion, and zeale, to your service then I."[15] Although she wrote frequently of her love and loyalty, Blennerhassett nonetheless had less money, fewer connections, and much weaker political and social influence—in Ireland or in England—than did members of the Hastings family. Perhaps for this reason she simultaneously employed language that emphasized her subservience and obedience to them. In 1656, when she was late responding to a letter, she cringed to Elizabeth Hastings that if she "weare any way guilty of [this offence] I should hate my selfe."[16] She cast herself in various letters as "the ungratfullst person in the world," completely "want[ing] of meirit,"[17] and "farre unworthy of that honourable kindnessess that I have receved from you."[18] Although this kind of language might seem groveling, it was done with deliberation and purpose. By positioning herself as an affectionate supplicant, Blennerhassett worked to flatter and honor the Hastings family and to maintain her alliance with them.

Blennerhassett stayed in contact with the Hastings family over many years and continued to speak of her affection for them even as it became increasingly clear that her emigration to Ireland had become permanent. In October 1656 she asked Mary Hastings to convey her good wishes to "my deare Lady Lucy [Hastings] and Lady Christiana [Hastings]" and to ask that they excuse her for "not writing to them at this time for I have out write my selfe."[19] Two years later she sent greetings to "my Lord and Lady [Hastings]" via Elizabeth Hastings and asked additionally to "lett me be mentioned to my Lady Elenor my Lady Lucy and the rest of my dear

Ladyes . . . [and] my pritty Deare Lord Theophilus."[20] And in 1660/61, after she had been married and had given birth to her first child, Eliza Blennerhassett asked Theophilus Hastings to give her "affectionate service to my deare Lady Elizabeth and the rest of my honoured Ladys."[21] Even five years after her departure from England, Eliza Blennerhassett thus worked to maintain her emotional bonds with multiple members of the Hastings family, describing what she believed was her continuing connection to them.

The alliance that Eliza Blennerhassett cultivated so carefully with the Hastings family was certainly maintained through these languages of subservience and love, but it was also nurtured in the interplay of objects, items chosen for their ability to speak to the supposedly identical qualities, tastes, and talents of both donor and recipient. In October 1656 Blennerhassett thanked Eleanor Hastings for the gift of a book, expressing her gratitude for "my Lady Newcastells booke that you pleased of your favor to send me."[22] This was likely a reference to a work by Margaret Cavendish, Duchess of Newcastle, and could have been any one of her early books: *Poems and Fancies* (1653), *The World's Olio* (1655), or *Philosophical and Physical Opinions* (1655). By sending Blennerhassett a copy of a book written by Cavendish, Eleanor Hastings helped to celebrate—and promote—elite women's contributions to studies of literature, language, philosophy, and science and suggested that she and Blennerhassett also shared a taste for those subjects.[23] The gifts exchanged between Blennerhassett and the Hastings women showcased their talents in medicine and cuisine as well as in literature and philosophy; in 1658 Blennerhassett thanked Elizabeth Hastings for "the recepts you honoured me with," expressing her gratitude by "returne[ing] my most humble thankes for them."[24] Gifts of "receipts," or recipes, should not be dismissed as quaint or banal, for in the early modern period they were powerful tools, used by women and men of many different backgrounds to share critical information about medical care, science, nutrition, and the natural environment.[25] The Blennerhassett-Hastings gift exchange referenced their mutual appreciation of and skills in creative and decorative art; in 1656 Blennerhassett asked Eleanor Hastings to send "some littell fancy drawne by your owne hand by the next [letter]."[26] Two years later Blennerhassett included "a locke of [my] haire" in her missive to Elizabeth Hastings. Hair locks or cuttings, often considered decorative objects, were popular gifts in the early modern period; freighted with meaning, they were intended to convey the lasting emotional ties that bound together friends, lovers, or family members even when they were physically separated.[27] Blennerhassett's gift exchanges with the Hastings family emphasized their mutual bonds, tastes, and qualities, celebrating their commonalities and attempting to mitigate any perceived cultural or geographic differences.

As if to provide further reassurance that her own interests and national identity lay firmly in England, Blennerhassett fed the Hastings family with a steady stream of information about military movements, reports on the successes (or failures) of settlement, and evidence of alliances forged between English and Irish families. Blennerhassett offered such a report to Eleanor Hastings in the fall of 1656, writing that a Lady Frances Butler had been "transplanted into Connaght" and was occupied in "farme[ing] her owne estate." Blennerhassett was disappointed that she had "not seen my Lady Frances Butler since I came into this country" but assured Hastings that she was in touch with her by letter, for "[I] have the content to heare from her somtimes."[28] Military men also received mention in Blennerhassett's letters; she wrote that a "Major Moor is gone Col[one]l into Hispaniola," probably a reference to William Moore, who was active in Cromwell's Western Design, a scheme that saw British troops stage a series of attacks on Spanish colonies in the Caribbean.[29] Blennerhassett sent news of aristocratic marriages, as when "the Earle of Killdars eldest daughter" had been "latly maried to one Captain Shane," and she provided the Hastings family with detailed information about the success of her own family's Irish investments.[30] In 1658 Blennerhassett explained that there were not enough profits coming in from their recently seized estate, as it would be "a yeare or tow till my brothers estate weare a littell better settled." And in June of that year Blennerhassett dutifully offered Lucy Hastings a detailed report on her own Irish income and annuities: "I am to receve the anuiety of 50 lb a year and at the end of three years 700 lb and in default of payment then the anuiety of 80 lb a year is to be continued till the 700 lb be payed."[31] By conveying information about settlement, military movements, marriage alliances, and investment patterns to the Hastings family, Blennerhassett attempted to prove both her loyalty and her indispensability as a source of on-the-ground intelligence.

To further convince the Hastings family that she allied herself with them and with England, Blennerhassett seeded her letters with strategic complaints about her new life in Ireland. She wrote to Elizabeth Hastings in 1658, "Madam, I must confesse I have a dislike to live in this Country."[32] Part of her discomfort stemmed from what she perceived were religious differences between the two countries; although Blennerhassett provided very few clues about the character of her own Protestant beliefs, she did complain frequently of the religious difficulties that she apparently faced in Ireland. She wrote in 1658 that "the want of hearing the word of god dispenced . . . makes [living here] uncomfortable to me" and explained that she was unable to listen to Protestant preaching because "there is not a minister under 10 or 12 miles round about us." Although Blennerhassett was able to find ministers who occasionally would "giv[e] us now and then a sermon," the lack of regular Protestant contact and support was troubling to her. She told the Hastings family that she had complained about this to her uncle Audley Mervyn, her mother's brother and a Speaker of Irish Parliament from 1661 to 1666, but she was still largely unsatisfied by his efforts: "my uncle says he will endeavor to gett [a minister] now that he goes up to Dubline but ther has wanted since I came into the country."[33]

Blennerhassett also complained about how isolated she felt. In 1658 she explained to Elizabeth Hastings that although the estates allotted to her family were fertile, she believed that they were underserved and depopulated, describing that "the harvest is great but labourers are very few."[34] She was also disappointed at the enormous length of time that it took to communicate with and travel to visit friends and family. It took a long "5 weekes" for her to "recev[e] the satisfaction and great happyness of a letter from [Eleanor Hastings]."[35] When she attempted to write letters to England, the "conveniencys" she "relyed on" had "failed me."[36] She complained that it was necessary to pray for "god to send a faire wind" before she could confidently send correspondence to England.[37] And her new life as an English person in Ireland was peripatetic; she suffered from "want of opertunitys"[38] to write to her friends, and she "had so littell time afforded"[39] to her, as her family members required her to travel repeatedly between their different, and distant, Irish properties, making her feel as if she was "so unsettelled not being constant in any place."[40] She wanted only "shuld it please god [to be] at the end of my jorney."[41] Eliza Blennerhassett emphasized the hardships that she believed she was experiencing in Ireland in an attempt to tie herself to the Hastings family and perhaps even to situate her life in Ireland in opposition to her previous life in England.

Blennerhassett played on her history and memories of the Hastings family—and the idea that her old life in England had afforded more opportunities for sociability with the Hastings family, opportunities that she now sorely missed—in a further attempt to maintain her old friendship with Lucy, Eleanor, Elizabeth, Mary, and Theophilus. She wrote to Elizabeth Hastings in 1658 that her "gratfull memory of you, [will] ever continue."[42] In 1659 she employed flowery, courtly language when hoping that ten-year-old Theophilus Hastings would "continue the memory of me, as of one that is extreamly in love with you."[43] And in 1660/61 she wrote again to Theophilus, hoping "that I have yett the happiness of some place in your memory."[44] Memories of the members of the Hastings family helped, she claimed, to mitigate the hardship of her separation from them. The letters that she received from Lucy Hastings and her children were "the only suports of my spirits," now that she was living in Ireland, and she begged them "not to debare me of them when occations are offered." In Blennerhassett's letters, life in Ireland was life in exile, and her continuing alliance to the Hastings—forged through the correspondence, the exchange of gifts, and the sharing of news and intelligence—was her saving grace. As she wrote to Eleanor Hastings soon after her arrival in 1656, "I am now in the worst part of Ierland, [and] I have the best company it can afford, werfor I have offten those thoughts that entertaine me with your La[dyshi]p."[45]

Blennerhassett's seven letters, which capture her thoughts, feelings, and self-stylings at a critical moment in history—both Ireland's and her own—help us to better understand one woman's Irish experiences. Blennerhassett traveled from England to Ireland and participated in Cromwell's settlement scheme, but, as she did so, she worked hard to maintain her connections to one prominent family she had left behind: the earls and countesses of Huntingdon. Blennerhassett saw herself as sharing a common past and a common identity with Lucy, Eleanor, Elizabeth, Mary, and Theophilus Hastings. Yet the Hastings family was in the process of shedding their ties to Ireland at the very same moment that Blennerhassett was tightening her own bonds to that country. Blennerhassett resisted this shift by writing to the Hastings of all their similarities and by attempting to demonstrate her usefulness to them as an on-the-ground observer of Ireland and its people. In the process she revealed the complexities of English-Irish women's senses of self and national identity. Despite our lack of biographical information about Eliza Blennerhassett and despite the fact that she left so few surviving letters, her writings reveal the introspective habits of someone trying to construct and manage a new English-Irish identity. By adding Blennerhassett's voice to the scholarly repertoire of life writing in early modern Ireland, we can begin to explore the ways that transmarine and archipelagic relationships and alliances affected these women's senses of self, place, and nation.

NOTES

1. Eliza Blennerhassett to Eleanor Hastings, October 30, 1656, Hastings Correspondence Box 20, Folder 840, Huntington Library (HL), San Marino CA.
2. Bernard Burke and Hugh Montgomery-Massingberd, *Burke's Irish Family Records* (London: Burke's Peerage, 1976), 134–35; William Shaw, *The Knights of England*, vol. 2 (London: Sherratt and Hughes, 1906), 204; Mary Agnes Hickson, *Selections from Old Kerry Records* (London: Watson and Hazell, 1872). Spelling of the family's name varies widely in historical records. For consistency's sake, I have chosen to use "Blennerhassett" throughout this piece.
3. The seven letters in the Hastings Family Papers are Eliza Blennerhassett to Mary Hastings, October 29, 1656, HAC 20(839), HL; Eliza Blennerhassett to Eleanor Hastings, October 30, 1656, HAC 20(840), HL; Eliza Blennerhassett to Elizabeth Hastings, 1658, HAC 20(841), HL; Eliza Blennerhassett to Elizabeth Hastings, ca. 1658, HAC 20(843), HL; Eliza Blennerhassett to Lucy Hastings (Countess Huntingdon), June 27, 1658, HAC 20(842), HL; Eliza [Blenner] Hayssett to Theophilus Hastings (Seventh Earl Huntingdon), October 30, 1659, HAC 21(6,244), HL; and Elizabeth Mervyn, née Blennerhassett, to Theophilus Hastings (Seventh Earl Huntingdon), February 11, 1660/61, HAC 22(9,245), HL.
4. Members of the family spelled their name Davis, Davies, and Davys.

5. Letter to John Blennerhassett, ca. 1650, HAC 19(4,629), HL.

6. William Davys to Lucy Hastings, Countess of Huntingdon, 1657, HAC 20(2,079), HL. The timing and topic of this letter suggest that the Henry Blennerhassett mentioned in the missive was Eliza Blennerhassett's brother Henry, high sheriff of County Fermanagh in 1658 and 1661 and member of Parliament for the same county in 1662. Henry Blennerhassett died in 1677, one year after his sister Eliza. See Burke and Montgomery-Massingberd, *Burke's Irish Family Records*, 134–35.

7. Tania Claire Jeffries, "Hastings [née Davies], Lucy, Countess of Huntingdon (1613–1679) Noblewoman," in *Oxford Dictionary of National Biography*, Oxford University Press, September 23, 2004, www.oxforddnb.com/view/10.1093/ref: odnb/9780198614128.001.0001/odnb-9780198614128-e-65147.

8. Jeffries, "Hastings [née Davies], Lucy."

9. Burke and Montgomery-Massingberd, *Burke's Irish Family Records*, 134–35.

10. The history of emotions is a relatively new and rapidly expanding field. For the most recent, representative work on this topic, especially in early modern British contexts, see Susan Broomhall, ed., *Spaces for Feeling: Emotions and Sociabilities in Britain, 1650–1850* (London: Routledge, 2015); Broomhall, ed., *Authority, Gender, and Emotions in Late Medieval and Early Modern England* (New York: Palgrave Macmillan, 2015); Thomas Dixon, *Weeping Britannia: Portrait of a Nation in Tears* (Oxford: Oxford University Press, 2015); Jan Plamper, *The History of Emotions: An Introduction*, trans. Keith Tribe (Oxford: Oxford University Press, 2015); Nicole Eustace, *Passion Is the Gale: Emotion, Power, and the Coming of the American Revolution* (Chapel Hill: University of North Carolina Press, 2008); and William M. Reddy, *The Navigation of Feeling: A Framework for the History of Emotions* (Cambridge: Cambridge University Press, 2001).

11. Finding reliable genealogical information on all ten of Lucy Hastings's children, many of whom did not survive infancy, childhood, or young adulthood, can be difficult. Eleanor, Elizabeth, and Mary were close in age, and Elizabeth was born in 1635. Theophilus Hastings was born in 1660 and died in 1701. See H. A. Doubleday, Duncan Warrand, and Howard de Walden, eds. *The Complete Peerage*, vol. 6 (London: St. Catherine Press, 1926), 661; Bernard Burke and Ashworth Burke, *A Genealogical and Heraldic History of the Peerage* (London: Burke's Peerage, 1931), 1296–97; and Jeffries, "Hastings [née Davies], Lucy."

12. On the ways that early modern women deployed gendered expressions of affection and love in their correspondence to construct and maintain alliances, see Amanda E. Herbert, *Female Alliances: Gender, Identity, and Friendship in Early Modern Britain* (New Haven: Yale University Press, 2014); on early modern women's correspondence more generally, see James Daybell, *Women Letter-Writers in Tudor England* (Oxford: Oxford University Press, 2006).

13. Anthony Fletcher, *Gender, Sex, and Subordination in England, 1500–1800* (New Haven: Yale University Press, 1995); Herbert, *Female Alliances*.

14. Blennerhassett to Elizabeth Hastings, ca. 1658, HAC 20(843), HL.

15. Blennerhassett to Lucy Hastings, June 27, 1658, HAC 20(842), HL.

16. Blennerhassett to Elizabeth Hastings, 1658, HAC 20(841), HL.

17. Blennerhassett to Elizabeth Hastings, ca. 1658, HAC 20(843), HL.

18. Blennerhassett to Elizabeth Hastings, 1658, HAC 20(841), HL.

19. Blennerhassett to Mary Hastings, October 29, 1656, HAC 20(839), HL.

20. Blennerhassett to Elizabeth Hastings, 1658, HAC 20(841), HL.

21. Mervyn to Theophilus Hastings, February 11, 1660/61, HAC 22(9,245), HL.

22. Blennerhassett to Eleanor Hastings, October 30, 1656, HAC 20(840), HL.

23. It is possible, but less likely, that the book was Cavendish's autobiographical *True Relation* or her work *Nature's Pictures*, as both texts appeared in 1656, the same year that this letter from Blennerhassett was sent. Lisa Walters, *Margaret Cavendish: Gender, Science and Politics* (Cambridge: Cambridge University Press, 2014); Emma Rees, *Margaret Cavendish: Gender, Genre, and Exile* (Manchester: University of Manchester Press, 2003).

24. Blennerhassett to Elizabeth Hastings, ca. 1658, HAC 20(843), HL.

25. Michelle DiMeo and Sara Pennell, eds., *Reading and Writing Recipe Books, 1550–1800* (Manchester: Manchester University Press, 2013); Elaine Leong and Alisha Rankin, eds., *Secrets and Knowledge in Medicine and Science, 1500–1800* (Burlington VT: Ashgate, 2011); Betty Travitsky and Anne Lake Prescott, eds., *Seventeenth-Century English Recipe Books: Cooking, Physic and Chirurgery in the Works of Elizabeth Talbot Grey and Aletheia Talbot Howard* (Burlington VT: Ashgate, 2008).

26. Blennerhassett to Eleanor Hastings, October 30, 1656, HAC 20(840), HL.

27. Blennerhassett to Elizabeth Hastings, 1658, HAC 20(841), HL. On the significance of gifts of hair in the long eighteenth century, see Angela Rosenthal, "Raising Hair," in "Hair," ed. Angela Rosenthal, special issue, *Eighteenth-Century Studies* 38, no. 1 (2004): 1–16.

28. Blennerhassett to Eleanor Hastings, October 30, 1656, HAC 20(840), HL.

29. Many thanks to Carla Pestana for her help with this reference. See Charles Firth, *The Regimental History of Cromwell's Army* (Oxford: Clarendon, 1940), 2:726. Blennerhassett to Eleanor Hastings, October 30, 1656, HAC 20(840), HL.

30. Blennerhassett to Eleanor Hastings, October 30, 1656, HAC 20(840), HL.

31. Blennerhassett to Elizabeth Hastings, ca. 1658, HAC 20 (843), HL; Blennerhassett to Lucy Hastings, June 27, 1658, HAC 20(842), HL.

32. Blennerhassett to Elizabeth Hastings, 1658, HAC 20(841), HL.

33. Burke and Montgomery-Massingberd, *Burke's Irish Family Records*, 134–35; Blennerhassett to Elizabeth Hastings, ca. 1658, HAC 20(843), HL.

34. Blennerhassett to Elizabeth Hastings, ca. 1658, HAC 20(843), HL.
35. Blennerhassett to Eleanor Hastings, October 30, 1656, HAC 20(840), HL.
36. Blennerhassett to Mary Hastings, October 29, 1656, HAC 20(839), HL.
37. Blennerhassett to Elizabeth Hastings, 1658, HAC 20(841), HL.
38. Blennerhassett to Elizabeth Hastings, ca. 1658, HAC 20(843), HL.
39. Blennerhassett to Mary Hastings, October 29, 1656, HAC 20(839), HL.
40. Blennerhassett to Lucy Hastings, June 27, 1658, HAC 20(842), HL.
41. Blennerhassett to Elizabeth Hastings, 1658, HAC 20(841), HL.
42. Blennerhassett to Elizabeth Hastings, 1658, HAC 20(841), HL.
43. Hayssett to Theophilus Hastings, October 30, 1659, HAC 21(6,244), HL.
44. Mervyn to Theophilus Hastings, February 11, 1660/61, HAC 22(9,245), HL.
45. Blennerhassett to Eleanor Hastings, October 30, 1656, HAC 20(840), HL.

8

Women's Letters in the Lyons Collection of the Correspondence of William King

JULIE A. ECKERLE

When Elizabeth Benson wrote in a 1698 letter to the bishop of Derry, William King (1650–1729), that "I am necessitated to make my complaynt to your Lop [Lordship]," she joined a legion of epistolary petitioners who complained to King in the hope that he could (and would) provide the critical assistance they needed.[1] For example, more than ten years earlier, in 1687 (when King was chancellor of Saint Patrick's Cathedral and rector of Saint Werburgh's), an otherwise unidentified "Eliz" wrote King to request a "small portion" for the bearer of the letter, an old crippled woman who was once a housekeeper (48), and in 1685 Ann Leavens similarly requested charity for Alice Owens, the bearer of her letter. According to Leavens, Owens was a "poor woman," widowed, "above threescore years of age," and "very deafe & darke sighted" (30).[2] King's sister Jean Lindsay wrote in 1703 (not long after King became archbishop of Dublin) because she believed her new husband deserved a better post (1010),[3] and Elinor Harrison in a 1705 letter asked King to help get the recently vacated dean of Saint Patrick's position for her husband (1135).[4]

Although these letters are just a tiny sample of the epistolary requests sent to King during his tenure as bishop of Derry (1691–1703) and archbishop of Dublin (1703–29), they are quite enough to explain why, according to correspondent Mrs. William Stoughton in 1705, King supposedly told a female friend of hers with whom he was visiting that he "thought all the beggers of Ireland found [him] out" (1182).[5] Indeed, King's correspondence from this period, much of which is collected at Trinity College Dublin in the Lyons Collection of the Correspondence of William King, is filled with what can be called "petitionary," or "suitors'," letters. Unfortunately, as King's purported word choice makes clear, there was a "stereotypical expectation that *women's* suitors' letters [would] be pitiful begging letters."[6] Yet, by whatever name, such letters provided a key means of problem solving in a period when individual agency was limited, especially for women. Letter writers of both genders, therefore, do not seem to have hesitated to take advantage of epistolary "begging," no matter the exasperation they might have engendered in the process.

The massive, multivolume Lyons Collection, which consists primarily of King's incoming correspondence, provides a case in point, as the collection contains roughly 150 female-authored letters from at least sixty-eight different women from 1683 to 1727, most of which are petitionary in nature.[7] In some cases the women responsible for these letters are not familiar to us and were not of high rank or import in their own time either. Thus, restoring these women's identities is often impossible, as the record leaves us with names (sometimes only partial names) and a random letter or two, nothing more. In other cases the women are the wives and widows of men who had active roles in Ascendancy Ireland, often in the church. And in still others, although not as many, the women are titled. In accordance with this range in the writers' status, women's petitionary letters in the Lyons Collection vary widely in degree of formality and skill. Yet in all cases they offer a unique opportunity to consider the rhetorical techniques used by many different women in a variety of circumstances who, in most cases, approached King from a position of vulnerability and great need. In contrast to the chapters in this volume that consider the epistolary techniques of a particular woman or circumstance, then, this chapter surveys and analyzes the strategies used by a range of women who wrote to the same man. It is King himself, in other words, who provides the common denominator. And King was his correspondents' chosen addressee in large part because he was rooted in the local Irish context that also informed their petitions.

Significantly, King was an Irishman—insofar as one can assign such labels in a period and context when national affiliation and identity were, as explained in the introduction to this volume, far from simple. Born in Antrim to Scottish parents, King converted to Anglicanism from Scots Presbyterianism sometime before 1671.[8] He was ordained in 1674 and subsequently devoted the whole of his life to spiritual work in Ireland.[9] He served as both chancellor (1679–89) and dean (1689–91) of Saint Patrick's Cathedral in Dublin before being promoted to his most distinguished positions as bishop of Derry and then archbishop of Dublin.[10] King never married but instead engaged passionately in person and in letters with the theological, intellectual, and political debates of his time. Indeed, in addition to his role as "*de facto* leader of the church in Ireland," King served four terms as lord justice and was "a pivotal political, intellectual and clerical personality not just in the Dublin of his day but also in intellectual circles throughout northern Europe."[11]

Accordingly, the extant correspondence of this "European man of letters" is extensive and wide ranging in its content, containing intellectual debate, ecclesiastical positions, evidence of "friendships of great strength and warm-heartedness," and even scientific ideas.[12] His correspondents included Charles Willoughby (d. 1694), a Dublin physician and naturalist; Francis Marsh (1627–93), archbishop of Dublin, 1681–93; Sir Robert Southwell (1635–1702), principal secretary of state for Ireland, 1690–1702, and president of the Royal Society, 1690–95; Jonathan Swift (1667–1745), the famous dean of Saint Patrick's, 1713–45; and James Bonnell (1653–99), accountant general of Ireland, whose widow, Jane (1660s–1745), became a voluminous correspondent of King in her own right. Indeed, Jane's letters are the most numerous of all the female correspondents whose missives appear in the Lyons Collection and thus offer an important case study within this chapter's larger focus on women's petitionary letters to King.

Put simply, King was an important man in late seventeenth- and early eighteenth-century Ireland. He was a representative of the Crown at a time when "Irish affairs of state and petitions from the citizens of Ireland could be addressed by the monarch's representatives in Ireland."[13] Yet King was much more than an English monarch's representative in Ireland. Rather, he was also an "Irish" man in Ireland, one who understood—through his own travels—how "visitors from Ireland were held in low regard in London" and how, "between 1689 and 1720, an unwholesome cultural dependency [of Ireland on England] had also deepened. This situation forced those from Ireland too often into the posture of entreaty."[14] Perhaps it makes sense, then, that King's rootedness in Irish politics, culture, and religion made him an obvious recipient of requests from those whose concerns were also rooted in an Irish context.

Therefore, although the letters examined here were not always written from Ireland, are not explicitly political, and often do not mention Ireland at all, the women nonetheless wrote within a distinctly Irish context informed by personal experience (often hardship) associated with life or business in Ireland. Furthermore, they wrote with an implicit trust in their addressee, an Irish-born Anglican who valued at least a degree of Irish autonomy, as evidenced by King's support for Irish parliamentary rights and his firm belief that the Church of Ireland, while "dependent upon the state . . . nonetheless had the right to preserve its identity."[15] Perhaps even more important, however, was King's familiarity with Ireland, since it was likely—in addition to his other qualities—to predispose him to answer favorably their various complaints and requests. In the case of spiritual matters, works of charity, and any number of mundane, individualized, and local needs—especially related to his diocese in Derry—King was his parishioners' go-to authority.

This is evident in a fascinating series of letters in which King is depicted as both villain and savior. The former can be seen in one of only two letters in the Lyons Collection in which both writer and addressee are women.[16] In 1704 Mary Colston wrote from England to her niece Mary Lane, in Ireland, to recount her horror upon learning of Lane's "apostasy" and to convey the family's certainty that the real villain behind this turn of events was "he who you falsly call archbishop of Dublin."[17] Indeed, Colston writes, "I desire you will aske yr great Muf[t]ie of Dublin from whene he received his ordination for if he is only a preist in name he can be noe true or lawful Bishop and doutles ye true church must haue a suceseon of bishops [fr]om ye apostles and I know he can deriue noe such, think of this, and for shame herd noe longer with wolffs in sheeps clothing." Colston's bitter sarcasm belies her deep concern for a young family member whose sojourn in Ireland has led her far from the family's traditional beliefs, a position underscored by the term *muftie*, which technically refers to a "Muslim cleric or expert in Islamic law empowered to give rulings on religious matters" but in this context pointedly lumps King with what Colston clearly sees as foreign and heathen religions.[18] She further claims that she has heard her niece has "become another creature," one "metamorfosed both in . . . looks and behauior" (2386). The situation is so dire that Lane's brother has been sent to her at once.

Yet of course Mary Lane, the recipient of this indignant letter, saw the situation quite differently and called on King in two extant letters in the aftermath of her aunt's missive for both advice (1090) and money (1116).[19] In the first case, she "beg[s]" to "be admitted ye honour of a short conferrence in order to arme me against the storme which threatens me. I hourly expect my Brother here, and in what manner I am to treat with him, I humbly beg yr Graces wise direction" (1090). In the latter, she requested money to pay for her lodging until her brother's arrival, at which point her future would be determined. Unlike Colston, who clearly saw Ireland as a den of heresy, Lane frets about having to "return to England. where I am more barbarously treate[d] by my Relations then is propper to tell" (1116). In this battle between one faith and country and another, King's authoritative position *in* and *on behalf of* Ireland clearly contributed to Lane looking to him for support.

The significance of King's association with Ireland is most clear at times of transition, as in a 1690 letter from Lady Frances Parker, who wrote to congratulate King on his appointment in Derry:

I have since I was in Ireland lived in hopes of seeing it again and nothing could more have increased that desire then your being so hapyly settled in that kingdom, which gives a vniversull sattisfaction to all that know you of which none must pretend to a greater share then my self. Pardon it Sr if there be a little self intrest in the case for I am apt to flatter my self, Sr Iohn Parker will never want a real Friend, so long as Ireland will be blest in haveing so good as well as so great A Prelate as my Lord Bishop of Londondery. (105)[20]

Letter writer Hannah Lloyd further reinforces the importance of King's Irish affiliation when, in a 1704 letter petitioning King for his assistance with her son's education, she says that "he hath no father either to admonnish or provide for him & my Husbands misfortunes where [were] so many since his comeing to this kingdome yt he had nothing to leave me either to maintain him or support my self in this my helples & mallencholy condition" (1070).[21] Since Lloyd wrote her letter from "lisnananah near Cavan," in the province of Ulster, "this kingdome" is clearly Ireland, and the specific historical context in which she and her potential benefactor operate is turn-of-the century Ireland, precisely early 1704, shortly after King has taken up his post as archbishop of Dublin. King is Lloyd's "local" authority, even if he is in Dublin and she in Ulster. The same is true when Margaret Lawrence writes in 1707 from England, where her husband is imprisoned, to remind King of a promise he had made to them when they lived in Derry (1253).[22]

Indeed, King's transition from his bishopric in Derry to his archbishopric in Dublin inspired a few particularly urgent letters by women who found such a shift in leadership to be anxiety producing. Mary Hill, for instance, "make[s] bold" in her husband's absence to write a relatively typical petitionary letter requesting King's assistance assuring that certain lands intended for her husband actually go to him when the current lease expires. Yet since she acknowledges at the beginning of her letter that King is moving "from this Diocess" to Dublin, the specific assistance she requires is for him to put in a word to his successor about the matter (990).[23] King correspondent Elizabeth Lloyd shared Hill's worry about unfinished business falling through with King's departure from Derry, writing just a few days earlier that she is particularly worried, since "my son Edward understanding yt your Ldshipp is Leaueing derry, and . . . you haue not settled him in his place for his life."[24] Lloyd pulls out all the stops here, noting not only how disastrous it would be for her son and his family if he were turned out of service but also how "it would bring me a poore widdow wth sorrow to my graue." She also reminds King of how he told her at their last meeting that he would do anything for her son (989). Rhetorically "beg[ing] . . . upon [her] knees" in this dramatic fashion thus reminds us of the importance of the local church administration in everyday life and of the concomitant tenuousness of that life, since one person's death, promotion, or move to a different locale could destabilize the existence of many others. And destabilization is precisely what leads to so-called begging letters.

Generally speaking, the genre of the petitionary letter ranges widely from state petition letters—formal negotiations with the state apparatus in which, to use Marie-Louise Coolahan's words, individuals could "narrate their political situations and elicit relief"—to just about any epistolary document in which the writer presents a suit to the addressee.[25] Not surprisingly, the more formal variety of the petitionary letter makes more extensive and more sophisticated use of rhetorical and generic conventions and is addressed, if not to an actual monarch, then to high-ranking officials who represent the monarch.[26] In contrast, the less formal type may be addressed to anyone in a position to offer the necessary assistance, including a kinsman or kinswoman, and also varies widely in terms of the writer's rhetorical skill, resources, particular context, and what Susan E. Whyman calls "epistolary literacy."[27]

Archives across Britain and Ireland are of course filled with such letters from the early modern period, when physical correspondence provided the primary means of communication and when constant conflict and warfare, especially in Ireland, created greater need for "petition-letters . . . , as networks of support could suddenly disintegrate."[28] Women were particularly vulnerable due to widowhood, loss of property, or simply being left alone to manage the home front while husbands and sons headed to battle, conducted diplomacy, went into exile, or left home and sometimes Ireland itself for any number of other reasons. Indeed, women were most often driven to epistolary petitions when, as Lynne Magnusson notes in her study of Elizabethan women's letters, they experienced loss of some sort and thus wrote "out of necessity in reactions to deprivations . . . of all kinds imaginable," such as "in response to their own imprisonment or their husbands'" or "in efforts to recover incomes, titles, properties, or leases."[29] That women in such predicaments would have written to an authority figure like King is thus not at all surprising. Yet his female correspondents and their letters have—with a few exceptions—gone overlooked, thus providing another instance of early modern women's life writing hiding in plain sight.[30]

The female-authored petitionary letters in the Lyons Collection tend to meet the expectations of the time for such letters, which meant following classical rhetorical structure (*exordium, narratio, propositio, petitio, confutatio,* and *peroratio*); "epistolary conventions in their use of opening and closing modes of address and salutations"; and a number of other requirements. Despite variance according to "the formality of the letter . . . and the social status of the letter writer in relation to the recipient," the common rhetorical strategies in letters of petition are clear. They include women's "depiction of themselves and other women as objects of pity, as victims of poverty and suffering," often through "overtly melancholic rhetoric"; reliance on their status as widows; "the use of negative female gender assumptions"; emphasis on "a range of domestic roles and ideal types of female behaviour, styling themselves as 'natural' mothers, and 'faithful' and 'dutiful' wives"; and personalized storytelling techniques in the narration (or *narratio*) section of their letters.[31] In whole, writers like King's petitioners relied "on a combination of *ethos* (the discursive presentation of self—specifically, of one's moral character—with the aim of obtaining the addressee's goodwill or favour) and *pathos* (affective persuasion) to the detriment of *logos*."[32]

Most important, however, as is always the case with rhetorical analysis, is context. For the women writing to King in late seventeenth- and early eighteenth-century Ireland, circumstances were urgent and highly personal. And, for most, King was their superior in power as well as rank. Thus, most of these letters fall into the category Magnusson describes (adapting labels used by Angel Day in *The English Secretorie*) as "humilitie and entreatie," undoubtedly the most appropriate category for petitionary letters written from an "inferior" to a "superior." Accordingly, King's female petitioners incorporate flattery, gratitude, the requisite narrative and request, emotional manipulation, spiritual manipulation, and—of course—ample use of the humility topos. Given the fact that the suitor's letter is, put simply, "a social action situated by exigence and audience,"[33] the letters witness to women acting in various degrees of desperation to manipulate the epistolary means available to them to convince King, the spiritual and political authority best known to them, to provide assistance.

Therefore, as already noted, most of the women's letters in the Lyons Collection involve personal requests, and most deal with practical concerns rather than abstract ideas. In one exception Jane Bonnell writes from London in 1712 to ask King's opinion of John Richardson's 1711 *A Proposal for the Conversion of the Popish Natives of Ireland, to the Establish'd Religion* (1422).[34] Bonnell, unlike many of her fellow petitioners, was intimately connected to the religious and political topics of her day, both through her late husband and her brother-in-law William Conolly (1662–1729), who was Speaker of the Irish House of Commons from 1715 to 1729. More often, however, the petitionary letters with which King dealt on a daily basis (including Bonnell's other letters) were more personal, more practically oriented, and less explicit in their acknowledgement of Ireland as the context in which they operate.

Elizabeth Benson's 1698 letter, briefly mentioned earlier, is a typical example. After "humbly craving [King's] assistance," she goes on to explain—in what is, strictly speaking, the *narratio* portion of her letter—how her son's education has been hampered by a broken agreement that has also cost her family a financial investment. Eventually, she builds to her request, or "petition," which is that King intervene in the legal proceedings on her family's behalf. Finally, Benson returns to the humble tone of her letter's opening by "begging your Lops pardon for my presumption in giving yow this trouble." She concludes with "mak[ing] bold to subscribe my self . . . your Lops most obedient humble Servant" (566). Here we see a clear, modesty-framed petition in which a woman seeks King's assistance for matters both financial and familial. "Ireland" seems to have no explicit role in the letter. But of course it does inform Benson's letter and predicament, since she writes from "Linsfortein, Enishowen" in Ireland and since the attorney to whom her son was apprenticed has left Ireland for England.[35]

This kind of indirect contextualization informs a great many of the letters in the Lyons Collection, whether the petitioners wrote on behalf of others, their loved ones (especially husbands and sons), or themselves.

Like Benson, most of King's female petitioners wrote on behalf of others. Examples include "Eliz" (48) and Leavens (30), mentioned earlier, as well as Elizabeth Crumy, who wrote in 1711 on behalf of a whole parish, Finvoy (County Antrim), to convey the parishioners' concern that the church-building project there was far exceeding the anticipated costs (1412).[36] More often the women wrote on behalf of family members, frequently asking that King help a son achieve an education or a husband secure a position. This subset of petitioners includes Lindsay (1010) and Harrison (1135), mentioned earlier, as well as Rebecca Berkeley, whose concern required two letters in 1691.[37] The first was a simple plea for King's patience, since—she informs him—her husband, the reverend James Berkeley, had accompanied King William III into Flanders and therefore would not be present when Bishop King visited Derry: "I therfore hope yr Losp will excuse his absence since he is in the Kings servis, as for his parishes your Lsps comands will carefully be obayed & nothing will be omitted that is for the go[o]d of the people" (118). Yet by December, eight months after the first letter, Berkeley wrote in a more urgent tone seemingly designed to keep the King from taking action against her husband: "I hope Mr Berk-ley has begd your pardon for his staying longer then he intended and given you an account that he desines to leave London about Christmus for though the King has dun him the honour to receive him as one of his Chaplens in ornery yet I doe n[ot] find that he intends to make use of the previlledge he has to attend at coort but resolves to cum home" (193).[38] Berkeley is perhaps disingenuous in implying that she does not know of her husband's communications with King but clearly not willing to leave the matter to chance.

Although Berkeley clearly has both her own and her husband's self-interest invested in her letters, plenty of other women wrote explicitly on their own behalf. Here again the petitioners' requests are both relatively routine and urgent, especially if the writers are widowed or otherwise estranged from male support. Such instances reveal the most about women's options for agency and negotiation in a context not predisposed to support their needs. Perhaps most poignant in this regard is the already mentioned letter from Mrs. William Stoughton, the widowed mother of ten children who in 1705 found herself feeling personally attacked by King's claim about beggars. After all, it was the gentlewoman she sent to call on King, apparently to remind him of a promise he had made to Stoughton, who was by that time in England and unable to visit herself, that led him to make this remark. Recognizing that she is likely the "beggar" that spurred King's comment, Stoughton faced a complex rhetorical situation, one she handles first by thanking him for a past favor and second by explaining why she sent her friend to call on him. Here she addresses his accusation head-on:

> my Lord I cannot but take notice of the reflections you made to the gentlewoman in saying you thought all the beggers of Ireland found you out I am sorry I should be stiled one of that number I thank God I have not had such occasion nor did I beg of any in all my Life nor was it ever in my thoughts to desire any thing of your grace in that nature all I desired of my friend when she went to you was what I have mentiond I [o]nst writ to your grace and desired ye favour of you to lend me two guineas to repair some loss I had with no other designe but to return the[m] againe with thanks as I shall this you were pleased to send me.

However, having restated the facts of the case, she must also defend her reputation. No, she has not ever been a beggar. Yes, she and her sons did experience great losses in Ireland. But, no, her Irish losses did not lead to her request (which, she claims, was based on her apparently misguided understanding that old widows in London could get a yearly allowance in certain circumstances), nor was her life in Ireland disrespectful in any way. On the contrary, she insists, "I was the mother of ten children and nursed nine of them so that I could not have much time for Idleness if I were that way inclined which I never was nor am I ashamed of the charecter I have Left behind me in Dublin" (1182). King may be frustrated by being constantly approached by so-called beggars—specifically, as he apparently said, beggars of *Ireland*. But Stoughton is also frustrated, and this frustration seeps into a letter that is her only means of managing from afar her reputation and at least some of her financial needs. Even sending an on-the-ground representative seems not to have yielded the results she had hoped for and, on the contrary, created more problems for her to deal with, once again by letter.

Stoughton's letter brings into sharp focus the bind in which female petitioners often found themselves, since speaking out on behalf of their own needs and desires often had in turn to be defended and justified. Self-defense became only more complicated once the petitioner had left Ireland, as Stoughton's insistence on her good character, "Left behind me in Dublin," suggests. In such matters it was no doubt helpful to have an Irish contact, someone like King whose reputation for piety and honesty was indubitable. Yet, in a somewhat circular fashion, one would have to maintain a respectful reputation in King's eyes to maintain his support.

This essential requirement for a successful petition likely explains a December 1699 letter to the then bishop of Derry in which Jane Bonnell found it necessary to defend herself against rumor:

> I must farther beg that yu will not upon heresay readilly believe an ill or undecent thing of me, for there are some bussy people that has nothing to doe but to sencure [censure] others, wch trully I shoud not much mind if I did not fear that some whose good opinion I vallue may be . . . influenced by hering ill storys how falce soever, among other & worse things they say of me that I am gon quit out of mourning & am now in collerd clothes, wch was as far from once entering my thoughts as the murthering my Brother was. (651)

Written within a year of her husband James's death on April 28, Bonnell recognizes the rumor as an affront to the very exemplary widowhood that she has already made the core of her identity.[39] Indeed, the construction of this identity is deeply entwined with her request that King publish James's life and letters—which in turn forms the primary topic of her letters to King over several years. Therefore, when Bonnell in a letter a few months later thanks King for saying "yt if [he] hard any ill of [her] [he] woud communicat it" but insists that "my humer is not to lay such things much to heart wn I am parfectly jnnocent of what is said of me" (657), the gap between the concern of one letter and the dismissal of the next is quite telling. Bonnell needed King not to take the rumor seriously, just as she needs King to help with her project.

Nearly everything Bonnell writes to King in the first few years after her husband's death must be understood within this context, even her frequent return to a spiritual matter that has become a source of debate in her correspondence with King:

> One part of yr letter has taken up some of my thoughts, & trully the same thing has don soe for severall months past, wch is how far I may be falty in more earnestly desiring to get to heaven for the love of a frend that is gon there, then for the desire of enjoying God himself, who gave me that frend & all the other blessings I enjoy, but how falty soever I may be in this it is wt I cannot get the mastry of, but I please my self with the hopes that it is such a desire as God will pas by as a frailty of human nature, but other times I think it is hardly to be called a falt to desire to . . . enjoy a frend in heaven who I loved here for his such qualitys as God himself loved him for. (657)

Although not a petition per se, Bonnell incorporates this concern in letters that are in every other respect petitionary. And the often-hyperbolic manner in which she describes her love for her late husband, the very "friend" she is so eager to meet in Heaven, implicitly marks her own devotion to James Bonnell as greater than King's. Such a characterization is one of many techniques she uses in her attempts to convince King to act.

Significantly, Bonnell's connection to King had originated in his own long-term friendship with James, accountant general of Ireland and a deeply devout man in his own right. It must have made great sense to Bonnell that, when she sought to publish her husband's life and letters, King would be the perfect man to ask. Yet he refused, and even though she was able to get William Hamilton (d. 1729), archdeacon of Armagh, to take on the project instead, the 1703 publication of *The Exemplary Life and Character of James Bonnell* seems not to have assuaged the bitterness and hurt she felt.[40] Thus, in the course of her long correspondence to King (which includes twenty-three letters in the Lyons Collection), Bonnell's bold tongue, quick wit, and remarkable capacity for rhetorical manipulation appear with stunning clarity and consistency.

Yet even with her bold tone, Bonnell's letters encapsulate many aspects of women's life writing in the seventeenth century, including the familiar turn to life writing as a means of coping with emotional distress and the even more commonplace decision to use life writing to construct or otherwise manage a husband's posthumous reputation, often by shepherding his textual remains into print.[41] For Bonnell, this work on behalf of her deceased husband seems to have become her main reason for living. In her first extant letter to King as a widow, written in late September 1699, she describes with great earnestness her desire to get James's papers "into order for the press" (625).[42] A couple of months later, she claims that gathering and compiling documents for this project is "the only thing in this world that I am much concerned for." Indeed, she adds, "I must confess I can take noe pleasure in any thing but in thinking, speaking or hearing others speak of him, & the more I think of him the more I love & honour his memory & bless God anew for making me the happy wife of such a saint" (640). Thus it becomes clear that writing and receiving letters about her husband provide not only a means to an end (the texts she hopes to have published) but also a means of keeping James's memory alive.

Even so, Bonnell goes far beyond both personal indulgence and the therapeutic benefits of life writing when she reaches out to numerous individuals over many years and with extraordinary persistence to make sure that James's memory lives on in others as well. Her reasoning—much like that behind all published lives of this period—is to make James's exemplary character and piety known to the world; she is further confident that, as his widow, "it lies upon me to make him known to after generations" (820). Thus she urges King to select those letters from James's correspondence that will be most "of use to the world" (631). Furthermore, given her belief that James was a very "patron" of goodness (645), she argues that the project is better done sooner than later: "for if one desires such a thing shoud doe good, it will have most effect upon people that loved him & remembers him; after generations may believe or not believe what may be said of one they did not know. but now every good & valluable thing thats said of him will be intirely credited, & I believe if yr Ldsp wd goe one [on] with that work nothing that has bin published of many years woud be more exceptable to the publick" (761). By this point in early 1701, King has made his resistance to the project quite clear in his letters, but Bonnell only escalates her rhetoric in the face of this resistance, asking in an April epistle if there are not, among James's letters, "many . . . wch have soe much of the composers spirit and piety, as might help to a waken and Reforme a Degenerate world" (783). Like so many of her fellow correspondents, Bonnell here attempts to play on King's spiritual devotion, having failed in earlier efforts to manipulate his loyalty to James as a friend.

In her efforts to persuade King to accept her petition, Bonnell tries nearly everything. She is conciliatory, offering to bring someone else on board to "ease [King] of the drudging part of" the project (625). She is aggressive (writing letters nearly every two weeks), repetitive, manipulative, and ver-bose.[43] On one occasion, when she still thinks King is leaning toward the project, she says, "I use no arguments to porswade yu to it because I please my self with the beleiff that yu . . . are forward to doe all that lies in yr power to preserve the memory of such a man who I may say deserved it from yu if the sincerest frendship may merrit any thing" (673). Of course, she is making an argument here, and she is also relying on numerous forms of manipu-lation to do it. Therefore, perhaps not surprisingly, when King ultimately fails to respond in the way Bonnell hopes, he is subjected to extraordinarily bold, angry, and self-righteous letters in a relentless epistolary campaign.

This is where Bonnell shows herself truly unique among the Lyons Collection's female writers. About one and a half years after Bonnell first mentions the publication project, she finally seems to understand that King does not want to do it, has, in fact, "persist[ed] in . . . den[c]ying"—to use Bonnell's words—"to doe Iustice to the memory of yr frend." Her response to this disappointment is remarkably cutting:

> I must acknowledge to be in a temper to writ such a Life woud need such recollection & sedeatness of temper as is not easilly to be attained in the midst of such incombrance as yu are engaged in, but the way to be in such a temper, woud be to set about such a work, the dwelling much

upon his life, & conversing with his heavenly remains, must put one in such a temper if they be not utterly lost to all sence of piety. My earnest desire was that yu shoud set about it when the sence of the loss yu had, was fresh in yr memory, & had made some impression on yu, then yu woud have neither wanted temper nor words to have represented him in a true Light, but alas we are all apt to let such things wear too soon of [off], . . . may I never forget [my loss] I humbly beg. (752)

In swift fashion, Bonnell calls into question King's loyalty, temperament, commitment to God's "desine," and even his piety. And despite asking King in this letter to return her husband's papers so that she can get a second opinion from Archdeacon Hamilton, she maintains her epistolary pressure through a barrage of her own arguments in defense of the project, others' opinions of the project's worthiness, and additional insults: "yr Ldsp may call this eagerness, but Love & gratitude . . . is its proper name; and it is an Eagerness wch I hope will live till I go to my gr[a]ve. But I am more concernd in the other part of yr letter concerning the life of yr frend, for so I will call him till I am forced to alter that name, and even let wt will happen he must still be called yr frend since he really was soe whether yu be his or no" (783).[44] Even as she further acknowledges that "these expostulations will be imputed to the womans Eagerness," Bonnell asks King to reconsider his decision.

Clearly, Bonnell and King's relationship was complicated, and King was not beyond snarky retorts of his own. For example, in a May 10, 1715, letter to Bonnell, he notes, "There is an art of complaining forth in wch I find you have made some proficiency, pray do you much frequent court for if you have I am afraid, wt is observd there, may have influenced you, to lay that to my charge of wch you only guilty."[45] Furthermore, as already noted, Bonnell felt it necessary from her earliest extant letters to King to defend herself against his concern that she was demonstrating excessive grief.[46] And then, of course, there is King's comment about beggars, a comment that he supposedly made to a woman about another woman. There is no doubt that gendered assumptions about appropriate female behavior are at work here, thus explaining why Bonnell might be on guard against gendered claims about "womans Eagerness." But there is also no doubt that Bonnell—while quite willing to fall back on tropes of femininity when necessary—also felt no need to subject herself to such restrictive codes of behavior.[47] She was a woman of very strong opinions and often quite hard to please.[48]

In the end, Bonnell's determined efforts were productive. Hamilton's *Exemplary Life and Character of James Bonnell* went through multiple editions and seemed to follow the guidelines and ideas she had initially proposed to King.[49] It further contributed to the construction of Bonnell as an exemplary widow, an endeavor Hamilton seemed more than willing to support with his comment that James "left behind him a truly afflicted widow, who, I am persuaded, will persevere to shew the world, how justly she prized his excellent qualities and tender love; and who has spared no pains to get his life and character published, that so some justice may be done to his memory."[50] Bonnell's efforts, then, not only memorialized James but also herself, as the devoted and pious widow. And her ultimately successful campaign underscores that, when it comes to petition letters, persistence is essential.[51] Despite the fact that circumstances took her frequently to England (where she often went to Bath for both her own and her daughter's health), her life's work—in the form of her publication projects—continued to send her back across the Irish Sea, whether in person or by letter.[52] First and foremost, this was because James's work was itself rooted in the Irish context. As Hamilton writes in *The Exemplary Life* of the response to his death, "so well was the character of his excellences confirmed among us; so generally was he known, esteemed, and loved in Ireland; . . . that I believe no private man was ever more lamented. . . . It was looked upon as a general loss."[53] But Bonnell's continual return to Ireland was also a result of her need for King, the premier Irish authority capable of helping her achieve her desires. If it is the local that matters most in an individual's life, and if it is most often the local authority to whom individuals turn for help, then King was Bonnell's guy. Although he disappointed her in the end, he was her go-to authority and would continue to receive her missives for years after their falling-out over the publication of James's life and papers.[54] Therefore, even if Bonnell's less-than-humble tone and the quantity of her epistolary output were not the norm, her persistent reliance on King—and on what he meant to Irish life and letters—*was*.

In other words, King's Irish context simply cannot be overstated, even though many of his female petitioners do not mention Ireland at all. The bottom line is that he is there, in Ireland, firmly embedded in theological and political networks, attentive to both abstract and concrete concerns that matter deeply to his constituents, and knowledgeable about the institutions and individuals with whom his petitioners need to interact. Thus, King's petitioners used goodwill gestures, offered prayer, flattered excessively, expressed gratitude for past favors (also excessively), played on King's emotions, presented requests both directly and indirectly, invoked Christian charity, played what a twenty-first-century cynic might call "the poor widow card," and did whatever else they thought might work to open King's eyes, ears, and hearts to their petitions—sometimes all in the same letter. Even when King does provide the requested assistance, his petitioners often come back for more. Elizabeth Lovelace, for example, who wrote in 1704 to ask King for help renewing her family's lease (1122), wrote about the same lease yet again in 1707, this time noting that the rent is far more than they used to pay. Even though she points out that, "as my Gratious God put it in yr hart to spek for me, I hope he will put me in a way to pay ye rent tho tis great," she has made her point. Thus, when she goes on to ask King to keep out an eye for employment opportunities for her son in Dublin (what began as her son's willingness to wait on King when he is in town in the body of the letter becomes a more straightforward request in the postscript) (1267), one can imagine that King was not at all surprised to find his work in this particular case not yet done.[55]

Yet he continues to write, to assist, and to maintain and cement relationships as necessary. After all, few men were in the position actually to grant individuals' petitions, especially those from women of lesser rank trying to make their way in turn-of-the-century Ireland, often without the husbands who would typically negotiate on their behalf and—if necessary—travel to Dublin or beyond to England to settle matters in person. Just as writing letters was likely their only means of securing King's assistance, so was reading and answering their so-called beggars' petitions simply his job to do. He was, after all, William King: bishop, archbishop, lord justice, intellectual, church leader, converted Anglican, writer, correspondent, friend, and brother. Most significant, for "all the beggers of Ireland," he was "a promoter & lover of Iustice" (1000).[56]

CHRONOLOGICAL LIST OF WOMEN'S LETTERS IN THE LYONS
COLLECTION OF THE CORRESPONDENCE OF WILLIAM KING
(MSS 1995–2008) AT TRINITY COLLEGE DUBLIN

Letters from Women to King

2302: before 1689, Elizabeth Dean[57]
2294: before 1689, Elizabeth Deniston
2300: before 1689, Elizabeth Lovelace
2362: before 1703,[58] Jane Hamilton
2409: before 1715, Elizabeth Wade
15: January 12, 1683, Anne Dowdall
30: April 20, 1685, Ann Leavens
48: November 9, 1687,[59] Eliz.[60]
96: October 30, 1690,[61] Jane Dean (from London)
105: December 13, 1690, Lady Frances Parker (*not* from Ireland)
118: April 7, 1691, Rebecca Berkeley
139: June 18, 1691, Lady Castalina Lambert
158: August 1, 1691, Lady Castalina Lambert
160: August 5, 1691, Lady Castalina Lambert
193: December 13, 1691, Rebecca Berkeley
276: May 13, 1693, Lady Elizabeth Lyndon
299: October 3, 1693, Mrs. Carwardine (from London)
479: November 1695,[62] Lady Mary Dillon
472: November 8, 1695, Lady Mary Dillon
490: 1695, Lady Mary Dillon
491: 1695, Lady Mary Dillon
492: 1695, Lady Mary Dillon
494: April 25, 1696, Honor Foley
566: March 25, 1698, Elizabeth Benson

597: February 22, 1699, Elizabeth Lovelace

2339: April 23, 1699(?),[63] Jane Bonnell

622: August 1, 1699, Mary Fisher

625: September 26, 1699, Jane Bonnell

631: October 24, 1699, Jane Bonnell

6333: October 30, 1699, Letitia Saunders

640: November 14, 1699, Jane Bonnell

645: November 28, 1699, Jane Bonnell

651: December 14, 1699, Jane Bonnell

2343: 1700?,[64] Jane Bonnell

657: February 3, 1700, Jane Bonnell

664: February 24, 1700, Anna Parnell[65]

666: February 29, 1700, Jane Bonnell

673: March 16, 1700, Jane Bonnell

675: March 23, 1700, Jane Bonnell

679: April 2, 1700, Jane Bonnell

694: June 11, 1700, Anna Parnell

705: July 29, 1700, Anna Parnell

711: August 9, 1700, Elizabeth Pratt

724: September 24, 1700, Jane Bonnell (from London)

752: January 28, 1701, Jane Bonnell

761: February 18, 1701, Jane Bonnell

765: February 25, 1701, Jane Bonnell

783: April 8, 1701, Jane Bonnell

790: April 27, 1701, Mildred Bernard[66]

794: May 3, 1701, Jane Bonnell

817: July 22, 1701, Elenor Brown

820: August 6, 1701, Jane Bonnell

826: August 30, 1701, Lady Nichola Sophia Beresford

828: September 8, 1701, Mrs.? Chapell[67]

833: September 14, 1701, Mildred Bernard

835: September 29, 1701, Ann Newburgh

905: April 15, 1702, Hannah Lloyd

925: July 9, 1702, Mildred Bernard

931: August 1, 1702, Frances Lane, Viscountess Dowager Lanesborough

935: August 28, 1702, Frances Lane, Viscountess Dowager
      Lanesborough (from London)

936a: September 1, 1702,[68] Jane Bonnell

2354: between September 2, 1702, and March 11, 1703,[69] Jane Bonnell

989: February 11, 1703, Elizabeth Lloyd

990: February 17, 1703, Mary Hill

1000: April 2, 1703, Ka. Heyland

1004: April 10, 1703, Elizabeth Lovelace

1005: April 11, 1703, Lady Nichola Sophia Beresford

1009: April 19, 1703, Ka. Heyland

1010: April 20, 1703, Jean Lindsay

1049: November 20, 1703, Mary Hill

1057: January 29, 1704, Frances Lane, Viscountess Dowager
      Lanesborough (from London)

1060: February 10, 1704, Honoria Whitley

1070: March 16, 1704, Hannah Lloyd

1072: March 18, 1704, Francis Lane, Viscountess Dowager
      Lanesborough (from London)

1075: April 8, 1704, Sophia Hamilton

1076: April 25, 1704, Frances Lane, Viscountess Dowager
      Lanesborough (from London)

1089: June 10, 1704, Sarah Neale

1090: June 19, 1704, Mary Lane

1116: October 2, 1704, Mary Lane

1122: November 18, 1704, Elizabeth Lovelace

1124: November 22, 1704, Sophia Hamilton

1127: December 27, 1704, Elizabeth Lovelace

1135: February 6, 1705, Elinor Harrison

1182: November 1705, Mrs. William Stoughton

1185: December 22, 1705, Lady Mary Dun

1186: December 23, 1705, Jane Evory

1188: January 10, 1706, Lady Mary Dun

1195: February 9, 1706, Lady Mary Dun

1205: April 22, 1706, Margaret Preston, Viscountess Dowager Gormanston

1211: May 23, 1706, Ellen Warren

1248: March 20, 1707, Jane Bonnell

1253: April 7, 1707, Margaret Lawrence (from London)

1254: April 10, 1707, Jane Asgill (from London)

1262: June 5, 1707, Mary Synge

1266: July 20, 1707, Mary Synge

1267: August 16, 1707, Elizabeth Lovelace

1290: March 6, 1708, Mary Synge

1293: May 27, 1708, Mary Synge

1319: May 25, 1709, Letitia Saunders

1336: December 3, 1709, Elizabeth Lovelace

1376: July 27, 1710, Frances Lane, Viscountess Dowager Lanesborough (from London)

1379: August 22, 1710, Frances Lane, Viscountess Dowager Lanesborough (from London)

1383: September 5, 1710, Mildred Bernard

1386: October 24, 1710, Frances Lane, Viscountess Dowager Lanesborough (from London)

1396: January 8, 1711, Lady Nichola Sophia Beresford

1412: November 5, 1711, Elizabeth Crumy

1418: December 17, 1711, Lady Nichola Sophia Beresford

1422: March 20, 1712,[70] Jane Bonnell (from London)

1427: May 27, 1712, Catherine Dent

1452: May 12, 1713,[71] Lady Nichola Sophia Beresford

1454: June 6, 1713, Lady Mary Dun

1458: June 23, 1713, Lady Mary Dun

1460: June 27, 1713, Lady Mary Dun

1461: July 2, 1713, Lady Mary Dun

1471: October 12, 1713, Margaret Monro

1489: June 3, 1714, Elizabeth Moore

1582: February 14, 1715,[72] Susanna Nugent

1604: March 25, 1715, Mary Hamilton-Moore, Dowager Countess of Drogheda

1630: May 2, 1715, Susanna Nugent

1631: May 4, 1715, Lucy Hamilton

1641: May 18, 1715, Susanna Nugent[73]

1760: [after May 18,] 1715,[74] Susanna Nugent

1674: July 5, 1715, Letitia Berry (from London)

1808: April 15, 1717, Elizabeth Harvey

1841: November 30, 1717, Lady Mary Dun

1897: December 30, 1718, Ann Saunders

1918: June 29, 1719, Mrs. M. Allen[75]

1934: November 17, 1719, Lady Meliona Southwell

1956: August 25, 1720, Dorothy [Leper or Forster][76]

1968: January 7, 1721, Mrs. Eliza Blake (from London)

1997: January 2, 1722, Frances Bellew, Countess Dowager of Newburgh

2018: November 15, 1722, Margaret Preston,
    Viscountess Dowager Gormanston[77]

2108: July 16, 1724, Lady Lavinia St. Leger

2128: May 28, 1725, Agnes Hamilton

2426: after September 12, 1725, Mrs. Mary Delany,
    alias Cary, alias Eustace

2167: August 7, 1727, Lady Meliona Southwell (from Hampton
    Court, Herefordshire)

Letters from Women to Other Addressees

2295: before 1689, Elizabeth Dominick to "Mr Sing"

2301: May 31, 1686, Elizabeth Dean to Mrs. King

411: March 10, 1695, Anna Margaret Dawson to ? Rowan, Esq.[78]

436: June 4, 1695, K. Hamilton to Dean Trench[79]

503: June 4, 1696, Marianna Leslie "Mr Ireland"

845: November 19, 1701, Mildred Bernard to Robert King[80]

854: December 28, 1701, Mildred Bernard to Robert King

875: February 8, 1702, Mildred Bernard to Robert King

958: November 9, 1702, A. Hamilton to Frances Annesley[81]

2386: June 7, 1704,[82] Mary Colston (from London) to Mary Lane

I conducted research for this chapter during three trips to Trinity College Dublin (TCD) (June 2012, June 2014, and October 2016) and one to the National Library of Ireland (NLI), Dublin (June 2016). I am immensely grateful to the research assistance of the archivists at both libraries and to the University of Minnesota Imagine Funds and Faculty Research Enhancement Funds, which made the research possible.

1. The writer's name appears at the end of the letter (Elizabeth Benson to William King, March 25, 1698, MSS 1995–2008/566, Lyons Collection, TCD) as "Eliza: Benson," in a seemingly different hand than the rest of the letter. It is likely that, as was often the case, someone else wrote the letter, and she simply signed it. Benson wrote from Linsfort, Inishowen, in County Donegal. Although this is the only letter from Benson in the collection, there are also letters from three male Bensons. All subsequent letters from the Lyons Collection referenced in the chapter are indicated by letter number in the body of the text.

2. This is the only letter from Leavens in the Lyons Collection.

3. The husband referenced was Lindsay's second, a Scottish clergyman whom she had married shortly before writing the letter (in which she also informs King of said marriage). This is the only letter in the Lyons Collection from her.

4. This is the only letter in the Lyons Collection from Harrison, whose signature appears on the letter as "Elli: Harrison," but there are three from her husband, Theophilus (d. 1720), who was then prebendary of Clonmethan in Saint Patrick's, Dublin, and dean of Clonmacnois; see Samuel Carlyle Hughes, *The Church of S. John the Evangelist, Dublin* (Dublin, 1889), 58. In the end, the position vacated by the death of Jerome Ryves (d. 1704) went to John Stearne (1660–1745), a kinsman of Ryves, who then served to 1713.

5. This is the only letter in the Lyons Collection from Stoughton, a widow, although there are two 1706 letters from a William Stoughton, perhaps a son.

6. Lynne Magnusson, "A Rhetoric of Requests: Genre and Linguistic Scripts in Elizabethan Women's Suitors, Letters," in *Women and Politics in Early Modern England, 1450–1700*, ed. James Daybell (Aldershot: Ashgate, 2004), 57 (emphasis added).

7. I have not included in this count letters by individuals whose gender cannot be clearly determined. Furthermore, although my count includes all letters regardless of date, my analysis focuses only on those written up to 1714, which—while somewhat arbitrary—nonetheless marks the end of an historical period, the Stuart dynasty. A complete list of the female-authored letters in the Lyons Collection is provided at the end of this chapter. Many of King's outgoing letters are also housed at TCD: 182 in the Lyons Collection and far more in other collections, especially MS 750 (outgoing correspondence when King was archbishop); MS 1,489 (a letter

book from King's time as bishop of Derry); and MS 2,009 (correspondence from King and others to the Second Duke of Ormonde).

8. Sandra Hynes, "Mapping Friendship and Dissent: The Letters from Joseph Boyse to Ralph Thoresby, 1680–1710," in *Varieties of Seventeenth- and Early Eighteenth-Century English Radicalism in Context,* ed. Ariel Hessayon and David Finnegan (Aldershot: Ashgate, 2011), 206n5; Joseph Richardson, "William King: European Man of Letters," in *Archbishop William King and the Anglican Irish Context, 1688–1729,* ed. Christopher J. Fauske (Dublin: Four Courts, 2004), 110.

9. Frank Leslie Cross and Elizabeth A. Livingstone, "King, William (1650–1729), Abp. of *Dublin," in *The Oxford Dictionary of the Christian Church,* ed. Frank Leslie Cross and Elizabeth A. Livingstone, 3rd ed., rev. ed. (Oxford: Oxford University Press, 2005), 934.

10. For a more detailed account of King's ecclesiastical career, see Fauske, *Archbishop William King,* esp. Richardson, "William King," 106.

11. Christopher J. Fauske, "'The angel of St. Patrick's is now the guardian of the kingdom,'" in Fauske, *Archbishop William King,* 18, 24. King's complex religious and political identity is described by Fauske as typical "of the Irish-born Anglicans who thought about their position. Native to Ireland by birth, they were, with few exceptions, not Irish by ancestry. They occupied lands seized from others, often within living memory, and . . . had to come to terms with a political reality in Westminster that did not correspond to their assumptions of the constitutional position they should have enjoyed" (13). King's support for William, Prince of Orange, led him to be imprisoned in Dublin Castle in 1689 and 1690. He has also been described as "a convinced patriot, resisting all attempts to introduce Englishmen into high office" (Cross and Livingstone, "King, William," in Cross and Livingstone, *Oxford Dictionary,* 934). In less polite terms, Philip O'Regan refers to this aspect of King's character as "anglophobia," in "William King as Bishop and Parliamentarian, 1691–7," in Fauske, *Archbishop William King,* 77. Even King's habits as a consumer had something of the "patriot" in them, according to Toby Barnard's brief treatment of King in *Making the Grand Figure: Lives and Possessions in Ireland, 1641–1770* (New Haven: Yale University Press, 2004). Especially during his tenure as archbishop, Barnard argues, "King became an increasingly strident champion of all things Irish, and . . . extended this attitude to goods" (122).

12. Richardson, "William King," in Fauske, *Archbishop William King,* 106; Fauske, "'angel of St. Patrick's,'" 27.

13. Fauske, "'angel of St. Patrick's,'" 13.

14. Barnard, *Making the Grand Figure,* 336, 337.

15. O'Regan, "William King," 100; Fauske, "'angel of St. Patrick's,'" 14.

16. The other is 2301, from Elizabeth Dean to Mrs. King. The latter is likely King's sister-in-law, Marion King, wife of his brother Robert.

17. This is the only letter by Mary Colston in the Lyons Collection.

18. *Oxford English Dictionary*, s.v. "Mufti, n.," def. 1., accessed April 5, 2018, www.oed .com. I am grateful to Estelle Gittins, of TCD Manuscripts and Archives Research Library, for her assistance with this term.

19. These are the only two letters from Lane in the Lyons Collection.

20. Parker was the second wife of Sir John Parker (d. 1696), son of King's "first clerical patron," John Parker, archbishop of Tuam (Fauske, "'angel of St. Patrick's,'" 12). King remained a friend of the archbishop's family throughout his life, as evidenced by the fact that he stayed with Frances and John Parker at their home in Fermoyle, County Roscommon, and by the extant correspondence, which includes letters like this one (the only one from Lady Frances Parker in the Lyons Collection) and five from Archbishop Parker's granddaughter Mary Dillon. Sir John Parker and his family were among the Protestants who left England in 1688. Charles Simeon King, ed., *A Great Archbishop of Dublin, William King, D. D., 1650–1729: His Autobiography, Family, and a Selection from His Correspondence* (London: 1908, 16n2).

21. There is one other letter from Lloyd in the Lyons Collection, from 1702.

22. This is the only letter from Lawrence in the Lyons Collection.

23. There are two letters from Mary Hill in the Lyons Collection, one from 1702/3 and one from 1703, and two from her husband, Samuel Hill. The successor mentioned in this letter was Charles Hickman (1648–1713), who remained in the position until his death. Another frequent King correspondent, Hickman did not enjoy his predecessor's favor; King apparently regarded him as "an habitual absentee who on one of his visits had uprooted for private gain a wood which King had planted for the future benefit of the diocese." Alan Acheson, *A History of the Church of Ireland, 1691–1996* (Dublin: Columbia, 1997, 47).

24. This is the only letter from Elizabeth Lloyd in the Lyons Collection, although there are several from her son. In fact, just two days before she wrote this letter to King, Edward wrote his own letter expressing his hope that King would keep the new bishop from dispossessing him (988).

25. Marie-Louise Coolahan, *Women, Writing, and Language in Early Modern Ireland* (Oxford: Oxford University Press, 2010), 4. Useful guides to the burgeoning scholarship on epistolary networks, conventions, and strategies—which has been led to a significant degree by James Daybell—are his articles "Recent Studies in Sixteenth-Century Letters," *English Literary Renaissance* 35, no. 2 (2005): 331–62; "Recent Studies in Seventeenth-Century Letters," *English Literary Renaissance* 36, no. 1 (2006): 135–70; and his co-edited collection, with Andrew Gordon, *Women*

and Epistolary Agency in Early Modern Culture, 1450–1690 (London: Routledge, 2016). For eighteenth-century epistolary culture among "lower- and middling-sort writers" (17), see Susan E. Whyman, *The Pen and the People: English Letter Writers, 1660–1800* (Oxford: Oxford University Press, 2009). And for work on early modern women's petitionary letters in particular, see Marie-Louise Coolahan, "Ideal Communities and Planter Women's Writing in Seventeenth-Century Ireland," *Parergon: Journal of the Australian and New Zealand Association for Medieval and Early Modern Studies* 29, no. 2 (2012): 69–91; Coolahan, *Women, Writing, and Language,* 102–39; James Daybell, "Scripting a Female Voice: Women's Epistolary Rhetoric in Sixteenth-Century Letters of Petition," *Women's Writing* 13, no. 1 (2006): 3–22; Magnusson, "A Rhetoric of Requests," in *Women and Politics in Early Modern England, 1450–1700,* ed. James Daybell (Aldershot: Ashgate, 2004), 51–66; and Alison Thorne, "Women's Petitionary Letters and Early Seventeenth-Century Treason Trials," *Women's Writing* 13, no. 1 (2006): 23–43.

26. Coolahan, *Women, Writing, and Language,* 10.

27. As Whyman explains the concept, "The possession of epistolary literacy meant far more than signing one's name. Those who enjoyed it could write coherent prose and engage in accepted epistolary conventions. With practice, they were able to conduct business and construct personal relationships. Epistolary literacy was thus a valuable skill" (*Pen and the People,* 76), one that incorporates both the material and intellectual aspects of letter writing. Petitionary elements, furthermore, "are found in almost every kind of Renaissance letter, which works to erode distinctions between 'domestic' or 'familiar' letters and letters of petition or 'practical' letters. The petitionary mode was commonly used in letters from daughters (and sons) to parents, from nieces to uncles and aunts, sometimes in letters from wives to husbands, as well as in other letters where the addressee was socially superior to the writer" (Daybell, "Scripting a Female Voice," 10).

28. Marie-Louise Coolahan, "Irish Women's Letters, 1641–1653," in Daybell and Gordon, *Women and Epistolary Agency,* 167.

29. Magnusson, "Rhetoric of Requests," 56. See also Daybell, "Scripting a Female Voice," 3–4.

30. One obstacle to studying women's letters, Magnusson points out, "is access to texts: not that they are few, but that they are so many" ("Rhetoric of Requests," 52).

31. Daybell, "Scripting a Female Voice," 8, 12, 14, 15–16, 17.

32. Thorne, "Women's Petitionary Letters," 27. Of course, as Magnusson usefully reminds us, women's letters "do not exist in a separate economy from men's" ("Rhetoric of Requests," 52). Both male and female petitioners use similar techniques—including professions of modesty, conventionally associated with

femininity—and sometimes work in tandem to make their requests: wives write when their husbands cannot; husbands pass along wives' comments; some letters are signed by both husband and wife, and so on.

33. Magnusson, "Rhetoric of Requests," 57, 54.

34. King *did* support using the Irish language for preaching and otherwise converting the native Irish, a highly controversial topic in the sixteenth and seventeenth centuries.

35. Likely the place Benson names is Inishowen, in County Donegal.

36. There is only one letter from Crumy in the Lyons Collection; however, a letter from King to a woman with a slightly differently spelled last name, "Crump" (William King to Elizabeth Crump, September 14, 1704, MS 750/3/1/30, William King Outgoing Correspondence, TCD), may well indicate the same individual.

37. These are the only two letters from Berkeley in the Lyons Collection.

38. The phrase "chaplain in ordinary" designates a position held in an official capacity. James Berkeley was appointed chaplain in ordinary November 25, 1691.

39. Barnard considers the power gained and demonstrated by Bonnell and her two sisters, Katherine Conolly and Mary Jones, in their respective widowhoods. See chapter 9, "A Tale of Three Sisters: Katherine Conolly of Castletown," of his *Irish Protestant Ascents and Descents, 1641–1770* (Dublin: Four Courts, 2004).

40. Intriguingly, D. W. Hayton's entry for James Bonnell in the *Oxford Dictionary of National Biography* ("Bonnell, James [1653–1699]," Oxford University Press, May 19, 2011, https://doi.org/10.1093/ref:odnb/2849) mistakenly claims that "William King, . . . in a somewhat proprietorial manner, proposed writing [James's] life, but the formidable Mrs Bonnell arranged for this honour to pass instead to Archdeacon William Hamilton of Armagh." Hamilton was a frequent correspondent of both King and Bonnell, who often refers to him as "cousin"; see, for example, her November 28, 1699, letter to King (645).

41. Of course, many early modern women actually wrote their husbands' lives themselves, as Lucy Hutchinson famously did with *The Life of John Hutchinson of Owthorpe, in the County of Nottingham, Esquire* (though her text was not published until 1806). In addition to the Lyons Collection, a great deal of Bonnell's correspondence is archived at the NLI; most important for the current purpose is MS 41,580 (letters to Bonnell within the Smythe of Barbavilla Papers), much of which correspondence regards subsequent editions of her husband's *Exemplary Life and Character*.

42. There were certainly earlier letters, however, which we know because Bonnell references them in the extant material.

43. Well aware of what might be deemed her epistolary excess, Bonnell self-effacingly notes in one letter that "I will for once endeavor not to cram the peaper as full as it can hold" (673).

44. This letter is dated April 8, 1701.
45. William King to Jane Bonnell, May 10, 1715, MS 41,580/14, Smythe of Barbavilla Papers, NLI.
46. See especially 625.
47. See, for example, 675, written March 23, 1700: "I am very sensable that I trespass too much upon yu, wch is generally the falt of my sex where wee meet with incoragem[e]nt we are apt to tire out our corraspondants."
48. In just one letter to King (631), for instance, she expresses her dissatisfaction with Rev. John Strype's account of her husband's last visit, which contains "a great many useless things"; the Bishop of Cork's funeral sermon, "for wch I know he expects my thanks but I am not to good a dissembler as to give it him"; and the print for the copper plate, which "was don from a picter yt I did not think very like."
49. For example, Bonnell wanted the volume to include James's meditations and prayers, the sermon preached at his funeral, and evidence from letters that James's piety in part descended from his parents.
50. William Hamilton, *The Exemplary Life and Character of James Bonnell*, 8th ed. (London, 1829), 68.
51. As Magnusson writes, the petitionary letter "is remarkable for its apparently limitless reiteration of the same request and for the length and extreme elaboration of the rhetoric of each request" ("Rhetoric of Requests," 54).
52. The Bonnells had three children: sons Albert and Samuel, both of whom died before their father, and daughter Rebekah, who died at age six.
53. Hamilton, *Exemplary Life*, 203.
54. The latest letter in the Lyons Collection from Bonnell to King is dated March 20, 1712 (1422). However, King wrote to her as late as June 15, 1727, in which letter he acknowledged having received hers of May 27 (William King to Jane Bonnell, MS 750/8/206, William King Outgoing Correspondence, TCD).
55. In all, there are seven letters from Lovelace in the Lyons Collection, dating from sometime before 1689 (see 2300) to 1709. Letters from two male Lovelaces, Arthur and Paul, are also included in the collection; one of these men is likely the son that Lovelace occasionally refers to in her missives.
56. This is how Ka. Heylan (or Heyland), writer of two letters in the Lyons Collection, describes King in 1703.
57. The letters are listed by letter number, then date and letter writer. I have included only those letters *obviously* written by women; therefore, it is possible that other letters by women *are* included in the collection. I have also updated the dates to new style where necessary and indicated (where possible) when letters were written from somewhere other than Ireland. Women's documents in the Lyons Collection that do not qualify as letters include 30a, the will of Mary Crooke,

widow of John Crooke, printer general; 297a, the answer of Anne Boardman to a bill of complaint; 1310a, a receipt from Mary Synge, daughter of Primate Michael Boyle (d. 1702) and wife of Samuel Synge (1655–1708), dean of Kildare, for two legal documents; and 2313, a draft deed by Dorris Gay. Items listed only in this appendix (and not discussed in the text) are not included individually in the bibliography.

58. Although the date is unclear, the letter was written to King as bishop of Derry, the position he left in 1703.
59. The calendar identifies the date as March 9, but November 9 is provided in the letter itself.
60. Only these first four letters of the writer's name are visible in the signature.
61. The calendar identifies the date as October 11.
62. In a series of five letters from Lady Mary Dillon, only one is fully dated. But, given the content of the letters, I believe this one to have been the first; the order of the others is more difficult to determine. This letter was endorsed November, 1695.
63. The year is not clear, but the calendar proposes 1699 (with a question mark), and this makes sense. Bonnell writes in the letter that her husband is gravely ill, and he died on April 28 of that year.
64. The date for this letter, which is in such poor condition that it is protected in a clear sleeve (unlike the rest of the letters in the collection) is unclear. The calendar proposes 1700 (with a question mark). It is written sometime after Bonnell's husband died (thus after April 28, 1699) and while King was still bishop of Derry (thus before 1703).
65. This letter has been printed in King, *Great Archbishop of Dublin*, 93–94.
66. There are also several earlier letters in the collection written to King from Rev. Andrew Hamilton on this correspondent's behalf, when she was still the widow Mildred Wallis and had not yet remarried.
67. All textual evidence—not least of which is the author's seeming reference to [her] self as a "woman" when ending the letter—points to female authorship, but it is not certain because the condition of the paper allows for only the letters "oman" to be legible. The calendar also has a question mark before "Mrs."
68. The letter was endorsed on this date.
69. The date is not clear, and the calendar provides only "[before 11 March 1703]." But we can be a little more specific, since Bonnell in the letter references one that King wrote to Andrew Hamilton, archdeacon of Raphoe, about his brother William Hamilton's plans to write a life of James Bonnell. A letter that fits this description (Lyons Collection 937) is dated September 2, 1702.
70. The calendar identifies the date as March 23.
71. The letter was endorsed on this date.

72. Both the letter and the calendar (which usually includes both old and new style dating) date this letter as 1714. However, given its placement in the chronologically organized collection, it is probably, according to the new style, 1715.

73. The calendar attributes this letter to Lucy, rather than Susanna, Nugent. But the hand, subject matter, and signature ("S Nugent") match Susanna's other letters in the collection.

74. The letter was endorsed with this year.

75. Due to a tear on the bottom right-hand portion of the paper, "MAll" is all that is visible of the writer's signature; however, she is identified as "Allen" in the calendar.

76. There is a discrepancy between the calendar, which identifies the letter writer as "Dorothy Leper," the wife of Rev. William Leper, and the signature, which is "Dorothy fforster." In the letter itself the writer refers to "ye last will & testament of ye said Iohn Forster." It is also important to note that the signature does not appear to be in the same hand as the body of the letter.

77. This letter is endorsed "Mrs Butler."

78. Based on both the calendar and the text of the letter, the addressee, whose full name is not available, is Dawson's father.

79. This was John Trench, dean of Raphoe.

80. This and the following two letters are to Robert King, William King's brother.

81. Although the letter is addressed to Annesley, Hamilton asks him to pass a message to King.

82. The calendar puts a question mark after the year. But 1704 makes sense, as the letter concerns Mary Lane, who encloses the letter and describes the same concerns in her own June 19, 1704, letter to King.

9

Ownership Inscriptions and Life Writing in the Books of Early Modern Women

JASON MCELLIGOTT

WOMEN AND BOOKS IN EARLY MODERN IRELAND

Over the past decade, pioneering work in an Irish context means that we know much more about women writers. Yet we still know comparatively little about women as readers and participants in book and print culture. Máire Kennedy has initiated research into the practices of women readers in Georgian Ireland, and work by Amy Prendergast on the literary salon in eighteenth-century Britain and Ireland shows what can be done with a sensitive use of a range of historical and literary sources: personal correspondence, family papers, private diaries, and original literary texts.[1] Such sources are very sparse for those who wish to explore the female experience in earlier centuries. One potentially very important source has not, as yet, been utilized in any systematic fashion in an Irish context: ownership marks and inscriptions in books owned by women.

Books were often valued as precious objects by their owners in both a financial and cultural sense; they could be rare or expensive items that bore witness to the power and status of their owners. They could have sentimental value in terms of personal and family connections or be important elements of the owners' religious, political, or national sense of themselves. The range of ways in which books and manuscripts could be valuable meant that owners often inscribed their names and other personal details into texts they owned. As one might expect, we know much more about male ownership of books in every period of history, but in a British context there has long been interest in the ownership of books by women as a subfield of the history of reading and of the history of the book.[2]

This chapter uses the holdings of Marsh's Library, Dublin, as a case study of how a broader history of female book ownership might be conceived and executed. It uses a sample of the twenty thousand early modern books in the founding collections to consider how common it is to find books owned by women in collections amassed by men. It examines what types of books these women owned and whether they acquired them actively (by purchase) or passively (by bequest or as gifts). Is it possible to say something about the significance that women might have attached to these books? What might we learn about a woman's life by examining the books she owned? Apart from the inscription of their names as marks of ownership, did women ever write anything else in their books? Might female-owned books be a useful source for the discovery of manuscript jottings, marginalia, and writings by women? In the context of this particular volume, might these inscriptions and jottings be read as life writing?

Marsh's Library provides a useful test case because the collection consists of the personal libraries of four scholars (Edward Stillingfleet, Elias Bouhéreau, Narcissus Marsh, and John Stearne), which have remained separate from one another and are almost entirely intact, apart from some thefts that occurred over the centuries. The library has never loaned books to the public. Readers must consult all items in situ. The four collections preserve echoes of their owners' familial, professional, social, and personal networks in the form of books inscribed with the names of earlier owners. These inscriptions are overwhelmingly male, but they do provide evidence for female ownership. Preowned books usually ended up in the libraries of these four scholars because they were presented as gifts, bequeathed by friends of family, or bought on the secondhand market. Some books were evidently loaned to the scholars by friends or family with the expectation that they would be returned, but they somehow never made their way back to their rightful owners. Many preowned books, usually those published shortly before they came into the hands of our collectors, contain the inscriptions of only one or, sometimes, two previous owners. Some items, however, particularly those published within the first hundred years of the invention of printing, bear evidence of multiple owners across several generations.

Marsh's Library aims to be the first rare-book library in the world to provide details of provenance and ownership evidence for every item in its collection. In doing so, it is particularly interested in logging every instance in which a female name has been written on or into a book or pamphlet. This project faces a series of well-documented, interlocking methodological problems when trying to assess the meaning and significance of ownership marks. It is evident that not all women (or men) signed their names or left any other marks in their personal books. The absence of a mark of ownership does not, therefore, signify an absence of ownership or a lack of interest on the part of an owner. It is obvious that women (and men) did not own every book that they read, so even a total history of book ownership—were such a thing possible—could not provide evidence about reading and readership in the early modern period. Very many items in rare-book libraries with an ownership mark do not contain any annotations or marginalia that might shed light on how the owners engaged with the text, if they happened to read it. Even if one does find an ownership inscription in a book alongside annotations and marginalia, it is often not possible to link those marks with the person or persons who have inscribed their name(s) into the book. The annotations could have been made by anybody, either before or after the book entered the library. An attempt to understand something about patterns of book ownership among women and girls in the early modern period is not, and cannot be, a history of that most elusive and fleeting of experiences: reading.

The collections in Marsh's Library have been remarkably static over the centuries. They have not suffered the same depredations as collections in many other libraries, which have been dispersed, depleted, or destroyed over time by a curious mixture of overuse, indifference, recycling, fire or water damage, accidents, and the sheer bad luck of being in the midst of sites of political or military conflict. Sometimes, however, fads in library collection management and a desire to update, rationalize, and make collections "relevant" to contemporary users can cause the loss or deaccessioning of valuable historical material. Until relatively recently, even professional conservators habitually destroyed much provenance information when rebacking and conserving damaged books, because inscription marks were often made on the flyleaves or the front and back boards of books, and these were usually discarded when books were "repaired." Even when scholars discover instances of female ownership among books that happen to have survived the centuries, it will often not be possible to find out anything about the women involved, let alone how or why they owned or used these books. For all its lacunae, however, a systematic study of ownership marks offers the possibility of breaking new ground in gender history, book history, and the history of possessions and consumerism. It will provide much new evidence for the breadth of book ownership in the early modern period. It will also suggest patterns of ownership, purchases, borrowings, and bequests and may also shed light—if used with proper care—on *aspects* of the history of reading.

At the time of writing, in early June 2016, staff at Marsh's Library had worked systematically through all 2,100 books bequeathed by John Stearne for evidence of provenance and ownership. This number constitutes slightly more than 10 percent of the 20,000 books in the core collections. The library began here because books fetched for readers over recent years suggested that an intriguing number of female names were present in Stearne's collection. No systematic survey of the books in the Stillingfleet, Bouhéreau, and Marsh collections has yet been undertaken, but the details in this article rely on careful observation of ownership marks in over 1,500 books fetched for readers from these subcollections over the past three years. In addition, we have been able to consult a printed list compiled during the 1920s by Newport B. White of signatures found in books in the library.[3] This list is by no means exhaustive, and it is now evident that it underrecords instances of female ownership, but when one considers it alongside the sampling across three subcollections and the systematic survey of Stearne's collection, it is possible to report on the presence of more than sixty female names in nearly fifty different books and pamphlets.

The research on women owners at Marsh's Library is at a relatively early stage, but it is possible to make some preliminary observations. It may be possible to write a history of books from the early modern period that happen to survive in Ireland, but this is very different from a study of book ownership in early modern Ireland, because only one of the four subcollections in the library (the books of John Stearne) was amassed by an Irish man. By contrast, Edward Stillingfleet was an Englishman who never visited Ireland. His collection was bought for the library after Stillingfleet's death and then transported across the Irish Sea. Two of the other collections (those of Bouhéreau and Marsh) belonged to men who went to Ireland only late in life. In other words, a book from the early modern period that happens to survive in a repository in Ireland often had no contact with, connection to, or bearing on Ireland in the early modern period. Furthermore, insofar as one might be able to envisage a history of aspects of book ownership in early modern Ireland, this will not be a study of *Irish* book ownership. There was no distinctly Irish print culture in the early modern period, and that is true whether one chooses to define *Irish* in a geographic or cultural sense.[4] It is perhaps more useful to see books in Ireland being produced and consumed within a broader geographically and culturally *British* context. So, for example, even the subcollection within Marsh's Library of the Dublin-born John Stearne is explicitly part of a broader British and Protestant culture, both in terms of the books collected and the assumptions and mindset of the collector himself. This is true of almost all collections of early modern books that happen to survive in Ireland.

It will be possible to reconstruct something of the extent of the engagement with print culture of the Irish Catholic religious who went into exile during this period from the records of their libraries in Irish colleges and institutions spread across the continent. Once again, though, there will be a wider context to this print culture; in this case, it will be explicitly and self-consciously European rather than British. As for educated lay Irish Catholics in Ireland and on the continent, the unfortunate reality of the frequent dispersal and destruction (both deliberate and accidental) of their book collections may mean that it will never be possible to attempt a study of Irish Catholic book ownership in general, let alone that of female

Irish Catholics. In the context of Marsh's Library, it is not evident that any of the more than sixty female names discovered in the books are those of Roman Catholics, and it is currently possible to suggest only that four of these women had any connection with Ireland. As will be discussed later, Grace Marsh was living in the archiepiscopal palace of Saint Sepulchre in Dublin with her English-born uncle in 1695. Jane Westmeath may have been the wife of the First Earl of Westmeath. Margaret Ussher almost certainly lived in Ireland during the 1670s and 1680s, but it is unclear whether she was born there, and Elizabeth Davys emigrated to the kingdom, almost certainly from somewhere in Britain, in May 1677.

SINGLE SURVIVING EXAMPLES OF FEMALE NAMES

The presence of a woman's name in a book does not always signify her ownership of the item. The name of "Lydia Measton" is written in black in large, thick letters on the flyleaf of a copy of the 1654 pamphlet *A Discourse Touching the Spanish Monarchy*, but some disjointed scribbles on the same page suggest that her name may have been written by a certain Henry James, who signed his name on December 16, 1659. James's marks on the flyleaf may also suggest that Measton, at the time he wrote her name, was a patient in a hospital, possibly in Bride Street in Dublin. There was probably a relationship of some type between Henry James and Lydia Measton, and the act of writing her name may have been inspired by ill health on the part of the latter, but the broader context, meaning, and significance of the inscription are lost to history.[5] It is equally difficult to decipher the context within which a seventeenth-century hand wrote the words "Sweet Mrs Lucy Cooke" into the back flyleaf of a copy of the 1579 *Compendium Scientiae Naturalis*.[6] It seems unlikely that Cooke would have described herself in these terms, so perhaps the inscription is the product of the admiration of a female friend or relative. It might conceivably be the product of a male named Cooke practicing what his sweetheart's name would look like if she were married to him. It is also possible that the inscription might refer to the scribbler's admiration for a married woman of that name. This inscription, like very many other examples of marginalia and annotation, is too fleeting, too fragmentary, and too highly personal to provide us with the necessary context.

There are several books that can be ascribed to a named, identifiable woman at a particular time and place. So, for example, a thick folio volume that contains two antipapal tracts has the name and armorial stamps of a certain Eleanor Beeston on the front and back boards of the book.[7] Book-plates as marks of ownership were unknown in the early modern period, but it was relatively common for high-status individuals to have an armorial design stamped onto the covering boards of a book. It was not unknown for women to have their own armorial stamps with their names or crests, but it was unusual and noteworthy, as it suggests the existence of a woman's library separate in some way from that of her male relatives.[8] In the volume stamped with the name of "Eleanor Beeston" in Marsh's Library, the later of the two polemical texts was published in 1612, so the texts must have been bound during or after that year. The owner may have been the Lady Eleanor Beeston who married Sir Thomas Roe, member of Parliament, in 1614. If this identification is correct, the volume in Marsh's Library must have been stamped with her name between 1612 and her marriage in 1614, when her surname would obviously have changed. The inscription "Grace Marsh Her Booke 1689" is written into the front of a quarto volume in Marsh's Library. The volume consists of two separate verse works from the 1610s. Grace was the niece of the founder of the library, Archbishop Marsh, and she famously caused him much "affliction" by running away to get married in a tavern in Castleknock outside Dublin.[9] "Her Booke," preserved in her uncle's collection, contains a series of verse elegies occasioned by the death of Prince Henry in 1612 and an edition, published in the following year, of Guillaume de Salluste Du Bartas's verse account of the first weeks of the creation of the universe by God. It was certainly not unusual for women to own items that were decades old, but this volume is unusual among the female-owned holdings in the library, both in terms of the length of the items (Du Bartas's text alone runs to almost nine hundred pages) and the fact that they are in verse rather than prose.[10]

It may well be possible to posit a provisional identification for the "Jane Westmeath" whose name appears in a seventeenth-century hand on the verso and recto of the title page of the rare incunabula *Fasciculus Temporum* from 1494.[11] She was probably the wife of the First Earl of Westmeath. Yet the vast majority of women are hard to trace, no matter how elevated their social standing or how broad their networks of friendship and kinship during their lives. The last page of the single surviving copy in the world of the 1507 apocryphal gospel of Nicodemus contains the inscription "Mistris ffrancys Saunder." The inscription is in a clear sixteenth-century hand, but it is unclear who Frances Saunders might have been or where this unusual book was before it came into the possession of Bishop Stearne and was bequeathed to the library on his death in 1745.[12] The woman who wrote "ye Lady Fenton her Book" at the front and back of a quarto volume containing several sermons published in the early 1630s may well be as hard to trace as the commoner "Mary Knight" who wrote her name seven times into the front and back of her copy of Thomas Shepard's *The Sincere Convert, Discovering the Paucity of True Beleevers*.[13]

It is sometimes possible to gain a fleeting glimpse of a woman's life from the inscriptions in her books. So, for example, when Alice Exton noted on her copy of Isaac Ambrose's *Prima, Media, & Ultima* that it was "her Booke bought the 30th of March 1668," she provides a specific date of acquisition, which may suggest that she had purchased it on the second-hand market.[14] James Raven has commented on the paucity of knowledge about the sale of used books in the early modern period, so evidence for female purchases could be very significant if a pattern of involvement were to emerge.[15] It may also be possible occasionally to detect momentous events in the lives of women through seemingly throwaway inscriptions in books. For example, a copy of Matthew Henry's *The Communicant's Companion: Or, Instructions and Helps for the Right Receiving of the Lord's Supper* was owned by a "Margaret Edwards," who signed her name on the title page and the flyleaf facing the title page. Yet the book also contains an inscription, apparently in the same hand, which reads "Margaret Stewart her book Anno Domini 1723."[16] This might conceivably reflect Margaret's change of surname after marriage.

It is a rare thing indeed to have only one ownership inscription in a book and for that owner to be a woman. It is much more common to find the name of a woman present among one or more male names. In these circumstances it is often difficult, and sometimes impossible, to ascertain the sequence of ownership and the relationship (if any) between the names on the page. For example, the title page of *Divinae plane expositiones* records the name of the female "Frances Loftus" alongside the signatures of Edward Edgeworth and Michael Jephson, as well as the personal motto of Archbishop Marsh himself.[17] Most instances of multiple female ownership in Marsh's Library relate to religious texts such as Bibles, prayer books, and other devotional literature passed down through families, and this will almost certainly be true in other rare-book libraries.[18] The library's 1625 folio copy of the prose romance *Barclay his Argenis: Or, The Loves of Poliarchus and Argenis* contains the inscriptions of three women: "Sarah Bruce" (or "Brace," the handwriting is unclear), "Doma Alicia Ayloffe," and "Mary Berkingham."[19] It would be useful to know of the links (if any) between these women. Was the book passed between friends or relatives, or did it pass through the generations of a family? Might it have been bought on one (or more) occasions on the secondhand market? The key to answering these questions may lie in linking the data collected in Marsh's with information in a range of other rare-book libraries and electronic platforms.

EVIDENCE FOR MULTIPLE BOOK OWNERSHIP BY WOMEN

There are four women whose names are inscribed in more than one book in Marsh's Library, suggesting that these women had personal collections of books, and it may well be the case that they owned a larger number of items that have either not survived or have not yet been identified in other rare-book collections. Their names appear in small numbers of items, certainly when compared with the size of surviving male collections, but recent work by Kate Loveman has shown what can be learned from analyzing small numbers of female-owned books. Loveman's analysis of reading, news gathering, and sociability in the late seventeenth century draws on Samuel Pepys's famous diary; his surviving collection of several thousand books in Magdalene College, Cambridge; and a variety of working manuscript letters and papers to investigate how, when, and where he and members of his circle read. Pepys has long been known as an avid reader, but it is Loveman's ability to sketch the contours of the place of books in the life of his wife, Elizabeth, that is of interest here. Something of her reading habits feature in the diary, but Loveman has also identified five books that belonged to a personal collection of Elizabeth's distinct from that of her husband. These three prose romances, an edition of Ovid's *Metamorphoses*, and John Guillim's *A Display of Heraldry* shed new light on her interests and pursuits and provide new contexts in which to understand her appearances as a reader in the diary.[20]

There are two books in Marsh's Library that belonged to a certain Sarah Batts. The inscription "Sarah Batts her book and pen" appears on the flyleaf of *Hymen's Praeludia: Or, Loves Master-Piece. Being the Ninth, and Tenth Part of that so much Admir'd Romance, Intituled Cleopatra*.[21] It was perhaps unremarkable for Batts to own this romance, yet it must surely have been unusual for her to own Joseph Moxon's *Mechanick Exercises: Or, The Doctrine of Handy-Works*, which describes the practice of traditional "manly" trades and skills such as blacksmithing, the making of tools, joinery, carpentry, and wood turning.[22] That she wrote such confident inscriptions about her book and "her pen" in two very different texts suggests that Batts may well have owned more books, items that have been either lost or destroyed over the centuries or that may be awaiting discovery in other libraries.

Elizabeth Stillingfleet, née Pedley, was the second wife of Bishop Edward Stillingfleet. Seven items survive within her husband's collection in Marsh's Library with her distinctive inscription, "Elizabeth Stillingfleet her book," and there is also an eighth item in the bishop's collection with the inscription "E. S. her book," which may be in the same hand. Some of the books were clearly bought new by Elizabeth, but at least one seems to have had a previous owner before she acquired it (possibly on the secondhand market). Two were presents that give an inkling of her social and kinship networks and the ways in which these overlapped with the professional networks of her husband. Elizabeth did not write in her books, and they do not seem to have been handled very much. They are both physically clean and, disappointingly for historians of reading, clear of annotations and marginalia. Yet Elizabeth did have a standard place in which she inscribed her name and ownership of a book: the front inside board. This is a prominent place and may well suggest that she had a strong sense of her own identity and social status and was used to, and comfortable with, delineating her ownership of goods and personal property. The contrast with the repeated, almost furtive scribbles of Mary Knight (described earlier) is striking. Elizabeth's confident inscription may also suggest that she had a relatively large collection of books. Unfortunately, the place where she chose to mark her books means that her ownership would have been erased from any of her books within Bishop Stillingfleet's collection that were repaired and rebacked before the advent of modern conservation practices and techniques.

Elizabeth's books include unremarkable works of contemporary Anglican religiosity and practical divinity by the likes of Richard Lucas, Henry More, and Bishop Seth Ward.[23] There was nothing particularly unusual about her ownership of a pamphlet by the quarrelsome Presbyterian clergyman Richard Baxter.[24] Yet two of her otherwise unexceptional religious books are interesting for the ways in which the ownership inscriptions within them can shed light on Elizabeth's social networks. Her copy of More's *Discourses on Several Texts of Scripture* records "Elizabeth Stillingfleet her Book, given her by the Most excellent Mrs. Berkley."[25] This was probably the author Elizabeth Berkley (1661–1709), the third wife of the prominent Anglican clergyman and historian Gilbert Burnet (1643–1715). Edward Stillingfleet and Gilbert Burnet were close friends, and the existence of some form of personal link between their wives is noteworthy, not least for the way in which it seems to have been iterated or reiterated by the gift of a book as a token of friendship and esteem. Similarly, Elizabeth's copy of Anthony Horneck's *The Happy Ascetick* contains the inscription "Elizabeth Stillingfleet Hers. Given me by my Couzen Mortlock."[26] This is presumably the Henry Mortlock who published *The Happy Ascetick* from his premises at the sign of the Phoenix in Saint Paul's Churchyard. Here, a book has again been used as a gift, this time between "cousins," but it may also have wider meaning in terms of the social circles in which Elizabeth and her husband moved. Mortlock published many of Edward Stillingfleet's sermons and theological works, as well as hundreds of texts by other Anglican writers, during his long and prosperous career. Elizabeth's copy of *The Happy Ascetick* preserves, therefore, clues to the interconnected nature of matrimonial, kinship, religious, and business links among the Anglican elite in the late seventeenth century.

Alongside these conventional works of Anglican religiosity, Elizabeth also owned some more intellectually stimulating items. She had Samuel

Parker's 1666 polemic against the works of the early Christian writer Origen (d. 253/54), who had argued that God created souls before he created the world and that these souls had become—depending on their degree of devotion to, and love for, God—devils, humans, or angels. Jesus Christ was, in Origen's view, a preexisting soul who had remained utterly loyal and devoted to God.[27] It need hardly be said that this heterodox theology was anathema to the church "as by law established." Elizabeth owned Thomas Browne's attack on Baruch Spinoza and Thomas Hobbes, titled *Miracles Work's Above and Contrary to Nature*.[28] This text might be considered as a relatively minor footnote to the prehistory of the early Enlightenment, but its ownership by a woman must have been unusual in the seventeenth century. Elizabeth's husband, the bishop, owned copies of works by both Spinoza and Hobbes, and he involved himself in polemical arguments against what he saw as their atheistic tendencies. It would be fascinating to discover whether Elizabeth had access to her husband's library of ten thousand books and whether she discussed these matters with him in any way. Because of the small number of surviving titles with Elizabeth's name on them, there must be a suspicion that she, like Elizabeth Pepys, probably had a collection of books kept separate from those of her husband and that somehow a small number of her books became enmeshed with those of her spouse, possibly because they were borrowed by him. Whatever the actual scale of her complete library, we have here a hint of the types of books to which Elizabeth was exposed and the social and personal contexts and networks in which these items were produced, encountered, bought, read, and exchanged as social gifts and tokens of esteem.

There are three books in Bishop Stillingfleet's library inscribed with the name of "Ann Stillingfleet." This was probably one of the daughters born to Elizabeth Stillingfleet. With Ann, as with her mother, one can use these few books to suggest a deeper, possibly more nuanced familiarity with print. Her duodecimo *Histoire de Soliman Troisieme* suggests an interest in the East and contemporary affairs in the Levant. It also suggests that she was proficient at reading French.[29] This is confirmed by the fact that Ann's octavo edition of the Book of Isaiah, *Traduit en Francois: Avec une explication tirée des ss. Peres, & des Auteurs Ecclesiastiques*, contains an inscription in French that it had been given to her by her father.[30] Her duodecimo of Louis Petit's *Dialogues Satyriques et Moraux* contains an inscription indicating that it had been given to her by "ye Right Revnd father in God Edward Lord Bpp of Worcester." She also recorded her opinion of the book as "A very pleasant one."[31] Here, with only three surviving books, we get a sense of a woman educated enough to read French, with access to continental printings. We also get a sense of the ways in which books were given as gifts and tokens of love between parents and children.

The largest number of female-owned books discovered so far in Marsh's Library belonged to a certain Margaret Ussher, whose name appears on fourteen separate books and pamphlets published between 1503 and 1687. Her surname indicates that she was of the Irish family whose members had long held prominent positions in Trinity College Dublin and the Anglican Church. Whether she was a member of the family by birth or by marriage is unclear, but inscriptions on several of the books demonstrate that she was actively acquiring texts between 1675 and 1682.[32] She may have been a relation of the Margaret Ussher of Dublin who died in 1664 and was probably related to Stearne, in whose collection all of her books in the library are found.[33] Her surviving books encompass a range of topics, genres, formats, and dates. Some were bought new at the time of publication, or soon after, but others were items of some rarity, antiquity, and bibliographical curiosity even when she owned them. Even though her older books must have passed through generations of owners, there are surprisingly few other inscriptions in them, which might suggest that she bought some of them from dealers in secondhand books. This raises the possibility that Ussher may have been an active collector of old and rare books, rather than a passive recipient of books handed down through the male line of her family. Some of Ussher's books have handwritten textual annotations or marginalia, but it is not possible definitively to assert that any of these marks were made by her. There are tantalizing instances, though, where it may be possible to suggest that she marked some of her books. Ussher (like Elizabeth Stillingfleet) had a standard place in which she signed her texts: the top right-hand corner of the title page. The last letter of her surname is always written with a distinctive flourish or tail. Without straying too far into the area of graphology, it seems self-evident that her signature shows Ussher was confident about her identity and status when marking her ownership of her books.

The only work of a literary nature with Ussher's name on it is the English edition of *The Choyce Letters of Monsieur De Balzac*.[34] The only polemical work of politics is a folio copy of Charles I's *A Large Declaration Concerning the Late Tumults in Scotland*, on which she wrote the date "1675."[35] Between 1675 and 1678 she inscribed her name and the year on an account of the life and beliefs of the Anglican clergyman Dr. Robert Sanderson, bishop of Lincoln, and on a pamphlet by Nathaniel Ingelo titled *A Discourse Concerning Repentance*.[36] She also had a half-century-old attack by the Puritan firebrand William Prynne on the alleged "Popish" inclinations of the Laudian cleric Dr. John Cousins.[37] She owned two works relating to the law or legal matters. *Two Dialogues in English, Between A Doctour of Divinity, and A Student in the Laws of England, of The Grounds of the said Laws, And of Conscience* is a lively, vernacular pamphlet that discusses the basic laws of England concerning the rights and obligations of property owners, as well as the basis of the laws regulating religious conscience. It was based on a popular text first published in 1528 by Christopher Saint Germain (d. 1540).[38] Ussher's copy of *The Learning Of Common Assurances* would have provided her with a basic insight into contractual law and the law of property conveyancing in England, but it would have had limited usefulness in helping readers to navigate the complexities of the land market in Restoration Ireland.[39] There can be no doubting the potential utility of Peter Lowe's *A Discourse of the Whole Art of Chyrurgery*. This vernacular, quarto pamphlet was not a learned medical treatise for professionals but instead was intended for a general readership that wanted to know something of first aid and minor medical procedures, as well as those who were interested in "preventing of Sicknesse, and recovery of Health."[40] There are no annotations or marginalia in this book, which may suggest that it was not actively used in a domestic setting by Ussher or any other member of her household.

Almost all the books owned by women in Marsh's Library were in English, but Ussher had a number of Latin items, such as a 1661 edition of the statutes of Oxford University and a 1687 edition of the public lectures by Johann Christoph Schambogen, a professor of law at Charles University in Prague.[41] She also had several weighty sixteenth-century tomes, three of which were produced on the continent. The earliest of these is a very rare edition (only four copies are recorded on the Universal Short Title Catalogue) of the legal text *Formulare Advocatorum et Procuratorum Romane Curie et Regii Perlamenti*.[42] Chronologically, the next of her Latin books is the devotional text *Postilla siue expositio*, on the title page of which there is a woodcut of Christ standing before the twelve kneeling Apostles.[43] There was also a 1526 printing of the hugely popular biblical history first penned by the French theologian Petrus Comestor in the third quarter of the twelfth century.[44] And, finally, Ussher owned a 1576 large folio edition of *Summa Aurea*, a work of Roman and canon law by the Italian lawyer Henry of Segusio (d. 1271), which was written largely during the 1250s.[45] These were rare books, even when Ussher owned them. Despite the subject matter and authorship of these texts, there is no reason to suspect that Ussher was a crypto–Roman Catholic. Instead, it is much more likely that she, as a member of a prominent intellectual Anglican family, valued the bibliographical rarity of these items more than she would have been concerned at the religious contents of these pre-Reformation texts.

If the fourteen books owned by Ussher found in Marsh's Library can tell us little about her life and inner thoughts, they do provide tantalizing clues about aspects of her interests and behavior. She seems to have actively acquired some items, possibly on the secondhand market, between 1675 and 1682, and did not confine herself to items considered by many contemporaries as appropriate for females: works of domestic and religious piety. Her ownership of learned Latin texts and books that were already old and rare by the 1680s is striking and must surely have been unusual in her day. All of Ussher's books in Marsh's Library are preserved within the collection bequeathed by Stearne; however, Marsh's does not possess the entirety of Stearne's books. Before his death his extensive collection of manuscripts and around 4,300 pamphlets were donated to Trinity College Dublin. Upon his death Marsh's Library picked around 2,100 of what were deemed the most desirable books from what was left of Stearne's collection, and the remaining items, the number of which is unknown, were sold to raise money for the benefit of curates in Stearne's diocese of

Clogher.[46] This sale explains why the library of Exeter Cathedral possesses a copy of a theological tract from 1593 that has the distinctive inscription of Ussher on its title page.[47] It seems likely that copies of other books owned by Ussher may survive in institutions that have not yet facilitated easy online searching of ownership records. There must surely be more of her possessions awaiting discovery among the Stearne pamphlets on the shelves of the Long Room in Trinity College Dublin. It will probably never be possible to write an intellectual biography of Ussher based on the books she owned, but it may well be possible to discover much more about the basic facts of her life and her range of preoccupations.

WOMEN'S MARGINALIA

In some exceptional cases readers' marginalia—occasionally extensive—constitute important literary or historical writings.[48] The vast majority of surviving marginalia, annotations, and jottings, however, are too fragmentary, fleeting, and isolated to say anything substantial about the inner mental life of the author. In actual fact, the vast majority of surviving books from any period of history contain no marginalia. If marginalia left by men are rare, evidence for annotations by females in books is very unusual, because books were often shared in family settings, and women commonly seem to have internalized a belief that they had no authority to make comments.[49]

Around 40 percent of the female-owned books uncovered so far in Marsh's Library have at least some evidence of marginalia or other markings within them, but it is almost never possible to decide who might have made these marks. There are extensive annotations in two of Ussher's oldest books, but as they are written in a neat hand typical of the early sixteenth century, they cannot have been made by her.[50] But two texts owned by Ussher, one from 1663 and the other from 1667, display dozens of textual emendations in a hand very similar to (and possibly identical to) that which signed her name in the books.[51] This would be potentially very exciting evidence of how a long-dead woman unknown to history engaged with a number of texts, were it not for the fact that all the corrections merely reflect the printers' lists of errata at the back of the books. In this context it is possible to suggest that Ussher may have been of a pedantic frame of mind, but it is impossible to understand whether or how she might have engaged intellectually with the texts.

As noted earlier, a copy of the 1625 romance *Barclay his Argenis* in Marsh's Library contains the inscriptions of three women. One of the names is that of Sarah "Bruce" or "Brace." Below this, in what looks like the same hand that wrote Sarah's name, there is a short text of nine words, which somebody has tried unsuccessfully to erase: "a man had better have a good prick then."[52] This is certainly amusing in its incongruity, but its broader significance is, to say the least, uncertain. The few other snippets of marginalia in the female-owned books surveyed at Marsh's are conventionally religious in nature. Margaret Dopping wrote the short phrase "O Christ hear us /o christ / hear us" beside her name on the front flyleaf of a book she owned.[53] A 1628 Holy Bible with several female inscriptions has the following prayer written on the verso of the title page of the New Testament: "Blessed Lord. Who hast caused all holy scriptures to be written for our learning, grant that we may in such wise hear them, read, mark learn & inwardly digest them that by patience and comfort of thy holy word we may embrace & ever hold fast that blessed hope of everlasting life which thou hast given us in thy Son Jesus Christ our Lord."[54] This is not an original composition but a prayer first written by Thomas Cranmer in the sixteenth century. It appeared in the Book of Common Prayer and was used as the Collect on the second Sunday of Advent. The copy of *Hymen's Praeludia* with the inscription "Sarah Batts her book and pen" also contains a handwritten prayer:

> O God that art my richasness [i.e., 'righteousness']
> Lord here me when I call
> Thou hast set me at Liberty
> When I was bound and thrall
> Have mersey Lord therefore one me.[55]

This text is taken from Psalm 4 of Sternhold and Hopkins's immensely popular sixteenth-century edition of the Psalms in English meter. Batts's orthography is sufficiently distinctive to suggest that she may have written from memory, rather than having a printed copy in front of her. Both fragments of writing testify to the enduring popularity of best-selling religious texts.[56] They also tend to suggest that further examples of women's marginalia in Marsh's Library are likely to be religious, and entirely conventional, in nature.

A certain Elizabeth Davys inscribed the following text on the front flyleaf of her copy of *A Perfect Abridgment of the Eleaven Bookes of Reports, of . . . Edw[ard] Cook*: "If thou relegon right would under Stand then have thes[e] answers all at thy command and they thy duty so well will te[a]ch that thou no farther ne[e]dst to re[a]ch."[57] This was probably intended as a positive comment on the legal text into which it was written, but this cannot be definitively asserted: it may conceivably be nothing more than a stock phrase reproduced by Davys from a still-unidentified catechism or other devotional work. Once again the necessary context is missing that would enable us to assess the meaning and significance of this snippet of female writing. One other inscription in Davys's book does, however, provide evidence for her internal emotions in response to a significant change in her personal circumstances: "We came into that ugely playce Ierland upon may ye 23 1677." It seems clear that Davys emigrated to Ireland from somewhere in Britain on that date, possibly due to a career move on the part of a husband or father, but that she was unhappy in her new surroundings. Her book subsequently ended up among the possessions of John Stearne and entered Marsh's Library after his death in 1745. It has now sat in the same place on the shelves for over 270 years, which in one sense qualifies it to be thought of as an *Irish* book, despite the antipathy to Ireland and the explicitly British (and non-Irish) identity of the book itself; its author, printer, and publisher; and the female owner who inscribed into it her response to the island. The case of Elizabeth Davys clearly demonstrates that an early modern book (or a piece of life writing found within that book) that happens to survive in a repository in Ireland is often difficult to classify as geographically or culturally "Irish."

NOTES

1. Máire Kennedy, "Women and Reading in Eighteenth-Century Ireland," in *The Experience of Reading: Irish Historical Perspectives*, ed. Bernadette Cunningham and Máire Kennedy (Dublin: Rare Books Group of the Library Association of Ireland/Economic and Social History Society of Ireland, 1999), 78–98; Kennedy, "Huguenot Readers in Eighteenth-Century Ireland," in *The Huguenots: France,*

Exile and Diaspora, ed. Jane McKee and Randolph Vigne (Eastbourne: Sussex Academic Press, 2013), 173–84; Amy Prendergast, *Literary Salons across Britain and Ireland in the Long Eighteenth Century* (London: Palgrave, 2015).

2. Paul Morgan, "Frances Wolfreston and 'Hor Bouks': A Seventeenth-Century Woman Book-Collector," *Library* 11, no. 3 (1989): 197–219; Jacqueline Pearson, "Women Reading, Reading Women," in *Women and Literature in Britain, 1500–1700*, ed. Helen Wilcox (Cambridge: Cambridge University Press, 1996), 80–99; David McKitterick, "Women and Their Books in Seventeenth-Century England: The Case of Elizabeth Puckering," *Library* 1, no. 4 (2000): 359–80; William Sherman, "What Did Renaissance Readers Write in Their Books?," in *Books and Readers in Early Modern England*, ed. Jennifer Andersen and Elisabeth Sauer (Philadelphia: University of Pennsylvania Press, 2002), 119–27; Edith Snook, *Women, Reading, and the Cultural Politics of Early Modern England* (Aldershot: Ashgate, 2005); Heidi Brayman Hackel, *Reading Material in Early Modern England: Print, Gender and Literacy* (Cambridge: Cambridge University Press, 2005); Heidi Brayman Hackel and Catherine E. Kelly, eds., *Reading Women: Literacy, Authorship, and Culture in the Atlantic World, 1500–1800* (Philadelphia: University of Pennsylvania Press, 2007); Snook, "Reading Women," in *The Cambridge Companion to Early Modern Women's Writing*, ed. Laura Lunger Knoppers (Cambridge: Cambridge University Press, 2009), 40–53.

3. Newport B. White, comp., *An Account of Archbishop Marsh's Library, Dublin . . . with a Note on Autographs* (Dublin: Hodges, Figgis, 1926).

4. See Raymond Gillespie and Andrew Hadfield, eds., *The Irish Book in English, 1550–1800*, vol. 3, *The Oxford History of the Irish Book* (Oxford: Oxford University Press, 2006); Marc Caball and Andrew Carpenter, eds., *Oral and Print Cultures in Ireland, 1600–1900* (Dublin: Four Courts, 2010).

5. Thomas Campanella, *A Discourse Touching the Spanish Monarchy* (London, 1654), Marsh's Library, H 4.6.1.

6. Hermolaus Barbarus, *Compendium Scientiae Naturalis* ([Lausanne], 1579), Marsh's Library, P1.7.44; Maria O'Shea, *The Unicorn and the Fencing Mouse: An Exhibition of Marginalia, Annotations and Doodles* (Dublin: Marsh's Library, 2015), 16.

7. The two texts bound in this volume, both by Philippe de Mornay, are *Fowre books, of the institution, use and doctrine of the Holy Sacrament of the Eucharist in the Old Church* (London, 1600), Marsh's Library, F3.3.4(1); and *The Mysterie of iniquitie: that is to say, the historie of the Papacie*, trans. Samson Lennard (London, 1612), Marsh's Library, F3.3.4(2).

8. See the British Armorial Bindings database, https://armorial.library.utoronto.ca/.

9. Qtd. in Raymond Gillespie, ed., *Scholar Bishop: The Recollections and Diary of Narcissus Marsh, 1638–1696* (Cork: Cork University Press, 2003), 55.

10. Guillaume de Salluste Du Bartas, *La Divina Settimana* (Venice, 1613), Marsh's Library, L3.2.15.

11. Werner Rolevinck, *Fasciculus Temporum* (Lyon, 1494), Marsh's Library, F4.4.25.

12. *Here Begynneth the Treatys of Nycodemus Gospell* (London, 1507), Marsh's Library, Z4.1.14(1).

13. The texts bound in the book signed by the "Lady Fenton" are by John Preston and include *The Saints daily exercise: a treatise, unfolding the whole dutie of prayer* (London, 1631), Marsh's Library, J4.7.23(1); *Life eternall: or, a treatise of the divine essence and attributes: delivered in XVIII sermons* (London, 1631), Marsh's Library, J4.7.23(2); *The Breast-plate of faith and love: a treatise, wherein the ground and exercise of faith and love . . . delivered in 18 sermons* (London, 1630), Marsh's Library, J4.7.23(3); *An Elegant and lively description of spirituall life and death: delivered in divers sermons in Lincolnes-Inne* (London, 1632), Marsh's Library, J4.7.23(4); and *Three sermons upon the sacrament of the Lords Supper* (London, 1631), Marsh's Library J4.7.23(5). See also Thomas Shepard, *The Sincere Convert, Discovering the Paucity of True Beleevers* (London, 1643), Marsh's Library, E3.5.11.

14. Isaac Ambrose, *Prima, Media, & Ultima* (London, 1654), Marsh's Library, E3.4.13(1).

15. James Raven, *The Business of Books: Booksellers and the English Book Trade, 1450–1850* (New Haven: Yale University Press, 2007), 136, 189.

16. Matthew Henry, *The Communicant's Companion: Or, Instructions and Helps for the Right Receiving of the Lord's Supper* (Dublin, 1716), Marsh's Library, J3.9.18.

17. Jaime Perez de Valencia, *Divinae plane expositiones* (Paris, 1521), Marsh's Library, A3.3.15; O'Shea, *Unicorn*, 8. Frances Loftus may be the individual mentioned in passing in Simon Loftus, *The Invention of Memory: An Irish Family Scrapbook, 1560–1934* (London: Daunt Books, 2013), 105, 122.

18. See, for example, the family Bible: *The Holy Bible containing the Old Testament and the New* (London, 1628), Marsh's Library, B2.8.54.

19. John Barclay, *Barclay his Argenis: Or, The Loves of Poliarchus and Argenis*, trans. Kingsmill Long (London, 1625), Marsh's Library, J4.7.26.

20. Kate Loveman, *Samuel Pepys and His Books: Reading, Newsgathering and Sociability, 1660–1703* (Oxford: Oxford University Press, 2015), 48, 49, 53, 63, 141, 142, 146.

21. Gauthier de Costes, *Hymen's Praeludia: Or, Loves Master-Piece. Being the Ninth, and Tenth Part of that so much Admir'd Romance, Intituled Cleopatra*, trans. J. D. (London, 1659), Marsh's Library, L3.2.33.

22. Joseph Moxon, *Mechanick Exercises: Or, The Doctrine of Handy-Works* (London, 1677), Marsh's Library, M3.3.29. On the central role of romance in female reading habits, see Helen Hackett, *Women and Romance Fiction in the English Renaissance* (Cambridge: Cambridge University Press, 2000); Lori Humphrey Newcomb,

Reading Popular Romance in Early Modern England (New York: Columbia University Press, 2002); and Pearson, "Women Reading, Reading Women," 91–93.

23. Richard Lucas, *Practical Christianity: Or, an Account of the Holiness which the Gospel Enjoins*, 3rd ed. (London, 1685), Marsh's Library, P2.4.33; Henry More, *An Exposition of the Seven Epistles to the Seven Churches: Together with A Brief Discourse of Idolatry; with Application to the Church of Rome* (London, 1669), Marsh's Library, B2.8.17; Seth Ward, *Six Sermons Preached by the Right Reverend Father in God, Seth Lord Bishop of Sarum* (London, 1672), Marsh's Library, B2.5.15.

24. Richard Baxter, *Certain Disputations Of Right to Sacraments, and the true nature of Visible Christianity*, 2nd ed. (London, 1658), Marsh's Library, E2.5.27.

25. Henry More, *Discourses on Several Texts of Scripture* (London, 1692), Marsh's Library, B2.5.5.

26. Anthony Horneck, *The Happy Ascetick* (London, 1681), Marsh's Library, P2.7.76.

27. Samuel Parker, *An Account of the Nature and Extent of the Divine Dominion & Goodnesse, Especially as they refer to the Origenian Hypothesis Concerning the Pre-existence of Souls* (Oxford, 1666), Marsh's Library, S3.3.17(2).

28. Thomas Browne, *Miracles Work's Above and Contrary to Nature* (London, 1683), Marsh's Library, T3.4.2(1).

29. *Histoire de Soliman Troisieme* (Amsterdam, 1688), Marsh's Library, O1.7.48.

30. *Traduit en Francois: Avec une explication tirée des SS. Peres, & des Auteurs Ecclesiastiques* (Paris, 1663), Marsh's Library, A.4.25.

31. Louis Petit, *Dialogues Satyriques et Moraux* (Amsterdam, 1688), Marsh's Library, P2.7.14.

32. Margaret wrote dates within the year "1675" alongside her name on both Charles I's *A Large Declaration Concerning the Late Tumults in Scotland* (London, 1639), Marsh's Library, G4.2.10; and William Prynne's *A Briefe Survay* (London, 1628), Marsh's Library, Z4.1.15(14). She wrote the year "1682" beside her name on her copy of Henricus Ostiensis's *Summa Aurea*, ed. Franciscus Accursius([Lyon], 1576), Marsh's Library, R*3.1.9.

33. Margaret Ussher, will, transcription, MS Z4.2.1(23), Marsh's Library, Dublin.

34. Jean-Louis Guez Balzac, *The Choyce Letters of Monsieur de Balzac* (London, 1658), Marsh's Library, F4.6.24.

35. Charles I, *Large Declaration*.

36. D.F., *Reason and Judgement: Or, Special Remarques of the Life of the Renowned Dr. Sanderson, Late Lord Bishop of Lincoln* (Oxford, 1663), Marsh's Library, C4.6.5(1); Nathaniel Ingelo, *A Discourse Concerning Repentance* (London, 1677), Marsh's Library, R*3.4.24.

37. Prynne, *Briefe Survay*.

38. Christopher Saint Germain, *Two Dialogues in English, Between A Doctour of Divinity, and A Student in the Laws of England, of The Grounds of the said Laws, And of Conscience* (1528; repr., London, 1673), Marsh's Library, E4.5.38.

39. William Sheppard, *The Learning Of Common Assurances* (London, 1648), Marsh's Library, E4.4.6.

40. Peter Lowe, *A Discourse of the Whole Art of Chyrurgery* (London, 1654), Marsh's Library, L4.5.17.

41. *Statuta selecta è compore statutorum universitatis Oxoniensis* (Oxford, 1661), Marsh's Library, E4.5.31; Johann Christoph Schambogen, *Prae-lectiones publicae in D. Justiniani institutiorum juris quatuor libros compositae et in universitatis Carolo-Ferdinandeae Pragensis magnae aulae Carolinae auditorio juridico dictatae* (Prague, 1687), Marsh's Library, E4.4.24.

42. *Formulare Advocatorum et Procuratorum Romane Curie et Regii Perlamenti* (Hagenau, 1503), Marsh's Library, E4.4.26.

43. Gulielmus Arvernus, *Postilla siue exposition* (London, 1509), Marsh's Library, Z1.2.17.

44. Petrus Comestor, *Historia Scholastica* ([Lyon], 1526), Marsh's Library, B4.6.8.

45. Ostiensis, *Summa Aurea.*

46. Peter Fox, *Trinity College Library Dublin: A History* (Cambridge: Cambridge University Press, 2014), 75–78.

47. Richard Cosin, *An Apologie For Sundrie Proceedings by Iurisdiction Ecclesiasticall* (London, 1593), Exeter Cathedral Library, Item E9900189678. This book was located because Exeter Cathedral Library has uploaded provenance information to COPAC (http://copac.jisc.ac.uk/), the combined online catalog of more than ninety UK and Irish national, academic, and specialist libraries. I am grateful to Peter Thomas and Ellie Jones of Exeter Cathedral for providing me with photographs of this book.

48. H. J. Jackson, *Marginalia: Readers Writing in Books* (New Haven: Yale University Press, 2001). The entries on Isaac Casaubon, Samuel Clemens, Samuel Taylor Coleridge, and John Dee are particularly appropriate in this context.

49. Snook, "Reading Women," 40.

50. *Formulare Advocatorum*; Comestor, *Historia Scholastica.*

51. D. F., *Reason and Judgement*; Ingelo, *Discourse Concerning Repentance.*

52. Barclay, *Barclay his Argenis.*

53. John Gailhard, *Two Discourses. The first concerning A Private Settlement at Home After Travel. The Second concerning the Statesman, Or Him who is in Publick Employments* (London, 1682), Marsh's Library, E4.6.7.

54. *Holy Bible Containing the Old Testament.*

55. De Costes, *Hymen's Praeludia.*

56. Ian Green, *Print and Protestantism in Early Modern England* (Oxford: Oxford University Press, 2000); Andy Kesson and Emma Smith, eds., *The Elizabethan Top Ten: Defining Print Popularity in Early Modern England* (London: Routledge, 2016).

57. Edward Coke, *A Perfect Abridgment of the Eleaven Bookes of Reports, of . . . Edw[ard] Cook* ([London], 1650), Marsh's Library, E4.5.35.

APPENDIX

Archives and Female Life Writers of Early Modern Ireland

As the chapters collected in this volume amply demonstrate, numerous archives across Ireland, England, Scotland, mainland Europe, and the United States house documents pertinent to the study of early modern women's life writing on and in Ireland. Yet many of these documents are not widely known, if at all. Furthermore, they are, like many female-authored documents of the early modern period, rarely available except in manuscript form. Finally, due to the vagaries of history that have scattered many documents germane to early modern Ireland, as well as inadequate or incorrect cataloging, individual scholars rarely have knowledge of every document by a single women. Greater systematization and communication are needed to truly make these rich materials both known and accessible. As a small step in this direction, we provide here brief descriptions of some of the most pertinent archives and women whose life writings await further scrutiny: in some cases this is because the *texts* have been underexamined; in other cases it is because the *Irish contexts* have been underexamined. Our aim is threefold: first, to showcase the important Irish contexts of some relatively well-known women life writers; second, to bring greater attention to lesser-known texts and archives; and, third, to facilitate further research on these and other life-writing texts. In short, we hope that this is a generative text that will support future scholarly research on the burgeoning field of women's life writing and early modern Ireland.

We have done our best to provide an overview of what is known about women's life writing in the Irish context at this point. But it bears repeating that this list is *selective* and *incomplete* and at times quite random. We have reassembled and built on the research of the pioneering literary scholars and historians who first asked questions about the lives and writings of women in early modern Ireland. We hope and expect that the information we have collected here will continue to be revised and expanded as more scholars engage in research in this area. In fact, we anticipate that this bibliographic appendix will support and inspire such research. We imagine that when some of the libraries and collections cited here are further explored by scholars attentive to both women and Ireland, many more treasures may be found. We also expect that scholars pursuing a particular woman writer through these and other archives will discover other gems. One resource likely to support these objectives is the Virtual Record Treasury, a virtual reconstruction of the archives lost in the 1922 destruction of the Public Record Office of Ireland that is currently underway as part of the Beyond 2022 project (https://beyond2022.ie/). In short, not only do we expect to have overlooked valuable material, but we hope that we have. The field is still young, and much remains to be uncovered.

We have focused on women's life writing from the sixteenth and seventeenth centuries, although there is no doubt that a higher proportion of material comes from the mid- and late seventeenth century. This is partly a reflection of our own research interests, but we suspect that it also reflects what survives in the archives. We have included women writers from different ethnic and religious backgrounds, and although we cite texts written in Irish and other European languages, the overwhelming majority of texts we have included are written in English. This reveals the deficiencies in our own knowledge of and engagement with the Gaelic culture of early modern Ireland, but it also reflects the poor survival rates of Irish-language material. Many English-language texts by women writing their lives in seventeenth-century Ireland contain Irish words and phrases, which demonstrates some level of engagement by settlers with their Irish neighbors and their native language. But work by Irish-language scholars is still needed to ensure that our understanding of women's life writing in early modern Ireland fully embraces the women who chose to write in Irish. When we have cited native Irish women we have tended to use the most familiar versions of their names, which are mostly but not always in English. Finally, for these brief summaries, we have drawn on existing research from other scholars (cited in the bibliography), as well as on invaluable resources like the *Oxford Dictionary of National Biography*, www.oxforddnb.com, and the *Dictionary of Irish Biography*, http://dib.cambridge.org/; we are not providing individual citations here to keep the focus on the sources and the individuals.

ARCHIVES

Archivo General de Simancas, Spain
This archive contains petitions of exiled Irish women. See Marie-Louise Coolahan, *Women, Writing, and Language in Early Modern Ireland* (Oxford: Oxford University Press, 2010).

Birr Castle, County Offaly
One of the treasures to be found among the letters and papers of the Parsons family in Birr Castle, County Offaly, is the receipt book of Dorothy Parsons (A/17). Tucked among the culinary and medicinal recipes in the small quarto volume is a pen-and-pencil drawing, dated 1668, that shows alterations to Parsonstown House along with the witty inscription: "An excellent receipt to spend 4,000 pound" (A/17). Other early modern recipes (1645–52) can be found in A/4. The Calendar is available at https://birrcastle .com/wp-content/uploads/2015/07/SummaryList-of-the-Calendar-of -the-Rosse-Papers.pdf.

Bodleian Library, Oxford
The Carte Papers is the most pertinent collection at the Bodleian Library, as it is a large, multivolume archive compiled by the historian Thomas Carte that contains the original papers of several men, including James Butler, First Duke of Ormonde and lord lieutenant of Ireland; Sir William Fitzwilliam, lord deputy of Ireland; and Sir John Davies, attorney general

of Ireland. The papers cover the period 1560–1715 and are particularly valuable for study of the Ormonde Butler family, both men and women, and the family's wide-ranging network. The papers of the Duke of Ormonde preserved among the Carte Papers chiefly relate to his political activities during the wars of the Three Kingdoms, so it follows that many of the female-authored documents represented in the collection have been included because of their political relevance. These include letters from Abbess Mary Knatchbull of Ghent, an important intermediary in the royalist intelligence network; letters from Queen Henrietta Maria from France; and life writings of women caught up in the wars in Ireland. Women such as [Mrs. Francis] Briver, wife of the mayor of Waterford; Lettice Digby, née Fitzgerald, of Geashill Castle, County Offaly; and Lady Alice Moore, née Loftus, of Drogheda all describe their different experiences of siege warfare. Beyond Ireland there are letters from powerful and well-connected women like Katherine, Duchess of Buckingham, a Catholic who took as her second husband Randall MacDonnell, First Earl of Antrim and an important Irish Confederate commander. There are also numerous petitions from various women in the collection (esp. MSS 104, 105). Edward Edwards's catalog for the period 1660–87 is available online at www.bodley .ox.ac.uk/dept/scwmss/projects/carte/carte.html. But for earlier and later periods, it is essential to consult Edwards's handwritten calendar at the Bodleian Library or on microfilm.

British Library, London
There is much of interest in the British Library, most of which is already well known, such as the autobiographies of Ann Fanshawe (Add. MS 41,161), Mary Rich (Add. MS 27,357), and Alice Thornton (Add. MS 88,897), as well as Rich's diaries (Add. MS 27,351–55) and "Occasional Meditations" (Add. MS 27, 356). Letters of Elizabeth Butler, née Preston, the First Duchess of Ormonde, to Sir Edward Nicholas are located in Egerton Manuscripts, 2,534. The Sloane Manuscripts include several items, most notably the siege narrative of Elizabeth Dowdall (Sloane MS 1,008), Dorothy Moore's "Of Education of Girles" (Sloane Add. MS 649), and the "choise receipts" of Katherine Ranelagh (Sloane MS 1,367). Other collections with items

relating to the Boyle and other women include the Althorp Papers (Add. MSS 75,354–55), Egmont Papers (Add. MSS 46,931–32), Hyde Papers (Add. MS 15,892), Petty Papers (Add. MS 72,884), and Stowe Papers (MSS 206–7): for a comprehensive list of the autobiographical texts of the Boyle women in the British Library, see Ann-Maria Walsh, "Writing Women's Lives: The Epistolary Cultures of the Daughters of the First Earl of Cork" (PhD diss., University College Dublin, 2017).

Chatsworth House, Derbyshire

This is the main repository of the Boyle family papers. Within the Cork Manuscripts is the correspondence of several generations of Boyle women, including Katherine Boyle, née Fenton, to her husband (vol. 1); Sara Moore, née Boyle, to her father (vol. 14); Joan, Countess of Kildare, to her father (vol. 19); Lettice Goring, née Boyle, to her father and brother (vol. 20); and Elizabeth Kinalmeaky to her father-in-law, Richard Boyle, First Earl of Cork (vol. 22), and to her sister, Katherine, Lady Ranelagh (vol. 31). The journal of Elizabeth Boyle, née Clifford, Countess of Cork and Burlington, 1659–88, can also be found here (Misc. Box 5) alongside her letters to her husband (vol. 31). For a comprehensive list of the autobiographical texts of the Boyle women at Chatsworth, see Walsh, "Writing Women's Lives."

Friends Historical Library, Dublin

The library contains the manuscript and printed archives of Quakers in Ireland since their establishment in the seventeenth century. There are congregational records including minutes of the women's meetings, as well as letters and spiritual autobiographies. Names of significant female friends include Sarah Cheevers (1655, 1659), Katherine Evans (1659), Elizabeth Fletcher (1656, 1657), and Katherine Norton (1677, 1678).

Huntington Library, San Marino, California

At least 125 letters from women appear in the Irish Papers series, a subset of the massive collection of Hastings Family Papers. Individual correspondents with multiple letters in the collection include Anne Conway, née Finch, Viscountess Conway; Frances Conway, née Popham, Viscountess

Conway; Agnes Graham, née Gray, Countess of Menteith and Airth; Lady Isabella Graham, née Bramhall; Mary Forbes, née Rawdon, Countess of Granard; and Rose MacDonnell, née O'Neill, Marchioness of Antrim. All the known letters by Eliza Blennerhassett are also at the Huntington; see Amanda E. Herbert's chapter, in this volume.

National Archives, Kew

Women's life-writing texts can be found among the State Papers, Ireland, with petitions particularly well represented (the Commonwealth petitions of the Duchess of Ormonde are among this number). Other materials include a letter by the Poor Clare Sister Magdalen Clare (1645) and some letters of Katherine Ranelagh to various recipients, including Elizabeth, Queen of Bohemia (TS 23/1/43). Find the State Papers Online, 1509-1714, at http:// www.gale.com/intl/primary-sources/state-papers-online-early-modern.

National Archives of Ireland, Dublin

This resource has, to date, been underexplored in regard to early modern women's writing. Yet there are several collections of family and estate papers, precisely the kind of collections in which women's papers can often be found, despite women's letters typically not being cataloged and the preponderance of deeds and other legal documents. Examples of women's life writing include two early eighteenth-century letters from a Clare Taylor, a 1662 letter from Mary Bellew to her husband, and a 1684 letter from Elizabeth to Christopher Bellew, all in a collection for the Bellew family of County Louth. Two letters from Jane Pottinger are also in the Sarsfield-Vesey Correspondence.

National Library of Ireland, Dublin

Female-authored letters and petitions appear in many of the National Library of Ireland's collections of family and estate papers, including letters to and from Jane Bonnell (MS 41,580); letters from Honora O'Brien to her brother Sir Donough O'Brien; other women's letters to Donough O'Brien (MS 45,325); Mary Vesey's 1694 letter to her father, Denny Muschamp; and a circa 1663 letter from Elizabeth Muschamp, née Boyle, to her husband, Denny Muschamp (MS 38, 868). The National Library also houses microfilm copies of the Orrery Papers (MSS 13,177–13,225), which includes letters from women such as Lady E. Ponsonby (1688). Perhaps the most significant collection in the library is the Ormond Papers, which were originally preserved at Kilkenny Castle until Thomas Carte took tranches of material to Oxford, where they now form part of the Carte Papers in the Bodleian Library. The Ormond Papers represent what was left behind and for this reason have been considered less valuable than the Carte Papers. But for scholars interested in women's writing, there is much of interest, particularly relating to the women of the Ormonde Butler family, whom Carte tended to overlook. The most significant Butler woman is probably Elizabeth, First Duchess of Ormonde. But her mother and mother-in-law, daughters and daughters-in-law, granddaughters, and sisters-in-law are also represented in the collection. Her daughters were important public figures: her eldest daughter, Elizabeth, as a celebrated courtier, and her second daughter, Mary, as a patron of the arts.

National Library of Scotland, Edinburgh
The prose narrative of "Mrs. Goodale," in which she writes about her experience in Ireland circa 1700, is included in this collection. It is also available online at Perdita Manuscripts, 1500–1700, www.amdigital.co.uk/primary -sources/perdita-manuscripts-1500-1700.

National Records of Scotland, Edinburgh
The National Records of Scotland—formerly the National Archives of Scotland—is another underexplored resource in regard to women's life writing in connection to Ireland. Pertinent documents include letters by Katherine Ranelagh (GD 45/14/237/1–5 and GD 406/1/3797).

Poor Clare Monastery, Nun's Island, Galway
A contemporary English translation of Mother Mary Bonaventure Browne's Irish-language chronicle of the Poor Clares in Ireland can be found at Nun's Island alongside other seventeenth-century materials, such as a copy of a letter from Mother Cecily Francis Dillon (December 1642).

Public Record Office of Northern Ireland, Belfast
Letters by women can be found among the correspondence of merchant families housed in the Public Record Office of Northern Ireland, such as the O'Haras of Sligo (T/2812), which includes letters to Kean O'Hara from Rose O'Hara (1674?) and Elizabeth O'Hara (1691); and of the Black family of Belfast (D/1950), which includes letters of Jane/Jean Eccles to her husband (1673). There are also letters to George, Sixteenth Earl of Kildare, from several women, including his aunt Elizabeth, Dowager Countess of Kildare (1628–33); see Aidan Clarke and Bríd McGrath, eds., *Letterbook of George, 16th Earl of Kildare* (Dublin: Irish Manuscripts Commission, 2013). The Public Record Office of Northern Ireland also houses receipt books, including one (ca. 1707) that contains Lady Ailesbury's recipe for "ye limbe watter" (D607/A/1).

Royal Society Library, London
Several texts by Katherine Ranelagh are housed here, including her "Discourse concerning the plague of 1665" (RB/1/14/1); a medical commonplace book containing several recipes filed under her name (RB/2/8); and letters to members of the Hartlib Circle (RB/3/5/6–14, RB/3/6/4).

Trinity College Dublin
Three collections are particularly significant. First, the 1641 Depositions—now available on a publicly accessible and fully searchable website (http://1641.tcd.ie/)—encompasses approximately 4,000 individual witness testimonies of (mainly) Protestant settlers of English and Scottish descent, recorded in the immediate aftermath of the 1641 rebellion. Since the website is searchable by the gender of the deponent, it is now possible to quickly identify (with reasonable accuracy) that women account for 817 documents in the collection across all the county groupings, from 3 female-authored depositions in County Tyrone to 150 in County Cork. Varying in length from half a page to eight or more pages, the depositions are the records of oral responses to preestablished questions, yet they also allow considerable room for the individual shaping of rebellion experiences. See Coolahan, *Women, Writing, and Language*. Second, the Lyons Collection

of the Correspondence of William King includes the incoming correspondence of William King (1650–1729). Although primarily written by men, there are an extraordinary number of letters by women, too. For a full list of these female correspondents, see Julie A. Eckerle's chapter, in this volume. Third, TCD Muniments is a collection of papers dealing with Trinity College Dublin. Although dominated by papers by and concerning men, a number of letters by women appear in the collection; most of these concern financial matters (such as Mary Lockhart's 1692/93 letter to Provost Browne regarding the rent of Ballywire, County Tipperary). The relevant indices can be consulted in the Manuscripts and Archives Research Library reading room.

University College Cork

A few letters by and about Katherine Villiers, née Fitzgerald, written both before and after her marriage to Edward Villiers, can be found in T3137 (see esp. A/15/3 and A/21/9). Both of these letters are written from England but either sent to or concerning Ireland.

LIFE WRITERS AND THEIR FAMILIES

Hannah Alexander, née Browne (fl. 1685)

Alexander lived in Dublin with her Scottish husband, James Alexander, clerk in the Exchequer Court of Dublin Castle, until they relocated to Paisley, Scotland, during the Williamite-Jacobite War. Her receipt book, *A Book of Cookery for dressing of Several Dishes of Meat and making of Several Sauces and Seasoning for Meat or Fowl*, was written in Dublin in the 1680s, with additional recipes later added by her daughter, Hannah Dorothea (b. Dublin, 1686). Text edited by Deirdre Nuttall (Westport: Evertype, 2014). The manuscript is privately owned.

Elizabeth Avery (fl. 1614–53)

Prophet and author of *Scripture-Prophecies Opened* (1647), Avery moved to Dublin in the early 1650s and became a member of John Rogers's Independent congregation in Dublin. Her conversion narrative, delivered before the Dublin congregation, was among those published in Rogers's *Ohel or*

Beth-shemesh: A Tabernacle for the Sun, 2 vols. (London, 1653); significantly, seventeen female-authored testimonies ranging in length from less than half a page to over three pages are included in Rogers's collection. Many of these women, like Avery, had only recently arrived in Ireland. Avery's edited testimony is published in *Lay by Your Needles Ladies, Take the Pen: Writing Women in England, 1500–1700*, ed. Suzanne Trill, Kate Chedgzoy, and Melanie Osborne (London: Arnold, 1997), but there is no extant manuscript. See also the sections on Elizabeth Chambers, Frances Curtis, and Mary Turrant. See Coolahan, *Women, Writing, and Language*; and Crawford Gribben, *God's Irishmen: Theological Debates in Cromwellian Ireland* (Oxford: Oxford University Press, 2007).

Brighid Ó Domhnaill Barnewall, née Fitzgerald (ca. 1589–1682)
The daughter of Henry Fitzgerald, Twelfth Earl of Kildare, Ó Domhnaill married first Rudhraighe Ó Domhnaill, Earl of Tyrconnell, in 1603 and was still in Ireland when he left during the 1607 Flight of the Earls. She spent a few years in England; was never reunited with her husband, who died in 1608; married second husband Sir Nicholas Barnewall in 1617; and wrote poetry. Her 1607 letter to Lord Deputy Arthur Chichester is printed in Angela Bourke et al., *The Field Day Anthology of Irish Writing*, vols. 4 and 5, *Irish Women's Writing and Traditions* (Cork: Cork University Press, 2002).

Alice Barrymore (1608–68)
The eldest daughter of the First Earl of Cork, Barrymore maintained a correspondence with her friend and member of Parliament Sir Ralph Verney over many years: this correspondence is preserved at the Verney home of Claydon Manor, Claydon, with copies available on microfilm in the British Library. There are also letters to members of her natal family among the Cork Manuscripts at Chatsworth House. See Ann-Maria Walsh's chapter, in this volume.

Barbara Blaugdone (ca. 1609–1704)
Blaugdone was an English Quaker who traveled and preached in England and Ireland during the Restoration and published *An Account of the Travels, Sufferings & Persecutions of Barbara Blaugdone: Given forth as a Testimony to*

the Lord's Power, and for the Encouragement of Friends (Shoreditch, 1691), reprinted in facsimile in Elizabeth Skerpan-Wheeler, ed., *Life Writings: The Early Modern Englishwoman; A Facsimile Library of Essential Works*, ser. 2, pt. 1, vols. 1–2 (Aldershot: Ashgate, 2001), vol. 2. See also Anne Fogarty's chapter, in this volume.

Jane Bonnell, née Conyngham (1660s–1745)
One of three daughters of Gen. Sir Albert Conyngham and wife of James Bonnell, accountant general of Ireland, Bonnell became a voluminous letter writer in her long widowhood. She was also the driving force behind the 1703 publication of her husband's life, William Hamilton's *The Exemplary Life and Character of James Bonnell*. Her manuscript letters are primarily archived at Trinity College Dublin and the National Library of Ireland and were sent from a range of locations, including Dublin, Finglas, Hillsborough, and London. See Eckerle's chapter, in this volume.

Lady Catherine Boyle, née Fenton, First Countess of Cork (ca. 1588–1630)
Daughter of Sir Geoffrey Fenton and wife of Richard Boyle, First Earl of Cork, Boyle spent most of her life in Ireland, with some extended trips to England. She died in Dublin and is buried at Saint Patrick's Cathedral there. Manuscript letters can be found among the Cork Manuscripts in Chatsworth House. See also Walsh's chapter, in this volume.

Elizabeth Boyle, née Clifford, Countess of Cork and Burlington (1613–90)
Heiress and daughter of Henry Clifford, Earl of Cumberland, and wife of Richard Boyle, Second Earl of Cork, Boyle managed estates and kept ample records, much like the other Boyle women. Letters written to her husband before and after their marriage can be found among the Althorp Papers in the British Library. Her manuscript memorandum book is in the Chatsworth House. See also Walsh's chapter, in this volume.

Elizabeth Boyle, née Fielding, Lady Kinalmeaky (1619–67)
Born and raised in England, Boyle's marriage to Lewis Boyle, Viscount Kinalmeaky, who was killed in the Battle of Liscarrol early in their marriage,

brought her temporarily into both Ireland and the Boyle family. Her manuscript letters are housed in the Carte Papers at the Bodleian Library and the Cork Manuscripts in Chatsworth House.

Margaret Boyle, née Howard, Countess of Orrery (1622–89)
Born and raised in England, Boyle's marriage to Roger Boyle, First Earl of Orrery, brought her into Ireland and the Boyle family. She is largely responsible for the collection of materials ultimately known as the Orrery Papers. See her manuscript letters at the National Library of Ireland. See also Walsh's chapter in this volume.

[Mrs. Francis] Briver (fl. 1641–42)
The wife of Francis Briver, mayor of Waterford in 1641–42, Briver wrote an epistolary account of the rebellion in Waterford, partly in defense of her husband. [Mrs. Francis] Briver, "An Epistolary Account of the Irish Rising of 1641 by the Wife of the Mayor of Waterford (with text)," ed. Naomi McAreavey, *English Literary Renaissance* 42, no. 1 (2012): 90–118. Her manuscripts are housed in the Carte Papers at the Bodleian Library. See also McAreavey, "'This is that I may remember what passings that Happind in Waterford': Inscribing the 1641 Rising in the Letters of the Wife of the Mayor of Waterford," *Early Modern Women: An Interdisciplinary Journal* 5 (2010): 77–109.

Mother Mary Bonaventure Browne (ca. 1610–ca. 1670)
Browne was the abbess of the Galway Poor Clares, who led the Irish order to exile in Spain in the 1650s and then wrote a chronicle of the order's experiences at home and abroad during the seventeenth century. The Irish-language original was destroyed, but a contemporary English translation survives: Celsus O'Brien, ed., *Recollections of an Irish Poor Clare in the Seventeenth Century* (Galway: Connaught Tribune, 1993). The manuscript is held in the Poor Clare Monastery in Galway. See also Marie-Louise Coolahan, "Identity Politics and Nuns' Writing." *Women's Writing* 14, no. 2 (2007): 306–20; Coolahan, *Women, Writing, and Language*; and Naomi McAreavey, "Irish Nuns and the Counter-Reformation Movement: The

Struggle between Nation and Vocation," in *Representing Women's Authority in the Early Modern World*, ed. Eavan O'Brien, 221–51 (Rome: Aracne, 2013).

Magdalen Bruce, née Faulkner (fl. 1642)
Faulkner's letters from the besieged Castle Lyon (March 1642) can be found with the Verney Papers, Claydon House, Middle Claydon, Buckinghamshire, with copies available on microfilm in the British Library.

Elizabeth Butler, née Preston, First Duchess of Ormonde (1615–84)
Butler was heiress and wife of James Butler, Twelfth Earl and First Duke of Ormonde, who served three times as lord lieutenant of Ireland. At least three hundred surviving letters covering six decades together provide insight into the public and private life and epistolary self-representation of a preeminent aristocratic Irish woman. Her manuscripts are in the Bodleian Library, British Library, National Library of Ireland, and elsewhere. See Elizabeth Butler, Duchess of Ormonde, *The Letters of the First Duchess of Ormonde*, ed. Naomi McAreavey (Tempe: Arizona Center for Medieval and Renaissance Studies, forthcoming). See also Eleanor O'Keeffe, "The Family and Marriage Strategies of James Butler, First Duke of Ormonde, 1658–1688" (PhD diss., University of Cambridge, 2000); and McAreavey's chapter, in this volume.

Margaret Butler, née Fitzgerald, Countess of
Ormond and Ossory (1458?–1542)
Daughter of the Eighth Earl of Kildare and wife of the Eighth Earl of Ormonde, Butler was known for her spiritual devotion and for restoring the Butler fortunes. Her 1540 letter to King Henry VIII is excerpted in Bourke et al., *Field Day Anthology*, vol. 4. See also Damien Duffy, "The Ormond Women: Family, Power, and Politics, c. 1450s–1660" (PhD diss., Maynooth University, 2018).

Mary Butler, née Somerset, Second Duchess of Ormonde (1665–1733)
Butler was less interested in spending her time in Ireland as her predecessor was, but her letters from Ireland (although less voluminous) nonetheless provide insight into the life of a woman transplanted from England to

Ireland through marriage. Her letters are archived at the British Library and the National Library of Ireland.

Elizabeth Cary, née Tanfield, Lady Falkland (1585–1639)
Cary spent 1622–25 in Ireland, as her husband, Sir Henry Cary, First Viscount Falkland, was lord deputy of Ireland 1622–24, and had her last two children there. Although only in Ireland for a short period, Cary studied Irish, connected with Irish and Old English Catholics, and was clearly impacted by her experiences in the country. Best known for her plays, Cary also wrote letters and was the subject of a biography written by one of her children. These documents are published in Heather Wolfe, ed., *Elizabeth Cary Lady Falkland: Life and Letters* (Tempe: Arizona Center for Medieval and Renaissance Studies, 2001). Cary's Irish connections have been considered by Deana Rankin, "'A More Worthy Patronesse': Elizabeth Cary and Ireland," in *The Literary Career and Legacy of Elizabeth Cary, 1613–1680*, ed. Heather Wolfe, 203–21 (London: Palgrave Macmillan, 2007); and Ramona Wray, "Memory, Materiality and Maternity in the Tanfield/Cary Archive," in *A History of Early Modern Women's Writing*, ed. Patricia Phillippy, 221–40 (Cambridge: Cambridge University Press, 2018).

Elizabeth Chambers (fl. ca. 1641)
Chambers was a member of the Independent congregation in Dublin and lived in Ireland before and after the 1641 rebellion; her spiritual testimony is included in John Rogers's *Ohel or Beth-shemesh*.

Sarah Cheevers (d. 1664)
Cheevers and fellow Society of Friends member Katharine Evans co-wrote the spiritual testimony, *This is a Short Relation Of Some of the Cruel Sufferings (For the Truth's Sake) of Katharine Evans and Sarah Chevers* (London, 1662), which includes a few references to Ireland, one of the many places to which they had traveled; she also maintained correspondence with other Quakers in Ireland. *A Short Relation* is excerpted in Elspeth Graham et al., eds., *Her Own Life: Autobiographical Writings by Seventeenth-Century Englishwomen*

(London: Routledge, 1989) and appears in facsimile in Skerpan-Wheeler, *Life Writings*, vol. 1.

Frances Cooke (fl. 1646–60)
Cooke's account of a dangerous Irish Sea crossing with her husband, John Cook, chief justice to the Court of Munster, was published in London as *Mris. Cookes Meditations* ([London, 1650]); it is included in Trill, Chedgzoy, and Osborne, *Lay by Your Needles*; and appears in facsimile in Skerpan-Wheeler, *Life Writings*, vol. 1.

Frances Curtis (fl. ca. 1650)
A member of the Independent congregation in Dublin, Curtis lived in Ireland before and after the 1641 rebellion; her spiritual testimony is included in John Rogers's *Ohel or Beth-shemesh*.

Mary Petty Conyngham Dallway, née Williams,
Lady Shelburne (1673–1710)
Born in England, Lady Shelburne married, first, Irish peer John Petty, Lord Shelburne; second, Irish brigadier Henry Conyngham, brother of Jane Bonnell; and, third, Col. Robert Dallway. Shelburne wrote many letters, the majority of which dealt with the Irish estates of the deceased Conyngham. Her manuscript letters are held in the Public Record Office of Northern Ireland, the National Library of Ireland, and the Castletown Papers at the Irish Architectural Archive.

Lady Eleanor Davies, née Touchet (1590–1652)
Davies moved with her family to Ulster as a teenager because of her father's administrative role in Ireland and remained there through her first decade of marriage, to Sir John Davies, poet and attorney general for Ireland. She also had three children in Ireland, including Lucy, who would become the Countess of Huntingdon and a prolific correspondent. Davies did not begin to publish her controversial prophesies until she returned to England, but they were shaped in part by her formative years in Ireland. She published

almost seventy tracts in her lifetime. See Esther Cope, ed., *Prophetic Writings of Eleanor Davies* (Oxford: Oxford University Press, 1995).

Lettice Digby, née Fitzgerald, Baroness of Offaly (ca. 1580–1658)
Digby defended Geashill Castle, County Offaly, during the 1641 rebellion. She eventually went to England, where she died. Her so-called siege letters are in manuscript in the 1641 Depositions at Trinity College Dublin and the Carte Papers at the Bodleian Library; the letters are published in Bourke et al., *Field Day Anthology*, vol. 5. See also Coolahan, *Women, Writing, and Language*, and McAreavey, "'Paper bullets': Gendering the 1641 Rebellion in the Writings of Lady Elizabeth Dowdall and Lettice Fitzgerald, Baroness of Offaly," in *Ireland in the Renaissance, c. 1540–1660*, ed. Thomas Herron and Michael Potterton, 311–24 (Dublin: Four Courts, 2007).

Mary/Marie Donovan, née Ogle (eighteenth century)
The daughter of Samuel Ogle, member of Parliament for Berswick and commissioner of the Irish Revenue, Ogle married, first, Capt. John Broughton and, second, Edward Donovan. Her second husband was a lawyer in Ireland, with whom she had twenty-one children. The recipe book that Ogle began in 1713, now known as the "Donovan Family Recipe Book," was maintained by multiple generations of the family and can be accessed online at https://arrow.dit.ie/gasbook/4/.

Lady Elizabeth Dowdall (fl. 1630–50)
The daughter of Sir Thomas Southwell and Lady Anne Southwell, Dowdall was born in Ireland as a member of the New English nobility. She married John Dowdall, who built Kilfinny Castle in County Limerick. During the 1641 rebellion, she defended this castle; her account of the siege is in the Sloane Manuscripts at the British Library. Her deposition is with the 1641 Depositions at Trinity College Dublin and in Bourke et al., *Field Day Anthology*, vol. 5. See also Coolahan, *Women, Writing, and Language*, and McAreavey, "Paper bullets," in Herron and Potterton, *Ireland in the Renaissance*, 311–24.

Katherine Evans (d. 1692)

Evans visited Ireland as part of her Quaker missionary travels with Sarah Cheevers, with whom she cowrote the spiritual testimony, *This Is a Short Relation Of Some of the Cruel Sufferings (For the Truth's Sake) of Katharine Evans and Sarah Chevers* (London, 1662), which includes a few references to Ireland. She also maintained correspondence with other Quakers in Ireland. *A Short Relation* is excerpted in Graham et al., eds., *Her Own Life;* and appears in facsimile in Skerpan-Wheeler, *Life Writings,* vol. 1.

Lady Ann Fanshawe (1625–80)

Although her actual time in Ireland was less than a year, Fanshawe's Irish episodes in her manuscript memoirs are memorable for their detail and adventure. They are housed in manuscript at the British Library, excerpted in multiple anthologies, and published in Ann Fanshawe, *The Memoirs of Ann, Lady Fanshawe,* in *The Memoirs of Anne, Lady Halkett and Ann, Lady Fanshawe,* ed. John Loftis, 89–192 (Oxford: Clarendon, 1979). See also Coolahan, *Women, Writing, and Language;* Fogarty's chapter, in this volume; and Lucy Moore's unique biographical treatment, built around Fanshawe's receipts and including her Irish experiences, in *Lady Ranelagh's Receipt Book: An Englishwoman's Life During the Civil War.*

Eleanor Fitzgerald, née Butler, Countess of Desmond (ca. 1545–1638)

The daughter of Edmund Butler, Lord Baron of Dunboyne, Fitzgerald was born at Kiltinan Castle, County Tipperary, as a member of the Old English nobility. She married first Garrett (Gerald) FitzJames Fitzgerald, the last Earl of Desmond, and endured imprisonment and other difficulties with him until his death in 1583. She married second husband, Sir Donough O'Connor Sligo, in 1596. Fitzgerald produced a substantive body of correspondence. Her manuscripts are housed at the National Archives at Kew, and a selection of her letters is in Bourke et al., *Field Day Anthology,* vol. 5. See also Anne Chambers, *Eleanor, Countess of Desmond, c. 1545–1638* (Dublin: Wolfhound, 1986).

Lady Joan Fitzgerald, Countess of Ormonde,
Ossory, and Desmond (1509?–65)
The daughter of the Eleventh Earl of Desmond and the wife of three powerful men (James Butler, Ninth Earl of Ormonde; Sir Francis Bryan, lord justice of Ireland; and Gerald Fitzgerald, Fifteenth Earl of Desmond), Fitzgerald played a significant role in the political life of sixteenth-century Ireland. She maintained a correspondence with Queen Elizabeth I. See Karen Ann Holland, "Joan Desmond, Ormond, and Ossory: The World of a Countess in Sixteenth-Century Ireland" (PhD diss., Providence College, 1996).

Lady Joan Fitzgerald, née Boyle, Countess Kildare (1611–1656/57)
Fourth daughter of the First Earl of Cork, Fitzgerald married George Fitzgerald, Sixteenth Earl of Kildare. Although she is relatively underrepresented in the Boyle family archives, at least one letter survives to her father. This letter can be found in the Cork Manuscripts, vol. 19, Chatsworth House. See also Walsh, "Writing Women's Lives."

Honor Fitzmaurice, née Fitzgerald, Lady Kerry (d. 1668)
Fitzmaurice and her husband, Patrick Fitzmaurice, Lord Kerry and Baron of Lixnaw, County Kerry, fled to England in the 1640s. Although her husband died in England, she returned to Ireland in 1660 and rebuilt Ardfert Cathedral, where she is buried. Her 1641 letter to Pierse Ferriter is included in Bourke et al., *Field Day Anthology*, vol. 4.

Ann Fowkes, née Geale (1692–1774)
Fowkes was born in Kilkenny, married minister Samuel Fowkes in 1712, and spent most of her life in Ireland, primarily in Waterford. Her autobiographical narrative, *A Memoir of Mistress Ann Fowkes née Geale, died aged 82 Years, with some recollections of her family, A.D. 1642–1774. Written by herself,* was published in Dublin in 1892, and is available in the National Folklore Collection in University College Dublin.

Elizabeth Freke (1641/42–1714)

Freke made several generally unhappy trips to Ireland during her marriage to her second cousin, Percy Freke. Although her autobiographical narratives are familiar to scholars of life writing, few have attended to her striking commentary on Ireland within these texts. In manuscript at the British Library, excerpted in multiple anthologies, and published as Elizabeth Freke, *The Remembrances of Elizabeth Freke, 1671–1714*, ed. Raymond A. Anselment (Cambridge: Cambridge University Press, 2001); see also Anselment's chapter, in this volume.

Martha Giffard, née Temple, Lady Giffard (1639–1722)

Martha, Lady Giffard, was the daughter of Sir John Temple, author of *The Irish Rebellion* (1646). She married Sir Thomas Giffard, Baronet of Castlejordan, County Meath, but was widowed two weeks later and never remarried. Thereafter she lived much of her life with her brother and sister-in-law, Sir William Temple and Dorothy Osborne. Lady Giffard was a prolific letter writer and also wrote a biography of her brother: *The Life and Character of Sir William Temple* (London, 1728). For her letters see Julia G. Longe, *Martha, Lady Giffard, Her Life and Correspondence, 1664–1722: A Sequel to the Letters of Dorothy Osborne* (London: G. Allen, 1911). Her correspondence is in the British Library and the library of the University of Southampton.

Mrs. Goodale (fl. ca. 1700)

Mrs. Goodale's memoirs cover her travels with her husband in both Ireland and Scotland in the late seventeenth century. This manuscript is online at Perdita Manuscripts and archived at the National Library of Scotland.

Lucy Hastings, née Davies, Countess of Huntingdon (1613–79)

Born in Dublin, Hastings was the daughter of the prophet Eleanor Davies, née Touchet, and Sir John Davies, poet and attorney general of Ireland. When Eleanor Davies was imprisoned, Hastings attempted to correct derisive accounts of her mother's reputation, drawing on the continuing family links with Ireland. As a widow, she had charge of land in Ireland, for which she received rents, dealt with tenants, and instructed solicitors and stewards. Her correspondence can be found among the Hastings Family Papers in the Huntington Library, including letters to her husband at the time of her marriage.

Lucy Hay, née Percy, Dowager Countess of Carlisle (1599–1660)
Hay inherited her husband's Irish holdings; helped her brother-in-law Robert Sidney, Second Earl of Leicester, be appointed lord deputy of Ireland; and engaged in a questionable relationship with Thomas Wentworth, Earl of Strafford and lord deputy of Ireland. Correspondence included in Dorothy Percy Sidney, *The Correspondence (c. 1626–1659) of Dorothy Percy Sidney, Countess of Leicester*, ed. Michael G. Brennan, Noel J. Kinnamon, and Margaret P. Hannay (Farnham: Ashgate, 2010).

Katherine Jones, née Boyle, Lady Ranelagh (1615–91)
Born in Youghal to Richard Boyle, First Earl of Cork, Jones married Arthur Jones, Second Viscount Ranelagh, in 1630/31 and had four children. She ultimately left her husband and spent the majority of her adulthood in England. A prodigious letter writer and an important member of the second generation of the Boyle family, Ranelagh's correspondents included family members such as brother Robert Boyle and members of the Hartlib Circle like Samuel Hartlib himself. Her letters can be found in the "Collection of State Papers Connected with Meath" in the Dopping Collection, Armagh Robinson Library; the Cork Manuscripts in Chatsworth House; the Petty Papers and Sloane Manuscripts at the British Library; the Royal Society Library, and elsewhere. Her recipes can be found in the Sloane Manuscripts in the British Library and in the Boyle Papers at the Royal Society Library. See also Evan Bourke's analysis of the women in the Hartlib Circle in "Female Involvement, Membership, and Centrality: A Social Network Analysis of the Hartlib Circle," *Literature Compass* 14, no. 4 (2017) and "A Godly Sybilla, an Erudite Wife and a Burdensome Sister: The Formation and Representation of Women's Reputations within the Hartlib Circle 1641-1661" (PhD diss., National University of Ireland Galway, 2018); and Ruth Connolly's and Amelia Zurcher's chapters, in this volume.

Lady Francis Keightley, née Hyde (b. ca. 1638)
The daughter of Edward Hyde, First Earl of Clarendon, and wife of Thomas Keightley, commissioner of the Irish Revenue, Keightley moved to Ireland in the late 1670s with her family. She ultimately separated from her husband and returned to England in the early eighteenth century. Some of her letters survive at the National Library of Ireland, including the lengthy "Advice to a daughter" for Catherine O'Brien.

Elizabeth Mathew, née Poyntz, Lady Thurles (1587–1673)
Mother of the First Duke of Ormonde from her first marriage to Thomas Butler, Viscount Thurles, Mathew later married Capt. George Mathew, who also predeceased her. Thereafter, she lived thirty-seven years as a dowager. She was a devout Catholic and, with the exception of her eldest son, all her children shared her Catholicism, and one daughter was a nun. Her letters, mainly to her eldest son, and other documents, including recipes, can be found in volumes 21, 23, and 28 in the Carte Papers at the Bodleian Library and in volumes 2,338 and 2,347 in the Ormond Papers at the National Library of Ireland.

Eliza Mervyn, née Blennerhassett (pre-1639–1676)
Mervyn came to Ireland during the Cromwellian settlement of the 1650s, but her family already had long roots in the country. She married in Ireland in 1660, had children, and seems to have remained in the country. Seven letters from the late 1650s survive, all written to the Hastings family, with whom she was related by birth. Her manuscript letters are in the Huntington Library (Hastings Family Papers). See also Herbert's chapter, in this volume.

Susan Montgomery, née Steynings (?–1615)
The wife of Scottish divine George Montgomery, who become the first Protestant bishop of Derry, Clogher, and Raphoe, Montgomery went to Derry with her husband in 1606 as a New English settler and died in Ireland in 1615. Her extant letters contain accounts of life in Ireland. Her manuscript letters are housed with John Willoughby's correspondence in the Trevelyan Papers, Somerset Record Office; see also George Hill, ed., *The Montgomery*

Manuscripts (1603–1706) (Belfast, 1869); and Marie-Louise Coolahan, "Ideal Communities and Planter Women's Writing in Seventeenth-Century Ireland," *Parergon: Journal of the Australian and New Zealand Association for Medieval and Early Modern Studies* 29, no. 2 (2012): 69–91.

Lady Alice Moore, née Loftus (1607–49)

The wife of Charles, Viscount Moore, who was killed in battle in Meath in 1643, Moore wrote several letters to the Marquess of Ormonde during the civil war period and especially after her husband's death. See Alice Moore, *A Declaration of Alice Vicecountess Moor Dowager of Drogheda, Concerning Her deceased Lord's faithful Service, and her Sufferings in Ireland* (London, 1648). Her manuscript letters can be found in volumes 5, 6, 7, 12, 13, and 18 in the Carte Papers at the Bodleian Library.

Dorothy Moore [Dury], née King (1612/13–64)

The daughter of Sir John King, an Irish administrator, Moore was born in Dublin, where her family lived near the Boyles. Her first husband was Arthur Moore, and her second was the itinerant Scottish minister John Dury. Moore engaged in extensive intellectual epistolary conversation with fellow intellects of her day, including Lady Ranelagh and members of the Hartlib Circle. She also petitioned the House of Lords in 1648 and wrote a treatise on girls' education, which is no longer extant. Although born in Ireland, she spent much of her adulthood in Utrecht. See also E. Bourke, "Female Involvement;" E. Bourke, "A Godly Sybilla;" and Dorothy Moore, *The Letters of Dorothy Moore, 1612–64: The Friendships, Marriage, and Intellectual Life of a Seventeenth-Century Woman*, ed. Lynette Hunter (Aldershot: Ashgate, 2004).

Katherine Norton, née McLoughlin (fl. 1671–79)

Norton was born in or near Coleraine, County Derry/Londonderry, but moved to Barbados at the age of sixteen, where she converted to Quakerism under the ministry of George Fox and became a preacher there. By 1676 she returned to Ireland, where she preached throughout the north of the country, including in the Irish language. One letter to the Dublin-based Quaker merchant, Anthony Sharp, dated March 30, 1678, survives. Her manuscripts are in the Sharp Manuscripts at the Friends Historical Library. See Phil Kilroy, *Protestant Dissent and Controversy in Ireland, 1660–1714* (Cork: Cork University Press, 1994); and Bernadette Whelan, "McLoughlin, Katherine (*fl.* 1671–1679)," in *Oxford Dictionary of National Biography*, Oxford University Press, September 23, 2004, https://doi.org/10.1093/ref:odnb/67223.

Catherine O'Brien, née Keightley (1676–ca. 1731)
As the daughter of Lady Frances Keightley, née Hyde, and Thomas Keightley, a commissioner of the Irish Revenue, lord treasurer, and lord justice, O'Brien was raised in Ireland from age five and ultimately married Lucius O'Brien in 1701/2. Beset with marital and financial problems, she wrote numerous letters, including a significant number to Jane Bonnell, which remain in the National Library of Ireland.

Gráinne O'Malley (ca. 1530–ca. 1603)
The subject of numerous legends, O'Malley's petition on behalf of her two sons is included in Bourke et al., *Field Day Anthology*, vol. 5.

Rosa O'Neill, née O'Doherty (ca. 1588–1660)
O'Neill left Ireland as part of the Flight of the Earls alongside her husband, Owen Roe O'Neill, who later returned to Ireland as a military commander for the Confederate Catholics; her scribally recorded Gaelic letter from September 1642 was first translated and published by Gilbert II and then reprinted in Bourke et al., *Field Day Anthology*, vol. 5. See also Jerrold Casway, "Rosa O Dogherty: A Gaelic Woman," *Seanchas Ard Mhacha* 10 (1980–82): 42–62.

Dorothy Parsons (1663–1749)
Born in Birr Castle, County Offaly, Dorothy Parsons was the daughter of Sir Laurence Parsons, First Baronet of Parsonstown (1637–98). Her receipt book, found among the Parsons family papers in Birr Castle, incorporates some suggestions of Lady Elizabeth Parsons, wife of Sir William Parsons, Second Baronet of Parsonstown (1661–1741).

Elizabeth Petty, née Waller (d. 1708)

The daughter of regicide Sir Hardress Waller, Petty was probably born in Ireland. Her first husband was Sir Maurice Fenton, and her second, whom she married in 1667, was Sir William Petty; he had led the Down Survey of Ireland in 1656–58 and was a founding member of the Royal Society. Elizabeth Petty's business diary records her travels and business activities on the couple's Irish estates in Limerick, Cork, and Kerry in June and July 1675. Her manuscript is in the Lansdowne Manuscripts at the British Library and online in Perdita Manuscripts.

Katherine Philips, née Fowler (1632–64)

A poet, playwright, and letter writer, Philips spent a prolific year in Ireland (where her family owned estates) in 1662–63 and became a leading member of a literary coterie based in the viceregal court at Dublin Castle. Although Philips is known primarily for the autobiography-inflected poetry that she composed under the pen name "Orinda" and addressed to the Irish nobility, including Lady Elizabeth Boyle, Lady Mary Butler, and the Countess of Roscommon, her correspondence also records her experiences in Ireland. Her epistolary addressees included Dorothy Temple, Edward Dering, Lady Fletcher, and Sir Charles Cotterrell. Her play *Pompey* was first performed in Dublin under the patronage of Roger Boyle, Earl of Orrery. Modern edition: Katherine Philips, *The Collected Works of Katherine Philips: The Matchless Orinda*, ed. Patrick Thomas, Germaine Greer, and Roger Little, 3 vols. (London: Stump Cross, 1990–93).

Jane Pottinger, née Faith (fl. Seventeenth Century)

The daughter of Solomon Faith, mayor of Carrickfergus, and the wife of Capt. Edward Pottinger, a merchant and ship's master of Belfast, Pottinger seems to have managed some of her husband's business when he was at sea. Two letters to her husband in France survive from November and December 1677. Her manuscripts are in the Sarsfield-Vesey Correspondence in the National Archives of Ireland. One letter is published in Bourke et al., *Field Day Anthology*, vol. 5.

Marguerite Preston, née de Namur (fl. 1647)
Preston was a native of Brussels and wife of Gen. Thomas Preston, who fought with the Confederate Catholics in Ireland. An April 24, 1647, letter in French to her husband is in the National Archives at Kew and printed in Bourke et al., *Field Day Anthology*, vol. 5.

Lady Dorothy Rawdon, née Conway (fl. mid-seventeenth century to early eighteenth century)
Rawdon, a frequent letter writer, wrote letters that survive in the Irish Papers series, a subset of the Hastings Family Papers at the Huntington Library.

Mary Rich, née Boyle, Countess of Warwick (1624/25–78)
A voluminous life writer and one of the daughters of Richard Boyle, First Earl of Cork, Rich has received a great deal of scholarly attention during the past few decades for her diaries, memoir ("Some Specialities"), and occasional meditations. Very little of her writing explicitly deals with Ireland, but there is no doubt that her girlhood experiences in Ireland influenced what she wrote. Her work is excerpted in multiple anthologies; print editions include Mary Rich, *The Occasional Meditations of Mary Rich, Countess of Warwick*, ed. Raymond A. Anselment (Tempe: Arizona Center for Medieval and Renaissance Studies, 2009); Rich, *Memoir of Lady Warwick, also her diary, from A.D. 1666–1672* (London: Religious Tract Society, 1847); and Rich, *The Autobiography of Mary Countess of Warwick*, ed. T. Crofton Croker (London: Percy Society, 1848). Her meditations, multivolume diary, and memoir are in manuscript in the Additional Manuscripts at the British Library. See Walsh's and Zurcher's chapters, in this volume.

Lady Cicely (or Cecilia) Ridgeway, née Macwilliam (d. 1628)
A one-time lady-in-waiting to Queen Elizabeth I, Ridgeway married Sir Thomas Ridgeway, treasurer of Ireland, 1606–16, and later Earl of Londonderry, and with him became involved with the Ulster plantation. She was a patron to the poet Anne Southwell, who was also among her correspondents; at least one letter is extant at the Huntington Library. See Coolahan, "Ideal Communities."

Dorothy Sidney, née Percy, Countess of Leicester (ca. 1626–59)
Sidney's correspondence with her husband, Robert Sidney, Second Earl of Leicester and lord lieutenant of Ireland, 1641–43, occasionally touches on Irish matters. See Brennan, Kinnamon, and Hannay, *Correspondence.*

Anne Southwell [Sibthorpe], née Harris (1574–1636)
Born and raised in England, Southwell moved to Ireland with her first husband, Sir Thomas Southwell, and spent most of her married life at Pool-na-long Castle, County Cork. In 1628 she left Ireland for England with second husband, Capt. Henry Sibthorp. She wrote letters and epistolary poetry and is best known for a commonplace book, which is in manuscript at the Folger Shakespeare Library; in modern edition Anne Southwell, *The Southwell-Sibthorpe Commonplace Book: Folger MS V.b.198*, ed. Jean Klene (Tempe: Arizona Center for Medieval and Renaissance Studies, 1997); and online at Perdita Manuscripts. See Coolahan, *Women, Writing, and Language*, on how Southwell's New English identity influenced her writing and vision.

Alice Stonier (fl. ca. 1600–50)
Stonier fled Ireland for her native parish of Leek in Staffordshire upon the outbreak of the 1641 rebellion. Her 1642 petition for poor relief is published in Bourke et al., *Field Day Anthology*, vol. 5.

Dorothy Temple, née Osborne (1627–95)
Temple's famous letters to her future husband, Sir William Temple (son of Sir John Temple, master of the rolls in Ireland and author of the 1646 *Irish Rebellion*) predate her move to Ireland as a young married woman. Nonetheless, some were sent to William in Ireland and contain much of Irish interest. Dorothy and William Temple lived in Ireland from 1656 to 1663. Her work is excerpted in multiple anthologies and edited and published as Dorothy Osborne, *Letters from Dorothy Osborne to Sir William Temple (1652–54)*, ed. Edward Abbott Parry (London: Dent, 1914); her manuscripts are in the Additional Manuscripts at the British Library .

Alice Thornton, née Wandesford (1626–1707)

Although she lived most of her life in England, Thornton spent several formative years of her youth in Ireland, where her father held administrative positions, and wrote about some of these experiences in her substantive life writings. For an excellent explanation of Thornton's very complicated textual corpus—which comprises four different manuscripts—see Raymond A. Anselment, "Seventeenth-Century Manuscript Sources of Alice Thornton's Life," *Studies in English Literature, 1500–1900* 45, no. 1 (2005): 135–55. For the manuscripts most pertinent to Ireland, see Anselment, in this volume. Thornton's two extant manuscripts are at the British Library; a no-longer-extant third is in microfilm at Sterling Memorial Library at Yale University; and a print edition of these materials is *My First Booke of My Life*, ed. Raymond A. Anselment (Lincoln: University of Nebraska Press, 2014). Thornton's work has been excerpted in multiple anthologies.

Mary Trye, née O'Dowde (fl. 1675)

Mary Trye is the author of *Medicatrix, or, The woman-physician* (London, 1675), which she wrote partly in defense of her physician father, Thomas O'Dowde, who had trained her. The Irish O'Dowde had lost his fortune during the 1640s, whereupon he entered the service of Charles I and then Charles II. *Medicatrix* is dedicated to Lady Fisher of Packington Hall in Warwickshire.

Katherine Villiers, née Fitzgerald, Viscountess Grandison (1674–1701)

Villiers's complicated path to marriage—which involved a betrothal to John, Lord Decies (later Second Earl of Tyrone) when she was twelve; a subsequent repudiation of said betrothal by John; and marriage instead to Edward Villiers when she was fourteen—is documented in part in an archive at University College Cork. At least two of her letters are included.

Joan Vokins (ca. 1630–1690)

A Quaker missionary who traveled and proselytized in Ireland, Vokins wrote an autobiography about her experience and sent letters to other

Quakers. Both autobiography and letters were published posthumously as Joan Vokins, *God's Mighty Power Magnified: As Manifested and Revealed in His Faithful Handmaid Joan Vokins* (Cockermouth, England, 1691); and online at Orlando: Women's Writing in the British Isles from the Beginnings to the Present, http://orlando.cambridge.org/svHomePage.

BIBLIOGRAPHY

MANUSCRIPTS

Archivo General de Simancas, Spain

Armagh Robinson Library, Armagh, Northern Ireland
    Dopping Collection

Birr Castle, County Offaly

Bodleian Library (Bodl.), Oxford
    Burnet Manuscripts
    Carte Papers
    Clarendon State Papers

British Library (BL), London
    Additional Manuscripts (Althorp, Boyle, Egmont, Hyde, Petty)
    Egerton Manuscripts
    Lansdowne Manuscripts
    Sloane Manuscripts
    Stowe Manuscripts

Chatsworth House, Derbyshire
    Boyle Papers
    Cork Manuscripts

Claydon House, Middle Claydon, Buckinghamshire
    Verney Papers

Folger Shakespeare Library, Washington DC

Friends Historical Library, Dublin

Sharp Manuscripts
Huntington Library (HL), San Marino, California
    Hastings Family Papers
Irish Architectural Archive, Dublin
    Castletown Papers
Marsh's Library, Dublin
National Archives (TNA), Kew, Surrey
National Archives of Ireland, Dublin
    Sarsfield-Vesey Correspondence
National Records of Scotland, Edinburgh
National Library of Ireland (NLI), Dublin
    Lismore Castle Estate Papers
    Ormond Papers
    Orrery Papers
    Smythe of Barbavilla Papers
National Library of Scotland, Edinburgh
Poor Clare Monastery, Nun's Island, Galway, Ireland
Public Record Office of Northern Ireland, Belfast
Royal Society Library (RSL), London
    Boyle Papers
Sheffield University Library, Sheffield
    Hartlib Papers
Society of Antiquaries, London
Somerset Record Office, Somerset
    Trevelyan Papers
Sterling Memorial Library, Yale University, New Haven
Trinity College Dublin (TCD)
    1641 Depositions
    Lyons Collection
    TCD Muniments
University College Cork
University College Dublin
    National Folklore Collection
University of Southhampton Special Collections
    MS 62 Broadlands Archive
Victoria and Albert Museum, London
    National Art Library
Wellcome Library, London
West Sussex Record Office (West Office RO), Chichester

Orrery Papers

Petworth House Collection (Howard Archive)

PRINTED PRIMARY SOURCES

Alexander, Hannah. *A Book of Cookery for dressing of Several Dishes of Meat and making of Several Sauces and Seasoning for Meat or Fowl*. Edited by Deirdre Nuttall. Westport: Evertype, 2014.

Ambrose, Isaac. *Prima, Media, & Ultima*. London, 1654. Marsh's Library, E3.4.13(1).

Avery, Elizabeth. *Scripture-Prophecies Opened, Which are to be accomplished in these last times, which do attend the second coming of Christ: in several Letters Written to Christian friends*. London, 1647.

Balzac, Jean-Louis Guez. *The Choyce Letters of Monsieur de Balzac*. London, 1658. Marsh's Library, F4.6.24.

Barbarus, Hermolaus. *Compendium Scientiae Naturalis*. [Lausanne], 1579. Marsh's Library, P1.7.44.

Barclay, John. *Barclay his Argenis: Or, The Loves of Poliarchus and Argenis*. Translated by Kingsmill Long. London, 1625. Marsh's Library, J4.7.26.

Baxter, Richard. *Certain Disputations Of Right to Sacraments, and the true nature of Visible Christianity*. 2nd ed. London, 1658. Marsh's Library, E2.5.27.

Berkeley, George. *Historical Applications and Occasional Meditations upon several subjects written by a person of honour*. London, 1667.

Birch, Thomas, ed. *A Collection of the State Papers of John Thurloe*. 7 vols. London, 1742.

Blaugdone, Barbara. *An Account of the Travels, Sufferings & Persecutions of Barbara Blaugdone: Given forth as a Testimony to the Lord's Power, and for the Encouragement of Friends*. Shoreditch, 1691.

Booy, David, ed. *Autobiographical Writings by Early Quaker Women*. Aldershot: Ashgate, 2004.

Boran, Elizabethanne, ed. *The Correspondence of James Ussher, 1600–1656*. Dublin: Irish Manuscripts Commission, 2015.

Borlase, Edmund. *The History of the Execrable Irish Rebellion*. London, 1680.

Bourke, Angela, Siobhán Kilfeather, Maria Luddy, Margaret MacCurtain, Gerardine Meaney, Máirín Ní Dhonnchadha, Mary O'Dowd, and Clair Wills, eds. *The Field Day Anthology of Irish Writing*. Vols. 4 and 5, *Irish Women's Writing and Traditions*. Cork: Cork University Press, 2002.

Boyle, Francis, *Discourses and Essays*. London, 1689.

Boyle, Richard. *True Remembrances* (1632). In *The Works of Robert Boyle*, edited by Thomas Birch, 1:vi–xi. 5 vols. London, 1774.

Boyle, Robert. "An Account of Philaretus during his Minority." In M. Hunter, *Robert Boyle by Himself*, 1–22.

———. *The Martyrdom of Theodora, and of Didymus*. In Hunter and Davis, *Works of Robert Boyle*, 11:3–79.

———. *Occasional Reflections*. In Hunter and Davis, *Works of Robert Boyle*, 5:3–187.

———. *Some Considerations Touching the Style of the Scriptures*. In Hunter and Davis, *Works of Robert Boyle*, 2:380–491.

———. *Some Motives and Incentives to the Love of God: Pathetically discours'd of, in A Letter to a Friend*. London, 1659.

———. *Some Motives and Incentives to the Love of God (Seraphic Love)* (1659), in Hunter and Davis, *Works of Robert Boyle* 1:51–141.

———. *Theodora*. In Hunter and Davis, *Works of Robert Boyle*, 11:3–79.

[Boyle, Roger.] *The Irish Colours Displayed*. London, 1662.

Boyle, Roger. *Poems on most of the festivals of the church composed by the Right Honourable Roger, Earl of Orrery*. London, 1681.

———. *A treatise of the art of war dedicated to the Kings Most Excellent Majesty and written by the Right Honourable Roger, Earl of Orrery*. London, 1677.

Brereton, William. *Travels in Holland the United Provinces England Scotland and Ireland MDCXXXIV–MDCXXXV*. Edited by Edward Hawkins. London: Chetham Society, 1844.

Briver, [Mrs. Francis]. "An Epistolary Account of the Irish Rising of 1641 by the Wife of the Mayor of Waterford (with text)." Edited by Naomi McAreavey. *English Literary Renaissance* 42, no. 1 (2012): 90–118.

Browne, Thomas. *Miracles Work's Above and Contrary to Nature*. London, 1683. Marsh's Library, T3.4.2(1).

Burkhead, Henry. *A Tragedy of Cola's Furie or Lirenda's Miserie*. Edited by Angelina Lynch. Dublin: Four Courts, 2009.

Burnell, Henry. *Landgartha: A Tragi-Comedy*. Edited by Deana Rankin. Dublin: Four Courts, 2014.

Burnet, Gilbert. "A Sermon at the Funeral of the Honourable Robert Boyle." In M. Hunter, *Robert Boyle by Himself*, 36–58.

Butler, Elizabeth, Duchess of Ormonde. *The Letters of the First Duchess of Ormonde*. Edited by Naomi McAreavey. Tempe: Arizona Center for Medieval and Renaissance Studies, forthcoming.

Campanella, Thomas. *A Discourse Touching the Spanish Monarchy*. London, 1654. Marsh's Library, H4.6.1.

Carbery, Mary. *Mary Carbery's West Cork Journal, 1898–1901*. Edited by Jeremy Sandford. Dublin: Lilliput, 1998.

Carpenter, Andrew, ed. *The Poems of Olivia Elder*. Dublin: Irish Manuscripts Commission, 2017.

———. *Verse in English from Tudor and Stuart Ireland*. Cork: Cork University Press, 2003.

Charles I. *A Large Declaration Concerning the Late Tumults in Scotland*. London, 1639. Marsh's Library, G 4.2.10.

Clarke, Aidan, and Bríd McGrath, eds. *Letterbook of George, 16th Earl of Kildare*. Dublin: Irish Manuscripts Commission, 2013.

Clarke, Elizabeth, Erica Longfellow, Nigel Smith, Jill Millman, and Alice Eardley, eds. *Constructing Elizabeth Isham*. Centre for the Study of the Renaissance. Warwick University. April 15, 2018. https://warwick.ac.uk/fac/arts/ren/projects/isham/.

Coke, Edward. *A Perfect Abridgment of the Eleaven Bookes of Reports, of ... Edw[ard] Cook*. [London], 1650. Marsh's Library, E4.5.35.

Comber, Thomas. *Memoirs of the Life and Death of the Right Honourable the Lord Deputy Wandesforde*. 2nd ed. Cambridge, 1778.

Comestor, Petrus. *Historia Scholastica*. [Lyon], 1526. Marsh's Library, B4.6.8.

Cook, John. *A True Relation of Mr. Iohn Cook's Passage by Sea from Wexford to Kinsale in that great Storm Ianuary 5*. London, 1650.

Cooke, Frances. *Mris. Cookes Meditations*. [London, 1650].

Cope, Esther, ed. *Prophetic Writings of Eleanor Davies*. Oxford: Oxford University Press, 1995.

Cosin, Richard. *An Apologie For Sundrie Proceedings by Iurisdiction Ecclesiasticall*. London, 1593. Exeter Cathedral Library, Item E9900189678.

Cox, Richard. *Hibernia Anglicana: or, the History of Ireland From the Conquest thereof by the English, To this Present Time*. 2nd ed. London, 1692.

Cranford, James. *The Teares of Ireland*. London, 1642.

De Costes, Gauthier. *Hymen's Praeludia: Or, Loves Master-Piece. Being the Ninth, and Tenth Part of that so much Admir'd Romance, Intituled Cleopatra*. Translated by J. D. London, 1659. Marsh's Library, L3.2.33.

De Mornay, Philippe. *Fowre books, of the institution, use and doctrine of the Holy Sacrament of the Eucharist in the Old Church*. London, 1600. Marsh's Library, F3.3.4(1).

———. *The Mysterie of iniquitie: that is to say, the historie of the Papacie*. Translated by Samson Lennard. London, 1612. Marsh's Library, F3.3.4(2).

D.F. *Reason and Judgement: Or, Special Remarques of the Life of the Renowned Dr. Sanderson, Late Lord Bishop of Lincoln*. Oxford, 1663. Marsh's Library, C4.6.5(1).

"Donovan Family Recipe Book." Dublin Institute of Technology. Gastronomy Archive. https://arrow.dit.ie/gasbook/4/

Dowdall, Elizabeth. "A true note." In Bourke et al., *Field Day Anthology*, 5:22–24.

Du Bartas, Guillaume de Salluste. *La Divina Settimana*. Venice, 1613. Marsh's Library, L3.2.15.

Dunkin, William. *The Parson's Revels*. Edited by Catherine Skeen. Dublin: Four Courts, 2010.

Edwards, David, ed. *Campaign Journals of the Elizabethan Irish Wars*. Dublin: Irish Manuscripts Commission, 2014.

Eliana. London, 1661.

Evans, Katharine, and Sarah Cheevers. *This Is a Short Relation Of Some of the Cruel Sufferings (For the Truth's Sake) of Katharine Evans and Sarah Chevers*. London, 1662.

Fanshawe, Ann. *The Memoirs of Ann, Lady Fanshawe*. In *The Memoirs of Anne, Lady Halkett and Ann, Lady Fanshawe*, edited by John Loftis, 89–192. Oxford: Clarendon, 1979.

Fitzgerald, Lettice. Letters. In Bourke et al., *Field Day Anthology*, 5:25–27.

Flood, John, ed. *The Works of Walter Quin: An Irishman at the Stuart Courts*. Dublin: Four Courts, 2014.

Formulare Advocatorum et Procuratorum Romane Curie et Regii Perlamenti. Hagenau, 1503. Marsh's Library, E4.4.26.

Fowkes, Ann. *A Memoir of Mistress Ann Fowkes née Geale, died aged 82 Years, with some recollections of her family, A.D. 1642–1774. Written by herself*. Dublin, 1892.

Freke, Arthur. "Siege of Rathbarry Castle, 1642." Edited by Herbert Webb Gillman. *Journal of the Cork Historical and Archaeological Society*. 2nd ser., 1 (1895): 1–20.

Freke, Elizabeth. *The Remembrances of Elizabeth Freke, 1671–1714*. Edited by Raymond A. Anselment. Cambridge: Cambridge University Press, 2001.

Gailhard, John. *Two Discourses. The first concerning A Private Settlement at Home After Travel. The Second concerning the Statesman, Or Him who is in Publick Employments*. London, 1682. Marsh's Library, E4.6.7.

Giffard, Lady Martha. *The Life and Character of Sir William Temple*. London, 1728.

Gilbert, John T., ed. *History of the Irish Confederation and the War in Ireland, 1641–1649*, 7 vols. Dublin, 1882–91.

Gillespie, Raymond, ed. *Scholar Bishop: The Recollections and Diary of Narcissus Marsh, 1638–1696*. Cork: Cork University Press, 2003.

Graham, Elspeth, Hilary Hinds, Elaine Hobby, and Helen Wilcox, eds. *Her Own Life: Autobiographical Writings by Seventeenth-Century Englishwomen*. London: Routledge, 1989.

Gulielmus, Arvernus. *Postilla siue expositio*. London, 1509. Marsh's Library, Z1.2.17.

Hallet, Nicky, ed. *Lives of Spirit: English Carmelite Self-Writing of the Early Modern Period*. Aldershot: Ashgate, 2007.

Hamilton, William. *The Exemplary Life and Character of James Bonnell*. 8th ed. London, 1829.

Henry, Matthew. *The Communicant's Companion: Or, Instructions and Helps for the Right Receiving of the Lord's Supper*. Dublin, 1716. Marsh's Library, J3.9.18.

Here Begynneth the Treatys of Nycodemus Gospell. London, 1507. Marsh's Library, Z4.1.14(1).

Hill, George, ed. *The Montgomery Manuscripts (1603–1706)*. Belfast, 1869.

Histoire de Soliman Troisieme. Amsterdam, 1688. Marsh's Library, O1.7.48.

Historical Manuscripts Commission. *Calendar of the Manuscripts of the Marquess of Ormonde*. N.s., 8 vols. London, 1902–20.

Holinshed, Raphael. *Holinshed's Irish Chronicle: The Historie of Irelande from the first inhabitation thereof, vnto the yeare 1509*. Edited by Liam Miller and Eileen Power. Atlantic Highlands NJ: Humanities, 1979.

The Holy Bible containing the Old Testament and the New. London, 1628. Marsh's Library, B2.8.54.

Horneck, Anthony. *The Happy Ascetick*. London, 1681. Marsh's Library, P2.7.76.

Hunter, Michael, and Edward B. Davis, eds. *The Works of Robert Boyle*. Electronic ed. 14 vols. Charlottesville VA: InteLex, 2003.

Hunter, Michael, Antonio Clericuzio, and Lawrence M. Principe, eds. *The Correspondence of Robert Boyle*. Electronic ed. 6 vols. Charlottesville VA: InteLex, 2004.

Hunter, Michael, ed. *Robert Boyle by Himself and His Friends*. Brookfield VT: Pickering, 1994.

Ingelo, Nathaniel. *A Discourse Concerning Repentance*. London, 1677. Marsh's Library, R*3.4.24.

Isham, Elizabeth. "Booke of Rememberance." In Clarke et al., *Constructing Elizabeth Isham*.

——— . Diary. In Clarke et al., *Constructing Elizabeth Isham*.

Longe, Julia G. *Martha, Lady Giffard, Her Life and Correspondence, 1664–1722: A Sequel to the Letters of Dorothy Osborne*. London: G. Allen, 1911.

Lowe, John, ed. *Letter-book of the Earl of Clanricarde, 1643–1647*. Dublin: Irish Manuscripts Commission, 1983.

Lowe, Peter. *A Discourse of the Whole Art of Chyrurgery*. London, 1654. Marsh's Library, L4.5.17.

Lucas, Richard. *Practical Christianity: Or, an Account of the Holiness which the Gospel Enjoins*. 3rd ed. London, 1685. Marsh's Library, P2.4.33.

McGrane, Kevin, ed. *An Account of the Life and Death of Mrs. Elizabeth Bury*. Grand Rapids MI: Reformation Heritage Books, 2006.

Moody, Joanna, ed. *The Private Correspondence of Jane Lady Cornwallis Bacon, 1613–1644*. London: Associated University Presses, 2003.

Moore, Alice. *A Declaration of Alice Vicecountess Moor Dowager of Drogheda, Concerning Her deceased Lord's faithful Service, and her Sufferings in Ireland*. London, 1648.

Moore, Dorothy. *The Letters of Dorothy Moore, 1612–64: The Friendships, Marriage, and Intellectual Life of a Seventeenth-Century Woman*. Edited by Lynette Hunter. Aldershot: Ashgate, 2004.

More, Henry. *Discourses on Several Texts of Scripture.* London, 1692. Marsh's Library, B2.5.5.

———. *An Exposition of the Seven Epistles to the Seven Churches: Together with A Brief Discourse of Idolatry; with Application to the Church of Rome.* London, 1669. Marsh's Library, B2.8.17.

Moxon, Joseph. *Mechanick Exercises: Or, The Doctrine of Handy-Works.* London, 1677. Marsh's Library, M3.3.29.

Mullan, David George, ed. *Women's Life Writing in Early Modern Scotland: Writing the Evangelical Self, c. 1670–c. 1730.* Aldershot: Ashgate, 2003.

Nugent, Richard. *Cynthia.* Edited by Angelina Lynch. Dublin: Four Courts, 2010.

O'Brien, Celsus, ed. *Recollections of an Irish Poor Clare in the Seventeenth Century.* Galway: Connaught Tribune, 1993.

O'Doherty, Rosa. Letter. In Bourke et al., *Field Day Anthology,* 5:30.

Osborne, Dorothy. *Letters from Dorothy Osborne to Sir William Temple (1652–54).* Edited by Edward Abbott Parry. London: Dent, 1914.

Ostiensis, Henricus. *Summa Aurea.* Edited by Franciscus Accursius. [Lyon], 1576. Marsh's Library, R*3.1.9.

Otten, Charlotte F., ed. *English Women's Voices, 1540–1700.* Miami: Florida International University Press, 1992.

Parker, Samuel. *An Account of the Nature and Extent of the Divine Dominion & Goodnesse, Especially as they refer to the Origenian Hypothesis Concerning the Preexistence of Souls.* Oxford, 1666. Marsh's Library, S3.3.17(2).

Perez de Valencia, Jaime. *Divinae plane expositiones.* Paris, 1521. Marsh's Library, A3.3.15.

Petit, Louis. *Dialogues Satyriques et Moraux.* Amsterdam, 1688. Marsh's Library, P2.7.14.

Philips, Katherine. *The Collected Works of Katherine Philips: The Matchless Orinda.* Edited by Thomas Patrick, Germaine Greer, and Roger Little. 3 vols. London: Stump Cross, 1990–93.

———. *The Collected Works of Katherine Philips: The Matchless Orinda.* Edited by Thomas Patrick. Vol. 1, *The Poems.* London: Stump Cross, 1990.

———. *Pompey.* In *The Collected Works of Katherine Philips: The Matchless Orinda.* Edited by Germaine Greer and Ruth Little. Vol. 3, *The Translations,* 1–91. London: Stump Cross, 1993.

Philo-Philippa. "To the Excellent Orinda." In Carpenter, *Verse in English,* 367–73.

Preston, John. *The Breast-plate of faith and love: a treatise, wherein the ground and exercise of faith and love . . . delivered in 18 sermons.* London, 1630. Marsh's Library, J4.7.23(3).

———. *An Elegant and lively description of spirituall life and death: delivered in divers sermons in Lincolnes-Inne.* London, 1632. Marsh's Library, J4.7.23(4).

———. *Life eternall: or, a treatise of the divine essence and attributes: delivered in XVIII sermons.* London, 1631. Marsh's Library, J4.7.23(2).

———. *The Saints daily exercise: a treatise, unfolding the whole dutie of prayer*. London, 1631. Marsh's Library, J4.7.23(1).

———. *Three sermons upon the sacrament of the Lords Supper*. London, 1631. Marsh's Library, J4.7.23(5).

Prynne, William. *A Briefe Survay*. London, 1628. Marsh's Library, Z4.1.15(14).

Rich, Barnabe. *A New Description of Ireland: Wherein is described the disposition of the Irish whereunto they are inclined*. London, 1610.

Rich, Mary. *The Autobiography of Mary Countess of Warwick*. Edited by T. Crofton Croker. London: Percy Society, 1848.

———. *Memoir of Lady Warwick, also her diary, from A.D. 1666–1672*. London: Religious Tract Society, 1847.

———. *The Occasional Meditations of Mary Rich, Countess of Warwick*. Edited by Raymond A. Anselment. Tempe: Arizona Center for Medieval and Renaissance Studies, 2009.

———. "Rules for holy living." In Berkeley, *Historical Applications*, 131–59.

———. *Some Specialities in the Life of M Warwicke*. In Rich, *Autobiography*, 1–38.

Robertson, William. *The First Gate, or, The Outward Door to the Holy Tongue, Opened in English*. London, 1654.

Rogers, John. *Ohel or Beth-shemesh: A Tabernacle for the Sun*. 2 vols. London, 1653.

Rolevinck, Werner. *Fasciculus Temporum*. Lyon, 1494. Marsh's Library, F4.4.25.

Ross, Sarah C. E., ed. *Katherine Austen's Book M: British Library Additional* MS *4454*. Tempe: Arizona Center for Medieval and Renaissance Studies, 2011.

Saint Germain, Christopher. *Two Dialogues in English, Between A Doctour of Divinity, and A Student in the Laws of England, of The Grounds of the said Laws, And of Conscience*. 1528. Reprint, London, 1673. Marsh's Library, E4.5.38.

Schambogen, Johann Christoph. *Prae-lectiones publicae in D. Justiniani institutiorum juris quatuor libros compositae et in universitatis Carolo-Ferdinandeae Pragensis magnae aulae Carolinae auditorio juridico dictatae*. Prague, 1687. Marsh's Library, E4.4.24.

Shepard, Thomas. *The Sincere Convert, Discovering the Paucity of True Beleevers*. London, 1643. Marsh's Library, E3.5.11.

Sheppard, William. *The Learning Of Common Assurances*. London, 1648. Marsh's Library, E4.4.6.

Sidney, Dorothy Percy. *The Correspondence (c. 1626–1659) of Dorothy Percy Sidney, Countess of Leicester*. Edited by Michael G. Brennan, Noel J. Kinnamon, and Margaret P. Hannay. Farnham: Ashgate, 2010.

Skerpan-Wheeler, Elizabeth, ed. *Life Writings: The Early Modern Englishwoman; A Facsimile Library of Essential Works*. Ser. 2. Pt. 1. Vols. 1–2. Aldershot: Ashgate, 2001.

Southwell, Anne. *The Southwell-Sibthorpe Commonplace Book: Folger* MS *V.b.198*. Edited by Jean Klene. Tempe: Arizona Center for Medieval and Renaissance Studies, 1997.

Spenser, Edmund. *A View of the Present State of Ireland*. Edited by Andrew Hadfield and Willy Maley. Oxford: Blackwell, 1997.

Statuta selecta è compore statutorum universitatis Oxoniensis. Oxford, 1661. Marsh's Library, E4.5.31.

Teate, Faithful. *Ter Tria*. Edited by Angelina Lynch. Dublin: Four Courts, 2007.

Temple, John. *The Irish Rebellion*. London, 1646.

Thornton, Alice. *My First Booke of My Life*. Edited by Raymond A. Anselment. Lincoln: University of Nebraska Press, 2014.

Traduit en Francois: Avec une explication tirée des ss. Peres, & des Auteurs Ecclesiastiques. Paris, 1663. Marsh's Library, A.4.25.

Trill, Suzanne, ed. *Lady Anne Halkett: Selected Self-Writings*. Aldershot: Ashgate, 2007.

Trill, Suzanne, Kate Chedgzoy, and Melanie Osborne, eds. *Lay by Your Needles Ladies, Take the Pen: Writing Women in England, 1500–1700*. London: Arnold, 1997.

Trye, Mary. *Medicatrix, or the Woman-Physician*. London, 1675.

Vokins, Joan. *God's Mighty Power Magnified: As Manifested and Revealed in His Faithful Handmaid Joan Vokins*. Cockermouth, England, 1691.

Walker, Anthony. *Eureka, Eureka the virtuous woman found*. London, 1678.

Ward, Seth. *Six Sermons Preached by the Right Reverend Father in God, Seth Lord Bishop of Sarum*. London, 1672. Marsh's Library, B2.5.15.

Wentworth, Thomas. *A Briefe and Perfect Relation, Of the Answeres and Replies of Thomas Earle of Strafford: To the Articles Exhibited against him, by the House of Commons on the thirteenth of Aprill, An. Dom. 1641*. London, 1647.

———. *The Earle of Straffords Speech on the Scaffold before he was beheaded on Tower-hill, the 12 of May, 1641*. London, 1641.

Whitelocke, Bulstrode. *The Diary of Bulstrode Whitelocke, 1605–1675*. Edited by Ruth Spalding. Oxford: Oxford University Press, 1990.

Wolfe, Heather, ed. *Elizabeth Cary Lady Falkland: Life and Letters*. Tempe: Arizona Center for Medieval and Renaissance Studies, 2001.

Woolf, Virginia. *A Room of One's Own and Three Guineas*. 1928. Reprint, Oxford: Oxford University Press, 1992.

SECONDARY SOURCES

Acheson, Alan. *A History of the Church of Ireland, 1691–1996*. Dublin: Columbia, 1997.

Anselment, Raymond A. "Feminine Self-Reflection and the Seventeenth-Century Occasional Meditation." *Seventeenth Century* 26, no. 1 (2013): 69–93.

———. Introduction to Rich, *Occasional Meditations*, 1–39.

———. Introduction to Thornton, *First Booke*, xvii–lxi.

———. "Robert Boyle and the Art of Occasional Meditation." *Renaissance and Reformation* 32, no. 4 (2009): 73–92.

————. "Seventeenth-Century Manuscript Sources of Alice Thornton's Life." *Studies in English Literature, 1500–1900* 45, no. 1 (2005): 135–55.

Appleby, John. "Merchants and Mariners, Pirates and Privateers." In McCaughan and Appleby, *Irish Sea*, 47–58.

Arab, Ronda, Michelle M. Dowd, and Adam Zucker, eds. *Historical Affects and the Early Modern Theater*. London: Routledge, 2016.

Armstrong, Robert. "Ormond, the Confederate Peace Talks and Protestant Royalism." In *Kingdoms in Crisis: Ireland in the 1640s*, edited by Micheál Ó Siochrú, 122–40. Dublin: Four Courts, 2001.

Arnold, L. J. *The Restoration Land Settlement in County Dublin, 1660–1688*. Dublin: Irish Academic Press, 1993.

Baker, David J., and Willy Maley, eds. *British Identities and English Renaissance Literature*. Cambridge: Cambridge University Press, 2002.

Barnard, Toby. "Boyle, Richard, First Earl of Burlington and Second Earl of Cork (1612–1698), Royalist Army Officer and Politician." In *Oxford Dictionary of National Biography*, Oxford University Press. January 3, 2008. www.oxforddnb.com/view/10.1093/ref:odnb/9780198614128.001.0001/odnb-9780198614128-e-3135.

————. "Boyle, Roger, First Earl of Orrery (1621–1679), Politician and Writer." In *Oxford Dictionary of National Biography*. Oxford University Press. September 23, 2004. www.oxforddnb.com/view/10.1093/ref:odnb/9780198614128.001.0001/odnb-9780198614128-e-3138.

————. "Crises of Identity among Irish Protestants, 1641–1685." *Past & Present* 127, no. 1 (1990): 39–83.

————. "The Hartlib Circle and the Cult and Culture of Improvement in Ireland." In Greengrass, Leslie, and Raylor, *Universal Reformation*, 281–97.

————. *Improving Ireland: Projectors, Prophets and Profiteers, 1641–1786*. Dublin: Four Courts, 2008.

————. *Irish Protestant Ascents and Descents, 1641–1770*. Dublin: Four Courts, 2004.

————. "Land and the Limits of Loyalty: The Second Earl of Cork and the First Earl of Burlington (1612–98)." In *Lord Burlington: Architecture, Art and Life*, edited by Barnard and Jane Clark, 167–200. London: Hambledon, 1995.

————. *Making the Grand Figure: Lives and Possessions in Ireland, 1641–1770*. New Haven: Yale University Press, 2004.

————. "New Opportunities for British Settlement: Ireland, 1650–1700." In *The Oxford History of the British Empire*, edited by William Roger Louis et al., 1:322–23. 5 vols. Oxford: Oxford University Press, 1998–99.

————. "The Political, Material and Mental Culture of the Cork Settlers, c. 1650–1700." In O'Flanagan and Buttimer, *Cork History and Society*, 309–65.

———. "A Tale of Three Sisters: Katherine Conolly of Castletown." Chapter 9 of *Irish Protestant Ascents*, 266–86.

Barnard, Toby, and Jane Fenlon, eds. *The Dukes of Ormonde, 1610–1745*. Woodbridge: Boydell and Brewer, 2000.

Bedford, Ronald, Lloyd Davis, and Philippa Kelly, eds. *Early Modern Autobiography: Theories, Genres, Practices*. Ann Arbor: University of Michigan Press, 2006.

Bourke, Evan. "Female Involvement, Membership, and Centrality: A Social Network Analysis of the Hartlib Circle." *Literature Compass* 14, no. 4 (2017).

———. "A Godly Sybilla, an Erudite Wife and a Burdensome Sister: The Formation and Representation of Women's Reputations within the Hartlib Circle 1641–1661." PhD diss., National University of Ireland Galway, 2018.

Bourke, Richard. "Pocock and the Presuppositions of the New British History." *Historical Journal* 53, no. 3 (2010): 747–70.

Brady, Ciarán, and Jane Ohlmeyer, eds. *British Interventions in Early Modern Ireland*. Cambridge: Cambridge University Press, 2005.

———. "Making Good: New Perspectives on the English in Early Modern Ireland." In Brady and Ohlmeyer, *British Interventions*, 1–27.

Brayman Hackel, Heidi. *Reading Material in Early Modern England: Print, Gender and Literacy*. Cambridge: Cambridge University Press, 2005.

Brayman Hackel, Heidi, and Catherine E. Kelly, eds. *Reading Women: Literacy, Authorship, and Culture in the Atlantic World, 1500–1800*. Philadelphia: University of Pennsylvania Press, 2007.

Broomhall, Susan, and Sarah Finn, eds. *Violence and Emotions in Early Modern Europe*. London: Routledge, 2016.

Broomhall, Susan, ed. *Authority, Gender, and Emotions in Late Medieval and Early Modern England*. New York: Palgrave Macmillan, 2015.

———, ed. *Early Modern Emotions: An Introduction*. London: Routledge, 2017.

———, ed. *Spaces for Feeling: Emotions and Sociabilities in Britain, 1650–1850*. London: Routledge, 2015.

Buchanan, Ronald H. "The Irish Sea: The Geographical Framework." In McCaughan and Appleby, *Irish Sea*, 1–11.

Burke, Bernard, and Ashworth Burke. *A Genealogical and Heraldic History of the Peerage* London: Burke's Peerage, 1931.

Burke, Bernard, and Hugh Montgomery-Massingberd. *Burke's Irish Family Records*. London: Burke's Peerage, 1976.

Burnett, Mark Thornton, and Ramona Wray, eds. *Shakespeare and Ireland: History, Politics, Culture*. Houndmills: Macmillan, 1997.

Burtchaell, Jack, and Daniel Dowling. "Social and Economic Conflict in County Kilkenny, 1600–1800." In *Kilkenny: History and Society; Interdisciplinary Essays on the History of an Irish County*, edited by William Nolan and Kevin Whelan, 251–72. Dublin: Geography, 1990.

Caball, Marc, and Andrew Carpenter, eds. *Oral and Print Cultures in Ireland, 1600–1900*. Dublin: Four Courts, 2010.

Campbell, Julie D., and Anne R. Larsen, eds. *Early Modern Women and Transnational Communities of Letters*. Aldershot: Ashgate, 2009.

Canny, Nicholas. "The 1641 Depositions as a Source for the Writing of Social History: County Cork as a Case Study." In O'Flanagan and Buttimer, *Cork History and Society*, 249–308.

———. "The Attempted Anglicisation of Ireland in the Seventeenth Century: An Exemplar of 'British History.'" In Merritt, *Political World*, 157–86.

———. *Making Ireland British, 1580–1650*. Oxford: Oxford University Press, 2009.

———. *The Upstart Earl*. Cambridge: Cambridge University Press, 1982.

Casway, Jerrold. "Rosa O Dogherty: A Gaelic Woman." *Seanchas Ard Mhacha* 10 (1980–82): 42–62.

Catterall, Douglas. "Drawing Lives and Memories from the Everyday Words of the Early Modern Era." *Sixteenth Century Journal* 36, no. 3 (2005): 651–72.

Chambers, Anne. *Eleanor, Countess of Desmond, c. 1545–1638*. Dublin: Wolfhound, 1986.

———. *Granuaile: The Life and Times of Grace O'Malley, c. 1530–1603*. 3rd ed. Dublin: Wolfhound, 1998.

Chedgzoy, Kate. "The Cultural Geographies of Early Modern Women's Writing: Journeys across Spaces and Times." *Literature Compass* 3, no. 4 (2006): 884–95.

———. *Women's Writing in the British Atlantic World: Memory, Place and History, 1550–1700*. Cambridge: Cambridge University Press, 2007.

Clarke, Aidan. "The Breakdown of Authority, 1640–1641." In Moody, Martin, and Byrne, *Early Modern Ireland*, 270–88.

———. "The Government of Wentworth, 1632–40." In Moody, Martin, and Byrne, *Early Modern Ireland*, 243–69.

———. *Prelude to Restoration in Ireland*. Cambridge: Cambridge University Press, 1999.

Clarke, Danielle. "Life Writing." In *The Oxford Handbook of Early Modern Prose, 1500–1640*, edited by Andrew Hadfield, 452–67. Oxford: Oxford University Press, 2013.

Condren, Conal. "Specifying the Subject in Early Modern Autobiography." In Bedford, Davis, and Kelly, *Early Modern Autobiography*, 35–48.

Connolly, Ruth. "A MS Treatise by Viscountess Ranelagh, 1614–91." *Notes and Queries* 53, no. 2 (2006): 170–72.

———. "A Proselytising Protestant Commonwealth: The Religious and Political Ideals of Katherine Jones, Viscountess Ranelagh (1614–1691)." *Seventeenth Century* 23, no. 2 (2008): 244–64.

———. "Viscountess Ranelagh and the Authorisation of Women's Knowledge in the Hartlib Circle." In *The Intellectual Culture of Puritan Women, 1558–1680*, edited by Johanna Harris and Elizabeth Scott-Baumann, 150–61. Basingstoke: Palgrave Macmillan, 2011.

———. "'A Wise and Godly Sybilla': Viscountess Ranelagh and the Politics of International Protestantism." In *Women, Gender, and Radical Religion in Early Modern Europe*, edited by Sylvia Brown, 285–306. Leiden: Brill, 2007.

Connolly, Sean J. *Contested Island: Ireland, 1460–1630*. Oxford: Oxford University Press, 2007.

Coolahan, Marie-Louise. "'And this deponent further sayeth': Orality, Print and the 1641 Depositions." In Caball and Carpenter, *Oral and Print Cultures*, 69–84.

———. "Archipelagic Identities in Europe: Irish Nuns in English Convents." In *English Convents in Exile, 1600–1800: Communities, Culture and Identity*, edited by Caroline Bowden and James Kelly, 211–28. Farnham: Ashgate, 2013.

———. "Early Modern Irish Autobiography." In Harte, *History of Irish Autobiography*, 38–53.

———. "Ideal Communities and Planter Women's Writing in Seventeenth-Century Ireland." *Parergon: Journal of the Australian and New Zealand Association for Medieval and Early Modern Studies* 29, no. 2 (2012): 69–91.

———. "Identity Politics and Nuns' Writing." *Women's Writing* 14, no. 2 (2007): 306–20.

———. "Irish Women's Letters, 1641–1653." In Daybell and Gordon, *Women and Epistolary Agency*, 167–81.

———. "Redeeming Parcels of Time: Aesthetics and Practice of Occasional Meditation." *Seventeenth Century* 22, no. 1 (2007): 124–43.

———. "Whither the Archipelago? Stops, Starts, Hurdles and Hiccups on the Four Nations Front." *Literature Compass* 15, no. 11 (2018).

———. *Women, Writing, and Language in Early Modern Ireland*. Oxford: Oxford University Press, 2010.

Coster, Will. *Family and Kinship in England, 1450–1800*. 2nd ed. London: Routledge, 2016.

Coughlan, Patricia. "Natural History and Historical Nature: The Project for a Natural History of Ireland." In Greengrass, Leslie, and Raylor, *Universal Reformation*, 298–317.

Cross, Frank Leslie, and Elizabeth A. Livingstone. "King, William (1650–1729), Abp. of *Dublin." In *The Oxford Dictionary of the Christian Church*, edited by Frank Leslie Cross and Elizabeth A. Livingstone, 934. 3rd ed. Rev. ed. Oxford: Oxford University Press, 2005.

Cust, Richard. "Honour and Politics in Early Stuart England: The Case of Beaumont vs. Hastings." *Past & Present* 149, no. 1 (1995): 57–94.

Davies, Stevie. *Unbridled Spirits: Women of the English Revolution, 1640–1660*. London: Women's Press, 1998.

Davis, Lloyd. "Critical Debates and Early Modern Autobiography." In Bedford, Davis, and Kelly, *Early Modern Autobiography*, 19–34.

Daybell, James. *The Material Letter: Manuscript Letters and the Culture and Practices of Letter-Writing in Early Modern England, 1580–1635*. Basingstoke: Palgrave, 2012.

———. "Recent Studies in Sixteenth-Century Letters." *English Literary Renaissance* 35, no. 2 (2005): 331–62.

———. "Recent Studies in Seventeenth-Century Letters." *English Literary Renaissance* 36, no. 1 (2006): 135–70.

———. "Scripting a Female Voice: Women's Epistolary Rhetoric in Sixteenth-Century Letters of Petition." *Women's Writing* 13, no. 1 (2006): 3–22.

———. *Women Letter-Writers in Tudor England*. Oxford: Oxford University Press, 2006.

Daybell, James, and Andrew Gordon, eds. *Women and Epistolary Agency in Early Modern Culture, 1450–1690*. London: Routledge, 2016.

Daybell, James, ed. *Early Modern Women's Letter Writing, 1450–1700*. Basingstoke: Palgrave, 2001.

Dickson, David. "Capital and Country: 1600–1800." In *Dublin through the Ages*, edited by Art Cosgrove, 63–76. Dublin: College Press, 1988.

———. *Dublin: The Making of a Capital City*. London: Profile Books, 2014.

———. *Old World Colony: Cork and South Munster, 1630–1830*. Cork: Cork University Press, 2005.

DiMeo, Michelle. "Katherine Jones, Lady Ranelagh (1615–91): Science and Medicine in a Seventeenth-Century Englishwoman's Writing." PhD diss., University of Warwick, 2009. http://wrap.warwick.ac.uk/3146/1/WRAP_THESIS_DiMeo_2009.pdf.

———. "Lady Ranelagh's Book of Kitchen-Physick? Reattributing Authorship for Wellcome Library MS 1340." *Huntington Library Quarterly* 77, no. 3 (2014): 331–46.

———. "The Rhetoric of Medical Authority in Lady Katherine Ranelagh's Letters." In Daybell and Gordon, *Women and Epistolary Agency*, 96–109.

———. "'Such a sister became such a brother': Lady Ranelagh's Influence on Robert Boyle." *Intellectual History Review* 25, no. 1 (2015): 21–36.

DiMeo, Michelle, and Sara Pennell, eds. *Reading and Writing Recipe Books, 1550–1800*. Manchester: Manchester University Press, 2013.

Dixon, Thomas. *Weeping Britannia: Portrait of a Nation in Tears*. Oxford: Oxford University Press, 2015.

Doubleday, H. A., Duncan Warrand, and Howard de Walden, eds. *The Complete Peerage*. Vol. 6. London: St. Catherine Press, 1926.

Dowd, Michelle, and Julie A. Eckerle. Introduction to Dowd and Eckerle, *Women's Life Writing*, 1–13.

———. "Recent Studies in Early Modern English Life Writing." *English Literary Renaissance* 40, no. 1 (2010): 132–62.

Dowd, Michelle M., and Julie A. Eckerle, eds. *Genre and Women's Life Writing in Early Modern England*. Aldershot: Ashgate, 2007.

Duffy, Damien. "The Ormond Women: Family, Power, and Politics, c. 1450s–1660." PhD diss., Maynooth University, 2018.

Eckerle, Julie A. "Prefacing Texts, Authorizing Authors, and Constructing Selves: The Preface as Autobiographical Space." In Dowd and Eckerle, *Women's Life Writing*, 97–113.

———. *Romancing the Self in Early Modern Englishwomen's Life Writing*. Farnham, England: Ashgate, 2013.

———. "Women Representing Ireland in the 17th Century: From English Idyll to Irish Nightmare." *Literature Compass* 15, no. 10 (2018).

Edwards, David. *The Ormond Lordship in County Kilkenny, 1515–1642: The Rise and Fall of Butler Feudal Power*. Dublin: Four Courts, 2003.

———. "The Poisoned Chalice: The Ormond Inheritance, Sectarian Division and the Emergence of James Butler, 1614–1642." In Barnard and Fenlon, *Dukes of Ormonde*, 58–64.

Edwards, David, and Colin Rynne, eds. *The Colonial World of Richard Boyle, First Earl of Cork*. Dublin: Four Courts, 2018.

Elias, Norbert. *The Civilizing Process*. Vol. 1, *The History of Manners*, translated by Edmund Jephcott. Oxford: Blackwell, 1978.

———. *The Civilizing Process*. Vol 2, *State Formation and Civilization*, translated by Edmund Jephcott. Oxford: Blackwell, 1982.

Eustace, Nicole. *Passion Is the Gale: Emotion, Power, and the Coming of the American Revolution*. Chapel Hill: University of North Carolina Press, 2008.

Fauske, Christopher J. "'The angel of St. Patrick's is now the guardian of the kingdom.'" In Fauske, *Archbishop William King*, 11–29.

———, ed. *Archbishop William King and the Anglican Irish Context, 1688–1729*. Dublin: Four Courts, 2004.

Fell-Smith, Charlotte. *Mary Rich, Countess of Warwick, Her Family and Friends*. London: Longmans, Green, 1901.

Fenlon, Jane. "The Duchess of Ormonde's House at Dunmore, County Kilkenny." In *Kilkenny: Studies in Honour of Margaret M. Phelan*, edited by John Kirwan, 79–87. Kilkenny: Kilkenny Archaeological Society, 1997.

Field, Catherine. "'Many hands hands': Writing the Self in Early Modern Women's Recipe Books." In Dowd and Eckerle, *Women's Life Writing*, 49–63.

Firth, Charles. *The Regimental History of Cromwell's Army*. Vol. 2. Oxford: Clarendon, 1940.

FitzGerald, Brian. *The Anglo-Irish: Three Representative Types: Cork, Ormonde, Swift, 1602–1745*. London: Staples, 1952.

Fletcher, Anthony. *Gender, Sex, and Subordination in England, 1500–1800*. New Haven: Yale University Press, 1995.

Fogarty, Anne. "Literature in English, 1550–1690: From the Elizabethan Settlement to the Battle of the Boyne." In *The Cambridge History of Irish Literature*, vol. 1, edited by Margaret Kelleher and Philip O'Leary, 140–90. Cambridge: Cambridge University Press, 2006.

Fox, Peter. *Trinity College Library Dublin: A History*. Cambridge: Cambridge University Press, 2014.

Fraser, Antonia. *The Weaker Vessel: Woman's Lot in Seventeenth-Century England*. London: Weidenfeld and Nicolson, 1984.

Fulton, Helen. "Autobiography and the Discourse of Urban Subjectivity: The Paston Letters." In Bedford, Davis, and Kelly, *Early Modern Autobiography*, 191–216.

Gardner, Winifred (Lady Burghclere). *The Life of James, First Duke of Ormonde, 1610–1688*. 2 vols. London: Murray, 1912.

Gibson, Jonathan. "Significant Space in Manuscript Letters." *Seventeenth Century* 12, no. 1 (1997): 1–10.

Gill, Catie. "Identities in Quaker Women's Writing, 1652–60." *Women's Writing* 9, no. 2 (2007): 267–84.

———. *Women in the Seventeenth-Century Quaker Community: A Literary Study of Political Identities*. London: Routledge, 2005.

Gillespie, Raymond. "Dublin, 1600–1700: A City and Its Hinterlands." In *Capital Cities and Their Hinterlands in Early Modern Europe*, edited by Peter Clark and Bernard Lepetit, 84–104. Aldershot: Scholar, 1996.

———. "The Religion of the First Duke of Ormond." In Barnard and Fenlon, *Dukes of Ormonde*, 101–14.

———. *Seventeenth Century Ireland: Making Ireland Modern*. Dublin: Gill and Macmillan, 2006.

———. "Temple's Fate: Reading *The Irish Rebellion* in Late Seventeenth-Century Ireland." In Brady and Ohlmeyer, *British Interventions*, 315–33.

Gillespie, Raymond, and Andrew Hadfield, eds. *The Irish Book in English, 1550–1800*. Vol. 3, *The Oxford History of the Irish Book*. Oxford: Oxford University Press, 2006.

Gray, Catharine. "Katherine Philips in Ireland." *English Literary Renaissance* 39, no. 3 (2009): 557–85.

Green, Ian. *Print and Protestantism in Early Modern England*. Oxford: Oxford University Press, 2000.

Greengrass, Mark. "Archive Refractions: Hartlib's Papers and the Workings of an Intelligencer." In M. Hunter, *Scientific Revolution*, 35–47.

Greengrass, Mark, Michael Leslie, and Timothy Raylor, eds. *Samuel Hartlib and Universal Reformation*. Cambridge: Cambridge University Press, 1994.

Gribben, Crawford. *God's Irishmen: Theological Debates in Cromwellian Ireland*. Oxford: Oxford University Press, 2007.

Hackett, Helen. *Women and Romance Fiction in the English Renaissance*. Cambridge: Cambridge University Press, 2000.

Hall, Dianne. "'Most barbarously and inhumaine maner butchered': Masculinity, Trauma, and Memory in Early Modern Ireland." In *The Body in Pain in Irish Literature and Culture*, edited by Fionnuala Dillane, Naomi McAreavey, and Emilie Pine, 39–55. London: Palgrave, 2016.

Hanson, Elizabeth. *Discovering the Subject in Renaissance England*. Cambridge: Cambridge University Press, 1998.

Haraway, Donna. "Situated Knowledges: The Science Question in Feminism and the Privilege of Partial Perspective." *Feminist Studies* 14, no. 3 (1988): 575–99.

Harris, Frances. "Ireland as a Laboratory: The Archive of Sir William Petty." In M. Hunter, *Scientific Revolution*, 73–90.

Harte, Liam, ed. *A History of Irish Autobiography*. Cambridge: Cambridge University Press, 2018.

Hayton, D. W. "Bonnell, James (1653–1699)." In *Oxford Dictionary of National Biography*, Oxford University Press. May 19, 2011. https://doi.org/10.1093/ref:odnb/2849.

Heal, Felicity. "Reputation and Honour in Court and Country: Lady Elizabeth Russell and Sir Thomas Hoby." *Transactions of the Royal Historical Society* 6 (1996): 161–78.

Herbert, Amanda E. *Female Alliances: Gender, Identity, and Friendship in Early Modern Britain*. New Haven: Yale University Press, 2014.

Hicks, David. *Irish Country Houses: A Chronicle of Change*. Cork: Collins, 2012.

Hickson, Mary Agnes. *Selections from Old Kerry Records*. London: Watson and Hazell, 1872.

Highley, Christopher. *Shakespeare, Spenser and the Crisis in Ireland*. Cambridge: Cambridge University Press, 1997.

Hindmarsh, Bruce. *The Evangelical Conversion Narrative: Spiritual Autobiography in Early Modern England*. Oxford: Oxford University Press, 2005.

Hinds, Hilary. *God's Englishwomen: Seventeenth-Century Radical Sectarian Writing and Feminist Criticism*. Manchester: Manchester University Press, 1996.

Hobby, Elaine. "Handmaids of the Lord and Mothers of Israel: Early Vindications of Quaker Women's Prophecy." In *The Emergence of Quaker Writing and Dissenting Literature in Seventeenth-Century England*, edited by Thomas N. Corns and David Loewenstein, 88–98. London: Cass, 1995.

———. *Virtue of Necessity: English Women's Writing, 1649–1688*. London: Virago, 1988.

Holland, Karen Ann. "Joan Desmond, Ormond, and Ossory: The World of a Countess in Sixteenth-Century Ireland." PhD diss., Providence College, 1996.

Howard, Sharon. "Imagining the Pain and Peril of Seventeenth-Century Childbirth: Travail and Deliverance in the Making of an Early Modern World." *Social History of Medicine* 16, no. 3 (2003): 367–82.

Hughes, Samuel Carlyle. *The Church of S. John the Evangelist, Dublin*. Dublin, 1889.

Hunter, Lynette. "Sisters of the Royal Society: The Circle of Katherine Jones, Lady Ranelagh." In *Women, Science and Medicine, 1500–1700: Mothers and Sisters of the Royal Society*, edited by Lynette Hunter and Sarah Hutton, 178–97. Stroud: Sutton, 1997.

Hunter, Michael, ed. *Archives of the Scientific Revolution*. Woodbridge: Boydell, 1998.

Hynes, Sandra. "Mapping Friendship and Dissent: The Letters from Joseph Boyse to Ralph Thoresby, 1680–1710." In *Varieties of Seventeenth- and Early Eighteenth-Century English Radicalism in Context*, edited by Ariel Hessayon and David Finnegan, 205–19. Aldershot: Ashgate, 2011.

Jackson, H. J. *Marginalia: Readers Writing in Books*. New Haven: Yale University Press, 2001.

Jeffries, Tania Claire. "Hastings [née Davies], Lucy, Countess of Huntingdon (1613–1679), Noblewoman." In *Oxford Dictionary of National Biography*. Oxford University Press. September 23, 2004. www.oxforddnb.com/view/10.1093/ref:odnb/9780198614128.001.0001/odnb-9780198614128-e-65147.

Jones, James Rees. *The Anglo-Dutch Wars of the Seventeenth Century*. London: Longman, 1996.

Kane, Brendan. *The Politics and Culture of Honour in Britain and Ireland, 1541–1641*. Cambridge: Cambridge University Press, 2010.

Kennedy, Máire. "Huguenot Readers in Eighteenth-Century Ireland." In *The Huguenots: France, Exile and Diaspora*, edited by Jane McKee and Randolph Vigne, 173–84. Eastbourne: Sussex Academic Press, 2013.

———. "Women and Reading in Eighteenth-Century Ireland." In *The Experience of Reading: Irish Historical Perspectives*, edited by Bernadette Cunningham and Máire Kennedy, 78–98. Dublin: Rare Books Group of the Library Association of Ireland/Economic and Social History Society of Ireland, 1999.

Kerrigan, John. *Archipelagic English: Literature, History, and Politics, 1603–1707*. Oxford: Oxford University Press, 2008.

Kesson, Andy, and Emma Smith, eds. *The Elizabethan Top Ten: Defining Print Popularity in Early Modern England*. London: Routledge, 2016.

Kilburn, Terence, and Anthony Milton. "The Public Context of the Trial and Execution of Strafford." In Merritt, *Political World*, 230–51.

Kilroy, Phil. *Protestant Dissent and Controversy in Ireland, 1660–1714*. Cork: Cork University Press, 1994.

King, Charles Simeon, ed. *A Great Archbishop of Dublin, William King, D. D., 1650–1729: His Autobiography, Family, and a Selection from His Correspondence*. London, 1908.

Lamb, Mary Ellen. "Merging the Secular and the Spiritual in Lady Anne Halkett's Memoirs." In Dowd and Eckerle, *Women's Life Writing*, 81–96.

Lear, Anne. "Thank God for Haemorrhoids! Illness and Identity in a Seventeenth-Century Woman's Autobiography." *Women's Writing* 12, no. 3 (2005): 337–44.

Leong, Elaine, and Alisha Rankin, eds. *Secrets and Knowledge in Medicine and Science, 1500–1800*. Burlington VT: Ashgate, 2011.

Little, Patrick. *Lord Broghill and the Cromwellian Union with Ireland and Scotland.* Woodbridge: Boydell, 2004.

Loftus, Simon. *The Invention of Memory: An Irish Family Scrapbook, 1560–1934*. London: Daunt Books, 2013.

Loveman, Kate. *Samuel Pepys and His Books. Reading, Newsgathering and Sociability, 1660–1703*. Oxford: Oxford University Press, 2015.

Lynch, Andrew. "Emotional Community." In Broomhall, *Early Modern Emotions*, 3–6.

Lynch, Kathleen M. *Roger Boyle: First Earl of Orrery.* Knoxville: University of Tennessee Press, 1965.

Lysaght, Patricia. *The Banshee: The Irish Supernatural Death Messenger.* Dublin: O'Brien, 1996.

MacCarthy Morrogh, Michael. "The English Presence in Early Seventeenth Century Munster." In *Natives and Newcomers: Essays on the Making of Irish Colonial Society, 1534–1641*, edited by Ciarán Brady and Raymond Gillespie, 171–90. Dublin: Irish Academic Press, 1986.

MacCurtain, Margaret, and Mary O'Dowd, eds. *Women in Early Modern Ireland.* Dublin: Wolfhound, 1991.

Mack, Phyllis. "Women as Prophets during the English Civil War." *Feminist Studies* 8, no. 1 (1982): 19–45.

MacLysaght, Edward, comp. and ed., *Calendar of the Orrery Papers.* Dublin: Stationary Office, 1941.

Magnusson, Lynne. "A Rhetoric of Requests: Genre and Linguistic Scripts in Elizabethan Women's Suitors' Letters." In *Women and Politics in Early Modern England, 1450–1700*, edited by James Daybell, 51–66. Aldershot: Ashgate, 2004.

Maley, Willy, and Rory Loughnane, eds. *Celtic Shakespeare: The Bard and the Borderers.* Farnham: Ashgate, 2013.

Manning, Conleth. "The 1653 Survey of the Lands Granted to the Countess of Ormond in Co. Kilkenny." *Journal of the Royal Society of Antiquaries of Ireland* 129 (1999): 40–66.

Matchinske, Megan. "Serial Identity: History, Gender, and Form in the Diary Writing of Lady Anne Clifford." In Dowd and Eckerle, *Women's Life Writing*, 65–80.

Maxwell, Felicity Lynn. "Calling for Collaboration: Women and Public Service in Dorothy Moore's Transnational Protestant Correspondence." *Literature Compass* 14, no. 4 (2017).

McAreavey, Naomi. "Irish Nuns and the Counter-Reformation Movement: The Struggle between Nation and Vocation." In *Representing Women's Authority in the Early Modern World*, edited by Eavan O'Brien, 221–51. Rome: Aracne, 2013.

———. "'Paper bullets': Gendering the 1641 Rebellion in the Writings of Lady Elizabeth Dowdall and Lettice Fitzgerald, Baroness of Offaly." In *Ireland in the Renaissance, c. 1540–1660*, edited by Thomas Herron and Michael Potterton, 311–24. Dublin: Four Courts, 2007.

———. "Re(-)membering Women: Protestant Women's Victim Testimonies during the Irish Rising of 1641." *Journal of the Northern Renaissance* 2 (2010).

———. "'This is that I may remember what passings that Happind in Waterford': Inscribing the 1641 Rising in the Letters of the Wife of the Mayor of Waterford." *Early Modern Women: An Interdisciplinary Journal* 5 (2010): 77–109.

McCabe, Richard. *Spenser's Monstrous Regiment: Elizabethan Ireland and the Poetics of Difference*. Oxford: Oxford University Press, 2002.

McCall, Hardy Bertram. *Story of the Family of Wandesforde of Kirklington & Castlecomer*. London: Simpkin, 1904.

McCaughan, Michael, and John Appleby, eds. *The Irish Sea: Aspects of Maritime History*. Belfast: Institute of Irish Studies, 1989.

McKitterick, David. "Women and Their Books in Seventeenth-Century England: The Case of Elizabeth Puckering." *Library* 1, no. 4 (2000): 359–80.

Mendelson, Sara Heller. *The Mental World of Stuart Women: Three Stories*. Amherst: University of Massachusetts Press, 1987.

Merritt, J. F., ed. *The Political World of Thomas Wentworth, Earl of Strafford, 1621–1641*. Cambridge: Cambridge University Press, 1996.

Mills, Sara. *Discourses of Difference: An Analysis of Women's Travel Writing and Colonialism*. London: Routledge, 1991.

Moody, Theodore W., Francis X. Martin, and Francis J. Byrne, eds. *A New History of Ireland*. Vol. 3, *Early Modern Ireland, 1534–1691*. Oxford: Oxford University Press, 1991.

Moore, Lucy. *Lady Fanshawe's Receipt Book: An Englishwoman's Life During the Civil War*. London: Atlantic Books, 2017.

Morgan, Paul. "Frances Wolfreston and 'Hor Bouks': A Seventeenth-Century Woman Book-Collector." *Library* 11, no. 3 (1989): 197–219.

Murphy, Andrew. *But the Irish Sea betwixt Us: Ireland, Colonialism and Renaissance Literature*. Lexington: University Press of Kentucky, 1999.

Newcomb, Lori Humphrey. *Reading Popular Romance in Early Modern England*. New York: Columbia University Press, 2002.

Nolan, William. "Castlecomer." In *Irish Country Towns*, edited by Anngret Simms and John H. Andrews, 120–30. Cork: Mercier, 1994.

———. *Fassadinin: Land, Settlement and Society in Southeast Ireland, 1600–1850*. Dublin: Geography, 1979.

O'Brien, Ivar. *O'Brien of Thomond: The O'Briens in Irish History, 1500–1865*. Chichester: Phillimore, 1986.

O'Dowd, Mary. *A History of Women in Ireland, 1500–1800*. Harlow: Pearson Longman, 2005.

O'Flanagan, Patrick. "Three Hundred Years of Urban Life: Villages and Towns in County Cork, c. 1600 to 1901." In O'Flanagan and Buttimer, *Cork History and Society*, 391–467.

O'Flanagan, Patrick, and Cornelius G. Buttimer, eds. *Cork History and Society: Interdisciplinary Essays on the History of an Irish County*. Dublin: Geography, 1993.

Ohlmeyer, Jane. *Making Ireland English: The Irish Aristocracy in the Seventeenth Century*. New Haven: Yale University Press, 2012.

———. "Strafford, the 'Londonderry Business' and the 'New British History.'" In Merritt, *Political World*, 209–28.

O'Keeffe, Eleanor. "The Family and Marriage Strategies of James Butler, First Duke of Ormonde, 1658–1688." PhD diss., University of Cambridge, 2000.

O'Regan, Philip. "William King as Bishop and Parliamentarian, 1691–7." In Fauske, *Archbishop William King*, 73–105.

O'Shea, Maria. *The Unicorn and the Fencing Mouse: An Exhibition of Marginalia, Annotations and Doodles*. Dublin: Marsh's Library, 2015.

Ó Siochrú, Micheál. *God's Executioner: Oliver Cromwell and the Conquest of Ireland*. London: Faber and Faber, 2008.

Oster, Malcolm. "Millenarianism and the New Science: The Case of Robert Boyle." In Greengrass, Leslie, and Raylor, *Universal Reformation*, 137–48.

Pal, Carol. *Republic of Women: Rethinking the Republic of Letters in the Seventeenth Century*. Cambridge: Cambridge University Press, 2012.

Palgrave, Mary E. *Mary Rich, Countess of Warwick*. New York: Dutton, 1901.

Palmer, Patricia. *The Severed Head and the Grafted Tongue: Literature, Translation and Violence in Early Modern Ireland*. Cambridge: Cambridge University Press, 2013.

Paster, Gail Kern, Katherine Rowe, and Mary Floyd-Wilson, eds. *Reading the Early Modern Passions: Essays in the Cultural History of Emotions*. Philadelphia: University of Pennsylvania Press, 2004.

Pearson, Jacqueline. "Women Reading, Reading Women." In *Women and Literature in Britain, 1500–1700*, edited by Helen Wilcox, 80–99. Cambridge: Cambridge University Press, 1996.

Perceval-Maxwell, Michael. *The Outbreak of the Irish Rebellion of 1641*. Montreal: McGill-Queen's University Press, 1994.

Plamper, Jan. *The History of Emotions: An Introduction*. Translated by Keith Tribe. Oxford: Oxford University Press, 2015.

————. "The History of Emotions: An Interview with William Reddy, Barbara Rosenwein and Peter Stearns." *History and Theory* 49, no. 2 (2010): 237–65.

Pocock, J. G. A. "British History: A Plea for a New Subject." *Journal of Modern History* 47, no. 4 (1975): 601–28.

Prendergast, Amy. *Literary Salons across Britain and Ireland in the Long Eighteenth Century*. London: Palgrave, 2015.

Prescott, Sarah. "Archipelagic Coterie Space: Katherine Philips and Welsh Women's Writing." *Tulsa Studies in Women's Literature* 33, no. 2 (2014): 51–76.

————. "Archipelagic Orinda? Katherine Philips and the Writing of Welsh Women's Literary History." *Literature Compass* 6, no. 6 (2009): 1167–76.

Preston, Claire. *The Poetics of Scientific Investigation in Seventeenth-Century England*. Oxford: Oxford University Press, 2015.

Rankin, Deana. *Between Spenser and Swift: English Writing in Seventeenth-Century Ireland*. Cambridge: Cambridge University Press, 2005.

————. "'A More Worthy Patronesse': Elizabeth Cary and Ireland." In *The Literary Career and Legacy of Elizabeth Cary, 1613–1680*, edited by Heather Wolfe, 203–21. London: Palgrave Macmillan, 2007.

Raven, James. *The Business of Books: Booksellers and the English Book Trade, 1450–1850*. New Haven: Yale University Press, 2007.

Reddy, William M. *The Navigation of Feeling: A Framework for the History of Emotions*. Cambridge: Cambridge University Press, 2001.

Rees, Emma. *Margaret Cavendish: Gender, Genre, and Exile*. Manchester: University of Manchester Press, 2003.

"Richard Barry, 2nd Earl of Barrymore." *Peerage*. Accessed May 16, 2018. www.thepeerage .com/p11658.htm#116575.

Richardson, Joseph. "William King: European Man of Letters." In Fauske, *Archbishop William King*, 106–22.

Rose, Mary Beth. *Gender and Heroism in Early Modern English Literature*. Chicago: Chicago University Press, 2001.

Rosenthal, Angela. "Raising Hair." In "Hair," edited by Angela Rosenthal. Special issue, *Eighteenth-Century Studies* 38, no. 1 (2004): 1–16.

Rosenwein, Barbara H. *Emotional Communities in the Early Middle Ages*. New York: Cornell University Press, 2008.

————. *Generations of Feeling: A History of Emotions, 600–1700*. Cambridge: Cambridge University Press, 2016.

————. "Problems and Methods in the History of Emotions." *Passions in Context: Journal of the History and Philosophy of the Emotions* 1, no. 1 (2001): 1–32.

————. "Worrying about Emotions in History." *American Historical Review* 107, no. 3 (2002): 821–45.

Schut, Rosalinde. "La Femme Forte: Katherine Philips and the Politics of Her Dublin Writings, 1662–1663." In *Early Modern Englishwomen Testing Ideas*, edited by Jo Wallwork and Paul Salzman, 107–20. Farnham: Ashgate, 2011.

Seelig, Sharon Cadman. *Autobiography and Gender in Early Modern Literature: Reading Women's Lives, 1600–1680*. Cambridge: Cambridge University Press, 2006.

Shaw, William. *The Knights of England*. Vol. 2. London: Sherratt and Hughes, 1906.

Sherman, William. "What Did Renaissance Readers Write in Their Books?" In *Books and Readers in Early Modern England*, edited by Jennifer Andersen and Elisabeth Sauer, 119–37. Philadelphia: University of Pennsylvania Press, 2002.

Simms, John G. *The Williamite Confiscation in Ireland, 1690–1703*. London: Faber and Faber, 1956.

Sloane, Thomas O. "Rhetorical Selfhood in Erasmus and Milton." In *A Companion to Rhetoric and Rhetorical Criticism*, edited by Walter Jost and Wendy Olmsted, 112–27. Oxford: Blackwell, 2006.

Smith, David Lee. *A History of the Modern British Isles, 1603–1707: The Double Crown*. Oxford: Blackwell, 1998.

Smyth, William J. "Ireland a Colony: Settlement Implications of the Revolution in Military-Administrative, Urban and Ecclesiastical Structures, c. 1550 to c. 1730." In *A History of Settlement in Ireland*, edited by Terry Barry, 158–86. London: Routledge, 2000.

——— . "Society and Settlement in Seventeenth Century Ireland: The Evidence of the '1659 Census.'" In *Common Ground: Essays on the Historical Geography of Ireland*, edited by William Smyth and Kevin Whelan, 55–83. Cork: Cork University Press, 1988.

Snook, Edith. "Reading Women." In *The Cambridge Companion to Early Modern Women's Writing*, edited by Laura Lunger Knoppers, 40–53. Cambridge: Cambridge University Press, 2009.

——— . *Women, Reading, and the Cultural Politics of Early Modern England*. Aldershot: Ashgate, 2005.

Stewart, Althea. "Good Quaker Women, Tearful Sentimental Spectators, Readers, and Auditors." *Prose Studies* 29, no. 1 (2007): 73–85.

Stone, Lawrence. *The Family, Sex and Marriage in England, 1500–1800*. London: Weidenfeld and Nicolson, 1977.

Stretton, Tim. "Marriage, Separation and the Common Law in England, 1540–1660." In *The Family in Early Modern England*, edited by Helen Berry and Elizabeth Foyster, 18–39. Cambridge: Cambridge University Press, 2007.

Tait, Clodagh. *Death, Burial and Commemoration in Ireland, 1550–1650*. New York: Palgrave Macmillan, 2002.

Tallon, Geraldine, ed. *Court of Claims, Submissions and Evidence, 1663*. Dublin: Irish Manuscripts Commission, 2006.

Taylor, Elizabeth Anne [Betsey Taylor-FitzSimon]. "Writing Women, Honour and Ireland, 1640–1715." PhD diss., University College Dublin, 1999.

Taylor-FitzSimon, Betsey. "Conversion, the Bible and the Irish Language: The Correspondence of Lady Ranelagh and Bishop Dopping." In *Converts and Conversion in Ireland, 1650–1850*, edited by Michael Brown, Charles I. McGrath, and Thomas P. Power, 157–82. Dublin: Four Courts, 2005.

Thorne, Alison. "Women's Petitionary Letters and Early Seventeenth-Century Treason Trials." *Women's Writing* 13, no. 1 (2006): 23–43.

Travitsky, Betty, and Anne Lake Prescott, eds. *Seventeenth-Century English Recipe Books: Cooking, Physic and Chirurgery in the Works of Elizabeth Talbot Grey and Aletheia Talbot Howard*. Burlington VT: Ashgate, 2008.

Trolander, Paul, and Zeynep Tenger. "Katherine Philips and Coterie Critical Practices." *Eighteenth-Century Studies* 37, no. 3 (2004): 367–87.

Walker, Garthine. "Expanding the Boundaries of Female Honour in Early Modern England." *Transactions of the Royal Historical Society* 6 (1996): 235–45.

Wall, Wendy. *The Imprint of Gender, Authorship and Publication in the English Renaissance*. Ithaca: Cornell University Press, 1993.

Walsh, Ann-Maria. "Writing Women's Lives: The Epistolary Cultures of the Daughters of the First Earl of Cork." PhD diss., University College Dublin, 2017.

Walters, Lisa. *Margaret Cavendish: Gender, Science and Politics*. Cambridge: Cambridge University Press, 2014.

Whelan, Bernadette. "McLoughlin, Katherine (*fl.* 1671–1679)." In *Oxford Dictionary of National Biography*. Oxford University Press. September 23, 2004. https://doi.org/10.1093/ref:odnb/67223.

White, Newport B., comp. *An Account of Archbishop Marsh's Library, Dublin . . . with a Note on Autographs*. Dublin: Hodges, Figgis, 1926.

Whyman, Susan E. *The Pen and the People: English Letter Writers, 1660–1800*. Oxford: Oxford University Press, 2009.

Wilks, Timothy. *Of Neighing Coursers and Trumpets Shrill: A Life of Richard, 1st Lord Dingwall and Earl of Desmond (c. 1570–1628)*. London: Lucas, 2012.

Williams, Mark R. F. *The King's Irishmen: The Irish in the Exiled Court of Charles II, 1649–1660*. Woodbridge: Boydell, 2014.

Wray, Ramona. "[Re]constructing the Past: The Diametric Lives of Mary Rich." In *Betraying Our Selves: Forms of Self-Representation in Early Modern English Texts*, edited by Henk Dragstra, Sheila Ottway, and Helen Wilcox, 148–65. London: Macmillan/St. Martin's Press, 2000.

———. "Memory, Materiality and Maternity in the Tanfield/Cary Archive." In *A History of Early Modern Women's Writing*, edited by Patricia Phillippy, 221–40. Cambridge: Cambridge University Press, 2018.

Zurcher, Amelia. *Seventeenth-Century English Romance: Allegory, Ethics, and Politics.* New York: Palgrave, 2007.

DATABASES

1641 Depositions. http://1641.tcd.ie.

British Armorial Bindings. https://armorial.library.utoronto.ca/.

Dictionary of Irish Biography. http://dib.cambridge.org/.

The Down Survey of Ireland. http://downsurvey.tcd.ie.

The Hartlib Papers. www.dhi.ac.uk/hartlib/.

Orlando: Women's Writing in the British Isles from the Beginnings to the Present. http://orlando.cambridge.org/svHomePage.

Oxford Dictionary of National Biography. www.oxforddnb.com.

Oxford English Dictionary. www.oed.com.

The Peerage. www.thepeerage.com.

Perdita Manuscripts, 1500–1700. www.amdigital.co.uk/primary-sources/perdita-manuscripts-1500-1700.

State Papers Online, 1509-1714. https://www.gale.com/intl/primary-sources/state-papers-online-early-modern.

CONTRIBUTORS

RAYMOND A. ANSELMENT, professor emeritus of English literature at the University of Connecticut, is the editor of Alice Thornton's *My First Booke of My Life, The Remembrances of Elizabeth Freke,* and *The Occasional Meditations of Mary Rich, Countess of Warwick.* Besides having written numerous essays on a range of writers and issues, he is the author of three books on early modern religious prose satire, poetic responses to the conflict of civil war, and seventeenth-century literature and medicine.

RUTH CONNOLLY is a senior lecturer in seventeenth-century literature at Newcastle University. She has published articles and book chapters on lyric poetry, textual editing, and early modern women's writing and edited a volume of Robert Herrick's complete poetry. She is currently coediting an edition of Ben Jonson's poetry for the Longman Annotated English Poets series and working on a larger study of matter, form, and affect in the poetry of Hester Pulter, John Milton, and Richard Lovelace.

JULIE A. ECKERLE is a professor of English and Gender, Women, and sexuality Studies at the University of Minnesota, Morris. She is the author of *Romancing the Self in Early Modern Englishwomen's Life Writing* and coeditor, with Michelle M. Dowd, of *Genre and Women's Life Writing in Early*

Modern England. She is currently working on a monograph on early modern women's life writing in the Irish context and editing *Calthorpe's Chapel,* a scholarly edition of seventeenth-century Englishwoman Dorothy Calthorpe's little-known manuscript.

ANNE FOGARTY is a professor of James Joyce studies at University College Dublin, co-founder with Luca Crispi of the *Dublin James Joyce Journal,* and academic director of the Dublin James Joyce Summer School. She is coeditor of *Joyce on the Threshold; Bloomsday 100: Essays on "Ulysses"; Imagination in the Classroom: Teaching and Learning Creative Writing in Ireland;* and *Voices on Joyce.* She has edited special issues of the *Irish University Review* on Spenser and Ireland, Lady Gregory, Eiléan Ní Chuilleanáin, and Benedict Kiely and has published widely on aspects of twentieth- and twenty-first-century Irish literature, especially fiction. She is currently coediting a collection of essays on Deirdre Madden.

AMANDA E. HERBERT is the assistant director at the Folger Institute of the Folger Shakespeare Library, where she runs the Fellowships Program. She holds a PhD in history from Johns Hopkins University and is the author of *Female Alliances: Gender, Identity, and Friendship in Early Modern Britain,* winner of the Best Book Award from the Society for the Study of Early Modern Women. She edits *The Recipes Project* online and is a co-director for "Before Farm to Table: Early Modern Foodways and Cultures," a $1.5 million Mellon Initiative in Collaborative Research. She is at work on her second book project, *Water Works: Faith, Public Health, and Medicine in the British Atlantic.*

NAOMI MCAREAVEY is a lecturer in Renaissance literature at University College Dublin and has written on women's writing in seventeenth-century Ireland, including journal articles for *English Literary Renaissance, Early Modern Women,* and the *Journal of the Northern Renaissance.* Her edition of *The Letters of the First Duchess of Ormonde* is forthcoming with the Renaissance English Text Society. She has related research interests in the cultural legacy of the 1641 rebellion, and she coedited, with Fionnuala Dillane and Emilie Pine, *The Body in Pain in Irish Literature and Culture.*

JASON MCELLIGOTT is the keeper of Marsh's Library in Dublin. He was educated at University College Dublin and St. John's College, Cambridge, and is a former fellow of Merton College, Oxford. He has published widely on British politics and print culture of the seventeenth century and is currently researching the Cato Street Plot of 1820 and writing a monograph on book theft in eighteenth-century Dublin.

ANN-MARIA WALSH teaches in the School of English, Drama and Film at University College Dublin. She obtained a PhD in English from UCD in 2017. Her areas of interest include the manuscript writings of seventeenth-century women and early modern Ireland. She is currently working on a monograph, *The Daughters of the First Earl of Cork: Writing Family, Faith, Politics, and Place*, and she is editing the Boyle women's letters for the Irish Manuscripts Commission.

AMELIA ZURCHER is an associate professor of English and director of the University Honors Program at Marquette University. She has published *Seventeenth-Century Romance: Allegory, Ethics, and Politics* and many articles on early modern romance and other seventeenth-century British literature. She is completing a book manuscript on the Boyle siblings titled *The Family as Intellectual Institution*.

INDEX

Balzac, Jean-Louis Guez, 242
Bandon, 35
banshee, 66–67
Barbados, 274
Barbarus, Hermolaus, 234
Barclay, John, 122, 237, 245
Barnard, Toby, 46n9, 139
Barnewall, Brighid Ó Domhnaill (née Fitzgerald), 262
Barnewall, Nicholas, 262
Barry, Richard, Second Earl of Barrymore, 48n36, 88–89, 97n40
Barrymore, Alice (née Boyle), Countess, 12, 84–85, 88–90, 91, 93, 144, 262
Barryscourt Castle, 98n44
Batts, Sarah, 238, 245
Baxter, Richard, 113, 116, 239
Beale, John, 83, 105
Beeston, Eleanor, 235
Belfast, 260, 276
Bellew, Elizabeth and Christopher, 258
Bellew, Frances, Countess Dowager of Newburgh, 219
Bellew, Mary, 258
Benson, Elizabeth, 197, 205, 206, 215
Beresford, Lady Nichola Sophia, 216, 217, 218
Berkeley, George, 86
Berkeley, James, 206
Berkeley, Rebecca, 206, 215
Berkingham, Mary, 237
Berkley, Elizabeth, 239
Bernard, Francis, 49n41
Bernard, Mary (née Freke), 49n41
Bernard, Mildred Wallis, 216, 218, 219
Berry, Letitia, 219
Beyond 2022 Project, 254
Bible, 26, 32–33, 47n12, 69, 70, 106, 114, 237, 243, 245
biography, 1, 4, 5, 27, 65, 208–14, 266, 271
Birr Castle, 255, 275

Black family, 260
Blake, Eliza, 219
Blaugdone, Barbara, 5, 11–12, 51–53, 56, 65, 67–73, 262–63
Blennerhassett, Deborah (née Mervyn), 184, 186, 191
Blennerhassett, Eliza/Elizabeth. See Mervyn, Eliza
Blennerhassett, Henry, 184, 190, 194n6
Blennerhassett, John, 185
Blennerhassett, Leonard, 184
Bleverhayssett, Henry, 185
Boate, Arnold, 104
Boate, Gerard, 104
Bodleian Library, 85, 255–56, 259, 264, 265
Bohemia, 104
Bonnell, James, 199, 205, 208–14, 263
Bonnell, Jane (née Conyngham), 5, 199, 205, 208–14, 216, 217, 218, 224nn42–43, 258, 267, 275
Bonnell, Rebekah, 213
Book of Common Prayer, 245
book ownership, 11, 13–14, 189, 229–51
Borlase, John, 33–34
Bouhéreau, Elias, 230, 232, 233
Bourke, Angela, 262, 265, 268, 269, 270, 275, 276, 277, 278
Bourke, Evan, 272, 274
Boyle, Alice. See Barrymore, Alice (née Boyle), Countess
Boyle, Anne, 82–83, 97n37
Boyle, Catherine (née Fenton), First Countess of Cork, 87, 88, 92–93, 99–100, 139, 257, 263
Boyle, Charles, 82–83
Boyle, Elizabeth (née Clifford), Second Countess of Cork and First Countess of Burlington, 5, 12, 81, 82–83, 85, 86, 94n6, 97n37, 263

Butler, Mary, Lady Cavendish, 173, 177, 259, 276

Butler, Thomas, Earl of Ossory, 151, 172–74, 175, 178,

Butler, Thomas, Tenth Earl of Ormonde, 160–61

Butler, Thomas, Viscount Thurles, 273

Butler, Walter, Eleventh Earl of Ormonde, 161

Campanella, Thomas, 234

Canny, Nicholas, 89, 99, 104, 144

Carbery, Mary, 45

Carew, George, 100

Carribean, 190

Carrick-on-Suir, 161, 163

Carrickfergus, 276

Carte Papers, 85, 255–56, 259, 264, 265

Carte, Thomas, 255–56, 259

Carwardine, Mrs., 215

Cary, Elizabeth (née Tanfield), Lady Falkland, 2, 266

Cary, Sir Henry, First Viscount Falkland, 2, 266

Cary, Lucius, Viscount Falkland, 103

Cary, Mary, See Delany, Mary

Castlecomer, 29, 32, 34, 62

Castle Freke, 44, 45

Castleknock, 235

Castlelyons [Castle Lyon], 88–90, 93, 265

Castlemartyr, 84

Casway, Jerrold, 275

catechism, 246

Catholicism, 8, 9, 10, 25, 30, 35, 40, 44, 61, 71, 89, 90, 100, 106, 140, 141, 143, 145, 151, 153, 154, 161, 162, 163–64, 166, 170, 233–34, 242, 243, 256, 265, 273

Cavalier, 167

Cavan, 202

Cavendish family, 81

Cavendish, Margaret, Duchess of Newcastle, 189

Chambers, Anne, 269

Chambers, Elizabeth, 262, 266

Chapell, Mrs., 216

Charles I, King, 30–31, 61, 110, 125, 161, 165–67, 242

Charles II, King, 13, 140, 148, 150–51, 153, 161, 162, 165–67, 169, 172, 174–77

Charles University, 242–43

Chatsworth House, 81–82, 85, 257, 262, 263

Chedgzoy, Kate, 2, 52, 80, 262, 267

Cheevers, Sarah, 257, 266–67, 269

Chichester, Arthur, 262

Christ Church, Dublin, 8, 10, 62

Church of England, 30, 44

Church of Ireland, 61, 200

Clare, 66, 67

Clare, Magdalen, 258

Clarendon State Papers, 85

Clarke, Aidan, 260

Clarke, Danielle, 54

Claydon Manor, 262

Clayton, Ann, 125

Clifford, Anne, Countess of Pembroke and Montgomery, 1, 83

Clifford, Henry, Earl of Cumberland, 263

Clogher, 243–44

Clonakilty, 37, 49n42

Clotworthy, John, 158n45

Coke, Edward, 246

Coleraine, 274

Colston, Mary, 200–201, 219

Comber, Thomas, 27, 57

Comenius, John, 103

Comestor, Petrus, 243

Commission of Assessment, 185

Commission for the Despoiled Subject, 10

commonplace books, 5, 57, 65, 84, 260, 278

Commonwealth, 101, 163, 167–69, 172, 186, 258

Giffard, Thomas, 271

gift exchange, 37, 116, 183, 189–90, 192, 230, 239, 240, 241

Gilbert, John, 275

Gill, Catie, 71

Gillespie, Raymond, 2

Glorious Revolution, 43–44

Goodale, Mrs., 259, 271

Gorges, Robert, 151

Goring, George, Lord Goring, 125

Goring, Lettice (née Boyle), 125, 126, 257

Goring, George (later First Earl of Norwich), 126, 127

Graham, Agnes (née Gray), Countess of Menteith and Airth, 258

Graham, Elspeth, 266–67, 269

Graham, Isabella (née Bramhall), 258

Greer, Germaine, 276

Grey, Lord Arthur, 139

Gribben, Crawford, 71, 262

Guillim, John, 238

Gulielmus, 243

hagiography, 65

The Hague, 173

Halkett, Lady Anne, 1

Hall, Joseph, 113

Hamilton, A., 219

Hamilton, Agnes, 219

Hamilton, Anne, Third Duchess of, 85

Hamilton, James, 126

Hamilton, Jane, 215

Hamilton, K., 219

Hamilton, Lucy, 219

Hamilton, Sophia, 217

Hamilton, William, 209, 212, 213, 263

Hamilton-Moore, Mary, Dowager Countess of Drogheda, 218

Hannay, Margaret P., 272, 278

Haraway, Donna, 117

Harrison, Elinor, 197, 206, 217

Harrison, Theophilus, 197

Harrison, Thomas, 71

Hartlib Circle, 4, 103–5, 121, 124, 153, 260, 272, 274

Hartlib Papers, 85

Hartlib, Samuel, 83, 103–4, 115, 133n63, 137, 272

Harvey, Elizabeth, 219

Hastings, Christiana, 188

Hastings, Eleanor, 185, 186, 187, 188–89, 190, 191, 192, 193, 194n11

Hastings, Elizabeth, 185, 186, 187, 188–90, 191, 192, 193, 194n11

Hastings family, 183–93, 273

Hastings Family Papers, 185, 257–58

Hastings, Ferdinando, Sixth Earl of Huntingdon, 186

Hastings, Henry, 186

Hastings, Lucy (née Davies), Countess of Huntingdon, 185–86, 187, 188–89, 190–91, 192, 193194n11, 267

Hastings, Mary, 185, 186, 187, 188–89, 192, 193194n11

Hastings, Theophilus, Seventh Earl of Huntingdon, 185, 186, 189, 192, 193194n11

Hay, Lucy (née Percy), Dowager Countess of Carlisle, 272

Haysett, Eliza. See Mervyn, Eliza

Heal, Felicity, 157n30

Hebrew, 105

Henrietta Maria, Queen, 125, 256

Henry VIII, King, 265

Henry, Matthew, 236

Herbert, Amanda E., 5, 13, 183–96, 258, 273

Herbert, Percy, 123

Here Begynneth the Treatys of Nycodemus Gospell, 236

Herron, Thomas, 268

Heyland, Ka., 217
Hill, George, 273
Hill, Mary, 202, 217
Hill, Samuel, 202
Hillsborough, 263
Hinds, Hilary, 69
Histoire de Soliman Troisieme, 240
Hobbes, Thomas, 240
Holinshed, Raphael, 25
Holland, Karen Ann, 270
Hopkins, John, 245
Horneck, Anthony, 239
House of Lords, 274
Howgill, Francis, 71
Hull, John, 36, 37
humanism, 105
Hume [Mathew], Anne (née French), 162, 176, 177
Huntington Library, 184–85, 257–58, 277
Hutchinson, Lucy, 1, 224n41
Hyde, Sir Edward, First Earl of Clarendon, 105, 144, 145, 148–49, 151, 152, 273
Hyde, Henry, Lord Cornbury, 151
Hyde Papers, 257

Idough, 62
imprisonment, 68, 69, 72, 105, 202, 204, 269, 271
Inchiquin, William O'Brien, Second Earl of, 36
Independent congregation, 5, 8, 10, 261–62, 266, 267
Ingelo, Nathaniel, 242
inscriptions, 11, 13–14, 229–51
Interregnum, 13, 52, 65, 67, 72, 159, 160, 165, 177–78, 186
Irish (language). *See* Gaelic (language)
Irish Revenue, 273, 275
Irish Sea, 24, 25–26, 35, 52, 60, 69–71, 72, 80, 85, 161, 178, 186, 213, 233, 267

Isham, Elizabeth, 1
Islam, 201
Isle of Wight, 91

Jacobean settlement, 8
Jacobite risings, 118
Jacobite, 44
James II, King, 36, 38, 40, 43, 44, 153–54
James VI and I, King, 161
James, Duke of York (later James II), 83
James, Henry, 234
Jephson, Michael, 237
Jones, Arthur, Second Viscount Ranelagh, 12, 103, 107–9, 125, 137–38, 141, 142–50, 154–55, 177, 272
Jones, Elizabeth, 143, 147
Jones, Katherine (née Boyle), Lady Ranelagh, 4, 10, 12–13, 18–79, 82, 83, 85, 86, 90–92, 93, 94, 99–100, 101–14, 115, 117, 118–20, 125, 126, 128, 137–55, 158n45, 170, 176, 177, 256, 257, 258, 259, 260, 272, 274
Jones, Richard, Viscount Ranelagh (later First Earl of Ranelagh), 151
Jones, Roger, First Viscount Ranelagh, 141–43, 145

Kane, Brendan, 145
keen/keening, 32, 62, 66
Keightley, Francis (née Hyde), 273, 275
Keightley, Thomas, 273, 275
Kelly, Frank, 63
Kennedy, Máire, 229
Kerrigan, John, 3, 4, 138–39
Kerry, 184, 185, 270, 276
Kildare, 28, 60
Kildare, Elizabeth, Dowager Countess of Kildare, 260
Kilfinny Castle, 10, 268
Kilkenny, 29, 76n27, 160, 163, 164, 169, 270
Kilkenny Castle, 161, 259

Killigrew, Elizabeth, 134n80
Kilroy, Phil, 275
Kiltinan Castle, 269
King, Charles Simeon, 222n20
King, John, 274
King, Marion, 219
King, Sir Robert, 169
King, Robert, 219
King, William, 5, 7, 13, 197–27, 260–61
Kinnamon, Noel J., 272, 278
Kinsale, 26, 65
Klene, Jean, 278
Knatchbull, Mary, 256
Knight, Mary, 236, 239

Lamb, Mary Ellen, 120
Lambert, Castalina, 215
Lane, Frances, Viscountess Dowager
    Lanesborough, 217, 218
Lane, Mary, 200–201, 217, 219
Latin, 104, 242–43
Lawrence, Margaret, 202, 218
Leavens, Ann, 197, 206, 215
Leper, Dorothy, 219
Leslie, Marianna, 219
letters, 2, 4, 5, 6, 8, 10, 11, 12–13, 23, 26, 41–
    42, 43, 79, 80, 81, 82–85, 86–93, 93n4,
    97n37, 102, 105, 106–11, 137–58, 159–81,
    183–96, 197–219, 223n27, 223n30,
    223n32, 237, 242, 255, 256, 257, 258, 259,
    260, 261, 262, 263, 264, 265, 267, 268,
    269, 270, 271, 272, 273, 274, 275, 276,
    277, 278, 279, 280
Levant, 240
Limerick, 10, 72, 268, 276
Lindsay, Jean, 197, 206, 217
Liscarroll, 142
Liscarroll, Battle of, 263
Lismore Castle, 93n1, 143, 146, 150
Lismore Castle Estate Papers, 85

Little, Patrick, 146
Little, Roger, 276
Lloyd, Edward, 202–3
Lloyd, Elizabeth, 202–3, 217
Lloyd, Hannah, 202, 216, 217
Lockhart, Mary, 261
Loftis, John, 269
Loftus, Adam, 145
Loftus, Robert, 145
Loftus, Frances, 237
Long Parliament, 61
Longe, Julia G., 271
Louth, 258
Lovelace, Elizabeth, 214, 215, 216, 217, 218
Loveman, Kate, 237–38
Lowe, Peter, 242
Lucas, Richard, 239
Lyndon, Elizabeth, 215
Lyons Collection of the Correspondence
    of William King. See King, William

MacDonnell, Katherine, 256
MacDonnell, Randall, First Earl of Ant-
    rim, 256
MacDonnell, Rose (née O'Neill), Mar-
    chioness of Antrim, 258
MacKenzie, George, 123
Magnusson, Lynne, 203–4, 223n30, 223n32
Maley, Willy, 6
Man, Judith, 122
marginal autobiography, 5
marginalia, 10, 13–14, 230, 231, 234, 238, 241,
    242, 244–46
Marsh, Francis, 199
Marsh, Grace, 234, 235
Marsh, Narcissus, 230, 232, 233, 234, 235, 237
Marsh's Library, 230–46
Mary of Modena, 83
Mathew, George, 162, 164, 273

Mathew, Elizabeth (née Poyntz), Lady
    Thurles, 273
McAreavey, Naomi, 1–21, 159–81, 253–80
McElligott, Jason, 5, 9–10, 13–14, 229–51
McGrath, Bríd, 260
Meade, Elizabeth. *See* Freke, Elizabeth
    (née Meade)
measles, 60
Measton, Lydia, 234
Meath, 271, 272, 274
medicine, 79, 84, 102–3, 105, 107, 183, 189,
    242, 260
meditations, 5, 31, 32–33, 53, 57, 59, 79, 82,
    86, 102, 111, 113–21, 123, 125, 256, 277
memoirs, 4, 23, 24, 45, 51, 52, 57, 63–64, 65,
    66, 68, 76n29, 82, 86, 269, 277
memorandum books, 5, 79, 81, 82, 86, 263
memory, 11, 13, 24, 31, 59, 183, 192, 245, 266
Meredith, Robert, 28
Mervyn, Audley, 191
Mervyn, Christian (née Touchet), 185
Mervyn, Eliza (née Blennerhassett), 5, 13,
    183–93, 258, 273
Mervyn, Henry, 184, 186
Mildmay, Grace, 1
millenarianism, 105
missionaries, 52, 68, 72
Monro, Margaret, 218
Montgomery, George, 273
Montgomery, Susan (née Steynings),
    273–74
Moore, Alice, nèe Loftus, 256, 274
Moore, Alice, 37, 41
Moore, Arthur, 274
Moore, Charles, Viscount Moore, 274
Moore, Dorothy [Dury] (née King), 4,
    104, 106–7, 109, 114, 274
Moore, Elizabeth, 218
Moore, Henry, Third Earl of Drogheda, 37, 41
Moore, Lucy, 269

Moore, Sara (née Boyle), 257
Moore, William, 190
More, Henry, 239
Mortlock, Henry, 239
Moxon, Joseph, 238
Mulgrave, Edmund Sheffield, Second Earl
    of, 168
Munster, 35, 87, 90, 92, 93, 100, 140, 267
Muschamp, Denny, 258–59
Muschamp, Elizabeth (née Boyle), 258–59

Naas, 28
National Archives, Kew, 83, 258
National Archives of Ireland, 258
National Archives of Scotland. *See*
    National Records of Scotland
National Art Library, 83
National Library of Ireland, 85, 258–59,
    263, 264
National Library of Scotland, 259
National Records of Scotland, 85, 259
natural philosophy, 99, 103, 107, 115,
    119–21, 137
Neale, Sarah, 217
Netherlands, 104, 172
New British History, 2–3, 6
Newburgh, Ann, 216
New English, 8, 9, 12, 61, 79, 89, 100–101,
    109, 121, 128, 138, 145, 148, 164–65, 267,
    268, 272, 278
New Protestants, 8, 13, 140
Nicholas, Sir Edward, 165–67, 169, 177, 256
Ní Mháille, Gráinne. *See* O'Malley,
    Grace/ Gráinne
nonconformists, 105–6
Norton, Katherine (née McLoughlin),
    257, 274–75
Nugent, Susanna, 218, 219
nuns' chronicles, 4, 5, 10, 259, 264–65
Nuttall, Deirdre, 261

O'Brennan family, 62

O'Brien, Catherine (née Keightley), 273, 275

O'Brien, Celsus, 264

O'Brien, Donough, 258

O'Brien family, 66

O'Brien, Honora, 66–67, 258

O'Brien, Lucius, 275

O'Brien, Murrough, First Earl of Inchiquin, 65

O'Brien, William, Second Earl of Inchiquin, 49n40

occasional meditations. See meditations

O'Doherty, Rosa. See O'Neill, Rosa

Ó Domhnaill, Rudhraighe, Earl of Tyrconnell, 262

O'Dowde, Thomas, 279

Offaly, Baroness. See Digby, Lettice

Offaly, 10, 255, 256, 268

Ogle, Mary/Marie. See Donovan, Mary/ Marie Broughton (née Ogle)

Ogle, Samuel, 268

O'Hara, Elizabeth, 260

O'Hara family, 260

O'Hara, Kean, 260

O'Hara, Rose, 260

Ohlmeyer, Jane, 89, 139

O'Keeffe, Eleanor, 265

Oldenburg, Henry, 83

Old English, 8–9, 61, 100, 109, 140, 145–46, 148, 164–65, 266, 269

Old Protestants, 71, 140

O'Malley, Grace/Gráinne, 8, 275

O'Neill, Owen Roe, 8, 275

O'Neill, Rosa (née O'Doherty), 8, 275

Orange, House of, 172

Origen, 240

Orinda. See Philips, Katherine (née Fowler)

Ormond Castle, 161

Ormond Papers, 259

Ormonde, First Earl of. See Butler, James

Ormonde, Elizabeth. See Butler, Elizabeth

Ormonde, First Duchess of. See Butler, Elizabeth

Orrery, First Countess of. See Boyle, Margaret

Orrery, First Earl of. See Boyle, Roger

Orrery Papers, 84–85, 259, 264

Osborne, Dorothy. See Temple, Dorothy (née Osborne)

Osborne, Melanie, 262, 267

Ostiensis, Henricus, 243

Ovid, 238

Owens, Alice, 197

ownership marks, 11, 13–14, 229–51

Oxford University, 242

the Palatinate, 104

pamphlets, 231, 232, 234, 239, 241, 242, 243, 244

Panmure, Margaret Maule, Countess of, 85

Parker, Frances, 7, 201–2, 215

Parker, John, 202, 222n20

Parker, Samuel: 239–40

Parliament, English, 29, 30, 61, 65, 85, 90, 110, 127, 140, 150, 152, 168, 262

Parliament, Irish, 25, 29, 32, 37, 43, 149, 151, 152, 169, 186, 191, 200, 205

Parliamentarians, 52, 127, 150, 168

Parnell, Anna, 216

Parry, Edward Abbott, 278

Parsons, Dorothy, 255, 275

Parsons, Elizabeth, 275

Parsons family, 275

Parsons, John, 33–34

Parsons, Laurence, First Baronet of Parsonstown, 275

Parsonstown House, 255

Raven, James, 236
Rawdon, Dorothy (née Conway), 277
receipts/receipt books. *See* recipe books
recipes/recipe books, 4–5, 79, 82, 103, 183, 189, 255, 260, 261, 273, 275
Reddy, William M., 55, 56
Reformation, 243
regicide, 276
Restoration, 11, 101, 105, 110, 148, 150, 153, 159, 160, 161, 162, 171, 174–77, 242, 262
Richard, John, 205
Rich, Charles, Fourth Earl of Warwick, 113, 121, 122, 124–28, 148
Rich, Henry, First Earl of Holland, 161
Rich, Mary (née Boyle), Countess of Warwick, 1, 2, 9, 12, 79, 82, 84, 85, 86, 99–100, 101–2, 105, 110–12, 113–28, 134n80, 256, 277
Rich, Robert, Second Earl of Warwick, 113, 122, 125, 126
Ridgeway, Cicely (née Macwilliam), Countess of Londonderry, 277
Ridgeway, Thomas, Earl of London-derry, 277
Roe, Thomas, 235
Rogers, John, 5, 8, 10, 261–62, 266, 267
Rolevinck, Werner, 235
romance, 102, 116, 122–25, 237, 238
Roscommon, Countess of. *See* Boyle, Frances
Rose, Mary Beth, 64
Rosenwein, Barbara H., 55–56, 57, 59–60, 68
Rosscarbery, 35
Rostellan, 35, 36, 37
Royal Society, 83, 121, 199, 276
Royal Society Library, 83–84, 260
royalism, 36, 52, 61, 64, 65, 67, 71, 72–73, 81, 88, 90, 122, 140, 148, 150–51, 153–54, 159, 160, 162, 165–68, 170, 174–75, 186, 256

Russell, Elizabeth, 157n30

Saint Germain, Christopher, 242
Saint Patrick's Cathedral, 197, 199, 263
Saint Sepulchre, 234
Saint Werburgh's, 197
Sanderson, Robert, 242
Sarsfield-Vesey Correspondence, 258
Saunders, Ann, 219
Saunders, Frances, 236
Saunders, Letitia, 216, 218
Savile, Anne, 176
Schambogen, Johann Christoph, 242–43
science, 102–3, 117, 119, 189
Scots Presbyterianism, 199
Scotland, 2, 5, 7, 8, 25, 61, 122–23, 140, 161, 162, 163, 166, 199, 242, 253, 259, 260, 261, 271, 273
Second Ormonde Peace, 166
Seelig, Sharon Cadman, 76n29
Segusio, Henry of. *See* Ostiensis, Henricus
sequestration, 7, 13, 44, 52, 64, 83, 150, 160, 168, 186
sermons, 86, 100, 113, 114, 127, 128, 236, 239
settlers. *See* plantation
Shakespeare, William, 3
Shane, Captain, 190
Sharp, Anthony, 274–75
Sheffield University Library, 85
Shepard, Thomas, 236
Sheppard, William, 242
Sibthorpe, Anne. *See* Southwell [Sib-thorpe], Lady Anne (née Harris)
Sibthorpe, Henry, 278
Sidney, Dorothy (née Percy), Countess of Leicester, 272, 278
Sidney, Robert, Second Earl of Leicester, 272, 278
siege warfare, 8, 10, 52, 89–90, 141, 142, 256, 265, 268

Verney, Ralph, 85, 88–90, 91, 262
Vernon, Colonel Edward, 152
Vesey, Mary, 258
Victoria and Albert Museum, 83
Villiers, Edward, 261, 279
Villiers, Katherine (née Fitzgerald), Viscountess Grandison, 261, 279
Virgin Islands, 65
Virtual Record Treasury, 254
Vokins, Joan, 279–80

Wade, Elizabeth, 215
Wales, 2, 3, 7, 162, 163
Walker, Anthony, 86, 113, 114, 127, 128
Walker, Garthine, 147
Waller, Hardress, 276
Wallis, Mildred, *See* Bernard, Mildred
Walsh, Ann-Maria, 5, 9, 12, 79–98, 257, 262, 263, 270, 277
Wandesford, Christopher, 23, 25, 26–27, 28, 29, 31–34, 45, 51, 58, 59, 61–62, 76n27
Warren, Ellen, 218
Warwick, Countess of. *See* Rich, Mary (née Boyle)
Waterford, 4, 86, 93n1, 256, 264, 270
Wellcome Library, 83
Wentworth, Thomas, Earl of Strafford, 25, 28, 29–31, 32, 33–34, 44, 58, 60, 61, 72, 75–106, 109–10, 122, 145, 148, 184, 272

Western Design, 190
Westmeath, Richard Nugent, First Earl of, 234, 235
Westmeath, Jane, 234, 235
West Sussex Record Office, 84
Wexford, 26
Whelan, Bernadette, 275
White, Newport B., 232
Whitelocke, Bulstrode, 106
Whitley, Honoria, 217
Whyman, Susan E., 203, 223n27
widowhood, 24, 35, 45, 58, 84, 128, 141, 162, 187, 197, 199, 203, 204, 206–7, 208–14, 263, 271–72
William III, King, 36, 43–44, 20
Williamite confiscations, 44
Williamite-Jacobite War, 44, 118, 261
Willoughby, Charles, 199
Willoughby, John, 273
Winthrop, John, 137
witches/witchcraft, 72
Wolfe, Heather, 266
Woolf, Virginia, 53
Worsley, Benjamin, 104
Wray, Ramona, 266

Youghal, 88, 94n6, 272

Zurcher, Amelia, 2, 9, 12, 99–135, 272, 277

In the Women and Gender in the Early Modern World series:

Pathologies of Love: Medicine and the Woman Question in Early Modern France
By Judy Kem

The Politics of Female Alliance in Early Modern England

Edited by Christina Luckyj and Niamh O'Leary

Women's Life Writing and Early Modern Ireland
Edited by Julie A. Eckerle and Naomi J. McAreavey

To order or obtain more information on these or other University of Nebraska Press titles, visit nebraskapress.unl.edu.